<u>Adve</u>
<u>I</u>
<u>Mind-Control</u>

<u>Finding freedom</u>
<u>from deceivers, manipulators</u>
<u>and parasites of the soul</u>

<u>By</u>

<u>Paul Arrowbank</u>

First Published United Kingdom
2013 by Paul Arrowbank

Printed by:
Orbital Print Ltd, Sittingbourne, Kent, UK

Proof-Reading: Nicci Crompton

Photography: Rhiannon 'Yanz' Vaughan

ISBN 978-0-9576754-0-7

www.paularrowbank.co.uk

Introduction

I once used to have a passing acquaintance with a great character in a pub who I called Squarehead. Squarehead was in his mid-forties and always used to sit at the same place at the end of the bar drinking real ale. He didn't drink lager: lager was for sissies. There was a slight tinge of Welsh to his tones.

Squarehead had been a rugby player in his formative years. His head was square because he still retained lantern-jawed good looks mixed in with a skull that had probably been remoulded by years of kicks from a thousand rugby boots in Saturday afternoon scrums and tackles up and down the land.

The thing about Squarehead I liked was that his smile was a beam that blinded everyone who walked through the door of that little drinking hole in the backstreets of the City of London. He'd sit there in his woollen v-necked pullover with its little crest, impeccable jeans and black shiny shoes, greeting all those who walked in like long-lost friends. There was a real sparkle in his kindly brown eyes as if he'd found out some great piece of information that everyone else had somehow simply missed. Whatever it was excited him but at the same time, he didn't feel the need to talk about it endlessly. Unlike many regulars of this watering hole who used to stand there with pints in their hands holding you right into conversations on topics that meant nothing to you and were at best irrelevant, Squarehead was self-aware enough to know that not everything was all about him. A conversation with him was a joy because he'd learned to pitch his chat to the perfect level according to who he was speaking to.

I used to meet friends in this pub back in the day and only knew Squarehead to return his beaming smile with a nod and a polite greeting. But one evening, the two of us had the chance to have a long conversation.

He told me he lived with his sister whom he'd rescued from an abusive husband. He admitted that when he was a boy, he'd bullied his sister mercilessly and had ignored the fact that she was also being hounded by tyrants at school.

"She was always so loving when she was a kid…" he admitted with a sigh, "…so forgiving. She has such a beautiful heart, my sister."

At some point, Squarehead had grown up and realised that he'd been "a complete and utter twat". One day, he'd taken his sister aside and hugged her with huge tears in his eyes. He begged her to forgive him and wouldn't let her go.

"I was so sorry about how I'd abused and upset her. For years I'd turned my back on her plight and sometimes even joined in with the bullies. I hated myself for that. I've always been a big bloke. I could've sorted them out there and then…"

As he spoke, a tiny tear forced itself to the corner of his eye which he wiped away with his big dinner plate of a hand. It was extraordinary to see this tough guy so humbled.

"As it turned out," he said, "there was nothing to forgive. She didn't hold even an ounce of malice in her heart for me. In fact, she hugged me back even harder than I hugged her…"

After that, Squarehead had vowed always to protect his sister. When it had come out that she was being regularly physically assaulted by her psychopathic Chef husband, he'd gone after the guy with his own meat cleaver (at least that's what he claimed!).

In order to prevent the psycho-chef from causing any more damage, Squarehead had moved in with his sister and stayed. That had happened some ten years earlier and they were still together.

"It just works so well," he explained. "She's a healer and I teach kids rugby. Not so fast on my feet any more, though!"

He chuckled as he patted a slight beer belly.

The conversation then became extremely enlightening.

"I say my sister's a healer, but she isn't what you call New Age, he said, rolling his eyes. Neither of us gets the New Age. It's just another scam of this matrix we're in, another bloody religion. All that's happened is New Agers have replaced an old abusive money-grabbing, angry, vengeful, hatred-fuelled, bigoted, war-mongering, racist, sexist demiurge of a god with a brand new set of masters. So now religions have been replaced with sects full of people who get on their knees to a sky-being from some fake plastic galactic federation. They think they're so free for escaping

4

from raging Priests in pulpits but all that's happened is these men have been replaced by gurus. The fear that these New Agers held before when they ventured into a confessional has now been replaced by pussy-footing around a supposedly enlightened guy in an orange dress.

"If these people are looking for something, why the hell don't they do it for themselves like I did? I didn't go off to India to look for enlightenment in some ashram. I found what I was looking for in London, right here in scumtown where the streets are paved with vomit and discarded beer cans, where the rich and powerful rub shoulders with the hopeless."

I loved Squarehead's turn of phrase and he knew that I was lapping it up. I told him I was also on a search but had never managed to conceive of exactly what I was searching for.

"Paul, just be a good man," he said. "Think with your heart and not your head. Your heart is multidimensional and can feel all possibilities. Your head is logical, two-dimensional in shape. It's not the head that does the loving. If you're going to find joy and wisdom it's inside *this*."

Chuckling, he grabbed hold of the crest on his jumper and yanked it backwards and forwards with the exaggerated motion of a beating heart.

"You just have to reach in and pull it out. You can't let anyone else do that. You have to do it for yourself, by yourself. As soon as you start expecting others to pile in and provide you with *their* solutions to your problems, you're no longer your own man. This is why the New Age is such a con. There are people within its ranks who imply that they can provide you with enlightenment, that they're the great hope for humanity and that it's their job to heal the world! How can this happen, Paul? The only way the world can improve is by people taking responsibility for their own crap and resolving their own issues. You can take advice and go for healing, but you should only allow those healers to guide you. If they tell you that they can only help you *so* far and then politely inform you that you must do the rest of the healing yourself, then you know you can trust them. On the other hand, if they or their work start to become your crutch, if they begin to give even the slightest hint that they're invalidating any other path or modality and telling you that only *they* can help you, then find your way out of their maze immediately and run a mile."

In so many ways I wish I'd listened to that advice. Like any institution, there are those within the framework who are fine individuals with honest-hearted motives: because of such people, it *is* possible to find a cure within the New Age and to uncover peace and love within a deeply meaningful moment of meditation. But finding that sublime moment or even an answer to the most pressing of problems is ultimately the result of a person simply detaching themselves from their monumental egos. For just a fleeting moment in the silence, they tap into the great consciousness that is our Universe.

Certainly, the New Age can promote moments of incredible lucidity. But more often than not, it's the strength of the individual that's brought them into such a place and not the institution itself.

The New Age is also full of people out of balance and hence out of touch with reality. Whilst some are actively working on all their negative traits in a laudable attempt to smooth out their interpersonal relationships and become much better humans, other New Agers are shouting: "*STOP!* A course of enquiry into your dark traits causes you negativity. You should never be concentrating on the negative, only the positive. If you're focussed on the negative side, you'll attract that vibration into your own life and it will destroy you!"

I'm confused. If you're concentrating on being a good person like Squarehead said, the "darkness" can't get anywhere near you, can it. Surely it can only get to you if you, as a person, are negative in your interaction with the world at large. If you're happy being the hero every minute of the waking day and living in that vibration, then surely you can delve into what remains of your traumatised psyche at will and not release demons from cages that will tear you limb from limb. All that will happen is they'll simply dissipate into thin air once the door of the cage has been kicked in.

This introverted terror of the dark and things that go bump in the night is at the very heart of my story.

Many New Agers cannot face themselves. They have all the answers to every single conundrum but their own. When my New Age friend read an early version of this book, she howled in protest:

"Paul, I felt awful after reading this. You mustn't keep using the word darkness and talking about darkness. All you're doing is bringing darkness in…"

She was genuinely horrified. It reminded me of so many kids of my generation who used to hide behind the sofa from *Doctor Who* because the Daleks were so terrifying to young, impressionable minds. But it's just a TV show!

I refuse to sanitise my life and experience in this book because others are not able to face themselves. New Agers often float around with their heads in the sand, never budging, ignoring the fact that dark deeds are being perpetrated around them (and even by them) every day of their lives. They may have an intellectual understanding that the entire world is run from the top down by those who practice the sorcery of mind-control through a Hegelian dialectic, but rather than shake themselves free from this control matrix by facing up to it, they keep their heads well and truly buried. With all this raging around them, they waste their lives concentrating on a bunch of angels from that plastic galactic federation, falling to their knees to an Ascended Master they've read about, begging for THE LIGHT. They then go off and spread this light, whatever it is, in offices, shops and places where people congregate, honestly thinking they're doing the world a favour. Whilst casting energy around like so much sparkly, spangly fairy dust, they're refusing to face themselves. The light they claim to bring in is no more than sludge. They're just too vain to admit it.

I pointed my friend who took such exception to his book in the direction of the Harry Potter series, telling her that Harry is a balanced character from day one as he doesn't pussyfoot around by referring to the bad guy as "he whose name dare not be mentioned" for fear that the very vibration of its utterance is enough to bring the darkness billowing in all around you. "*LORD VOLDEMORT!*" says Harry, fully aware, even at a young age, that it's your own attitude towards fear that's stopping you from finding genuine courage and ultimately a solution to your problems and the prize of freedom. Congratulations to Jo Rowling for teaching kids that bad stuff goes down in this world, *so deal with it.*

That evening with Squarehead was amazing. He taught me so much, but I just didn't allow his words to filter through enough to my everyday life. It was many years before he made any sense to me, long, long after I'd moved from London and forgotten about him completely until one day when someone used the word "squarehead" out of the blue. The word brought back a rush of memories....

Squarehead gave me a model of the Universe which now makes perfect sense. He told me that an enlightened man is one who understands that this world is Dark and Light, that there are souls who walk the path of Service to Self and some who choose Service to Others, that Dark teaches Light and that the enlightened man has simply learned to synthesise all energies. In doing so, he's learned not to fight against the Dark, but simply let...it...all...be...

"After all's said and done, you don't have to be anyone special," Squarehead said. "You just let everyone be who they need to be and know that if they want to walk the Service to Self path, you just have to let them get on with it. One day such people will wake up by themselves if you leave a few little clues lying about the place. The wise man is an integrated soul who's accepted the Light and the Dark within him and treads lightly on the path by letting those others do their own thing, helping them when they call for help. As he's in balance, he'll pick up his sword if he has to and only when his intuition tells him that "justice" must prevail. Otherwise, he'll simply accept that all experience, joyous or deeply wounding, is a lesson. He doesn't have to do anything else other than be the good guy..!

"Accept the fact that we're all deeply loved and this life is just a temporal school preparing us for entry into the greater Universe. While we're at that school, we pass our exams by simply respecting the world at large. You don't have to love everyone like you love your mum. Unconditional love is just honouring everyone's need to be individuals, to be the fat ones, the stupid ones, the hideous and unsightly, the boring, the bigots, the posh ones, the common ones, the pig-ignorant, the social outcasts, the poofs, the slags, the rat boys, the weirdos, the self-obsessed, the narcissists, the ones desperate to walk in the shadows, the legends in their own bloody dinnertimes and the mild-mannered with their kind hearts and caring ways. All are worthy of respect. When you know this, you're enlightened, Paul. *That's* when your life fills up with all you ever dreamed of. If you feel all this in your heart, you're there, mate!"

I often wonder where Squarehead is these days and whatever became of him. I'd love to meet him now and tell him that I've found out, after all these years, that he was so right.

This is a book about my experiences with those in the shadows. I admit, I should have walked on as Squarehead said, but lacked awareness and hadn't yet allowed his words to filter through to my conscious world. In all my spiritual naivety (which was New Age at first, I also admit) I allowed myself to be controlled and bamboozled by two unbalanced New Age scam artists: one who thought she could control Light and Dark like a mad scientist in the hope that it would cause money to fall like rain into her bank account and another who was of such dark and evil intent, that he actually declared a love for some character called Satan. This was a man who was in almost constant pain from years of Service to Self but still couldn't put down his dark instruments and was determined to go to his grave clutching tightly onto the materials of his own suffering.

I like to think I allowed myself to be lowered into a pit built by these two people. I was lowered right to the bottom, but didn't feel in the least bit inclined to jump out of the bucket. Instead, I pulled on the emergency cord when I'd seen enough. When I discovered there was no one left to pull me up, I did it myself, somehow; God only knows how.

When I reached the top, I found the New Age had mercifully dissipated and I was free from all bondage. I learned to respect and honour those who had shown me the pit and rejoiced in my new-found sovereignty.

I've really pushed the boat out with this book and in places been unnervingly frank. In other places, in order to keep the book light-hearted, I've been downright sarcastic which you'll tell me is the lowest form of wit. Well, if wit was in a barrel, I've definitely scraped my way to the very bottom.

I've done this in order to bring us all catalyst. The two people who this book exposes brought down an enormous amount of catalyst to my life; in fact, so much I nearly collapsed beneath the weight of it. It's now my turn to do everyone a favour and expose the tricks, the control, the lies, the manipulation, the hypocrisy and the general spiritual stink and squalor which is the stock in trade of the psychopathic cult leader.

You may then decide you want to advance like I did and beat a path to the door of someone similar. I wouldn't recommend it, but it does work for some people. On the other hand, you may learn something from my experiences and decide that now you know what's involved, you'll never have to go through such a gruesome set of lessons yourselves. You may even write to me and say "thanks for sharing. I've learned from you and from your dark experiences!"

Just to make sure we're all clear, I bear these characters no ill will at all. The work they've done for me is phenomenal; you just cannot put a price on it. If I'm rude about them, please run with it. They knew before they took on their lives as controllers that they would be playing the game with me and the exposé is as much a part of the game as their attempts to control me and ultimately to fail. One day, maybe in ten life times, they'll probably expose their own manipulators in the same way and finally reach that exalted state of perfection we all yearn for, whether we accept that or not. In the grand scheme of things, outside of this veil that holds us in place, we have all reached that state already. The end has already happened, and it's a triumph for us all. We just have to get there now…

Chapter One

I was brought up as a Catholic in the days before happy clappy acoustic guitars and uptempo hymns. In my childhood it was still all about guilt, humiliation and little devils that popped up if you admired yourself for too long in the mirror. In those days, the priest was the ultimate spiritual arbiter and his word was sacrosanct. It was amazing how people used to cowtow to the clergy.

The whole religious thing posed a major problem for me from an early age, because I just never felt comfortable with it. The very sound of the word 'Catholic' felt somehow alienating. Even as a seven year-old, I found it oppressive, if not downright scary. The superlatives offered up to some invisible, but angry god were just too strong for me. The hours and hours of singing praises to some demiurge that didn't seem to give a damn about me and was more angry than caring, were so empty and wasted. I really didn't like the fact that I felt I was a good person but was being made to feel defiled and filthy. Often I had to drum up some sins quickly before going into the confessional just so I would have something to talk about. Really, there wasn't that much to confess, aside from whatever sin it was that I was born with and I never really knew what I was accused of.

When I was about ten, I used to feel incredibly faint during mass. Sometimes, I'd have to run out of the church as I felt I was about to throw up. The whole service went on too long and the sheer terror of being told that if my eye caused me to sin I was supposed to pluck it out was enough to make me sick to the stomach. All the more so for being told it was better to enter the kingdom of God eyeless than to keep both eyes and wallow in torment for eternity where there was apparently something called "a worm that never dies".

The fainting thing was partly resolved when I bizarrely stepped forward to become an altar boy. The problem with that was I never really did concentrate on the job in hand. I was always missing the correct moment to ring the bell and often seemed to incur the wrath of the priest for standing in the wrong place. One time at mass during the Easter holidays, I swung the thurifer (that large brass incense burner on a long chain) so hard I nearly broke noses.

Despite rejecting the whole scene at a very young age, the guilt that ties one into this religion stayed with me during the years of my atheism. As a teenager and in my early twenties, I loved being an atheist. It gave me something to bang on about at parties and I got a kind of childish enjoyment out of riling the faithful. But atheism wasn't me either. I didn't just think there was something out there, I was convinced there was. It simply wasn't the *thing* that people said it was. I felt I'd been lied to for years. I knew my atheism was a passing fad and that some day, something genuine would come along to replace it. I had no idea what.

In the spring of 1988, I found myself on my own in Rome. I had a day off from my studies at a little language school in the centre of the city and was wandering around the splendid Cathedral of San Giovanni in Laterano which had been the seat of the popes before they'd built St Peters. It was whilst I was in that magnificent baroque church, that I passed a confessional box.

For some time, I'd been feeling guilty about my atheism. I'd given the Catholic god such a rare old public drubbing that I felt terrible about it and was revisiting the guilt of my earlier years, still unsure how to replace this Catholic idol with his terrifying demands for subservience and money.

Outside this particular confessional box was a little light on warning that there was a priest inside waiting to hear confessions. The sign above the door said simply: INGLESE, English.

I really wanted a chat. The problem was, I didn't quite have the linguistic reach with my Italian at the time to say what I wanted, so I wondered if this "inglese" sign augured help. If there was a priest inside who could speak some English, this was the perfect moment for me to offload some concerns.

Carefully, I stepped into the confessional and knelt down. Out of respect, I spoke in Italian at first, asking if we could continue in English as I had an important question to ask.

What happened next shocked me to the core. There was an outraged roar from the other side of the curtain.

"NON PARLO INGLESE!"

I stammered an apology and tried to explain, but it was too late.

There was the sound of a chair scraping and a door being thrown open. Whoever this "man of God" was, he was furious with me. Ranting at me with words that barely made sense, he fled, slamming the door of the confessional.

Mortified, I opened my own door a crack and peered out through the tiny space. A giant black-clad fire-breathing dragon with a shock of white hair was stamping down the aisle, cursing me to high heaven, his arms flailing madly at his sides.

Throwing my own door open, I too fled. I charged the exit at the rear of the church, flung myself through the door and fairly flew down the short flight of stone steps into the piazza below. I stopped at the bottom and looked back and up at the Cathedral. I had a moment of clarity in which I really wondered what the point of it was. It was stunningly beautiful and old, but didn't serve any discernible purpose for me or anyone with any real burning questions.

I made up my mind never to set foot voluntarily into such a place again. In fact, as I found my way to the bus stop to take me back to the Circus Maximus where I could catch the Metro home, I think I made a very specific unconscious decision: I would find the truth behind this "God" if it killed me.

So I set out on a journey of discovery. I took nothing with me but a sense of wonder which everyone around me saw as complete unbridled naivety. I peeled back the lids of many a belief system, jumped inside, saw the sights and smelled the smells. I got my clothes filthy and got bored. I jumped out again and ran for cover. Each time, the ones who know better tutted and shook their heads. I was accused of never having any money, of letting everyone down for not getting a swanky job in the Foreign and Commonwealth Office, for allying myself with the great foolish of the world.

And thereby hangs the tale!

Chapter Two

My story really begins on a very wet Tuesday night, the week before Christmas, 1997. I was living in Rundown Street just off Discarded Needle Road in West Reading. I'd recently returned from living the high life in Greece where I'd been thriving, loving the food, the weather, the Greek people and their light-hearted ways and the fact that I had few worries and even fewer personal troubles. I'd been called back to the UK by a strange and inexplicable stirring. It was time for me to peel back the layers of mystery and find the wisdom that was eluding me.

As I walked up the hill, shivering under my umbrella, I reflected on the circumstances that had dragged me back to rainy old England. I was *still* looking for answers: in fact, I was desperate for them. I wanted more than ever to know why I was alive. Who was I? More to the point, where was I going and why? My greatest question was this: was I mad and totally alone for trying to be spiritual in my approach to life?

As I made my way through the threatening gloom of the badly lit road (one of Reading's roughest areas) I honestly believed I was on the verge of an adventure that would lead me to the answers to such questions and many more besides. I was excited.

My good friend at the time, Kat, was about to introduce me to a woman she'd been talking about with such admiration for months. I was incredibly curious to meet this person now. Apparently, she had all the answers. Through a life of terrible suffering and hardship, she'd found what I was looking for - the source of all life, an infinite consciousness of pure unconditional love and eternal wisdom.

As I walked down Hovel View Road, it no longer mattered that I'd turned my back on my great life in Greece. For the moment, I'd stopped noticing the cold. In fact I didn't care. This meeting was the important thing now. It felt like my whole life had led up to this very moment.

I found this lady's house. It was your classic late Victorian British terrace, slightly shabby and uncared for. Her tired old banger sat in the rainy street outside.

I sometimes wonder if I should have paid attention to the number on the front door which was thirteen. If I had, if I'd been even just a little bit superstitious, I may have just walked away there and then and probably saved myself many years of misery. But then, life is for living and sometimes your moments of extreme anguish can also be ones which you look back on in hindsight and say: *how well I learned my lessons...*

Kat let me in that evening. She'd already warned me earlier in the day to take off my shoes and leave them by the door as I was now treading on consecrated ground. Smiling, she pointed to the door at the foot of the stairs that led into the reception room. I remember gently pushing that door open and carefully putting my head around first before venturing in. For some days, Kat had been prepping me for this moment. I was to be very careful what I said: I was not to speak unless spoken to, I was never to use bad language or even express an opinion. The first thing I was to do was put my hands together and do a light bow as one would do to a guru in India.

Actually, I hated the thought of cow-towing to anyone. Later on, it would make me think I was the cowardly lion or the tin man shaking like leaves as they made their way up the long hallway to consult the Wizard. All the time, this "great" magician was just some ordinary Joe frantically working machinery behind the scenes that amplified his voice and persona. Unknowingly, I'd already built a giant mythical closet in my head ready to cram in a cartload of "facts" I knew I wouldn't understand about these bizarre circumstances. There I would leave all that junk until either I had proof positive of this lady's credibility or until I was sufficiently wise to know how to cope with it all. In the meantime, I was so desperate for it all to be working in the way that I wanted, I utterly suspended even the slightest disbelief and crushed any intuitive thoughts out of existence.

Feeling very at odds with this 'namaste' bowing thing, I bent down too low as I placed my hands together and made out that I was prostrating myself in front of the haughty, terrifying Queen Of Hearts in Lewis Carroll's *Alice In Wonderland*. If I'd listened to my inner thoughts I'm sure I'd have heard her howling: OFF WITH HIS HEAD!

I was quite relieved by what I saw in those first few moments. The one I would come to know as "Holy Mother" was a lovely looking lady in her mid forties. She was positively radiant that night. Her black hair was quite long and free flowing and she seemed so amazingly young and serene. I was impressed as well that she was wearing a sari. I thought: *this lady means business.*

A week earlier I'd finished her biography and had been deeply shocked by it. It's an extremely sad book, charting her lonely childhood, the isolation of being an only child, unwanted by an uncaring mother, often the victim of a father who had a tendency to lash out violently at her in a jealous rage. As a young adult, she'd been the victim of unreliable and even predatory men and had had a series of disastrous relationships. However, the book had seemed to end on a positive note. Despite all her hardships and trials, the "Holy Mother" had prevailed with her spiritual path and once she'd turned away from the life that had brought her such personal and emotional hardship, in the quiet and solitude, she'd become an enlightened being and was able to "hear the voice of God". I didn't have a clue what that meant at the time and was absolutely desperate to find out. I couldn't wait to speak to her.

I sat down in a dining room chair placed in the centre of the room opposite her and waited for her to start talking to me. When she did address me, it was in a very measured way, almost over-practiced. She told me she was glad to meet me at last as Kat had been talking about me for at least four months.

The "Holy Mother" didn't waste any time that evening. I told her I'd come about my back pain which was being exacerbated by the fact that in all my free time, I was beavering away writing a novel. Unfortunately, my PC at the time was perched on a dressing table and for seating I'd been using a plastic patio chair with a thin spongy squab. My posture was extremely lax and often, I would sit there with the keyboard on my lap. In fact, I was so excited about this great novel I was writing, I'd neglected everything: my fitness, my health, my physical pain and even my appearance.

The "Holy Mother" took a deep breath and seemed to steel herself for something. She then asked me carefully if I could entertain the possibility that I may have lived before. I frowned slightly at that point. There was an awkward five seconds.

"I know you Catholics don't teach reincarnation," she said, quite out of the blue.

I began to wonder what on earth Kat had told her. She knew full well that I'd turned my back on Catholicism years earlier and that I was more into a kind of free-flowing, hippy spirituality. Reincarnation was an intrinsic part of that.

As it turned out, Kat had given the Holy Mother a lot of information about me, but very little of it was correct. I'd told Kat many times that I'd taught "English as a Foreign Language" in Greece, that I'd been born in Zambia to an English father and an Irish mother and that I'd studied French and Italian at Reading University. The problem with Kat was that she was so wrapped up in herself she never ever listened to anything I said and was more concerned with herself as the focus of her own extremely Kat-centred world. Even though we were friends, I'd often noticed that she struggled to accept others, to align herself with the possibility that her friends were like her, ordinary people who were *also* unique, trying their best to live life, to advance, to make a difference. Because she'd effectively shut out all my words and hence my individuality to contemplate "Kat", all the information I'd given about myself was translated across to this Holy Mother as:

Paul is South African. He's a qualified teacher of English who studied English at Oxford University.

The "Holy Mother" herself, who didn't know me from Adam, had somehow managed - as I was to discover - to embellish this faulty image yet further. In the Mother's mind, this had bizarrely come to mean:

Paul is from a rich family who are dripping in gold and jewels. Because they're from South Africa, that must mean that they all live on an enormous plantation crammed with slaves that do their exact bidding at the crack of a whip. Therefore, this Paul has never had to lift a finger for himself, is spoilt rotten, overeducated and needs to be taken down a few pegs.

In return for helping me to recover from my back pain, the "Holy Mother" asked very politely if I would put aside some time to help her young son with his reading. She also suggested I look into something that I'd done in a past life when I'd been a spoilt,

17

selfish, precocious brat who'd grown up to become a sorcerer and had taken revenge on his own family by sending a hailstorm to destroy their house with them inside.

A certain image is doubtless bubbling upwards in the imagination at this point: what a perfect victim this "Paul" is! Watch carefully as the spider spins her web. How deftly the bright-eyed young seeker is assumed into the fold. The man is gold dust; see his wallet fly open at the slightest request. At the same time, notice how he's belittled and subjugated with guilt. Observe as he's emotionally beaten down like a dog for being a hoity-toity private school-educated type with no common sense who would probably cry if he got his hands dirty.

In reality, the seeker was as poor as a church mouse at the time. I never asked for cash from my parents (who are *not* rolling in money) and did all my own cleaning, gardening, shopping, ironing and washing. I knew what was good for me. Well, at least, I thought I did...

The "Holy Mother" asked me to take off just my outer shirt and lie down on my front in the middle of her living room floor.

I did as I was told and breathed a sigh of relief. I wasn't in the mood for nakedness. Luckily, for added insulation that evening, I'd put a T-shirt on under my shirt. When I removed my main shirt, the "Holy Mother" would have seen a picture of a giant evil-looking bat gazing blood-thirstily down on a muscle-bound biker riding a demonic bike, speeding off to rescue a scantily-clad angel lashed to the top of a skyscraper.

She set to work on my back and I felt incredibly relaxed. There was incense burning in the holder but I could smell another scent; it was incredibly sweet and like nothing I'd ever smelt before. When she finished, I was asked to carry on lying there for a few minutes until I felt ready to get up. The "Holy Mother" retired to her reception room to talk to Kat.

When I did stand up and walked out through the sliding doors into where the "Holy Mother" was now sitting, I felt really good. I also felt quite light-headed and relaxed and began to chatter like a schoolboy. The Mother smiled sweetly and I was told to go home and meditate. I said goodbye to them both and was ushered out by Kat who told me she would phone me later. On my way home, I felt on top of the world and as soon as I got in, I was so entranced by everything, I forgot about the meditation completely, prepared myself a bowl of cereal and settled down to watch *Eastenders*. It was only once I'd been treated to half an hour of good old East End pub shenanigans and implausibly murderous plot lines that I got up to put my cereal bowl in the sink. That's when I realised that my backache was gone.

I was utterly thrilled.

A short time later the phone rang. It was Kat. In a calm and prepared voice, she ripped right into me:

"Paul…why didn't you leave Holy Mother any money at all? You have made a terrible, terrible mistake tonight and she's furious with you. You should have left at the very least £30!"

I had no idea I was going to be charged. I'd read this woman's book on practical spirituality and she claimed to be a lady of Universal compassion and mercy. Honestly, I thought people like that healed or helped people out of unconditional love for humanity and not as some kind of money-making operation. I was totally thrown and apologised profusely, promising to leave some cash for the Mother as soon as I could draw it out from the cash point.

I went to bed feeling terrible that night. I hadn't even started out on my spiritual path yet and already this woman's God was fulminating and furious with me.

After the great back-curing incident, I was hooked. Of course, it never occurred to me that there might be another explanation for such a miracle, that actually, all that had happened was that I'd gone to HM's[1] house expecting a cure and that was what had occurred because I'd brought about such a scenario by my own volition. I wasn't sure that the placebo effect even existed in those days, let alone could work for me.

This isn't to say that HM wasn't a good healer. In reality, she occasionally was and one or two of her successes were well known. However, this isn't a straight case of 'is she a fake or is she

---

[1] From now on I will refer to the Mother as HM so that I don't have to continue to use the word holy to describe her. I think we are ALL holy in one sense or another and some people are definitely NOT more *holy* than others, which is what this idiotic name implies….

genuine?' In order to explain that, you need to stay with this story as the reality of the situation is incredibly subtle; there are certain shades of light, of distinct and also overlapping truths and untruths that need to be explored before we fully answer that question. As a novice to spirituality, it was incredibly difficult for me at the time to make of sense of it all. My only suggestion for you, as the reader, is to put your reservations on hold and ride the crest of this particular wave as I tried to do at the time.

I'd met HM on Tuesday 16th December 1997. I told her I was going to my parents' house for Christmas and that I'd be back on December 27th as I had to work. At the time I had a temp job and if I didn't work, I didn't get paid; it was as simple as that.

By the weekend, a book had turned up from her. It was only on loan, but I was ordered to read it from cover to cover. It was called, *Tibet's Great Yogi Milarepa*, by *W Y Evans Ventz*. Apparently, as Kat told me when she handed me the book, it was a true story and that in a past life I'd been Milarepa. Milarepa was the one who HM had referred to in my first meeting with her, the one who'd destroyed a house with all his family inside.

The book was fascinating. I discovered that this Yogi was so sorry after summoning up the destructive and deadly hailstorm, he eventually retired to a cave and lived in seclusion, surviving by drinking nettle tea. In the quiet and isolation two things happened. One: he became enlightened and achieved great spiritual gifts and two: he turned green from the tea.

Did I think I'd been this character once I'd read the book? All I can say is that, at the time, I had no choice but to put that piece of information somewhere until I could believe it, so I booted it straight into my "on hold" closet along with everything else.

If I'd had my wits about me and had not been so baffled and confused, I'd have realised there was a clever little game being played with a wireless controller. When I think back on it, I almost love it myself for its sheer ingenuity. What better way to manipulate someone in a situation like this than to "big them up" and belittle them all at the same time. Milarepa was a beautifully chosen example. On the one hand, his anger and arrogance were undeniable: these were the very traits that HM wanted to expose in me, whether I had them or not. By telling me that my soul was capable of mass murder, I was held in check. This was a time when

20

the notion of reaching enlightenment was all that mattered to me. The implication was that only a high guru like HM could possibly help me to pay off all that "sin" before I could even contemplate training for enlightenment. I therefore had "no choice" but to bind myself to her for good or ill.

On the other hand, I was being told I'd been a very important Yogi and believe it or not, one who, legend has it, could even take to the air and fly. What better way to hook a person in! Tell them their soul has such a fine and wonderful heritage! The implication was that I was this great being that desperately needed help and the only person available for such a dangerous mission was Britain's very own Holy Mother.

I was meant to feel honoured and extremely privileged whilst at the same time no better than a piece of crap lying in wait on the pavement.[2]

---

[2] Around this time, she also told me I'd been one of Jesus's disciples. Awesome! Oh, wait a moment. It turned out to be a lesser one - James the Less…(Oh, well…)

Chapter Three

Like an idiot, I secretly went to the doctor and got myself a flu shot that winter. It turned out to be one of the biggest mistakes of my life. To this day, I honestly believe there was something in that injection that did harm to me on the deepest level. Some eight years later, I realised that I'd developed an overactive thyroid gland and went into health meltdown. But up to that point, and starting almost immediately after the flu shot, I became ravenous. In those days, if anyone was asking "who ate all the pies?" the answer was inevitably Paul Arrowbank. I could stuff as much food down my gullet as I wanted and stay, well...not skinny, but relatively slim. I had always been a chubby kid and to have this added bonus as an adult was great. I developed a deep and lasting love of sponge, particularly carrot cake.

Joking aside, my adrenaline was now pumping away nineteen to the dozen and I was hyperactive. I chatted away like a little monkey and often made a fool of myself. I charged around town with so much energy during the day, that by five in the evening, I was almost a gonner. This state of affairs lasted for years and went unnoticed by HM. All she could focus on was how greedy I was and suggested I cut down on my food intake. I tried that, but failed utterly. It was so bad I'd have eaten the flowers in my own garden, given half the chance.

The reason why I went for this flu jab was because I was worried that I wouldn't be able to acclimatise back to Old Blighty temperatures after coming back from Greece. Although I wasn't that bothered by the cold in myself, there were times when it would still affect me whether I acknowledged it or not. My little garden flat was quite damp and forbidding. It was just a small building with a conservatory, tucked away at the bottom of a garden. The main dwelling was a large three-storey town house that had been converted into flats. I was the one who had drawn the short straw. Not only was my place unhealthy and at times unfit for human habitation, it was constantly being invaded by slugs and creepy crawlies: I would often wake up at night with a spider crawling over my face. Worse still, the place stank of cat wee and some nasty teenage girls (egged on by a psychotic mother) from the neighbouring council flat had taken to throwing stones from the roof of the garages over the wall onto the top of the conservatory.

So much for South African plantations, slaves and dripping in gold and jewels.

Life really wasn't easy in terms of finances. I was earning £600 a month, just enough to pay my bills and rent and buy some food. I had the feeling that I was about to be tapped up for every single last penny I had, so I had to have that flu jab. To miss a day off work would have probably sunk me without trace.

I went to my parents' house for Christmas on the 24th. Whilst there, I wittered on about my encounter with an enlightened lady, about all the healing she could do and how great she was. Both my parents kind of glanced at each other but kept a diplomatic silence. Only my brother had anything to say on the matter:

"Sounds like she's going to get you doing stuff for her!"

And how right he was. Almost the moment I returned home after Christmas, the spiritual slavery for the organ grinder's monkey began in earnest.

Firstly, on the Sunday, I was called around to HM's house to help her hook up her new video recorder. This turned out to be a great day as I met two very important people there. The first was the bright and bouncy young girl who answered the door when I first arrived. She was absolutely gorgeous and very bubbly with a lively personality. This was HM's daughter, Rosie. I'd heard that she was a bit of a handful, extremely wilful and not very obedient. I saw no sign of such character traits on that day.

The other character was HM's little boy, Scooter[3]. As I went in through the door of the reception room I greeted HM with the bowing thing and said "good morning" using her first name. I

---

[3] This is my own current nickname for HM's son and not his real name. It's been taken from a song called *Tenth Avenue Freeze Out* on *Bruce Springsteen's Born to Run* album, a record that I've always loved. "Scooter", I have to say, is not a name that HM would consider giving her son in a million years…

23

caught sight of the little guy for the first time and his eyes held a fleeting moment of shock. He turned to his mother and pulled on her sleeve, whispering, "Mum…Mum...he called you *********".

HM rolled her eyes and patted him on the head, smiling with enforced patience. Later when I got back home, the phone rang and it was Kat.

"I *told* you not to address the Holy Mother by her first name. She is *furious* with you…"

I said to Kat: "Wait a minute, excuse me… I asked you how you address the Holy Mother and you said, 'use her first name.'"

"No, I didn't," she snapped. I snapped back, "Oh, yes you did!"

As it turned out, Kat had got the wrong end of the stick. I had posed the question thus: "how do you address the Holy Mother?"

Kat had immediately assumed that I'd meant "how do *you* (Kat) address the Holy Mother." It didn't seem to occur to her that I might be asking from the point of view of the general "you" as in "one". She just hadn't been able to drag herself away from contemplation of her own ego for long enough to appreciate that this conversation wasn't in fact all about her.

As Kat was something called "the chief disciple" apparently she was allowed to use HM's first name. I was staggered. Both these funny ladies were obsessed with themselves and their own places in the world and weren't listening to a word I told them. Already communications were breaking down inexorably.

My faux pas with the name aside, I was very happy to have met Scooter. He was a very cute-looking kid with lots of black untidy hair and big brown, curious eyes. He was also a chatty little monkey and as HM left the two of us to put this video recorder together, he gave me some background about presents he'd received for Christmas. I felt a little sad for him. I knew there wasn't much money in his home, but listening to him talk it sounded like a 19th century street urchin telling me with glee that he'd received an orange and a spinning top. Whilst most kids had computer games and gadgets, little Scooter had educationally sound toys and sensible, conservative gifts. It didn't seem to bother him, I noticed.

Little did I know at the time, Scooter and I would become great buddies. This story is about him as well and also to a lesser extent about Rosie. Rosie, I could sense, was very much a girly girl. I

24

knew I would love her to bits, but by this time, she was already quite independent and liked her own arty, creative-young-lady pastimes. Scooter, though, was my kind of kid. He was a bit cheeky and over assertive, but very loveable and certainly easier for me to get on with, being a boy.

When I failed to get the video working, Scooter shouted out to his mum that I'd botched it. He also chided me for letting him down as he had a pile of cartoons to watch. He wasn't being rude, of course. This was just a typical six year-old kid who wanted everything NOW with no questions asked.

What I didn't know at the time was that the video player was faulty. It was a cheap one anyway and had been bought by someone who HM referred to as "one of my disciples". This sounded to me like HM was surrounded, like Jesus, by holy men in robes. In fact, there were no disciples, as no one was that bothered, interested or even mug enough to put themselves forward for such an ordeal. This particular chap wasn't a disciple at all - just someone who was often "around" but didn't hold any discernible role. HM did her best to keep the two of us apart for some weeks, worried that our combined energies could spawn some kind of rebellious monster that would topple her regime. Both she and Kat talked about this "disciple" as if he was some kind of uncontrollable jungle-dweller; I came to the conclusion there was every likelihood the video recorder came from some dodgy source and was never destined to work properly in the first place.

So that's the story of my second bunch of blunders and foolish mishaps. Great start! Already I was proving myself to be that spoilt privately educated boy that HM had so expected to find: no common sense, no sense of anything at all. In order to underline my incompetence, HM then set me up again for a fall. A couple of days later, she rang up and asked if I'd come with her to the filling station to fill up her car and check the oil and water. She told me she'd be around my place at 2pm the following Saturday and we'd all go together, Scooter included.

The hour arrived but the door bell failed to ring. I became worried and wondered what on earth had happened. At 2.30, I took the door bell down to check the battery and lo and behold got acid all over my hands and T-shirt. I hadn't checked the appliance since I moved in and as few people were visiting me, had no idea if it was functional or not. My heart jumped into my mouth as I realised HM had obviously come by and must have been ringing on my bell without my knowledge.

Sure enough, around 3pm the phone rang and it was Kat.

"Holy Mother is furious with you!"

Seemingly by now HM was convinced I was an idiot and clearly had this vision of me cowering indoors, afraid to come out in case I got my lovely soft little private school hands all oily.

There was a real pattern emerging now. I'd get an order, promise to carry it out, be frustrated and foiled by Universal events beyond my control and then get a complete rollicking. Someone upstairs was having fun with me.

Such was the situation for literally years to come...

Chapter Four

The 1998 New Year celebrations came and went and there was an eerie silence from HM. I kept in touch with Kat and she avoided the entire subject of Paul by doing what she did best: talking about Kat. Then one evening she phoned me:

"Holy Mother is furious with you!"

Oh no... Not again! *Off with his head!*

Apparently I'd failed to give her a Christmas donation. I was supposedly doubly selfish for my failure knowing what a precarious financial situation she was in. I popped some money through her door that evening and the following day she phoned me and I was back in favour.

I can hear what you're thinking now: *this is a cult like the Moonies! The woman is brainwashing fools into parting with cash.*

To be fair, that's only a partly correct assessment of the situation. As you continue with this book, you'll begin to see that there's a lot more to this theme of money in HM's life than is evident at first glance. However, you're right in one respect: spiritual teachers should NEVER, EVER *demand* money off people for the help they give. Certainly, there are always cases where people want to express their gratitude for help that's been given to them by someone who's reached a high level of spiritual attainment, but that money is given spontaneously out of love and kindness and doesn't have to be demanded.

Let me just add here, and apologies if you're not a believer in a Source Consciousness, but that consciousness and the spiritual "help" that comes from it cannot have a price. A teacher who makes charges for those who are on a path to find the essence of the Source is misrepresenting it and cashing in on the idealism of spiritual seekers. Therefore, put simply, what HM was doing by constantly demanding cash is an offence, through and through. More fool me for not realising that sooner. No wonder so many people are sick and tired of spiritual folks when they hear stories like this. For every person who's been put off finding answers to life's mysteries by the discovery that a certain guru is *expecting* cash for being who they are, then that guru will, at some point, have to foot the bill.

The "Moonying" of Paul Arrowbank began in earnest in - I think - the second or third week in January 1998.

Believe it or not, it wasn't all bad at first, mainly thanks to the shenanigans of Scooter. My main task was to help him with his reading and writing and many an evening was spent in such a pastime. Because I was still being seen as an over-educated Oxford graduate, for some reason I was expected to pull a rabbit from a hat as far as this was concerned. Worse luck for me, progress was just a little slow...

Scooter was very intelligent but bone blooming idle. He was such a loveable, cute kid and I relished spending time with him, but his laziness was legendary. HM was concerned that he was lagging behind and I was pressed into spending at least half an hour with him for several evenings a week listening to him reading.

He would do anything he could to get out of it. Once we'd settled down with a book, he would rest his head on his arm splayed out across the table and read aloud in the dullest possible monotone just to wind me up. Rolling his eyes and sighing, sometimes he would mispronounce words for a laugh or speak in a funny voice. Meanwhile, HM was listening from upstairs whilst tapping away on her old Amstrad. Then I would hear her voice calling down:

"Scooter! Read properly or you can go to bed early!"

Scooter would make an effort for a few seconds and then find something else to distract himself. A classic was for him to say:

"Paul, I just need to go upstairs a sec. I'll be back soon."

I would let him go and wait. Five baffling minutes later, I would still be sitting there on my own like a stuffed dummy. Then HM's voice would call down from the landing:

"Paul, what on earth are you doing? Why is Scooter playing with Lego in his bedroom?"

Having managed to entice him back into his chair, I would somehow trick him into reading a few more lines. To punish me, he'd then get bored again and start to ask me impertinent questions:

28

"Paul, have you ever heard of the Teletubbies?"

"Can't say I have, Scooter. What are they?"

"Oh, it's a programme for babies about some stuffed coloured things that run around in a garden. They have a hoover and they make baby noises and one of them's called Stinky Winky…"

Scooter wasn't a malicious chap. It was all just a joke for most of the time as far as he was concerned. I just couldn't bring myself to be angry with him.

After the reading, he Rosie and I would be allowed to play games and chat before bathtime. As Scooter was born in the Chinese year of the Goat (or Sheep), a big joke was to call bath time Sheep Dip. It kind of suited him because sometimes he was such a little farm animal.

One thing I always remember about Scooter and Rosie at that age was their total lack of organisation. For example, when we were socialising in the front room, one of them would go out to the kitchen, get a glass of water and then come back and put it on the floor. As these were little people who couldn't sit still for five seconds, inevitably the glass would get kicked across the carpet. HM's carpet was nearly always sopping wet in those days. The kids would then make it worse by grazing like goats on snacks and grinding crumbs into this mess. Sometimes I used to think it would be quicker just to go out to the garden, get the hose, spray a few gallons of water around and be done with it.

Despite my best efforts, I did go down with flu that winter. Scooter got it first from school. I went round in the second week in February and found him coughing and spluttering all over the place. In those days, being so young and bouncy, he didn't think twice about being tactile with adults and he was at his most comfortable when sitting on my crossed legs on the floor playing a game or watching TV. When I moved away to get the blood flowing again and sat on one of HM's bashed up old wing chairs, he would give me two minutes and then jump on me and stay there.

On reflection, what Scooter needed was a dad and there had never really been anyone like that in his life. I think I was the first male to appear, who could, at least in part, come close to that role and I think he realised that pretty quickly. For my part, I already knew it was going to be very hard just to walk away.

After all that coughing and spluttering, within days I was stricken with flu. HM found out and phoned me. When I mentioned - off the cuff - that Scooter had passed on his germs, she gave me a thorough dressing down. She told me that you become ill because of your attitude and because you've called in the illness with your thoughts and negativity. She explained that illness is also brought on by bad eating habits and made sure I was in no doubt: the reason I was stricken so low myself was because I was absolutely riddled with anger, hatred and resentment towards her.

I double-checked that I'd understood: you mean we don't make each other ill by coughing and spluttering over one another?

"It's your attitude!" she repeated.

I had a problem with this. Of course we make each other ill. In fact, there's flu raging as I write and we're passing it on in offices and shops and public transport. What she should have explained is that as harmful viruses and bacteria are as much an essence of "God" as we are, it's ultimately our own choice as to whether we accept them into our bodies and lives or not. If we're going with the flow, we'll simply say: *I'm healthy and radiating love and Light.* With such a positive mental attitude, we're more likely to avoid illness.

Instead, what HM was doing was using this situation as a way to hound me. She explained that I'd made myself ill by own thoughts, but hadn't explained that in order to overcome the illness, I needed to take a more constructive and creative approach to life. She focused in on the negative aspect and conveniently overlooked the positive lessons I could have learned from the situation. So I was made to feel "down" about myself for calling in the illness. This turned out to be typical of the angle she took in so many ways. It was always the destructive element of what people did that she homed in on. Rarely did she take the chance to inform them of more meaningful reasons behind difficult situations, such as how they could be used as a springboard to understanding the inner man. It was as though she couldn't wait to use the down side of the situation to harass people and put them in their place. In my case, I was made to feel doubly guilty for hating her and wanting to murder her in her bed. I was confused because my feelings towards her were at the very most neutral.

This was a classic example of the blurred nature of HM's teachings. Many years later she was to attack me quite bitterly when I stood up against her in a debate over AIDS. She told me it was, at least in part, a punishment from her "God" for Gays being immoral. I was incensed when I heard that. I told her that AIDS was a genetically engineered disease, that it was just a bastardisation of science and also affected other groups in the community.

She rounded on me and shouted: You know I don't give any credence to science! This is spirituality. You're logical and therefore *ignorant*..."

Once again, such was her intention to expose the negative side of the situation, she shut out the true essence of it, which was that it wasn't a punishment at all, just a soul taking on a situation that would allow it to focus on what it needed to learn and grow.

This sort of approach to illness is an example of someone who cobbled together a few teachings, some fag ends of spiritual wisdom and a whole lot of religious bigotry and intolerance. Fly-by-night teachers who are going around oppressing others by focusing in on the "blame" aspect of illness are pushing away the chance to inspire them to learn the deeper reasons for why they're suffering. There are lessons in every single situation, that's why we're here: to learn and progress. On top of that, although we *can* make ourselves better by changing our thoughts and lifestyles and by being positive, we do sometimes need to trust science and technology as well as be wary of it. Those souls that do find a cure from science and conventional medicine have probably learned the spiritual lessons they've set themselves after all!

There's another nice little adjunct to the tale of Scooter's flu virus. When she heard I was ill, HM sent some fruit around to me via Kat. I thought it was a lovely gesture and asked Kat to thank her for me. There followed an eerie silence from HM for about three days. Then, lo and behold, it was OFF WITH HIS HEAD again. The phone rang and it was Kat:

"Holy Mother is furious with you. She went out and bought you all that fruit and you haven't contacted her to thank her or given her any money! You *know* how hard up she is..."

31

One day, Kat phoned me up to tell me that HM had been saying I was too soft and private school. I thought, *"oh no, not this bloody subject again!"* HM was obsessed with emanating a sort of haughty disdain of posh privately-educated types; I should have been suspicious because she barely even knew me and had clearly not observed me with any great depth. I came to the conclusion that there was a kind of inverted snobbery about her which I explained perversely by chalking it up to her gritty, down-to-earth manner supposedly designed to draw out weaknesses in people so she could teach them.

That evening Kat announced that HM had had an idea. I was to be told to go and live out on the street as a homeless person for a whole week. This would apparently teach me to stop being such a soft little weakling. Personally I thought she'd gone bonkers, but Kat was serious.

"Don't worry," she said. "I'll come and get you in my car once the week's up. If you're smelly, I'll have some deodorant ready..."

Somewhat bemused, I happened to mention this to a bunch of people in my office who all went extremely quiet. Then one of the girls, Jane, who was very intelligent and extremely socially aware, suddenly piped up:

"For God's sake! Who is this woman she thinks she can ask someone to do that? That's the most pathetic thing I've ever heard! I'd hate the thought of anyone going out on the street and *pretending* to be homeless when they've got a nice warm flat to go home to after a week. How bloody patronising!"

Her words hit home hard. It *was* pathetic. Not only had HM completely misunderstood my nature, but she was enforcing an entirely unnecessary lesson on me that was every bit as sick an idea as Jane claimed.

I discussed Jane's opinion with Kat who I believe then told HM herself. Unsurprisingly, the stupid homelessness idea was suddenly dropped, probably because if I told anyone else what the plan was, word would get round and people would accuse HM of telling her disciples to do sick things in the name of "God". That would not have been good for her reputation. I was later given a good old-fashioned HM reprimand for discussing what plans she had for my spiritual path with anyone outside our circle.

During this period, HM started to make claims that she was being incredibly "nice" towards me. She insisted that indulgence and leniency were not part of her teaching agenda and that if she gave me the full force of the grief she was prepared to give her "disciples" I would buckle because I was too sensitive. But then, think about it: she *was* being abusive. Her histrionics made Cruella DeVil look like a pussy. The Starlight was definitely barking!

One day, Rosie was showing me cross-stitch and we had some needles out. HM explained to me that she wanted me to be extra careful of the needles and not to leave them lying about in case one of the kids was hurt. Obviously, she was within her rights to do that as she was a mother doing what comes naturally: caring for her children. But there was such a threat behind her words, a sort of emotional violence being transmitted that I think, inevitably, she brought about the very circumstances required for a problem with those needles! It's like when parents warn kids with too much emphasis to be *extra careful* not to get tea all over their best clothes: they then get so nervous that they end up losing control of their muscles in their fearsome state and spew tea all over themselves and those around them.

At some point, I dropped a needle. The next thing that happened, Scooter distracted me and almost in an instant, I clean forgot to search for it. It sat there on the chair and lay in wait for some hapless victim. I went home and was all calm until that phone rang again. This time, it wasn't Kat phoning to say that HM was furious with me. It was the furious one herself. And oh boy, was she mad! She screamed at the top of her lungs that I'd disobeyed her, that I'd put her and her children in danger, that I was absent-minded, selfish and lacking in awareness. You could then hear her throwing that phone down halfway across Reading. Although I admit it was extremely remiss of me, I was flabbergasted at her aggression. She was later to refer to such outbursts as "righteous anger" and claimed that they were her prerogative as a divine being, but to me, unconsciously, it came across as the behaviour of someone with a psychopathic tendency. She always claimed in those days that every time I went near her, she could feel my resentment towards her. I always wanted to say this: "I'm not a resentful person. But if your behaviour is alienating towards those who are trying to do the right thing in your regard, then resentment is what you inspire."

HM was her own worst enemy. As a spiritual person, she was always telling us that thoughts are a creative power in themselves, that if your thought patterns are set to negative then you bring about negative circumstances in your life. Why it was that she was incapable of understanding that principle in her own life is beyond me. She saw threat in everyone, especially in men. Consequently, she always felt menaced and aggressed and brought into being the circumstances of her own poverty and misery.

Look at the difference between these two thoughts:

I won't find any obstacles on my way when I drive into town and the car park won't be full so I won't have problems and struggle to find a parking space

and

I will have an easy journey into town and will find a parking space in just the right spot.

On the surface of it, both sentences seem positive. But in reality, the first sentence is full of negative words like "won't", "obstacles" "struggle" and "problems". By concentrating on the negative side of every situation, the positive cannot shine through. However, the second sentence is one that's full of good vibration and is more likely to bring about the positive outcome, even if that outcome may not be exactly as you envisage it.

HM was already negative when I first met her. Her constant stressing over her lack of money, her lack of quality personnel to help her achieve her aims - such as they were - her continual complaints about the immorality and idiocy of those around her caused her to bring into her life the misery that she was so desperate to escape from. With me, her negativity was such that rather than benefiting from my eagerness to help, it ended up causing her extra suffering.

Eventually a point would come when she would lash out at me in the most vicious way for not being the person that she required me to be.

Chapter Five

One day, Kat rang to tell me to go round to HM's in the evening. She informed me that she wasn't allowed to tell me what it was about, but that I was to have a good shower first. I was intrigued and followed this order to the letter.

I arrived at HM's that evening at 7.30 to find both children had been sent upstairs so that HM would not be disturbed. I was then asked to take my socks off.

I blanched. Suddenly I knew what this was all about. Some years earlier, HM had invented an "extremely efficient" way of getting people to view their past lives through reflexology, massaging the soles of the feet. She told me that there was an experience that she thought it was essential I revisit from *this life*, in fact, a scene that I'd apparently blocked out of all conscious memory due to its violence. She warned me that when I was about seven years old, I'd witnessed a child being abused at boarding school; she told me that I'd been walking through a corridor, heard a cry for help and had gone to investigate by opening a door into a room. Where this room was at my school I couldn't remember, but apparently what had happened was enough to set up trauma and an emotional block that I still had raging some twenty-five years later. When I opened the door, I disturbed a teacher in flagrante delictu with a young lad. This teacher had rounded on me, screaming at me that if I ever dared tell anyone what I'd seen, he'd come and kill me and then kill both my parents. I'd been so horrified, not only by this threat, but also by what I'd witnessed, that I fled the scene and instantly suppressed it from memory.

As I lay down on the sofabed ready for my reflexology, I was already struggling. My first thought was that it wasn't possible that any of this abuse had happened because I'd still been living at home when I was seven. Secondly, I really had to ask myself if the treatment would work. For one thing, I didn't want anyone fiddling around with my feet. I saw it as an invasion of privacy, particularly when I hadn't come forward to ask for it to be done of my own accord. Also, I thought it was up to me to come to the conclusion about whether or not I had childhood trauma and not to be told that was the case. My behaviour has never been such that I've shown traits caused by childhood trauma. I've never felt the urge to visit a psychiatrist or even had any kind of recurring nightmares. I knew there was one incident that had left me with a great deal of emotional sadness, but that isn't trauma and I have a conscious memory of it, even though it was something I'd simply stopped thinking about, NOT suppressed. That incident was when I witnessed a rape, but the rape of a woman, not a child. It was nothing to do with that particular school.

As HM carried out her reflexology, I tried to relax, but it just wasn't working for me. I was plain embarrassed. All I wanted to do was put my socks back on and flee. I wasn't scared of what I was supposed to see, just very uncomfortable.

After some minutes, she gave up with a sigh and told me, quite succinctly, that I was her first "failure" with the treatment. She immediately wrote the whole incident off as me being awkward and was not of a mind to face a simple fact: I hadn't wanted her fiddling around with me in the first place. I have an excellent long-term memory and although I can honestly say there were things going on at this particular school that were just plain wrong, the abuse was deeply emotional, not physical.

That evening, HM gave me strict orders to go home and see if I could view the scene for myself in meditation. This, she said, would then release the block and help me get on with my path.

I tried my hardest, I really did. In my meditation, I walked around and around that school but to no avail. I could see absolutely nothing and was totally at a loss. It just didn't seem right to me and I was very confused why HM would want to bring this into my life.

With hindsight, I can see what her little game was: she'd cooked up the whole thing so that she'd have a chance to do her regression therapy and charge me for it. Clearly she'd needed the cash and felt that not only was I "milkable", but also so stupid, I'd actually fall for the scam and honestly believe that there was some trauma to be tapped into. In her mind, she'd have justified lying to me by telling herself that she needed the money to do "God's" work and therefore, by throwing some challenges into my life, it

36

would be good for me on my spiritual path and a nice little earner for her.

I had no idea of this little ruse at the time. Because it had been sold to me by someone I thought I could trust, I immediately took it to be a self-evident truth and was determined to give it some honest investigation. In order to resolve the problem and get "this incident" confronted and behind me, I took drastic action. In London at the time, there was a lovely lady called Barbara who had a spiritual shop where I would buy books and incense. I always had a chat with her and thought she had a beautiful heart. One evening, Barbara opened up her shop and allowed a lady called Ruth to give a talk to about twenty people. The talk was about Ruth's therapy for viewing past lives. She told us how she put people into a state of hypnosis and gradually regressed them to whatever past lives they needed to see for the issues they were dealing with in their current lives. I was totally hooked by the idea of trying this and as soon as the talk was over, I booked myself a session.

All excited and chomping at the bit, I went and told Kat what I'd done. She said she thought it was a good idea, but she warned me: whatever I did, I wasn't to tell HM as I'd be in deep trouble for not doing the work myself. After all, I was on a spiritual path and had to realise that I was supposed to be doing all this sort of personal investigation on my own. If I didn't have a method, I was to learn one. At the time, HM was really pushing me to get this past event viewed, confronted and accepted so she could get on with her teaching. The suggestion was that I was holding her back. I can only imagine, with hindsight, that even though I hadn't paid her for her foot-prodding session, she felt she still had to push the lie on me in the hope that there would be something at the end of it for her.

Ruth had given me a date for my consultation which was about a month away and Kat advised me to write to Ruth and ask if she could possibly bring it forward. So I wrote her a letter the very next day.

The letter was roundly ignored which I thought was very odd. Instead, I ended up waiting the whole month and prevaricated whenever HM asked me how I was doing with my regression. On reflection, I was being incredibly duplicitous in not telling her what my real plan was, but I just didn't think I was up to finding the method for regression myself. I really thought I was spiritually incompetent at the time.

Eventually, the day came for my appointment and I took a train to Ruth's house in London. When she opened the door, I was met with a wall of ice. I walked into her large neat home and felt immediately unwelcome. She was stiff and formal with me and made no effort to help me relax. I mentioned my letter to her and she cut me short:

"I don't have time to answer letters or change appointment times," she said gruffly. I wanted to run out at that point. I felt I was on a complete hiding to nothing.

After lecturing me about ancient South American cultures and talking down to me like I knew nothing, this lady eventually got around to regressing me.

As it turned out, I liked her regression method very much and it did actually work. I saw three lives, all of which, if you don't mind, are quite personal and not within the scope of this particular book. In many respects, it was an extraordinary experience as it helped me to put a lot of missing pieces into my life puzzle about who I am and where I've been. I also realised afterwards that a lot of the people I saw in the visions were friends and family I recognised from my present life and the difficulties I faced with them in those lives were still being worked through in our current incarnations. A few years after this regression session, I met loads more of them as well and two people in particular who were very good friends of mine in one life I viewed, later became excellent friends in this life.

One of the last lives I saw in that session was a difficult one for me. I saw myself drowning and began to panic. Ruth had to bring me round very gently and when I came back, it took me a little while to recover.

That recovery, however, was short lived. I'd been to a cashpoint earlier in the day and raided my account for nearly all my previous week's earnings. It was lucky I did. For a therapy session that lasted no more than twenty-five minutes, Ruth ripped me off for £80! When I'd asked her previously how much the session would cost, she'd given me a very vague answer which I just brushed over, such was my desperation to get answers for HM.

I staggered out of that house reeling. For £80 I could have fed myself for two whole weeks and in that time, somehow found the method for myself. I learned a terrible lesson that day. There's greed and immorality amongst people who call themselves spiritual in the New Age scene. This lady gave herself airs and graces and reckoned she was worthy of fleecing people for doing nothing but just sit there. I was so green at the time. That naivety was to be my undoing for a long time to come.

HM appeared - on the face of it - to be thrilled when I told her of the lives I'd seen and congratulated me on succeeding in doing that all by myself. But I also came out with my second whopping great fib. I told her I'd also succeeded in viewing the abuse scene. I did that to get her off my back whilst I worked through it in my own time. I felt terrible about treating her so shoddily, but I was getting desperate and wanted things to go smoothly between us.

It seemed strange at the time, but when I mentioned it, she went all quiet. As I say, I hadn't "donated" any money for the reflexology that she'd given me, so that plan had backfired for her. She must really have been wondering at this point what was going on. She knew she'd lied to me about the abuse scene and then for me to turn it up suddenly as if it had actually happened must have thrown her completely!

A few days later, I went to a Mind Body Spirit fair in Reading Town Hall. Ruth the therapist was there and gave me a steely look as I went to talk to her to see if she remembered me. She deigned to speak to me for a few minutes but was incredibly cold and looked through and past me the whole time. I knew I was persona non grata and fled, determined never to darken her door again. I hope the ruthless woman enjoyed all that filthy lucre...

Later that day, Kat came over to my flat to see me before walking around the corner to spend the afternoon with HM. I nonchalantly mentioned that I'd been to the fair and really didn't think that such a revelation would have any kind of consequence.

Half an hour later, the phone rang. It was Kat. She told me solemnly she had to come around immediately as she had something urgent to tell me. She also asked me to meet her halfway up the street rather than let her in.

I followed her request to the letter and met her just down from the church. She was very agitated and almost shaking in fear. She said:

"Holy Mother knows you've lied to her. She knows all about the regression therapist and she knows you lied about seeing your school experience. She picked all this up herself in meditation. You're in so, so much trouble. She's thinking of banning you for life; she can't trust you and she's also told me she thinks you're violent. That's why I'm not coming in to your place, Paul. Holy Mother reckons you'll lose your temper and kill me with a knife."

I was aghast. I'm not a violent person at all. How could this lady, who always maintained she was in touch with Universal "information sources" make such a fundamental error of judgement?

If anyone was picking up "information" from the Field that afternoon, it was me. I knew Kat was lying. She'd promised me she'd never tell HM that I'd lied to her about the therapist, but she'd simply *not* been able to keep her mouth shut. Kat called herself my friend, but in truth, her priorities lay in keeping in with the Holy Mother. To do that, she was prepared to wheeler deal, duck and dive and betray. This was great kudos for her. She'd reported me and done an almighty deed. Worse still, *both* of them were now lying as they were trying to claim that HM had picked up what had really happened whilst in a state of meditation. I wasn't stupid. Of course Kat had told her.

To cap it all, she claimed that HM also knew that I'd visited a psychic fair without her permission. As a consequence, HM had been attacked by the dark side and nearly died. This had *supposedly* happened because I'd passed on some kind of devilish non-physical mischief-maker to Kat when I'd seen her earlier that afternoon. This entity was one that apparently recognised HM as an extremely high being and was intent on causing as much destruction as it could.

Kat handed me a letter from HM that venomously attacked me for my behaviour and I read it there and then out in the street. Kat seemed genuinely sorry about what had happened to me and promised to keep in touch. As she walked up the street, I watched her disappear and knew that I'd been well and truly stabbed in the back.

This theme of HM being attacked by the dark side was to return time and time again over the next few years. More often than not, I was the one who stood accused of bringing these dark entities in and I was always to blame for my immorality that attracted demonic forces.

It was a long time before I had an angle on just how that works which would show me that more often than not, I was just an innocent party. But for the moment, it suited everyone involved to make sure that I was known to be a dangerous, incompetent spiritual seeker that needed a good lesson. I was always reminded of that fact and it certainly kept me in my place.

Chapter Six

In the spring of 1998, HM's landlady gave her notice to quit her house in Hovel View Road. HM took this as a sign from her god that he was moving her out of a dump that she hated. Seemingly she'd petitioned him for somewhere more salubrious as she was sick and tired of living in a place she equated with bad student accommodation. The new house was going to be positively palatial. After so many years of poverty, HM was about to be rewarded. For several weeks, all Kat would say was:

"There's money coming now! This is it, Paul. HM is on the rise. There'll be an ashram, lots of people and money. Perhaps I can get some new kitchen cupboards..."

Weeks passed and no cash appeared. The kitchen cupboards would clearly have to wait as God wasn't of a mind to cough up.

When it was clear the celestial wallet wouldn't be opening, there began a desperate search for housing that caused a stressful situation to become almost a crisis. Once again, HM's "glass half empty" attitude caused delays, extra misery and a frightful outcome.

As she was so hard up, it became evident that to find a house in the "right" area was going to be impossible. HM, who was so hard-focussed on the unruly behaviour of the masses with their foul language and insulting manners, refused to move to an estate. Even though she detested the middle classes for pettiness, for lacking in humanity and care for their fellow men, she was still holding out for a nice little semi in leafy suburbia with lovely, genteel neighbours. The dichotomy behind this attitude meant that she blocked herself from day one. Over the next few months as the day closed in for her to move, she turned her nose up at a succession of properties. The negativity around her became almost tangible.

Scooter began to suffer himself. One day, he and I were playing with Lego and chatting and he asked me what a bay leaf did. I thought for a moment and realised that he was talking about a bailiff. His innocent little face looked so downcast. I also realised something else. Although HM was concerned enough for the welfare of her children that she was prepared to scream the place down if there was danger from a needle, she didn't think twice about haranguing her own son with damaging imagery of desperate poverty and the overhanging threat of homelessness. I knew she'd obviously discussed it with him, but instead of trying to bring comfort, she'd selfishly offloaded all her negative concerns onto him and imparted the full force of the seriousness behind the problem rather than attempt to talk him through it with love. Consequently, poor little Scooter thought that he was going to be sleeping in the freezing cold street with all his toys and clothes taken away from him by horrible men in dark suits. Honestly believing he'd forever be a victim of crushing poverty, he was just plain terrified. I tried to get him to understand that this wouldn't be the outcome but I could tell from his dejected eyes that the damage had already been done. For years, HM offloaded negativity onto her children in this way.

Realising that no suitable accommodation would be forthcoming in the private sector, HM went to the council for help. At the time, there was a long list of people waiting for houses and she had to join the back of that queue. If I remember correctly, she and Kat tried to convince the council that as she was a "minister of God" (?) she should be given priority; of course, that pretext just did not wash.

One of the houses that she was eventually offered was in a rough area of town. She and Kat went to look at it and walked out in disgust. Apparently, due to the extreme unpleasantness of previous occupants of the property, there was a vicious red entity in the kitchen that attacked HM almost the moment she walked through the front door.

I can understand why someone as sensitive as HM was unwilling to bring up her children in such an area. However, if she'd been more positive, she could have taken the house as a stop gap, cleared it of its negative influences (which should have been possible given all the claims she made about her spiritual abilities) and then bought herself some time to look for the place she wanted. But by then, HM was convinced of her role as an almost messianic figure in global spirituality and wasn't prepared to compromise, even for a moment.

Once she'd turned this property down, the council lost interest in helping her and wouldn't hear any excuses. As she'd long passed her deadline to move out of the terraced house, the landlady, knowing her predicament, had given her some extra time to sort herself out, but inevitably a day came when all such goodwill had been used up. The situation became so fraught with difficulty, the council became involved again and she and the children were offered what's called temporary emergency housing in a stop gap home. This house was a small semi a few miles away. It wasn't in leafy suburbia and there were no middle classes to be seen. HM reluctantly accepted.

I didn't see the house until the day she moved in; surprisingly she seemed quite pleased with it as the street it was in wasn't rough, just slightly run down, a little like her in so many respects.

A few days before her moving date, I finally met the "disciple" who had bought her the dodgy video recorder the previous winter. This was her friend Gary[4]. As soon as I met Gary I had this terrible feeling of foreboding. He was spectacularly stiff and formal to the point of being downright rude to me almost from the start. He began ordering me about like some kind of all-powerful patriarch; you wouldn't have believed he was a month younger.

After that first meeting which was engineered by HM so that we could discuss the logistics of her imminent house move, the patriarch offered to give me a lift home. As we sat in the car he said:

"Paul, you ain't gonna like me very much cos I'm from a working class background, right. I call a spade a bloody spade!"

I thought: *You know what, street boy? You don't fool me...*

I could tell that he had a lot of spiritual gifts and despite his rough exterior was someone with some wisdom. I also came to the conclusion that the reason why he was a little brusque with me initially was because HM had prepared him to meet a soft little private school idiot with no common sense.

---

[4] Not his real name. I chose Gary because it has a certain gritty quality, unlike Charles or Edward for example which would be slightly too uppercrust for this particular character and he would be furious with me...

As it turned out, on the day of the move, that's what he got! I was as weak as a kitten and definitely not up for the job of moving washing machines and heavy boxes. I think it was because I wasn't feeling very well and it showed. Once I'd ruptured myself enough to help him in his hired van to move all HM's rather battered belongings into her new home, he took pity on me and gave me some healing which turned out to be incredibly beneficial.

I mustn't get too excited with my description. With Gary, there was always a sting in the tail and that day was no exception. He and a friend of his, who was helping with the move, mocked and sneered at me nearly the whole time. I tried to turn it into a joke and go along with everything, but felt like a fish out of water. At one point, the twosome started swearing and like a fool I joined in.

By way of a lesson for me, he took HM aside some time later and reported my little verbal indiscretions to her. Consequently, two days after the move, it was *off with his head* again. I received a phone call from Kat:

"Holy Mother is furious with you. Apparently you were swearing and ogling girls..."

I found this surprising. Because I was apparently so soft, Gary assumed that I had to be a bit of a sissy. So why he took it upon himself to report me as a sort of rough-builder-type-wolf-whistler to HM, I don't know.

Actually, yes, I do know. Gary is one of life's "mick takers". I believe that he understood on a very deep level what sort of a character HM was. Instead of using his considerable wisdom to steer her right, he took it upon himself to be part of the lesson for me and therefore to go along with HM's abuse.

One day Kat decided to tell me why HM was so keen to keep me and Gary apart: she was terrified that our combined forces of violence would be lethal to her. She even went around telling people that both of us had murdered her in several lifetimes for being a beautiful, vulnerable soul that only ever wanted to do right.

I'll let you to make up your own mind about me, but as for Gary, the most I can say is that he was nothing more than a spiritual loose cannon with a self-appointed role as the devil's advocate and the cat amongst the pigeons.

HM's approval of her new house was short-lived. It was cold. By now it was spring 1998 and still not the warmest time. The only source of heating in the house was a gas fire in the front room. I've never liked that sort of heating myself as it produces so much condensation. This was certainly the case in this house. It was incredibly damp and poor old Scooter, who ended up with a miniscule bedroom, also ended up with the worst of it. Scooter being Scooter made the most of it, probably because he was relieved not to be on the streets with a bay leaf pointing a gun to his little face.

Rosie settled in quickly. She's always been such an adaptable person and everything seemed to wash through her in the most spiritual way. She really was a credit to her mum but just wasn't appreciated. When Rosie was born, she was a crier. According to HM's autobiographies she cried the house down from morning to night and would just never settle. These days I believe there are very deep reasons for this and for why, even at an incredibly young age, she was unhappy in this incarnative experience. I'll leave you to work that one out for yourselves as this story progresses. For the moment, all you need to know is that she was a little girl like so many little girls these days who just wanted to have some fun, go to school and hang out with friends.

In those days (and you really cannot fault HM's devotion to duty here) she was driving both children daily to a village school at least ten miles outside Reading. She'd picked this school for them because it had an excellent reputation and fostered a very loving and caring environment. Hats off to her for this choice because, to a certain extent, it was the making of those two in their early years and it really gave them both an excellent start.

However, by the time I arrived on the scene, the driving was taking a toll on her. She was such a delicate person and could be knocked aside so easily. She always claimed that it was the high spiritual vibration she'd achieved that caused this sensitivity. But I can say that people who achieve this high vibration due to spiritual advancement can still cope with life's problems. If anything, they cope better than anyone else as they have added strength and inner creativity, know exactly what to do in any situation and can manage the unpredictability of daily life with real mastery.

Not HM. For her, everything was an uphill struggle and a reason to shout: I CAN'T COPE! From the outside looking in, it seemed to be no more than a refusal to get on with life and a call for everyone else around her to take away her personal responsibilities so she could concentrate on herself as a great messianic being. She constantly used this daily journey as a pretext to make out that she was grinding away at life harder than anyone, especially to me, the privileged one with a legion of slaves to dust his bedroom.

As she'd worked herself into a state where she no longer felt she could cope with the drive, let alone with a trip to Asda, she decided to take the children out of school and teach them herself. Rosie didn't like this situation. She's always been a gregarious type and didn't get on with this new form of isolationism at all. On reflection, I believe that even aged nine, she knew there was something unnatural about it. All she wanted to do was mix with ordinary folk and muck in with other kids.

Because she'd always been painted as the problem kid, that's unwittingly what she became in those days. She just wouldn't co-operate and made her feelings abundantly clear about how she didn't want to be corralled up at home. After a few months of this rebellion, HM decided to let her go to a local school that didn't have the same loving atmosphere that the first one did. Ironically, Rosie ended up enjoying herself there and just got on with her life as best as she could.

As for Scooter, he was pleased he didn't have to go to school because he was such a lazy little scamp. Instead, he put up with the school work that HM gave him as part and parcel of getting on with his mum and keeping her happy. But he was also becoming more and more despondent and I was too preoccupied with myself to notice. I would go around and he would be fractious and even less co-operative than he'd been in the first days I'd known him. By and large, I think he was mostly an upbeat chap, though. I did notice he could be brought round and cheered up fairly quickly. He still relished my company and would play some horrible jokes on me like stealing and hiding my wallet, my shoes, my signet ring, in fact anything I left lying around.

Around this time, HM took me aside and announced that the reason why nothing was happening for her on the spiritual front was partly because she still had training to do which could involve much meditation and self-analysis. Because of this, she asked me to get a permanent job at the company where I was temping. I readily agreed as I needed the money. I liked working for this company as it was an organisation with a good history and had a dignity and fairness about it that's lacking in so many firms. I went for an interview and got a job straight away which suited me perfectly. According to HM, this arrangement would only be for a year or so as her ministry was due to start in earnest and I would be assumed in glory into some great spiritual community or ashram, as they call it.

When HM had first moved in to the new house, she was still desperately hard up and utterly incapable of creating the spiritual vibration that would improve her life from the financial point of view. If she'd have been more aware, she'd have been able to understand that what she was supposed to do was get down from her ivory tower, stop calling herself holy and a divine being and just plain get on with the job of healing people and helping them with their spiritual paths. She was still labouring under the impression that she had to make a splash and hit people right between the eyes with the full on "I AM DIVINE" scene. Every time someone pointed out that she was being ridiculous, rather than seeing it as an extremely useful Universal message, she would twist it around and say that it was her God's decree that she should meet with adversity and criticism from others. Her suffering was a kind of Jesus-like stamp of approval on her role as Britain's foremost spiritual being.

I didn't know it at the time, but here in the UK we have a fair few spiritually evolved people; none of them are as brazen about their abilities as HM was. The way to find such people is to be utterly humble in your approach and they will appear in your life synchronistically. At the time, I can't have been ready to meet such a person as the Universe had pointed me in the direction of a monster not a master. In retrospect, that was clearly HM's role in my life: to be the freak that kicked my ass so soundly it would do me a world of good and provide me with the lessons I needed to advance. She, of course, had no clue whatsoever about just how that was working and to be frank, neither did I! But then, not to put too fine a point on it, this was not about me. It was all about her, pure and simple.

After the great Sweary Mary incident when my potty mouth had been well and truly exposed by Gary, I was banned from seeing HM for a month. In fact, it turned out to be more like a week as she'd come to rely on me. It was suggested to me that I "donate" £60 a month to the cause and now that I was imminently working full time, that was within my budget. I was asked to give this money to Kat as she spent so much time doing chores for HM that she didn't have enough energy to do more of her own private jobs. That felt weird. Kat had her own house and there I was, hardly able to put two pennies together, living in rented accommodation and subsidising her mortgage. All the same, I still cared about her; I thought it was the best I could do.

I think in those early days of the new house, Kat was suffering in her own way. She was becoming quite ratty and unable to cope, but then, she was under far too much pressure. Her own daughter was a very bright and bubbly young girl who, like Rosie, wanted to live a normal life and mix with other kids. She saw Kat's involvement with HM as a hindrance to her and couldn't bear the sound of her name. On occasion, when I'd go round to Kat's house to look after her when Kat had some kind of engagement, she'd make me laugh till tears streamed down my face by mocking the concept of HM. Dancing around the sitting room, she'd wave her hands in the air and shout in a posh voice: "Oh, look at me! I'm a *Hooooly* Mother! Get out of my way! I'm the *Hooooly* one! *I'm sooo sooo Hooooly!*"

HM had no time for Kat's daughter. She would constantly berate Kat for not bringing her up in a morally correct environment. Kat was determined to stick to her guns and give her daughter the upbringing she wanted, keeping her many "indiscretions" in this regard quiet from HM. She took the view that if she wanted to listen to the *Spice Girls* who were all the rage at the time, then she should be allowed to. Rosie was not allowed anywhere near the *Spice Girls*. Scooter thought they were stupid anyway which kind of made life easier in so many respects.

I'll never forget walking into that house on the first day and going up to the main bedroom to find Kat on her hands and knees, her hair in her eyes, cleaning up thick dust from the closet and throwing away piles of unwanted garbage left behind by previous tenants.

Kat was straining under the yoke and perhaps some of her impatient behaviour from that time could be put down to the stress she was suffering. She and I remained reasonably close and in her more lucid moments, she tried to talk me through HM's bizarre behaviour with patience and the promise of better days to come when there'd be an ashram, when we'd all be working for the greater good in healthy surroundings. I'm sure she must have known deep down that was just never meant to be. She knew HM's thing wasn't healthy, that it was deeply damaging. Inevitably, one of the first people I was acquainted with to be damaged by HM turned out to be Kat herself.

That summer, Kat and her daughter went abroad on holiday. Before she left, HM told her that she was going to start pushing her when she came back to the UK. By this, HM was saying that she wanted to move her up to Spiritual Master, a level of spiritual attainment that New Agers say is the one of the first stages of enlightenment. Personally, I don't "do" levels. Very often, it's another reason for people to start giving themselves labels and there's great potential for misunderstandings by using such a wide term of reference. However, for the moment, all you need to know is that HM wanted more out of Kat. She needed someone to be her right hand, a person who had a good healing ability, good clairaudience and clairvoyance, had a sharpened intuition and enough unconditional love to help the sick and the lost, people who were supposedly going to be beating a path to HM's door in the very near future.

Kat was so excited and phoned me to say that she would be making it to Spiritual Master in six months time. I was thrilled for her and could really feel her exhilaration. It was the first time in months that I'd seen her that animated.

What I didn't realise is that it doesn't work like that. Soul evolution comes as a very subtle process of inner opening to the Light, the important word there being *inner*. You cannot put a timetable on this inner movement. It doesn't just happen because you've pencilled it in for a certain time and place. HM always looked for advancement from the point of view of externals. From someone who was supposed to be enlightened herself, it was

50

extraordinary behaviour. This kind of vast spiritual awakening doesn't come suddenly, out of the blue. You have to work on your attitudes towards others and yourself, as well as find some kind of meditative path to sharpen your general awareness[5]. Kat was just too stressed out by all the donkey work she was doing for HM and too loyal to her daughter to be able to create the circumstances for this inner unfolding of realisation. I felt she needed time and space and had neither. Some people can reach a high level of wisdom and awareness whilst totally surrounded by noise, hassle and distraction. But to me, it was always as if Kat needed to be left alone from outside influence.

When she returned from holiday, HM pitched in to her almost immediately and that's when the resentment kicked in. In retrospect, it was clear why HM felt the need to do this. With a week's absence, Kat would have had time to take stock of her life and to reassess. Once outside of HM's strong sphere of energy, there's every chance that Kat would have started to regain her own sense of identity and quite possibly return with a more independent head on her shoulders. In order to maintain her position of authority, HM brought through the full brute force of her control in order to boot her back to her position as slave. This was done deftly with swingeing emotional drama tactics disguised as "strictness". HM would claim that this device was designed to inspire Kat to move up to the level of Spiritual Master – at least that's how it was sold to her. There were days when Kat understood that. But then, there were other times when to lie down and accept it was just completely unrealistic.

---

[5] My good friend from Germany, Anna (whose amazing role in this story will later become apparent) had this to say on the subject of meditation: "From my experience, I didn't meditate a lot in the classical sense. All these things came to me just like that. My boyfriend goes for a run - that's his meditation. A friend of mine paints - that's her meditation. For some people, who've chosen a meditative path, meditation is of course all-important, and that meditation is not just done by sitting on the floor in the lotus position. It can be done anywhere where you feel silence in the mind. Enlightenment is not just one big bang - there's no such thing as one enlightenment. It's a continuous path because after the first enlightenment there are different levels after that: different awarenesses, wider understandings. What in the past was a longing for Nirvana is now outdated."

51

Kat's initial excitement abated swiftly. In no time at all, she began to see the whole Spiritual Master scenario as pointless. The HM spiritual bandwagon had slowed right down for her and she was beginning to feel she was on a complete hiding to nothing. Her frustration and resentment were a manifestation of this deep inner realisation. The problem was, she just hadn't reached the point where she could completely let go.

HM phoned her and had a go at her over some trivial matter and Kat finally snapped. An argument ensued and this time, for a change, it was Kat who was up for a good beheading. HM tried pulling the banning tactic out of her armoury and brought her usual tired old brand of indignation down on Kat in an effort to scare her into thinking that her god was furious with her. Kat threw the phone down and was so unspeakably furious, she phoned me up and shouted with thinly disguised outrage:

"You know what that bitch said to me...?"

I was really shocked because up to that point, Kat had always been so loyal to HM. But beneath the surface that loyalty had been inspired by the fact that HM had hooked her in by promising that she would be a great spiritual person, forever remembered for being the handmaiden of the Messiah for the Aquarian age. I don't think I'm exaggerating here. HM and Kat had been so hand in glove for a long time, I think it's inevitable that between the two of them, a plan had been hatched for world domination. Kat must have been swept along by this and I don't blame her. I think she was motivated by the right kind of ideologies and there was a caring side to her that sometimes emerged. The problem was that she still had too much inner work left undone, too much detritus from her past to sift through and of course, the biggest block of all: HM herself. The fact that Kat could collapse so easily over one disagreement with HM was a sign that all was far from well.

On top of that, the Messianic thing was dangerous and clearly never, ever destined to happen. This isn't 33AD. The sort of ministry that HM was aiming for, where she was this divine oracle speaking down to humanity after sweeping majestically into a room in a sari, would have your chattering classes spitting with mockery. The whole plan was conceived in complete naivety.

That evening, Kat told me some things about HM that she should have kept to herself. I promised to keep the information under my hat and felt my heart sink as it showed that HM had, at some time in past, done something that undermined her claim to have been a celibate "holy" person. To be honest, I was angry with both of them: HM for not being the person I wanted her to be and Kat for undermining herself by going from the loyal handmaiden one moment to the disloyal revealer of painful truths the next.

I tried to talk her through her new-found impasse with HM and told her not to react badly. After all, by this time I was the one who was the most experienced at having his head regularly removed from his torso in ignominy.

After a few days, Kat somehow managed to shift back into gear. She gritted her teeth and decided - God knows how - to soldier on. Eventually she was back in favour and we did try to pick up where we left off, but in all fairness, it was incredibly hard for her. That initial euphoria you get when you've been assumed back into the fold after a period of exile can be incredibly uplifting at first. This was a very effective control tactic and a prime example of how a psychopathic controller works: send the victim into exile, shut down on them completely. After a period where they're left to stew in their own juices, welcome them back with open arms and in doing so, bind them even more tightly to you while they ride that wave of relief for the forgiveness you've granted them. Watch as it washes over them. Observe how they pander to you in gratitude and indulge your every whim. You are their lord and master and they know it. As they bask in the glow of your love regained, prepare yourself for the next period of isolation and anticipate, with wringing hands, the sight of them returning yet again, panting like a puppy for more of you.

Kat's return was not a glorious one for me; I'd come to the conclusion that our friendship was now permanently damaged. On the one hand, she wanted to be my friend and confidante and on the other, she was back being as thick as thieves with HM having effectively stabbed her in the back. Now it was my turn to be furious. I think a part of me had really wanted her to stand up to HM and give her a good emotional slap in the face by not coming back. My frustration with Kat for returning was frustration with myself for not having the guts to deliver that slap myself. I said nothing and threw the whole incident into my "on hold" closet to be dealt with at a later date.

Kat would be horrified to know that I thought she betrayed me terribly in those days. She would take me into her confidence and then go running to HM and report what I'd said, usually with embellishments that put entirely the wrong angle on a situation. For example, I told her that I was having trouble with a boss at work and once that piece of information had been filtered through all the various channels in the Ministry of Disinformation that worked overtime in her head (and in HM's head where there was still so much resentment towards me for being such an over-privileged toff) I was in trouble for not being spiritual enough in my working environment. By being the unwitting traitor, I see with hindsight that Kat was terrified, because within herself - subconsciously - she believed that HM's god would punish her and not love her if she didn't do exactly as she was told.

As a result of the stress that this layer of complication was causing, I rang Kat one evening and told her that our one-to-one chats would have to stop as I wanted some space for myself. She was disappointed by this and quite put out, but I was just sick and tired of someone saying I was their best friend and then booting me into touch behind my back. Unfortunately, it was the beginning of the end of what could have been a very beneficial friendship.

Another thing that happened that summer sends shivers down my spine. I still don't know how it came about, but a reporter from the local paper phoned to say he was interested in doing an article about HM. To this day, I believe that she and Kat may have been doing some shameless promotion of the HM bandwagon and when this opportunity came forward, they jumped at it, probably thinking that it would get that juggernaut rolling into town ready for the full-on ministry. They were so bowled over by this opportunity that HM didn't stop to work out if it was the correct thing to do.

And of course it wasn't. The journalist duly arrived one morning with a cameraman and interviewed HM about her work and her hopes for a proper home. HM gave an open interview in all innocence, honestly believing that once people found out that there was a Holy Mother in town, a steady stream of them would beat a path to her door with offers of help.

As it turned out, the article was quite a snide little piece of writing, implying that she was making all sorts of claims about herself as being like Mother Theresa of Calcutta. HM had used that analogy in an attempt to try and put forward the healing side of her work, but it just seemed to backfire completely. I've no doubt that this journalist was trying to make a name for himself and knew full well the subtlety of language. He also must have believed he was doing the community a service by undermining someone who was giving herself airs and graces.

I felt sorry for HM. She took the article badly and became extremely forlorn. I took it upon myself to ring the chief editor of this paper to tell him that he had unfairly damaged an innocent woman's reputation.

"You're malicious," I said. "You've no idea of the damage you've done. If anyone is put off from going to see this lady because of the actions of your paper, you'll be held accountable!"

I slammed the phone down in my new-found indignation, all high and mighty on my own burgeoning sense of self-importance.

At the time, I honestly thought I was doing special work and that I had to stick my neck out. Already, I was a little zealot in the making. When I look back, I cringe to the very depths of my being, but also forgive myself, as really, I thought I was doing the right thing at the time and saw it as trying to help a worthy cause. It's only when you have the benefit of hindsight that you start to berate yourself and that's when you need to stand back and take stock. Life is for living and we all make mistakes. Mine were just a little more spectacular than most.

Although HM was upset with the situation, about a year or so later, she fell into an identical trap. In many respects, it shows that she was prepared to stop at nothing to get herself known and was so desperate to achieve her goals that her intuition failed her utterly and became entirely overruled by her overwhelming, obsessive ambition. I'll just temporarily jump ahead one year now in order to tell part two of the newspaper saga.

Even though HM had had her fingers burned the first time with enthusiastic young journalists, a very similar thing happened when she tried to push her boat out even further in 1999. One day, she rang me and told me that she'd written what she called a "press release" to say that there was a Holy Mother living in town who desperately needed to be housed. In the text she said she could do a lot of good for the community and was looking for people to give her a house rent free or at least to give her money towards one. She'd meditated on this, she told me, and been given orders for me, by God himself, to distribute this "press release" in all the houses along the road where she lived. I wasn't expected to deliver these pieces of paper anywhere else, just her road. I thought the idea was bonkers as this wasn't the most affluent neighbourhood.

I was so scared at the prospect of doing this delivery job that I couldn't get to sleep at night. But by this time, I was so hooked in, I just couldn't extricate myself enough to stand up and say what I should have said all along: "Holy Mother, you're as mad as a March Hare and this latest ruse to strive for global domination will bring you trouble!"

So one fine summer's day, with my heart in my mouth, I set off with a bag full of papers and posted them through the letterboxes of about fifty to seventy houses. The following day, I returned and did the rest of the street. Only this second day, the neighbours had had time to talk about what was going on. Inevitably, there were one or two people lying in wait for me and I was given some quite unpleasant abuse.

Unsurprisingly, not a single person stepped forward with any ideas or money. In fact, what did happen was that some of the neighbours banded together and phoned another local paper. Immediately, a journalist rang HM and told her he was sympathetic with her plight and could he come over and interview her. The previous year's shenanigans now well and truly forgotten, HM invited him over and let him in. Like a child who just won't learn her lesson for sheer lack of self-discipline, basic understanding and life experience, once again she handed herself over to the cynical on a silver platter. In her desperation for global domination, she proceeded to allow herself to be served up to public ridicule, yet again. This time, the paper pulled no punches. It interviewed her and heard her story about wanting to set up a spiritual centre that would benefit the entire community. But on the sly, the journalist also interviewed the neighbours who had alerted him to the goings on. They decided to remain anonymous but said they thought she was being silly: it was wrong to expect people just to hand over money to a complete stranger; it could potentially exploit the naïve. If I remember correctly, there was also an implication that the show she was presiding over was not a genuine one and that she was running a knocking shop.

HM should have seen this as a shot across her bows. Anyone with their head screwed on at this point would have understood it as the Universe telling them to give up this "Holy Mother thing" and to stop trying to strike for what some would see as a position of privilege that she was basically never destined for, or ever even merited. Instead, along with all the fury and the screaming and shouting that this situation caused, she decided to blame me for not using my intuition to stop her from making such a mistake and for not putting my foot down. Think about it, if I *had* put my foot down, she'd have screamed and shouted even more and my life and the children's lives would have been even more hell. I hated the way that she used to stamp her foot like a spoilt brat when she didn't get what she wanted. But could I do anything about it? I wanted to, but it was not worth the emotional grief for any of us.

As it turned out, neither of these brushes with the world of celebrity in the shape of the local rags had any long term affect, positive or negative. If anything, they just made HM more bitter and equally more determined not to let the negative ones grind her down. She dealt with the disappointment by becoming even more zealous and stuck in her ways. She dug her heels in and gritted her teeth hard.

Chapter Seven

Most of the rest of 1998 remains somewhat of a blur. I tried to get on at my new job and to live a normal life alongside the increasingly bizarre circumstances of my spiritual world. By this time, those close to me were totally baffled by the goings on, but kept themselves at a safe distance and maintained a diplomatic silence.

As summer became autumn and the weather cooled, the disadvantages of the house really began to become apparent. It was even more freezing and damp than it had been when HM moved in and Scooter's room was unbearable. HM said she'd "picked up" that a previous occupant of the room had been a little boy who used to cry himself to sleep as he was so sad about the state of his life. His emotions had left an imprint on the room and consequently the bedding was always sopping and the whole atmosphere was gloomy and sad. If anything, it wasn't a child's emotional imprint at all, but the sadness that she created due to her inability to push through with her plans and the sorrow that poured out of her own children for not being able to be the little people they so needed to be in such abnormal circumstances.

Despite everything, somehow, the two of them just tried to get on with the business of being kids. I used to come around and play with them and was now using all my annual holiday entitlement to take days off to teach Scooter which was never really a problem – just a little...*exhausting*...

By that time, my life was completely hers. If she ever found out that I had any time to myself, she'd suddenly come up with something for me to do. I was either sent shopping for her or ordered to type up some leaflet or booklet advertising all her services. Whenever I came around, she'd ask me to go to the supermarket for her, even if it was only a loaf of bread or some milk. She'd always give me money for such items, but I began to notice she would frown as she did so. One day, it was "off with his head" time again and Kat phoned:

"Holy Mother is furious with you. You must never take money off a holy person. You know how hard up she is."

HM hadn't worked for years and had no intention of working. She did make some cash from a few people who came for help and healing, but by and large, she lived on benefits. I coughed up on essentials and was always thanked, but never remunerated in those days. I kept my own financial situation quiet and said nothing about how strange it felt to know "God" was standing in the dole queue with Joe Public.

One strange thing I remember from that time is how she decided one day, out of the blue, to give the kids sex lessons. Scooter was seven and Rosie was ten by this time. The reason for this was she wanted them to grow up with a mature attitude to sex and not to have to learn about it in lurid terms from other kids. She sat both children down one evening and spoke to them very carefully about the subject.

Rosie couldn't be bothered with such a discussion and it meant nothing to her. She ignored the whole incident and got on with her childhood. Scooter was just plain not ready for it. Some years later, he recounted with horror about what he'd been told and how uncomfortable it had made him feel. The irony was that later on, as a youngish teenager, he beat most of his peers in the race to have sex for the first time with a girl and was initiated into the joys of it while most lads of his age were still retiring slyly to the gents with a magazine. But that, as they say, is another story!

I often wondered why HM didn't tend to sit *me* down and give me teaching. I thought that was what this guru-student thing was all about, after all. In fact, I only ever remember her doing it once and when it happened, it wasn't what I was expecting at all.

One evening, Kat phoned to say that we were both invited around to HM's house as she wanted to talk to us about something called Advaita Vedanta. I'm not sure that Kat was all that pleased as evenings belonged to her and her daughter and this would mean getting a neighbour to babysit.

As I remember it, Kat and I were asked to sit at HM's feet and listen to her as she gave a well-prepared monologue. Now I come to think about it, this was what HM had always wanted: in her search for unquestioning obedience from a group of devoted slaves, there was nothing more satisfying then to sit there like Jesus with those followers sitting at her feet, hanging onto her every word. The energy to be vamped from such a set-up must be phenomenal.

The talk was quite short, I recall. She told us how "God" was all things and not some separate agent sitting distant and aloof from creation on a throne in an unattainable heaven in the sky. The essence of "God" permeates everything we see, hear and touch and is an intrinsic part of us: we ourselves are individualised sparks of the Divine.

This means that we have goodness and the Light which our religions have always explained is the essence of "God". However, what they'd failed to explain is that because all things are "God", that must mean that evil and the darkness are also a manifestation of "God".

For the life of me, I can't remember that she said anything else that night and I remember going away feeling unfulfilled as if there was somehow more to the whole doctrine than that. And why, when HM wasn't inclined to show patience enough to spend time teaching her students in those days, was this suddenly relevant?

It was at least a couple of years before I discovered the answer to that question. I was not to understand it at the time, but this "dark side" was already beginning to play an important role in my spiritual training and one day would make itself extremely evident in my life, a story I shall relate later in this book.

Kat gave me a lift home that night and had nothing to say about what we'd been told which I also found strange as she was supposed to be working hell for leather to reach this thing called Spiritual Master. All she could talk about was her stressful life and all the pressure she was under. I became convinced that she only reason she stayed with HM was that she'd been completely hooked in by the promise of becoming the Messianic handmaiden. Nothing else seemed to matter to her.

Over the years, my path has brought me to a place now where I can build on the sketchy outline that HM had given me that night. If you'll permit, in order to understand how the next few years were going to pan out in terms of the sheer hard slog of it all, we just need to take a quick look at some spiritual concepts and theories[6].

We are all divine beings having a glorious and gruelling human experience. "God" is us. It's not, and never has been, some bearded patriarch in the sky. We are the Creator. We are the Creator experiencing itself.

Imagine us all existing - outside of a physical universe - as one infinite consciousness, knowing no Linear Time, just being - in complete bliss and perfection. In such a state, we all know that negative emotions exist, but we have yet to experience them. This could be considered an issue, as to have experienced such emotions as true hatred, resentment, fear, rejection and anger, and then to have faced them and stopped co-operating with them, makes us stronger and all the wiser. We decide that some platform of learning is required...

The best tense to use to explain how we proceed with our lessons in this regard is the present. I do this because all the universes and states that exist are all operating at once and not according to any linear earthly time frame.

So we envisage a Universe. We shine it into a void like an image from a projector and prepare ourselves to move into the film, thinking it's real. The Universe is in fact just a hologram but one that's so real, we know that when we enter it, we'll forget that it is not. Once the projector starts up, we take our first baby steps into the movie.

Imagine this entire Universe as one all-encompassing unit of consciousness. As you step in, imagine you're a perfect being existing as an integral part of that consciousness unit. As you're all space and all time, you're actually in any space and in any place in time just by pinpointing your intentions to your desired moment and location within the Universe. For you, time would only exist in that one particular space you choose to be. But as your essence is

---

[6] The section you're about to read is based on my own research. At the time of writing, I feel it to be the explanation that I most resonate with. However, please be warned that you have to use your own discernment. What's true for me may not be true for you where you stand in your life at the moment. In no way, shape or form is this an invitation for me to promote anyone's teachings or to force my own opinions on the world at large. That goes for any of the spiritual explanations mentioned in this book.

the "all", therefore time is relative to where you pinpoint your attention!

As I've said, this consciousness that we're all an integral part of and which we shall refer to as The Source Field or The Creator (or even the light from the movie projector!), creates a platform on which to experience itself and to explore the challenges of "negative" emotions. I purposefully avoid using the word "God" as that word can mean anything from an idol to some religious fear figure. I myself associate it with blind sacrifice, with separation and hence the kind of spiritual oppression that our religions have inflicted upon us for centuries and at the time of writing, still do.

We're aware that we've envisaged more than one universe and that each one is subtly different from the next. Some of these universes are states where no "evil" exists. We understand that these universes are vital stages of learning for us as the Creator but some of us feel that they're no more than an extension of the joyful existence that we individualised sparks of the Infinite experience in our perfect state outside our realms of learning. They're blissful and seamless, but an extremely slow platform for advancement in terms of spiritual evolution.

The Universe we're in however, has been brought about because what some of us want is catalyst, in other words, situations where we can all evolve by exploring the paths of Light *and* of the shadows (ie evil, darkness). By experiencing the essence of this darkness or "dimmed Light" (by putting ourselves through some quite hellish circumstances) we're able to challenge ourselves to the very core of our being. By becoming deeply involved in this game, we're in a position to intensify our experience in physical creation. Our goal is to integrate both the Light and the Shadow within us and in so doing, understand the nature of unconditional love by playing a subtle game where the fully Dark/Light integrated-individual just allows everything and everyone to be. This evolved being loves all, whatever game is being played, no matter how hideous and morally corrupt the player. Because this soul has been all things and played all sides of the game, he knows all experience leads to soul evolution. He therefore allows life just to happen and learns to dip in and out of the game whilst unconditionally loving all and not interfering with the free will of any other soul wishing to learn the same lessons.

If you hear your typical New Ager saying that they must set up an army of Lightworkers to fight against the darkness, run a mile from them. They aren't souls in balance and don't understand the game. This is a sign of someone like HM, who's stuck in unresolved duality. A person who isn't in true equilibrium is still swinging like a pendulum from side to side in the game of Light versus Dark; they still haven't learned to find true peace in the "Now Moment". This is when an evolving individual learns to quieten the mind and exist only in the present. All regrets of the past melt away, hopes and dreams for the future fade into insignificance. In the Now Moment, the soul can step back and just *be* in one endless moment of complete understanding: in such a place, all things are shown to be utterly perfect.

From now on, we can refer to those who dip into the Light side of the game as "Service to Others" and those who doggedly play the game in the Shadows as "Service to Self". At the same time, perhaps it would be beneficial to refer to souls who've learned all their lessons on both sides of this game and have "brought balance to the Force" as they say in *Star Wars*, as existing in "refined Light" or Unity Consciousness. Such people will be Service to Others when the need arises and stand up and fight their corner when their sense of justice (and also their intuition) calls them to. They'll have a very keen understanding of when to be involved and when just to walk on. Ultimately, such people will have stopped actively playing the game on a Service to Self polarity and will be what we call "spiritually evolved".

This explanation of how the game is played was far more subtle than the superficial, plagiarised explanation given by HM. For years, I was desperate for wisdom that felt so Universally sound, it would make my heart sing. I was constantly sitting there waiting for this "holy" person to provide them for me, but I might just as well have been waiting for a number 10 bus at the bottom of the Atlantic. It's possible that HM knew exactly what I've just explained but dumbed it down or held back information as a form of oppression, ultimately to control. Alternatively, there's every chance she didn't know because she was just plain unevolved. The wisdom was out there, but effectively, as she thought she was already perfect, she didn't go and search for it and was happy just to rest on her laurels.

There are "forces", let's call them, which don't want the human race to advance. We've allowed them to come into existence to train us. As I explain later, these forces have existed for millennia and are of an extreme Service to Self orientation. They've taken it upon themselves to try and hold back human spiritual evolution; that's their work, their modus operandi. We're still talking of catalyst here, where the more resistance that's applied, the harder the entity has to push itself. A Service to Self soul hard at work applying this resistance, will NEVER admit to itself that it's operating to help the advancement of souls. It cannot see beyond its immediate desire to get what it wants, to vampirise and feed off a mass of "fools" in bondage.

So in our world under the yoke of those Service to Self souls who hold sway, all desire for advancement is suppressed. Consciousness is dumbed down, lives are humdrum and dull; there is little to inspire your human to think of anything outside his immediate environment. These "forces" encourage people to think only of themselves and their needs, of their misery and illnesses. Those on the path of Service to Self create an ambiance of ignorance to make sure there is no true knowledge around so that souls struggle to lift their spirits to higher thoughts. Love is oppressed with fear and fear is food for them.

If you look around, you'll now see why our society has moved in the way it has. The Service to Self-oriented who have pushed their way into governments and positions of power, have constantly been working over the last few thousand years to make us obsessed with the petty and the pointless. This is why people would much rather watch trash TV and use drink, food and sex as a crutch to forget about reality, than decide to move onwards and upwards. Whilst we look the other way, those in the know plunder and pillage at will.

It *is* important to understand however, that this life plan is what we souls have chosen for our evolutionary path: there are those of us who opt for an incredibly tough route on purpose, knowing eventually we'll tire of adversity and finally say, "This cannot be the 'be all and end all'. There has to be more…"

HM was her own version of the Service to Self orientation. She gravitated towards control and manipulation and in doing so, was actually, and I don't mean this lightly, using those around her as pawns in her own game. I've hinted that she had plans for a kind of almost Messianic role where she was this great holy being with all her minions like me at her feet hanging on to her every word. She was never interested in my spiritual advancement, only in what I could do for her in terms of typing and desktop publishing and providing her with the money to get her bandwagon rolling. It was never her intention to tell me anything about the deeper side of spiritual advancement.

Aren't we all in the same position? Look around you at how your world is run. You are pre-programmed to sneer at these pages because those who run your world don't want you to have any thoughts other than the ones they tell you to have. What you need to do then, rather than rejecting these words, is just keep an open mind. Watch and listen. Do some research of your own and keep it to yourself if necessary. It's the ones that keep their minds open who are in a position to grasp opportunities when they arise and those are the souls that advance. There's no need to show blind faith, certainly. But at the same time, don't be closed-minded.

Just to complete the picture before we move on with my story, this understanding of how we lower ourselves into a hostile pit to create lessons for ourselves just needs a small amount of explanation. I shall use the wording that's common within the general New Consciousness forum, so that if you see it again, you know what's being explained.

It would seem that the lessons conducted in this part of the Universe all occur in various vibrations or densities. Density is a good word because the lighter the density, the lighter the physical body, the more subtle the vibration. In dimensions where the vibration is lighter and higher, the lessons are also more subtle and sublime. Souls in these densities have a high level of soul attainment and are more in touch with the Source Field/Creator. They're not bound up within a control matrix as we currently are and can, for example, shift their consciousness, as explained above, to any time or place within the Consciousness Unit that is this Universe.

As vibration slows, denser dimensions of existence produce a new set of lessons for a soul evolving through all the possibilities offered. Our own dimension is currently spanning a range of these vibrations. Many people say that the human is in a density where only a tiny range of vibrations are detectable to our human senses. This is true certainly, as if this was a pit that we've been allowing ourselves to be lowered into from higher dimensions, then we're more constricted the deeper we travel. The walls of the pit are closing in the further we descend. As we move to the bottom, the vibration is darker, we have more difficulty in perceiving the wider Universe.

It sounds as though I'm saying we've descended into a biblical hell, almost as if we're being punished.

We're most certainly not being punished. We've allowed this to happen. Over the last few millennia of recorded history, the human soul has been exploring the deepest recesses. We've allowed ourselves to pack into an extremely truncated life-span experience of suffering, pain and humiliation. We've seen wars, famine, disease, genocide. We truly have scraped the bottom and been cut off from the daylight.

This was never meant to last. As we'll see later in this book, monster controllers have been allowed to hold sway in this world of ours since a cataclysmic event thousands of years ago. Both we and those controllers are in a density which we shall refer to as the density of base consciousness, one where there's a physical body as opposed to the Light Body of higher dimensions. The density of base consciousness is one that's also marked by the existence of duality, the intense interplay between good and "evil" where the learn/teach ethos of karmic lessons is prevalent. If you look at human history over the last few thousand years, it's been all about despotic rulers, violent religions, oppressors, psychopaths, institutional liars, mass poisoning, mass indoctrination, mass slavery. This is the density of base consciousness, the most stringent, the toughest and most volatile place to incarnate.

Having bounced along the bottom for this allotted period of time, the human soul is starting to rise again in vibration and we're gradually cranking the pulley that's bringing most of us up into some fresh air for the first time in thousands of years. Certainly there are those who are not ready to do this, and those souls are being honoured by those whose time has come to rise.

These rising ones are now beginning to live within the densities of a more subtle vibration. They're finding that thoughts create and are therefore extremely careful how they perceive the reality around them. For having risen out of a thick density where thoughts take time to bring manifestation in all the fug and mist, they're now surprised to find that intention of a more elevated vibration can make experience more immediate, finer and more subtle then was the case during the darkest times of the human base consciousness era. They're finding that it's possible to cut through all the religious nonsense, the petty laws and observances that thicken the soup. Only one thing matters: the secret is in being nothing more than a totally decent, loving and caring person.

The time has therefore come for a rise in consciousness for those who choose it. The psychopathic ones that rushed in when experience was at the bottom of the pit, who cremated care and promoted hatred, are now finding their attempts at control harder to roll out. There is a war on consciousness as they try to arrest dominion from an awakening human.

Meanwhile, the new human doesn't have to declare war against the control matrix at this time; the secret is in focussing on change, on finding soul sovereignty and hence freedom. True freedom is the exact opposite of that condition that we formerly knew as "evil".

In terms of this Universal layout, HM's issue was that she was desperate to be on the path of Service to Others in this rising vibration; however, her block was that her constant obsession with money and control put her firmly on the path of Service to Self. The irony of this is you cannot serve two masters. If she reads this now, she might understand something. The reason why she never succeeded in getting that ashram, those disciples, enough money to run her spiritual centre and to travel the world as a teacher surrounded by followers was because she tried to use the shadow side of the game to get what *she* wanted through mental control of those around her. This, she erroneously believed, was her role as a divine being entitled to do whatever she wanted in the name of her god. In other words, she believed that "God" had given her carte blanche to use whatever tools at her disposal to bring her interpretation of Light into the world. To her mind, it was fine to summon up demonic energies and ask for a pot of cash so she could go and buy a house. She felt this was acceptable as ultimately she was doing her god's will. It seemed to have escaped her entirely that playing the game on the shadow side doesn't get you a free lunch. Consequently, with such a twisted approach, she bounced back and forth from Light to Shadow, drifting for years and years, unable to find balance or to stop interfering in the free will of others. If she'd stood back and stopped desiring, stopped giving herself fancy titles, stopped swooping around like a bird of prey in the name of "God", everything she needed would have come of its own accord without a struggle. For all those years, decades even, she blocked herself and never moved an inch.

Chapter Eight

The winter of 98/99 wasn't easy for any of us. Both the children became quite difficult as the issues that beset their mother caused her to be miserable and frustrated. Hardly anyone was battering down her door with requests for healing or emptying fat wallets onto the collection plate. Consequently, the cupboard was almost permanently bare.

In desperation, HM came up with an idea to ask a wealthy uncle for some cash, but her mother got wind of this communication and immediately put a stop to it. To this day, I'm not sure how much HM's mother knew of the life her daughter lived, but you could tell from a distance, the mutual suspicion that existed between the two of them had clearly brought about some major ructions. HM didn't have a single positive thing to say about her mother and blamed her for absolutely every hang up, every life disappointment and just about every disastrous relationship she'd ever had.

To try and lift herself out of the doldrums, HM had hired a hall in the Southcote area of Reading to give Darshan. Darshan is a service in which a guru gives a blessing to those who are keen to follow a spiritual path. One by one, those seekers can approach the guru: this often involves, certainly for a female evolved soul, being hugged and having holy water placed on their third eye at the centre of the forehead.

This sort of blessing is common in India where there are so many gurus. Some of them like the Holy Mothers Amma and Meera spend time travelling the world giving the blessing and they have many followers who report that they find the energy during the gatherings incredibly uplifting and deeply moving.[7] However,

---

[7] Amma was the first guru to use the hug. For women it was forbidden to touch men outside their family. She was the first to touch the "untouchables". In India a guru never touched their followers. Darshan is a Sanskrit term meaning "sight" or "vision." Many Hindus believe the act of seeing a saint or guru confers a spiritual blessing, and when the spiritual leader makes eye-contact with a devotee an important psychic link

Darshan is only really for those who are keen to follow a spiritual teacher and the practice does seem somewhat alienating to Western minds. People can accidentally associate it with a sect or cult and can easily think of it as giving away your energy and sovereignty to some controlling preacher intent on riding your guilt trip. This obviously isn't always the case. It would be unreasonable for me to say that all gurus who use these methods have underhand intentions. In HM's case, she simply didn't have the wherewithal to carry it off with any authenticity.

I'm not sure why she seemed surprised when no one apart from one or two acquaintances turned up to that Darshan in Southcote. She'd put so much energy into the undertaking, but hadn't taken something important into account. Few people know what Darshan is and even fewer believe it's of any use to them whatsoever. I think deep down she blocked herself even further by hoping that people would come in for a hug and throw cash into the pot. This was a completely unrealistic outlook and the whole undertaking was naturally doomed to failure.

I felt sorry for her at the time. Despite the mental anguish she dished out to me on a daily basis, I just couldn't bring myself to dislike her. It's hard to explain, but I had come to care about her and most of the time, in between the abuse, we would have some great conversations and many, many laughs. That's probably surprised you. But you have to remember that HM was only a part time tyrant. There was a gentle side to her and a caring side that appeared every now and then – maybe once a month. The problem was that over the years, her desperation to get on, her ambition and desire to get things done her way caused her, as I've said, to block herself. The more blocks there were in her path, the more frustrated she became. And of course the more that frustration abounded, the more difficult she was to be with.

This caused an extremely difficult situation for her family dynamic. There was just never enough energy around for her children. What little there was, both children fought bitterly for and it was awful to see. For one thing, Scooter was always the one

is established. Mother Meera touches your head and looks into your eyes when she imparts her blessing.

70

who could do no wrong. He was the boy who - *she* said - would be like her one day. For her own reasons, HM saw Scooter as a child who was full of Light and born to have an almost messianic role in his own right. Rosie on the other hand, in her mother's eyes, was the one who blocked her. HM always said that Rosie didn't want a spiritual life because she wanted to do things her way and fall into the distractions that others girls her age enjoyed like makeup and pop music. That was certainly true. But what HM missed was the fact that Rosie really did try to do what her mother wanted and *was* prepared to go to school in a skirt that was conservatively long. She wanted to please and obey her mother because she loved her. But energy for Rosie was not in abundance and that made her sad. If she had a scrap with Scooter and hit him, even lightly, there would be an investigation. If it ever turned out that Scooter had hit her back or even hit her first, HM would chastise Rosie. Don't get me wrong; HM was never violent to her children. But she could send them to Coventry and invariably, it was Rosie who had to make that journey, time and time again. Scooter, whose love for his mother was so pure in those days, got some of the energy he needed from this situation and would occasionally milk it to the limit. He must never blame himself for this as it was a typical reaction for a seven/eight year-old living in an environment where love was stifled. Invariably, with Rosie far away in Coventry, Scooter got at least some of the energy he needed by being the good boy.

I hope that people who read this will understand something important about HM. There were times when she genuinely did try to be a good mother. I often saw her spending time with both kids, playing with them and talking with them. She would take them out on outings and look after them brilliantly when they were ill. There was always a healthy meal on the table for them and they were never denied food unless it was something incredibly unhealthy. The problem was, even though the will was there, more often than not, HM's efforts came to nought because there was no underlying enthusiasm for the parenting process. She was always so woebegone about her desperate circumstances, it stopped her from enjoying the present and hence taking a proper and devoted part in their upbringing.

The favouritism side of the issue was always a sore point for me though. I could see it going on and was powerless to do anything to prevent it. I didn't dare broach the subject with HM. I always tried to be nice to Rosie and would give her a hug when I gave one to Scooter. But my problem was this: I didn't want to be accused of sidling up to her. I wasn't her father and was desperately worried that I would be accused of inappropriate behaviour if I got too close. Consequently, poor old Rosie missed out from me as well and it was always Scooter who seemed to get my attention, being younger and a boy. Rosie then, naturally I suppose, began to see me as someone who couldn't really be trusted. She still loved me, but it was from a distance. Gradually, as the years passed, poor Rosie slipped away from us all and eventually gave up. That was when something happened that caused her to change dramatically - a story that I shall come to soon.

The only person who was prepared to stand up to HM in those days was Gary. If HM made a decision that he thought would be a disaster, he'd tell her to her face. On several occasions, I heard them argue bitterly as HM was so determined, for good or ill, to do things her way. On one occasion, they began an argument in the kitchen. I was upstairs with the children and suddenly HM screamed out my name at the top of her voice. I ran downstairs and found her in the front room. The sight of her terrified me. She looked psychopathic, her eyes ablaze with godless fury. She howled at me for not protecting her against this monster Gary and yelled at me to get the hell out of her house before she called the Police. I was so scared that I tried to talk but my voice came out really high pitched and strangled. I decided not to stick around: ramming my feet into my shoes, I fled, not even bothering to say goodbye to the children.

Later that day, Kat phoned me with the "off with his head routine" and the infamous "Holy Mother is furious with you" outburst. I couldn't believe it when she sneered at me for speaking to HM in a strangled, terrified voice.

That's when I realised: I could never trust Kat. I felt betrayed by her yet again and I hate to say it, actually began to dislike her intensely. I covered it as well as I could, but every time she came near me, I bristled. I really began to resent helping to pay part of her mortgage whilst I froze in my rented garden flat crawling with slugs and stinking of cat wee.

All this time, Reading Borough Council were trying to evict HM from the stop-gap home. The problem they faced was that there was just no unseating her because, simply put, there was absolutely nowhere for her to go.

Once again, no council properties "suited" her. The private sector didn't want a single mother on benefits and as there was also absolutely no money, even if a house had come up, there just wasn't enough cash for a deposit.

HM and Kat fought the council for months. They faced angry judges and officials who wouldn't listen to a word HM said about her condition. She told everyone she had a highly sensitive son who needed to be in a caring environment, but her pleas fell on deaf ears. This may have been because HM was so open and insistent that everyone understood she was a Holy Mother and address her as such. The problem with that was that most of the people she came up against were inwardly sneering from the very depths of their being at such a gross display of arrogance. They clearly hated her for it and unconsciously did all they could within the bounds of the powers accorded to them to put the blocks on anything she wanted. HM counteracted this by digging her heels in and becoming even more doggedly "holy".

In the summer of 1999, out of the blue and within weeks of some serious imminent "bay leaf" intervention, a house came up. Like the one in Hovel View Road, this house was in a part of Reading which was notorious as a gathering place for drug users, prostitutes and criminals of all shapes and sizes. A lot of young professionals live there because they can buy cheapish houses and turn them into a kind of home from home until things look up and they can flee to a more salubrious area. So it isn't quite as bad as it sounds. But to HM, it was absolute hell on earth and a sentence of death.

The house that she rented was right in the thick of it. I went around there on the Sunday before she moved in and was horrified. It was filthy and in a shocking state of repair. Seemingly a previous tenant had been violent and had taken out his frustrations on some of the fixtures and fittings.

Gary and I were charged with the job of cleaning the place up. It was the hottest day of the year and I would have loved to have been wearing shorts, but HM viewed such a garment as disgusting. So I turned up in jeans with all my cleaning gear and literally fried.

Something happened on that day which made me start to dislike Gary for quite a while, I regret to say. Because he always saw me as soft, that meant that in his mind, I had to be bending towards the pansy side of camp. At one point, he removed his shirt and I just happened to be looking in his direction. The problem was he mistook my observation of him as something akin to enjoyment. Actually, I didn't enjoy the sight at all and was only looking at him because we were talking. He gave me a look as if to say: *there is something very wrong with you...*

I was incredibly annoyed at that and wanted to punch his lights out, but then Gary and me in a fight? Well, let's just say that I might as well call 999 for myself in advance. I went into the bathroom and shut the door for a while, determined to bite my knuckles off in sheer frustration for his attitude. He later pointed out as I carefully cleaned the front room that I was a little too good at housework. There was just no stopping his sneering that day. I put him in his place by calling him sexist for implying that housework was a girls' task and unmanly. Luckily, he shut up in case I reported him to HM; though to be honest, he might just as well have carried on wittering in my ear. I wasn't a grass. It was always Gary that reported me to HM and not the other way around.

As the reader, you must be thinking now: *this woman – whoever she is – appears to be running your classic dictatorship, where everyone snitches on and oppresses everyone else.* That would actually be a very fair assessment of the situation. It was the outer edge of the perfect Service to Self operation for the psychopathic cult leader.

Once Gary had been pressed into laying a new carpet in HM's work room and done any number of DIY jobs (which he was always good at), HM arranged a screaming argument with him and he disappeared off the scene for a long, long time. After a while, my negative feelings towards him abated and I missed him - though not the trouble he caused or the sissy accusations! Perhaps if he'd been around, he may somehow have tempered HM's behaviour at a time when, slowly and inexorably, she began to go extremely wild.

Within days of HM and the children moving into Ryan Street, I was in the doghouse again. HM had given me several pieces of paper to turn into the beginning of a book called *Our Violent World* and I was having trouble making sense of all the annotations and the bits of scrap with afterthought paragraphs slotted into spaces with sellotape and glue. HM always made out that her books came from her god and just flowed out via some kind of miraculous communication. I remember thinking as I ploughed through this particular work what a thoroughly disorganised bloke this god was and wondered how on earth he managed to keep a watchful eye on all the universes of his co-creators if he was always in such an almighty tizz.

As I read through what HM had written, I had a problem with it immediately. HM always claimed I was an intellectual snob, but having taught English to Greek kids, I think I developed an eye and an ear for grammar and syntax. I also prided myself on being a writer, but I hadn't had anything published at that point. I can be a bit over-zealous in correcting poor English, I admit it. In fact, I can be downright pedantic about it which is hypocritical as I've been known to make some shocking howlers myself over the years. But this was something I felt I had to be pedantic about. I didn't think the writing was professional enough for HM to be taken seriously, so I took it upon myself to change her words. All I intended to do was make it clearer and less like treacle to swim through.

HM wasn't stupid. She was certainly intelligent enough; but she had this view that she needed to get down to brass tacks and talk to the masses in their own language. That's fine as long as you don't talk DOWN to the masses. If people read a book containing serious material about how to control kids with behavioural problems, they're unlikely to take it seriously if it reads like an idle conversation in a laundrette.

I do think I should have approached HM with this issue and thrashed it out with her instead of haughtily taking it upon myself to change her words, but would she have listened to me? HM never listened to anyone; shout and lash out at them certainly, but have a normal debate based around a sensible and adult exchange of views? Forget it.

Inevitably the phone rang. It was Kat for one of those precious "off with his head" moments:

"Holy Mother is furious with you. She says: *how dare you presume to change her words!* She also says you're an intellectual snob."

I protested that the book read badly and for the first time, even knowing that Kat was in the habit of reporting back everything I said to HM, really stuck my neck out. But HM was insistent. I was never to change her words again. There was no question of her asking what was wrong with the work, or any kind of investigation into how to make it more readable. My opinion didn't matter anyway as I wasn't holy. I decided to grit my teeth and just got on with it.

The point is, I really wanted HM's "thing" to work. At the time, I had such complete and utter blind faith in what she was doing that I was desperate to see her succeed and make at least some difference. Consequently, I ignored the fact that she wasn't really up to the job. If anyone ever criticised her, she would crumble and become woeful and depressed. I was always wondering how on earth she thought she could push herself forwards so brazenly when she must have known she wouldn't be able to deal with the inevitable fallout of her extremely controversial views.

For example: one of her biggest problems with modern society was the fact that she felt everyone was immoral. She saw this in everything from the use of bad language in public places to the way that people watch violent TV and wear provocative clothing. She would visibly bristle with indignation when she saw girls running around town dressed in skimpy skirts and tops. She hated going into a newsagent and catching site of porn on the top shelf, claiming that men who read or watch porn are potential rapists.

This is a reason why I was beginning to struggle with her books and teachings. Provocative clothing and foul language are all examples of behaviours in modern society which are now the norm. I'm not saying that we should be blindly accepting of this situation: after all, it's still unacceptable to turn up to work in an office dressed in a T-shirt with an offensive slogan on it or a "pelmet" and high heels and then proceed to speak to customers by swearing liberally at them. Certainly in the company where I work, you could be on disciplinary for that sort of behaviour or be sacked on the spot. Surely the way to solve this issue isn't to oppose it through oppression, but to make sure that your own behaviour is as good as it can be. I always wanted to say to HM: Ask yourself; do you exude an attitude of negativity? Are you rude and aggressive in your dealings with others? The answer to that with HM was a qualified "yes". To be fair, she never, ever swore and always wore respectable clothes. Considering she had little money, HM always tried to dress nicely. But when she was out and about, she would lose her rag so quickly.

One day she went into Halifax Building Society in Reading's Broad Street. For one reason or another she didn't get the service that she felt she deserved and decided to "put her foot down." This she did by screaming at the poor employee at the desk at the top of her voice, stamping her foot and storming out. She made a total spectacle of herself in front of all the other customers and Scooter, who was with her at the time, was mortified.

HM believed that this was valid behaviour for someone as a pillar of the community. However, it sends out a vicious message. How can someone who complains about aggression in language and lax, immoral behaviour in others, go about her business shouting and screaming when she doesn't get the service she demands? I always thought this was hypocritical in the extreme. It shows a complete lack of love and common courtesy, all attributes that HM claimed she had in abundance as a Holy Mother.

If you're to change the world, you have to change yourself. If you want unconditional love to abound on planet earth, you have to exude that vibration yourself in everything you do. Everywhere she went and in nearly all her undertakings, HM was rude, brash and impatient and so, inevitably, negativity followed her like a dark cloud. She believed that because she had transcended such traits in her own personality, having reached a state of divine grace, it was her right and her privilege to swing the axe of disapproval. She did that by breaking her own rules and bringing back in abundance all those negative traits of shouting and sneering, using them as a way to teach the fools around her a jolly good divine lesson. But no one accepted her because they couldn't see the divinity in her due to her atrocious behaviour; all she ended up doing was misrepresenting her god and alienating everyone from spirituality.

It really was a case of "do as I say, but don't do as I do". As the "mouthpiece of God" all she was doing was making people feel dirty and guilty about themselves. It always made me feel uncomfortable when she implied that you couldn't reach the level of Spiritual Master and be in a sexual relationship because the energy expended in sex would lessen your healing ability. To me, that just didn't seem right. Neither did her assertion that nudity and sexuality in general were "unspiritual".

When a girl is ready to start toning down her dress sense she'll do it because she wants to and not because someone who shows no love and compassion is ordering her to. Likewise, teenagers who read porn should never be written off as potential rapists when they're at a delicate stage and still finding themselves sexually. If they're going to become rapists, it's for a myriad of reasons and not just because they retired to the loos with a girly magazine.

HM just didn't understand young people, and she didn't understand men. What's more, she had no intention of finding out how any of us tick. If she'd bothered to make some proper observations, once again, she'd have lifted a massive block and become more loving and accepting of people for their individuality: finally, she may have succeeded in becoming the teacher she desperately wanted to be.

Chapter Nine

In the autumn of 1999, I decided I'd had enough of Rundown Street, of slugs and cat wee. I looked around town for somewhere a little more salubrious and decided I wanted space and to spread out a little. I was tired of studio flats, doing my cooking in the same room where I went to bed. Eventually, a place came up that that fitted my bill. Once again though, I ignored my intuition and took it because it suited my plans and desires and not because it was a suitable place for me. It also turned out to be in an even rougher area of West Reading than I'd been in before and literally thirty seconds away from HM on foot. By this time, I was spending most evenings around her house and I'd come to the conclusion that it would be convenient if I wasn't constantly taking buses every time she called me over. This meant that I had, by then, turned myself and my whole life over to HM completely. From that day on, she would be able to call on me whenever she felt like it and there would be absolutely no escape. I hadn't thought of that when I signed the contract.

However, there was also an altruistic reason for my choosing this particular flat: I could keep an eye on the children. Both of them were struggling. Rosie kept her feelings to herself but Scooter was becoming stressed out and tearful. This was a child who had gone from a bouncy young character to one that was beginning to see and hear things that most young people of his age are kept away from. I'm not talking about anything untoward or illegal. It's more an observation of how much his mother's self-inflicted suffering was rubbing off on him and how much he was having to bear himself.

My dad came and helped me to move and was horrified at the state of my new flat. Personally, I thought it was a palace compared to my old one and I loved the fact that I had a large living room. But there was a kind of gloomy depressing feel to the place that had not been there when the previous tenants had all their furniture around. Still, I soon settled in and so did Scooter.

He was around whenever he could make it, which was most days, nestling himself in front of a Surround Sound Toshiba TV that I'd bought cheaply from someone at work. Scooter took an instant liking to it. On some days, we attached an old PS1 to it and played our own version of *Grand Theft Auto* where we took it in turns to see how quickly we could smash up our cars. I used to laugh so hard at Scooter's amazing ability to cause utter destruction. It seemed to come so naturally to him.

The truth is, despite everything, I really enjoyed the company of both children and was always glad to have them. I often let them do their own thing whilst I spent my evenings working on all the books that HM was now writing. I had a Pentium 150 in those days which was a great machine that unfortunately ran on Windows 95. It could never *really* cope with the tasks that I demanded of it.

HM had asked me to find out how to set up and upload a website and I was spending many hours reading magazines and trying to piece together the information on how it all worked. In the end, I succeeded and set up HM's first site. It wasn't the most professional-looking site, but it served her purposes. Using the site, she could advertise her Darshans and spiritual workshops and inform people of all the various kinds of work she did. It didn't take off immediately, as in those days, the search engines seemed to take ages to spider new sites. But when it did, it started to attract attention from various quarters, not all of them positive, I have to say. One particular internet group that appeared to attract mainly men, set out on a campaign of harassment when they discovered there was a "holy" person standing up against violence in the media. This was an anti-censorship organisation that bombarded HM with sad emails suggesting that she grow up and "get a life". To this day, I can't bring myself to condone their methods. It's so easy to hide behind the anonymity of the internet and troll anyone who offends your sensibilities. It's also incredibly cowardly. I went and had a look at this group's forum and felt immediately sick. Although on the face of it, the site was purely for those with a kind of anarchic view of the world who revelled in the more sordid underbelly of life, there was a slight feeling that it was the sort of meeting place that functioned as an introduction for those seeking relationships with the underaged. What was chilling about it was that they just didn't seem to care or understand that their attitudes were abnormal.

Life became quite humdrum for a few months. I was often in trouble with HM for my attitude and for not pulling my weight. If I accidentally let out a swear word or ate something that I was not supposed to eat (HM had me on a diet!) both the children would report my actions to her and she would give me a scolding. She often used to complain that all the negativity I caused by being disobedient was dragging her down and I was made to feel as though her lack of funds and inability to get on with her work were entirely my fault. She was also blaming Rosie at the time, who didn't have a clue where she was going wrong. Certainly she could be wilful and her bedroom was always a complete tip; getting her to tidy it up was a big task in itself. But she was not the unruly child that she was made out to be. To be honest, neither of the children liked tidying up their rooms and Scooter, who was also a bit lax in that direction, developed a little ploy to get out of it. He would break the hoover. I lost count of the number of second hand hoovers I had to buy from the house clearance shop in West Reading to replace the latest casualty. Funnily enough, you could get items like that for a fiver and it was a great place to browse. I still have some of the junk I bought there over the years. But the hoover thing was just plain bizarre.

He also had this terrible habit of mixing up his clean laundry with the soiled stuff. One of the funniest things was watching him trying to sort through it. He would pick up a pair of undies and press his nose right into the crotch. If they were clean, he would obediently put them in the drawer. If they were "used" he would pull a little mock face of disgust and discard them onto a separate pile for the laundry basket. Just how efficient this system was I will never know, but it was classic Scooter. To make matters worse, he had a small teddy bear that was in the style of a good quality Steiff bear. Unfortunately, he'd given this bear a rather unkind name (which I don't want to repeat as it's upsetting for certain sections of the community.) This bear had been given to Scooter by someone he had absolutely no time for. Part of the joke was to keep this bear in the undies drawer, unloved, his little face pressed hard into the crotch of a pair of pants. I joshed about this with HM and quoted the *Rocky Horror Picture Show*:

> *When Eddie said he didn't like his teddy,*
> *They knew he was a no good kid…*

That was a standing joke for quite a while.

One side of life that I wasn't finding funny was my disastrous relations with Kat. Around the time that HM had moved into Ryan Street, Kat had gradually disappeared off the scene. She and HM had not seen eye to eye and she was buckling under the strain. She was incensed that HM had criticised the way she was bringing up her daughter, but as Kat had always said, she didn't feel it was right for her to impose her own spiritual beliefs on one so young. Her daughter was absolutely full of beans, had loads of friends and was doing exceedingly well at school. The last thing that Kat wanted was to see any of that compromised.

One day, out of the blue, she phoned me at work and I could tell she was shaking with fury. She told me in between gasps that she'd just thrown the phone down on HM. I talked to her for a while and tried to be helpful, but something told me that this was the straw that had broken the camel's back. HM had pushed her too far.

That evening, I went around to Kat's house to look after her daughter whilst Kat went and had a heart to heart with HM. She was gone for hours and when she came back, she seemed heavy-hearted. I don't know what they talked about, but I think they decided to call it a day in terms of their guru/chief disciple relationship. They'd parted on amicable terms as far as I could make out and had obviously talked about keeping in touch, but I knew it wasn't going to be the same. I think the situation was hard for HM as she relied on Kat quite a lot. They were quite good friends and shared a lot together, but their friendship had been put under strain by the fact that HM wanted Kat to become a spiritual master and the latter was just not ready. As I've said, spiritual advancement can't be foisted on anyone. It comes when you're prepared and not before. HM was being far too exigent in just expecting it to happen, like pulling a rabbit from a hat.

A week or so later, HM and I discussed the future of my monthly donation to Kat. HM believed that whilst Kat had been in the fold, it was only fair that she had a bit of help with her mortgage. But now that she'd effectively bailed, HM felt she needed the money for herself. I was totally in agreement with her and reckoned now that Kat had more time on her hands, she'd be able to increase her hours at work and make a little more money.

When I'd failed to give Kat her monthly cheque, she phoned me to talk about it. I told her that I'd decided to give it to HM and there was a moment's silence. She seemed to accept my decision and tried to sound resigned to the situation. Quietly, at first, she said: *I thought we were friends.* I told her that I didn't see it like that, as first and foremost, she'd told HM everything I'd mentioned in confidence to her and therefore for some months, for my own sanity, I'd had to see her, not as a friend, but as someone to appease, like a chief disciple. When she heard this, Kat went ballistic and screamed at me that I'd let her down.

I can't remember the rest of the conversation, but do remember how it ended. Kat, HM-style, could be heard throwing her phone down on me right across town.

Now it was my turn to be furious. I honestly believed that she was actually expecting me to carry on paying her money, even though she knew that it was going to be impossible for me to continue giving it to her. I thought: *I see. You only wanted me as a friend so you could milk me. Charming!*

To this day I don't know if it's true or not that Kat only put up with me for the cash. But for a long time in those days, I was convinced of it. From that night on, I nursed such an incredibly unhealthy dislike of Kat that it was affecting my peace of mind. I just couldn't settle. I felt utterly betrayed. I'd so needed a friend in those days and I really wanted it to be her.

The following day, I went around to see HM about it and she was sympathetic but also shocked. She asked me to record my feelings in a notebook which the two of us reviewed over the next few weeks. I didn't hide anything in the book either; I let it all come out. If HM helped me in those days, it was to encourage me to open up emotionally and I could see why she was doing it. I'd never learned to express myself and my inner anxiety. If I ever complained about school when I was a kid (and there was one educational establishment I was sent to which threw me into a kind of nervous breakdown when I was only twelve), I was told pretty much to put up with it as "it won't last forever." Don't get me wrong, I don't blame my folks for this; they just had no idea what was going on and those were the days (the seventies) when no one ever complained about anything. Writing down my inner thoughts and frustrations was a very useful task at the time and I released a lot of blocks.

Two good friends of mine who helped me edit this book have pointed out that there was something else at work in this situation with the notebook. I never appreciated it at the time, but HM was lapping up the information I imparted to her in my musings. It was such a useful little exercise for her to get a glimpse into the inner mind of Paul. By finding out what made me tick, where my fears lay, what my weaknesses were (and I was brutally frank in those writings), I handed myself over to her on a plate to be manipulated and controlled. I just never saw it at the time.

HM also took some knocks over Kat's departure too. After my screaming match with her, Kat – apparently – was so incensed at how she felt she'd been treated that she threw away everything that HM had ever given her and obliterated HM from her life totally. When I heard this I was doubly angry. For over a year, Kat had utterly sold herself to the HM experience. It had become her whole life. To have thrown it up in the air so fast and so completely implied that all her talk had been nothing but a sham. I began to think of her as being incredibly superficial and lacking in conviction.

With the benefit of hindsight however, I can honestly say that she was just as much drawn in by HM as I was. The only difference between me and Kat on the day that she fled HM was that she'd escaped and I hadn't. *She* woke up and *I* was still very much the one with the blindfold tied tightly around my head. If I hadn't been so indoctrinated, I'd have exalted in such a triumphant ending to her HM story.

All the same, these negative emotions went on for months and whenever I thought about Kat, I would seethe. It was some years before I saw her again and we did try to get it together as friends. But then, Kat did something which ruined our friendship once and for all – a story I can only relate once the time comes to explain what happened when young Scooter reached the age of fifteen.

Chapter Ten

By Christmas 1999, HM and I had settled into a routine. I went to my parents' house and was given a new coat and a really warm hat for presents. I didn't think I'd really need them, but my flat wasn't the warmest place in the winter and I took to wearing the hat indoors.

On New Years Eve, I ushered in the New Millennium on my own. HM was not of a mind to celebrate, as to her, it was just another date. I stayed in and watched the rain lashing against my window. Ordinarily the street outside was buzzing with traffic and people of all races, creeds and colours. The sex shop opposite was also well frequented with its gaudy Christmas tree lights shining in the darkness all year round. The takeaways did a roaring trade with the fine aroma of curry and Chinese wafting into my flat. But that night, everything was deserted. Everyone was packed into pubs and clubs and obviously celebrating like there was no tomorrow. At midnight, the sky exploded with fireworks. I looked out at the deserted rain-washed street and wished I was back in Greece.

The year 2000 saw me sell my soul completely to HM. For the entire year, I didn't step outside Reading town once. I was either at work, shopping in Sainsbury's, at home hunched over my PC updating HM's site and working on her books and leaflets or hanging out with the children. To be honest, most of the time I was as happy as Larry as I thought it was all going to lead somewhere spectacular and that a day would come when all my efforts would be rewarded. Instead, the whole year passed in the doldrums for her.

Gary was off the scene and there was no Kat. I did the running around and most of the time, HM still had to get her own shopping. Any extra cash I earned I was giving to HM. I was always concerned about the children and wanted them to have presents if it was their birthday and clothes if they needed them. If HM wanted help with the purchase of presents for them, I'd give her some money, but she'd always say that the present came from her and not me. I'd then purposely betray her by telling the kids where the money came from! They already knew, to be honest. Both of them, despite being untidy and disorganised were pretty switched on for youngsters of their age.

When the summer came, HM seemed convinced that things were about to look up for all of us. She began to suggest that it was time for me to leave work because when August came, there would be people almost breaking down the door to come and take spiritual training and healing. I didn't realise it at the time, but this was a bit of a clever ruse to try and get *all* my time and energy to look after the children during the summer holidays, a task that she didn't feel she could cope with on her own. By this time, Scooter, fed up with lessons at home, had convinced her to send him back to school and she was getting used to having time on her own again and was dreading the summer holidays.

In July, she insisted that I resign from my job. I was incredibly reluctant to do that as personally, I could see no end in sight from the doldrums. I decided to get around the issue by asking my manager if I could take a month off unpaid. The answer was simple: no! I was told if I wanted time off, I'd have to resign. As I was effectively sold to HM by this time, I had no choice but to do just that.

On my leaving day, I was given an excellent present and wished well by a lot of colleagues who'd accepted my rather bizarre circumstances by maintaining a wary silence about them. I kept the fact that my life was no longer my own a secret but they knew, and were all the more diplomatic for understanding that I was reluctant to talk about it.

The month of August was surprisingly warm. I didn't have much money but still enjoyed myself, living on some savings and hanging out with the children. The four of us played tennis in Prospect Park and watched TV whilst I set aside my worries for the future. Inevitably, there were no callers and no folks queuing up for all this spiritual training that HM had pencilled in for herself.

One incident that I remember from that time was the day that Rosie went swimming in the Central Pool with a little friend from around the corner. There was silence for most of the afternoon until about five in the evening when Rosie suddenly rang from a phonebox to say some kids were bullying her and she was trapped. I was horrified and so was HM. We sped around there in the car and I got out to see a bunch of kids, nasty-looking types, hanging around. I approached them and started shouting at them. They sort of backed off and moved down the road, but I was so incensed I gave chase. You should have heard the language and abuse they gave me. I was appalled and all the more so for wishing that people would stop being nasty to Rosie. Her life was difficult enough already without some total strangers turning on her. As I approached, they started throwing stones at me and I threatened to call the Police. At that point, they melted away into the distance and I had no choice but to give up the chase.

Rosie was incredibly resilient and didn't complain. I guess by this time, she was so resigned to life's difficulties that she barely noticed yet another act of treachery being perpetrated against her. When we got home, I was talking to HM in the hallway and suddenly remembered I'd left a pan of brown rice boiling on my hob. HM, let me go and I got home to find the water had boiled away, but no other damage. A lucky escape! I was sure there were "friends" watching over me in those days. In fact, now I *know* there were. But that's a piece of information we shall save for another time.

One day, we all went to Prospect Park for an afternoon walk. Scooter found a lovely grassy bank he couldn't resist rolling down and behind his mum's back, did just that, gleefully landing at the bottom in the filthiest, most stinky patch of mud he could possibly have come across. When he stood up, honest to God, he looked like the monster from the black lagoon. HM, who you may have given up on as a totally humourless old hag, laughed like a drain at this sight and I joined in with abandon.

Somehow we managed to get the Scooter into the car, having asked him to remove the worst of his clothing. Even though it was a hot day, his mum wrapped him up in a towel and we drove home. On arriving back at Ryan Street, Scooter got himself out of the car and abandoned the towel. Thinking it was all one big Scooter-like joke, he proceeded to run down the street waving his arms in the air and shouting like a complete lunatic, covered in slime. All he had on was a pair of undies.

HM and I laughed properly for the first time in ages.

In July 2000, Rosie had broken up from the local school and was due to start at a local secondary school a little further out of town. Before the beginning of term, she was expected to turn up with a parent or parents to meet one of the teachers and to be given a little preparatory interview to introduce her to the school. Unfortunately, an event that should have helped Rosie to make a smooth transition from primary into secondary education, ended up being turned into a fiasco.

As the day for the interview approached, HM asked me if I'd accompany her so that I could introduce her to the teacher conducting the interview as a "Holy Person" and in doing so, tell everyone that she was, under no circumstances, to be kept waiting in a queue, was to be addressed as "Holy Mother" and was not, for any reason whatsoever, to be touched, even to shake hands. I was supposed to explain that because of her high level, the low vibrations of ordinary mortals with their desire natures would cause her pain.

Deep down, I found this whole situation utterly ridiculous. I was furious that HM was about to wreck what should have been a positive start at Rosie's new school, by sweeping in like Cleopatra and demanding to be treated like royalty. It was probably the single most crass example of shameless and outrageous self-promotion that she'd ever made and it sickened me to the stomach. I also knew that far from inspiring interest in her teachings amongst intelligent free-thinking people, it would bring in an unprecedented level of ridicule by a group who live and work in an environment of political correctness where the old values of doffing your cap to some spoilt aristocrat have been swept away in favour of a more humane approach to society. To think that HM honestly believed she could make a splash in this world shows just how intrinsically out-of-touch she was with reality and how hopelessly damaging her car-crash spiritual policies really were. It was a sickening display of the cult of the personality that society nowadays associates with the swaggering arrogance of divas and super-spoiled Hollywood glitterati. HM didn't discuss with me the real reason why she wanted to play the Diva role, but even to this day, I believe that she doesn't understand what makes university-educated people tick. Her behaviour towards me when I first

89

arrived was to assume immediately that I was impressed by showy displays, by fine clothes, by holding high level conversations about literary subjects that showed off how well read you are. In reality, it's far more down-to-earth than that. HM assumed, never having been to university, that teachers and intellectual types in general look down on the rest of the world and put themselves on a pedestal for their achievements. But most graduates keep their qualifications to themselves and don't spend all their time revelling in superficial shows of intellectual greatness.

In an effort to make a ripple in this world, HM showed herself up and it was frankly embarrassing. When the day came, I was sick with worry. I knew what was going to happen.

When we arrived at the school, I ushered HM in and did as I was told. I went to the receptionist and demanded that she be seen immediately as she was not to be kept waiting. The receptionist who must have seen every kind of behaviour over the years from both unruly kids and overbearing parents, frowned, shook her head and told us to sit down and wait. HM in turn, frowned at me for not pushing her case and I knew I was already in trouble.

Eventually, Rosie's teacher came in and walked up to us. I stood up and trotted out the pre-prepared speech about HM's position, stammering and almost losing my voice in shame. The look on the teacher's face was a picture. He just couldn't cover his disgusted reaction and frowned deeply, curling his lip for about five seconds, just enough for everyone present to be in no doubt at all what he was thinking:

Cuckoo!!

He then somehow uttered his first word which came out similar to Doctor Evil's "riii-iiight" in the *Austin Powers* films. The whole interview was destined to be a farce from that moment.

We went into a room and all took a seat. I just sat there like a stuffed dummy wishing a hole would open and swallow me up. At one point, the teacher, having taken HM through some business as usual-type topics, turned to Rosie and gave her a warning that his school did not accept unruly behaviour amongst its pupils. HM rounded on him:

"You're talking to the daughter of a Holy Mother! Her behaviour is impeccable!"

That shut him up.

The interview ended and we were ushered out. The teacher, by this time almost biting his tongue in an effort to hold back his rising sneer, dispatched HM as fast as he could and ran inside, no doubt to tell all and sundry he'd just met the freakiest people in the whole wide world.

Inevitably, HM was not impressed with this school. As soon as she could, she enrolled Rosie in a completely different school which was miles away on the other side of town and this time, there was no turning up for an interview like hallowed ancient Egyptian royalty and no excruciating displays of fake grandeur. I think HM had been cut down by her experience with the sneering teacher and somehow came to her senses just for long enough to realise that showy spiritual histrionics don't work amongst intellectuals after all.

At the end of August, HM, having used me as a free babysitter for a month, then suggested something that she knew was going to happen all along; namely that I should go back into the world of work and get myself a job as soon as I could. Her hordes of spiritual seekers that were supposed to be bashing down her door that summer were just nowhere to be seen.

Immediately, I signed on at an agency and told them the name of the company I'd previously worked for. More fools they, one of their staff rang my old department at the company and asked them if they'd have me back. Rather than paying the agency money for employing me, one of the managers rang me direct and offered me my old job, bypassing the agency completely. It was quite sneaky, but I was deeply complimented.

So, in the first week of September, there I was again, administering a banking system as if nothing had happened. A number of colleagues wanted to know what the point was of my having accepted a leaving present and many was the time they came up to me and jokingly demanded the 5p back that they'd put in my collection envelope for the leaving gift! I was highly amused and deeply mortified at the same time. I was also overjoyed to have an excellent manager, a lovely lady who was to be unwittingly very supportive of me the following year when I was going to need all the help I could get.

Now that Scooter had gone back to school a new set of problems arose. He absolutely hated it. At first, HM had sent him to Rosie's primary school and from day one, there were ructions. Part of the problem was that Scooter – certainly in those days – was just not interested in academia. I'm sure he was being given homework to do at the time, but he always denied he had any. He would then be in trouble at school for not producing the goods on demand. As he could be quite a sensitive kid at times, if any of the teachers were in any way strict with him, he would get upset and then refuse to co-operate at all. HM was often up at the school trying to sort out problems that were cropping up because of what she called his sensitivity. To me, Scooter was simply "on strike".

Other kids sometimes had a go at Scooter and at first he was at a loss to know how on earth to deal with it. His inclination was to use his fists and fight his way out of the problem; this wouldn't have been a challenge for Scooter as he was always big for his age. However, he was also exceptionally loyal to his mum and his priority was never to do anything that would put her in a negative light. He doesn't talk about it much, but I suspect that he probably took quite a lot of grief from other kids in those days, but tried his best to take it on the chin and not retaliate. I'm certain that none of the kids knew the nature of his mother's life or work, but they would certainly have sensed something different about Scooter himself. The best way I can describe it is by saying that he was a boy like any other boy who was prepared to play the game in the rough and tumble world of primary school, but on the other hand, a child who felt he had at least to try to be the person that his mum – as a spiritual teacher – expected him to be. He didn't want to compromise her position in any way and constantly had to walk the line between being the tearaway that he could have been (had he been in a normal fully functional family unit) and the angelic son of a "Holy" Mother. It was hard for him and some of the abuse he took from teachers and peers alike would often make him tearful and sad.

Rosie on the other hand just got on with it. I never really heard any complaints from her, even though I'm sure there must have been issues. She's always been gregarious, but at the same time, she has this habit of clamming up and trying to get any information out of her about how she's feeling is like pulling teeth. I think with

Rosie, if she doesn't like a situation, just walks away and finds other fish to fry. This is often, if you're in a difficult place (and Rosie was to find herself in some very difficult places in the years to come) a good policy.

That autumn, Scooter started at a primary school outside town that his mother always had high hopes for as she seemed to like the way it was run. At first, things appeared to be fine. Initially HM would drop Scooter off every morning in her car, but eventually, she decided it was easier for her to put him on a bus. She would always see him off and then, by necessity, come and meet him at the bus stop when he returned after school. I say "by necessity" because the problem was, Scooter just didn't have a clue where he lived. He had no idea of direction, no memory at all for landmarks and no feel for time and duration. I can honestly tell you for example that he didn't know the months of the year for a long, long time after his peers had got them under their belts in infant school! It was almost like he was a visitor to this planet from a far off galaxy, as the concept of time and space that we're so bound by on this planetary system in its base consciousness state, meant absolutely nothing to Scooter. Consequently, when it was time for him to alight from the bus after school, unless his mum was there to distract his attention outside the window, he would just carry on sitting there being cool. If he ended up in Outer Mongolia, then so be it.

There is a certain irony in this situation, however. If you told Scooter to look out for a giant chocolate cake at the very spot where he was supposed to have jumped off the bus, you can bet your bottom dollar he'd have been off that bus at exactly the right time and in the right place. Really, it was all about motivation and sometimes getting Scooter interested enough to contemplate reality meant appealing to his desire nature!

Chapter Eleven

I was not to know, as 2000 became 2001, that the new year would be hell for us. I went to my parents for Christmas 2000 and realised that I hadn't seen them once that whole year. They'd kept in touch but kept their distance as they didn't want to witness me being swallowed up by a mad cult and were powerless to do anything to prevent it.

HM was becoming desperate. Her situation was showing no sign of improvement and she was still penniless and still alone, with only me for company, the most bloody useless disciple in the world. I really was useless too. She'd ask me to do something like get her a loaf of bread on the way home from work and I'd forget in an instant. I got behind with all the paperwork, writing and secretarial tasks I was supposed to be doing and consistently had to be chased up. I also used to lie my socks off to get out of situations when I'd failed to do something. I came up with some horrendous excuses for not doing things such as my PC breaking down, or having to work overtime. I'm sure she always knew what a fibber I was and often she would just roll her eyes and repeat the order. If she was already in a state because she was having a bad day, I'd be screamed at and kicked out of her house. In those days, if I did something wrong, she would ignore me for a week and send me a letter telling me that I was making no headway on the path, that I was a burden to her and taking up too much of her time and energy.

By way of an aside, I have to say that over the years, the letters began to have less and less effect on me. In the early days, I used to dread them as they often threatened a ban for life and that was a terrifying prospect. To me, being banned for life meant being rejected from the spiritual fold completely and becoming an outcast, not only from my supposed charmed life as being trained by the world's most "powerful" spiritual being, but in the eyes of her god, which, at the time, was also indubitably *my* god. When I think back, I cringe at the thought of how "God" was misrepresented. It was like religion all over again. It was all guilt and fear and threats and banishment. This is absolutely everything that "God" is not. An Infinite Source Consciousness of unconditional love and compassion would never cast anyone out, especially not someone who was trying to find the nature of the Universe like I was, wholeheartedly. Why didn't I see that? More to the point, why didn't *she*..?

One thing I did see was the decline in Scooter's behaviour. He became demanding and controlling. By this time, he'd worked out how to get around me and became extremely manipulative. I can't blame him for that. He was a nine year-old kid who had to put up with a lot of grief and misery.

If Scooter wanted to come over and I said "no", the phone would ring five minutes later with a threat from HM. Then Scooter would come over...

If I said or did anything that he knew his mother would disapprove of, five minutes later, the phone would ring. "Scooter says you did this, that, the other...blah...blah...blah".

I loved both of those kids to pieces, but they had me right where they wanted me. HM had, in Scooter, a very useful spy and in turn, the spy had a mother he could manipulate to get me to do what he wanted. This makes him sound nasty, but of course he wasn't. I knew full well that all kids are like this given half the chance. Also, to be honest, he was only copying the behaviour of his own mother. One of her greatest tricks was to play people off against each other as part of her need for control.

This was to become abundantly clear as spring became summer in 2001. Gary, albeit briefly, appeared on the scene again. When Gary appeared, it almost always augured trouble. He's an intelligent chap, although he'd deny it as he wants everyone to think of him as a streetwise working class lad with brawn before brains. He certainly had enough grey matter to know exactly which buttons to press to get me into the maximum amount of hot water.

One day, he came around for a chat to see how I was. I believe there was also a lecture buried in there as well as HM often used him to go and give me a thorough dressing down over my attitude. When she got him to do that, she would also warn him that because I suppressed all my emotions it meant that I was highly dangerous, violent and psychopathic. She would warn him that he needed to be on his guard in case I attacked him with a knife when his back was turned. Gary would always maintain that he was from the street and he could rearrange my face before that ever happened. Of course Gary knew I wasn't going to attack him. But he went along with the HM fear-factor thing because, like her, he loved to move us all about on a chessboard. For him it was all a laugh. For HM, it was a deadly serious part of playing her shoddy little game.

Whilst he was giving me his HM-inspired lecture, he suddenly stopped and pointed to my CD shelf.

"Oh, you've got *Once Around the World* by *It Bites*!" he exclaimed.

I told him that since seeing the band at Reading University in the Eighties I'd always loved them and their amazing mixture of pop/progressive anthemic stadium rock. Apparently, Gary had liked them too and came out with a piece of information that had me rolling around in laughter: we'd both seen them at the same gig in February 1987 at the Majestic in Reading.

"I spliffed up with them after the gig," he said. "Yeah, me and my mate got into their dressing room."

Suddenly, I could almost have worshipped Gary. He was human! After hearing he liked *It Bites*, I stupidly forgave him all his betrayals of me.

Just as he was about to leave, he played a really nasty trick on me. He goes:

"Oh! Holy Mother is coming up the stairs!"

I rushed over to the landing and couldn't see anything.

He seemed to come over all strange and looked visibly shaken. I said:

"Um...I take it you've just had a vision of her?"

He confirmed that that was exactly what had happened and, on the face of it, looked like he'd just been given an almighty spiritual lesson. He told me that the best thing I could do was tell HM what had happened, that her spirit had paid him a visit. He warned me that there was every chance she wouldn't know.

Later that day, when I went around to her house, I informed her of Gary's experience. She was quite shocked and warned me excitedly that as a Holy Mother, she was sure that she often appeared to people in spirit, either in their hour of need or at times when they had something to learn. She herself would have no conscious memory of this happening.

"Exactly what did Gary see?" she asked.

As Gary had said that HM was coming up the stairs at the time, I kind of lied and told her that it had been just her head, which effectively was possible for someone making an appearance towards observers standing a little bit away from the top of the stairs. Unfortunately, HM – as usual – wasn't listening to a word I said and assumed that I meant she'd been just this sort of floaty head thing, moving mysteriously and bodiless around my flat.

Later when she cross-questioned Gary, he gave a completely different story and said she'd appeared in her entirety. It was all getting very confusing and HM was apoplectic with rage.

I knew that I was in the doghouse the very next morning. As I was leaving for work, I passed HM on the road where she'd just been saying goodbye to Scooter who was off to school. Our eyes met and I did that namaste bowing thing that she still expected me to do. But rather than greet me, she glared at me with eyes of complete distaste and fury. My heart jumped into my mouth. I knew that something had gone wrong and that I was in trouble again; this did not look good.

All day at work, I couldn't concentrate for worrying about what was going to happen next. And sure enough, that evening, I was in so much trouble. I can't recall what she said to me, but if I remember correctly, Gary came around and pitched into me for the way I'd handled the whole business. I was told I was banned and then given a really vicious letter from HM almost threatening me with a promise of irredeemable hell fire for lying to her. Of course, I took it very seriously and was incredibly upset and downcast.

It was a long, long time before HM forgave me for that incident and she never let me forget it.

Had Gary lied about the apparition on the stairs? You bet he had! He was playing devil's advocate again. It was just Gary being Gary: he was such a terrible trouble-maker. But you know what? He liked *It Bites*, so I overlooked his idiocy.

I know I'm making light of the situation around this time, but it's helping me to come to terms with it. In truth, everything was just beginning to fall apart.

Gary was around for some weeks and his presence caused problems for me and HM, not least because he was loving the discord between us. Around this time, he played his part in an incident that seriously damaged my faith in everyone.

One Sunday night, Rosie called me to ask me if I could come around and iron her school blouses. I was so tired and despondent from all the hassle, it was not what I wanted to hear. All I could think of as I crossed the zebra crossing to the other side of the road was, *why doesn't HM do it herself? She doesn't work; she has all that time on her hands; all she ever does is sit around and moan and complain at everyone.*

By the time I got to her house, I was fuming. Rosie opened the door and gave me the blouses, saying that her mum was too tired and ill. I can't remember what I said, but it was something that an over-sensitive person like HM would understand as lacking in respect.

I took the blouses home, ironed them and brought them back. When Rosie answered the door, she was curt with me, snatched the blouses and slammed it shut. I knew she'd been ordered to be like that. I thought: *Damn! HM has obviously heard my outburst from earlier.*

And sure enough, it was a right royal case of "off with his head" this time. HM didn't speak to me for days and then Gary phoned. He was stiff and formal with me and ordered me around to HM's house that night when she would be channelling my guide who "had something to tell me".

If you're new to the spiritual thing, you need to know that apparently, everyone has a spiritual guide. If you're not pre-disposed towards spirituality, you still have a guide, but it's likely that you share one with others, especially as there's not much point in a highly evolved entity getting personally involved in your case if you're not plain interested!

In my case, I had my own guide. According to HM, he was not from this planetary system and I was meant to feel extremely honoured to have him give me such personal attention. A part of me felt that to have him take an interest in me such that he would allow himself to be channelled, meant that he must have something serious to impart.

The problem is, on the other hand, I just wasn't having it. My "On Hold" closet was absolutely chockablock by this time and there just wasn't enough room for me to suspend my disbelief in anything else. To be honest, by the time I was standing outside HM's house that evening ready to ring the bell and be let in by Gary, I was already saying this one word in my head: *bollocks*.

Gary had been well prepped by HM to be strict and distant with me. As he was playing his role as Devil's Advocate to its maximum effect, he put on such an act that he came over not as strict but as downright abusive. It only served to make me even more terrified. But, as I took off my shoes, bizarrely, the terror abated. Instead, quite inexplicably, I began to feel calm and then resigned. Resignation was then taken over by a brand new emotion that was very different for me in my experiences with the "holy" lady. I found myself in mocking mode. I was just *not* having any of this.

When I went into HM's work room, she was seated stiff and formal in her chair. There was a stern look on her face and clearly, in her mind at least, she was already bringing the guide through. What a brilliant act! And all for the greatest sucker ever!

The accent she spoke in was definitely not of this world. It sounded like a mishmash of every Western European language all rolled into one. It also wasn't flowing as it would have been if the channelling had been genuine. As she spoke, you could see she was still there and concentrating hard. Occasionally, she would hesitate. If it had been a true channelling, you'd have known immediately as the voice would have been emanating smoothly from her, but at the same time, her words would have been originating from some place well beyond her. Even I, in my state of complete blind faith, could see this was not the real article.

HM told me that if I scrubbed her floor for a hundred years, I wouldn't even begin to pay off all the Universal debts I owed her. Apparently, throughout a succession of lifetimes, I hurt her in every way possible and killed her many times. I'd imprisoned her and done genetic experiments on her, keeping her in a cage and letting her out only to inflict terrible pain on her; all because she'd refused me when I asked her for spiritual training. As I'd been

99

resentful towards her, I'd decided to turn my anger against her and had joined the dark side. Seemingly, since then, I'd been on the dark side for centuries and was now being given a final chance to put things right before handing myself over for literally millennia of suffering.

On the face of it, I should have been terrified given the way that I'd been so cleverly and utterly sucked in. But I was really struggling to take it all seriously this time. All I could think of was to mock this ridiculous situation. So I was rude. I sat there like a disobedient schoolboy and answered in a monotone, at times curling my lip in a sneer. HM in her "state" chose to ignore this stance and instead, obviously realising that I was struggling with this whole situation, tried a different tactic, becoming more gentle and conciliatory towards me.

When the channelling was finished, I was duly dismissed. I walked out of the door and Gary was sitting on the stairs. I knew he'd heard us talking and had obviously homed in on my backchat. He warned me that he was coming over to see me after a few minutes in conversation with HM and looked at me as if to say: *you're never going to get out of this one!*

As I walked up the street, I began to wake up from my spell. For the first time, I'd been pushed too far. A word from earlier moved its way to the front of my head:

Bollocks...

I crossed the road at the zebra crossing and repeated it again with more seriousness. By the time I reached my place and was putting the key into the lock, I was repeating it over and over again in my head: bollocks, bollocks, utter, utter, utter BOLLOCKS!

When Gary came over, he didn't give me a dressing down at all. Instead he kind of brushed over the whole thing and I was immediately suspicious. To this day, I'm certain that HM had told him to be nice to me and overlook my disobedient schoolboy stance. I think she must have known the game was up and that she'd pushed the bounds of credulity too far.

When Gary left that evening, he seemed quite bouncy as if he'd had some fun. And I, like a fool, moved back into my usual state of denial. HM had always told me that as a Holy Mother, she could take on any role she liked in order to get a trainee to the place he needed to be in for spiritual learning. To me, that meant that if she

100

had to tell barefaced lies, which was what the whole evening had been about, that's exactly what she would do. After all, the end would justify the means, especially if the end brought about "enlightenment" in the individual concerned.

So I accepted that it had all been a sham. Instead of using it as a springboard to realisation of the web of deceit that bound me, I conned myself back into the matrix all over again. By the following day, it was business as usual for Paul and Holy Mother and I was, once again, the serf held right under the thumb of the omnipotent lord.

Chapter Twelve

After the floating head debacle, there was war. Gary stayed around for a few more weeks and most of the time there was trouble for me. I'm sure that as part of his game, he was whipping HM up into a fury and most of his pawns were moving inexorably against what few pieces I had left on the board. Every single day I'd be trashed for something: getting the wrong food from the supermarket, forgetting to do the simplest of tasks, saying the wrong things, being at the wrong place at the wrong time, breathing, existing.

Gary had to take over the responsibility of doing the shopping as - supposedly - I could never get it right. This didn't mean that he paid for the items, of course. I was still coughing up as that was all I was good for.

One day, HM phoned me at work and asked me quite aggressively to get a certain packet of biscuits for her after I'd finished. Over the course of the day, I became so busy that in the melee I totally forgot what brand of biscuits I'd been asked to get. HM was incredibly fussy about things. You had to get exactly the right brand of whatever she wanted or her whole world would cave in. This was not her being strict as a teacher. It was a case of one being utterly stuck in her ways and unable to compromise even for a moment like a spoilt, demanding child. That afternoon, just before I was due to set off home, I had no choice but to ring her and ask her to remind me what brand of biscuits she needed. When she heard my question, she let off a torrent of abuse and was spiteful and vicious to me.

I purposely didn't buy those biscuits that day. I was so upset and angry, I walked straight past Sainsbury's and stomped off home. By the time I got back to my flat, I'd worked myself into such a state that I'd decided enough was enough. By this time, I think I'd begun to detest her like Kat. I just couldn't take the pressure anymore.

I ran indoors and grabbed a bunch of floppy disks which contained a load of files on them relating to books and leaflets that I was typing up for her. I rammed them into an envelope and set off for her house.

As I walked, I really questioned my motives. This would mean I would never see the children again and open up a torrent of abuse and unpleasantness I didn't think I would be able to stand. I knew that Rosie would take this latest blow on the chin and deal with it quietly in her own little way. But I also knew that Scooter would be devastated. It would be like losing a dad for him. I'm sure after all these years, he would confirm that. I reached HM's front door, shoved the envelope through the letterbox and fled.

About half an hour later the phone rang. It was her.

"What was all that about?" she snapped. "Have you left?"

"Err...yes," I stammered. "I can't take this any more."

She then started on me, sneering and spitting at me with all her dark venom. I can't remember everything she said but I believe that in between the vicious outbursts, she was implying that I'd let her down after everything she'd done for me. The fact that she'd never in fact done anything at all for me was not relevant. Neither was the fact that it had always been me that had put energy into this venture.

For all the money I'd chucked in her direction over the years, for all the time and effort I'd put into trying to serve her, for all the times she'd used me as a whipping boy, she thanked me by throwing the phone down.

I sat down and thought about things for a long, long time. A part of me felt extremely relieved to be free, but the greater part was terrified. I began to realise that my overriding emotion was now one I simply hadn't anticipated in the turmoil of the afternoon: regret. I came to the conclusion that I'd completely blown it in terms of my spiritual path. I had visions of burning in hell, of spending the rest of my life tumbling down into misery and poverty beneath the weight of all the debts I now owed the Universe for my part in the destruction of "God's messenger on earth".

You probably think I'm exaggerating at this point, but believe me, I most certainly am not. By day I was a normal person working for one of the UK's most respected companies. By evening and all weekend, I was naïve and easily manipulated. To her, I was no more than an ugly little rag doll to be tossed around and sucked into her dark drama. Because I was too lacking in conviction to stick up for myself, I felt I was hardly a man at all.

The phone rang and it was Scooter. He asked me if it was true that I'd left and I apologised to him but confirmed that it was true. I tried to make him understand but he was too upset. The last thing he said to me in a quivering voice, was "thanks a lot, Paul." This time, it was his turn to throw down the phone. I felt like I'd slapped an innocent child right in the face and was deeply ashamed of myself for betraying him.

The drama didn't end there. After another half an hour, he was over at my place knocking on the door. I let him in and we sat down to talk. He was incredibly sanguine and trying to put on a mature face. He told me that his mum was shouting the house down and was so angry that she was becoming dangerous. There was also a hint that if she ever saw me again, she would call the Police and accuse me of harming all three of them. When he delivered this piece of information, there was a slight warning behind his voice that the two of us were going to have a lot of diplomacy to work through. He knew his mother could be emotionally dangerous and he wanted to avoid such a scenario at all costs. Suddenly I knew why he was there. He was concerned about me and didn't want his mother to ruin my life and his.

I was absolutely horrified. My friends had always hated my involvement with "that woman" and had often warned me about getting close to her in case someone so obviously unhinged would turn around and accuse me of attacking the children. And now, here it was: I'd ignored them and set aside their concerns believing that they just didn't have a clue about what I was trying to achieve. As for her, she'd stooped to the lowest point ever.

So, bending beneath the pressure of this intimidation, I felt I had no choice but to attempt to put everything back together again. I had to backtrack. I couldn't bear the thought of being falsely accused of anything.

I often wonder if HM had "prepped" Scooter to come over with the Police threat, knowing that it would work perfectly as a ploy to lure me back. In his own turn, Scooter would have fallen for it and willingly run over to see me so that he could play his own little part in bringing me back into the fold. Even today, I do believe that he cared about me and was only too keen to make sure I was still in his life. There was no one else who would provide an occasional antidote to the bizarreness of his personal circumstances. I rented videos for him to watch, allowed him to get away with things that he couldn't get away with at home and indulged his little whims. I think he admired me for that and was glad for those little distractions to his routine. HM of course, needed the cash and a "gofer".

I felt so sorry for Scooter that evening. I told him to go home and tell his mother that I was prepared to "recant" and asked him to tell her I'd changed my mind. It was all I could think of to resolve the situation. I knew by doing that, she would take all my energy from me in one giant gulp and that I would be made to pay for months and months. She would never let me forget my mistake and it would be held against me in an effort to imply that her terrible life was officially all my fault. If I came back, of course, it would be under sufferance. She'd be leaning low into the gutter to fish me out and I'd better be incredibly grateful for another bite at the apple.

As it turned out, that was exactly what happened. Over the next few days, I had to endure one of her vicious letters and both children were banned from seeing me.

However, Scooter, who was learning from the greatest trickster ever, came up with a ruse to put her right into the palm of his little hand. As I've said, he is and always has been, a master manipulator. He knows exactly which buttons to press and when to get people where he needs them. I understand why he felt the need to hone such "skills". In those crazy days when everything was falling apart for him and his sister, he decided to pull out all the stops. He told HM that he was in contact with an ancient spiritual teacher whose name I'll withhold as I'm sure Scooter doesn't want to make a big thing of this. He told his mother, strictly and in the sternest voice possible that there was an order from on high: Paul was not to be thrown out for his error of judgement. He was to be kept on, "if only to keep Scooter company".

HM was always desperately scrabbling around for celestial signs that were telling her what to do and where to be. She believed that by following channelled information, it would bring her to that pot of gold at the end of the rainbow that would be the answer to all her financial and housing problems. As she'd effectively sanctified Scooter for years, claiming that he would one day be her successor, she would often bow to his will and take his words seriously, especially when he "channelled". Scooter couldn't really channel anyone. He pretended he could as he knew he could get away with it and his face was always so cute and believable!

So she went along with it and did as she was told. Looking back, this was a sign of one of her biggest problems and the reason why she was barking up the wrong tree for years. She just didn't have the strength of her own convictions and was clutching at straws, scrabbling around for celestial signs, *anything* to show that she wasn't deluded. Had she really heard the voice of "God" as she always claimed? Let's just say at this point that if a demonic energy had been whispering orders into her ear whilst pretending to be "God" himself, she'd have believed it. This, by the way, is a clue as to what we'll have to explore later in this book.

For the moment, all you need to know is that she took me back. Even though she'd received what she believed was a celestial message, it didn't stop her from continuing to make my life a misery, from stepping up her rudeness towards me and intensifying that guilt trip. What's more, our breakdown in communications was about to get a lot worse.

Previously that summer, she and I had travelled to London to an exhibition that she really wanted to see at Olympia devoted to arts and crafts. I paid for the tickets and looked after her with the same care and attention I wanted to show to my own mother. She had responded very positively that day and on the way back, had shown a soft side to her character, thanking me for being a true friend to her.

She was never, ever to say anything like that to me again.

Over the next few weeks, HM became convinced that I was now officially the source of all her problems. She was making no headway at all with getting the house she wanted, in finding spiritual students to train and in sorting out her woeful financial situation. Time and again she warned me that if I didn't pull up my socks and clean up my act, that I would be banned for life. This was said with a look of total disdain.

By now, she'd realised that Gary was probably causing more problems than he was solving and he mysteriously disappeared off the scene again. This meant that she was now holed up with me, someone she'd come to mistrust but at the same time, felt she had to keep within her sphere of influence. I think she was in a real quandary. She'd begun to wish she could see the back of me after all, but just wasn't in a position to jettison me for good. There was also pressure from Scooter who did want me around.

Scooter himself was learning to play the game very well. When I wasn't around and she was pitching into me, as was her wont, he would pacify her by agreeing with her wholeheartedly that I was a damaging influence on her situation in general. He did this because he wanted to keep in with his mum and keep her sweet. Sometimes the best way to do that was just to go along with everything she said. In many ways, he's always guarded his mother like a lion, watching over her and trying his best to protect her. I think from a very young age, he realised just how vulnerable she was. As his love for her was so unconditional, he was prepared to play the game to keep her happy or risk losing her.

One day in August I got back from work. When I walked into my sitting room, a horrific sight met my eyes. She'd come around in my absence using the key I'd given her when I first moved in. With me out of the way, she'd been through all my belongings, my cupboards, everything. There were piles of stuff pulled out on a table and all over the computer desk with angrily scribbled notes on torn pieces of paper lying on top. The messages read something like: "what are you doing using this? You know it's bad Feng Shui..." "Why are you listening to immoral music? Get rid of all these records and CD's."

In the kitchen, she'd taken items of food I kept in the fridge and thrown them in the bin, saying that I wasn't eating properly and sticking to the diet she'd prescribed for me.

The whole flat was a mess. The worst thing she did was switch on my PC and put a Windows password on in a pathetic attempt to prevent me from using it. I think that may have been Scooter's idea as a way of appeasing her. However, he didn't know much about how PC's operated in those days and didn't realise that I could get around the problem by simply pressing cancel.

I was meant to feel violated. She was totally hard-focused on the damage she thought I was doing to her by not obeying even the most miniscule rule of Feng Shui, by not being the most subservient disciple. What she expected of me was nothing short of complete and total slavery. To waver at all from any of the draconian rules that she reckoned she had to foist on me was to block her utterly. Her penury was my fault, her misery all my doing. I was the millstone around her neck that was preventing her and hence the whole planet from advancing.

The flat trashing thing was a ploy to see how far I could be pushed and to remind me that she owned me outright. The fact that Scooter had had to go along with it suggested that he was not his own man either. She owned him as well and he had no choice but to play her game or risk her turning on him too.

As for Rosie, she was *always* to blame. Rosie was to blame just by existing. I'm really not sure how she shouldered that "responsibility", but I think by that time, she'd already started a new tactic to get through life and that was to lie extremely low and keep herself to herself. This was a very good idea as it kept her well out of trouble.

One evening, just as I was settling down to do some meditation, the phone rang. HM was psychotic again and screamed at me that I was to tell Rosie she was being kicked out for the night and had to sleep on my living room floor. I was worried about that. I wasn't her father and it just didn't look right at all. But once again, it was all about keeping HM from going off the rails, so I agreed. I went round to HM's to pick Rosie up. HM had barricaded herself in her bedroom and sadly and with a heavy heart, I helped her to gather some clothes and her duvet and carry them all over to my place with her in tow. On the way across the road, I asked her to tell me what had happened and she just shrugged. Later, Scooter rang me and told me that HM had had enough of her as she was to blame for blocking her. I didn't get another explanation for the circumstances of the fall out.

Later, at about half past ten, Scooter was sent around with some medicine for Rosie which HM had made up to regulate her behaviour patterns. I wouldn't be surprised if she'd looked up "hyperactivity in children" in her natural medicine books and decided to treat Rosie herself. Rosie wasn't hyperactive. She just didn't want anything to do with her mother's "thing". But HM was convinced she was ill and deeply disturbed[8].

The problem was, this medicine turned out to be an envelope of something that looked like grit or that ash you get from burning incense sticks. In fact, HM claimed it was something called Vibhuti, which is a kind of ash that was produced out of thin air by the Indian Saint Sai Baba. I don't know anything about that particular guru or his "miracles", but HM seemed to believe that this grit would transform her daughter and make her more placid and obedient.

Rosie wasn't having it. She watched in horror as Scooter mixed this grit with water as his mother had insisted and handed it to her. Understandably, she refused to take it and shouted at Scooter to go away. Scooter shouted back. He was frustrated because he just wanted to go home, tell his mother he'd done what she'd asked and then go to bed as he was obviously tired. The more Rosie shouted, the more Scooter shouted. The problem was, there was a tone of total panic and genuine horror in Rosie's voice that was difficult to ignore. She seemed petrified. Worse still, she began screaming and her voice sounded like someone was attacking her physically.

I began to get incredibly uneasy. If this hadn't been a rundown area where people often ignored screams in the night, the Police would have been called immediately by concerned neighbours.

I knew I had to intervene, so I shouted at Scooter: "All right! That's enough!"

I turned to Rosie and told her to sit tight and then I ordered Scooter to get his coat as I was taking him home. As we left the room, I heard Rosie behind me sobbing her heart out and I was so incredibly disheartened. I tried, but I just couldn't think of a way to resolve her issues without causing ructions and mayhem. If I'd supported Rosie against HM, the latter would have swung her axe

---

[8] What I didn't realise at the time were the deeper reasons for HM trying to demonise her daughter by casting her in the role of "the naughty little girl". Rosie was everything that HM wasn't and she resented her for it.

of vengeance against both of us. All I could do was try not to rock the applecart.

I was a little short with Scooter as I dropped him back. But he was also fed up and I think he went straight to bed when he got in. Meanwhile, I went home and went in to see Rosie. She'd stopped crying and I tried to talk to her and ask her gently once again to hold her nose and take the bloody grit, if only to shut her mother up. But she just turned away from me.

The damage had been done.

HM made it crystal clear over the next few weeks that she was officially holding me to account for all her woes and how she wished she'd done that all along. She honestly believed that if she hadn't been so blind to my general uselessness, she'd have avoided years of suffering by just nipping me in the bud sooner and dumping me. One day, she discovered that I'd been connecting my PC to the internet with a phone extension that I had to trail across the centre of the living room. On occasion this wire would just be left lying there when I forgot to disconnect it and wind it up. This action in itself was also highlighted as me causing her a block through my lack of respect for the laws of Feng Shui. Having read a couple of books on this subject, HM reckoned she was suddenly what they call a Feng Shui Master and tried to set herself up in business. Her first client was me. I didn't ask her to come over and sneer at the position of my furniture, she *told* me was coming. Having then toured my flat and pointed out everything that was wrong using a sack load of Feng Shui jargon, I was left financially lighter and baffled as to what exactly I'd got for my money. When she mispronounced the word Bagua as Bagooah, I corrected her thinking that it would be important if she was calling herself a master at this art that everyone saw her as completely professional. She didn't see it like that and lost her rag with me, accusing me of being a know-all. Because I felt most of her observations of my flat were wrong, I ignored her advice and was then accused of causing her money to fly down my bathroom loo by accidentally leaving the lid open.

What all this boils down to is that HM was utterly unable to face herself. Deep down, I still believe she *must* have realised that her blocks were all self-induced. But she was so entrenched in self-

110

denial that she was incapable, even for a moment, of standing back far enough to see the situation for what it was; namely that her absolutely abominable behaviour, her pettiness, her nastiness, anger and resentment were all still the root cause of her inability to move forward. This was on top of the fact that she had laid claim to a spiritual level of attainment that she was absolutely nowhere near. It was so much easier simply to blame someone else for her abject failure.

I'll never forget her words and actions on the day the Twin Towers were destroyed. I remember feeling incredibly alienated that afternoon sitting at work and looking at the internet, aghast at this horrific drama playing out in front of all our eyes. I was also angry as I felt there was something incredibly fishy about it and that no one would tell us the truth. In those days there was a TV rental shop in Reading's Broad Street and as I walked past it on my way home, I joined a crowd of people gazing in at the four or five TV sets that had not yet been switched off for the night. I checked out one woman's face as she turned away from the sight and set off up the street. She was actually smiling. I was incredibly shocked and shouted out after her: "Glad you find it so funny..."

I should have realised what was happening there and not been so lacking in understanding. When people are scared, their faces can show an opposite emotion in a subconscious effort to mask their true feelings. I guess it's why kids sometimes smirk when they're being told off. This woman, like me, was wondering what the hell was happening. A lot of people were feeling helpless, all the more so for knowing that this sort of event just emphasises how powerless individuals *seem* to be in the face of those who want to undermine our world.

Unfortunately, my own upset was to double later in the day when HM turned a world crisis into her very own drama. As soon as I got in, Scooter came around and we watched as the news was now showing pictures of the towers crashing down. He ran home to tell her and she phoned and demanded to know what the score was as she hadn't seen the news all day. At this point, information was very confused and there was a rumour going around that there were still planes in the air carrying terrorists to all sorts of targets. People were talking in terms of a massive invasion of the US. I told her all this and she went off to do some meditation in an

111

effort to use her "power" to stop any more attacks. Later she rang again and asked for an update. I told her that it was all quiet and there was nothing new to report, at which point she absolutely exploded and shouted:

"I thought you said there were thousands of planes in the air dropping bombs all over the States. So what's happening? What's wrong with you? Why don't you get your facts right!"

There I was, gazing horrified at the TV and wondering how many people had died in those towers and at the Pentagon and in my ear was this mad voice *still* complaining that I was making life difficult for her and blocking her. I wanted to shout out loud that for once, this wasn't all about *her.*

When I look back, I realise that 9/11 marked a turning point for her. From that day until Christmas she was totally thrown, seeing nothing but darkness all around her, slipping further and further down into depression and helplessness. I remember her saying at the time that the dark side now had a foothold and was moving in on all of us. She seemed to take the situation personally and although I'm sure she was *trying* to meditate, she just felt entirely surrounded by darkness.

Scooter, for his part, was now refusing to stay at school for an entire day. He'd always suffered from asthma and when he got anxious, he would bring on an attack that would last for days. In the autumn of that year, he was picking up on his mother's upset and was ill with it nearly all the time. He would have whole nights up wheezing and fighting for air and there were occasions when HM would have to ring Gary after he'd gone to bed and ask him to rush around and give him healing. As Gary had such a strong male vibration which is really what Scooter needed for company, his presence often helped to calm Scooter down as it brought a kind of protective reassurance that a child likes. If HM had allowed Scooter to use a ventolin inhaler in those days it would have helped him enormously, but she held back for years, honestly believing that it would harm his extremely sensitive body.

Scooter's behaviour became desperate. He would demand to come over and see me when I got in from work, hang out with me for a few minutes and then ask to go home. I would accompany him back to his place, get home and the phone would ring. It would be Scooter asking if he could come back over. I would go and get him, he'd stay for half an hour and then ask to be taken home again. This situation would repeat itself sometimes three times during the course of an evening.

Something similar was also happening at school. He'd start off the morning fine and then at about ten o'clock, HM would have to go and get him as he'd be suffering from a sudden asthma attack.

It was some time before I realised what all this was about. He was completely unable to settle as he thought something was going to happen to his mum. Either that or he thought she would try something desperate and end it all.

One day, as it turned out, I discovered that his fears in this regard were not in the least bit unfounded.

It was a Saturday night in November, if I remember correctly. I was at home trying to do some quiet meditation when the phone rang. Scooter was in floods of tears and begged to come over immediately. I asked him what was wrong and he told me: *Mum's tried to kill herself.*

I told him to get round to my place immediately. Without delay, he went into Rosie's room and told her he was going to mine and not to tell mum unless she specifically asked. Closing the front door quietly, he ran over the zebra crossing and hared around to mine as fast as his legs would carry him. As soon as he came in through the front door he collapsed in a heap on my hall floor, his head in his hands sobbing like I'd never seen a kid sob before. In between gasps for breath he managed to force out the story of what happened.

HM had been in a bad mood all day and had locked herself in her room. She was refusing any food and was just sitting there in a heap, completely uncommunicative. At some point, she'd come downstairs and had taken a knife from the kitchen drawer. Then, in front of Scooter, she'd proceeded to try and slash her wrists.

"The knife was blunt, though," Scooter sobbed. "She couldn't draw any blood."

I was a terrible mix of emotions. I knew deep down what this was all about. HM had chosen a blunt knife because she had no intention of ending it all. She had also committed this act in front of another party which meant it was a cry for help.

My first really clear thought was "why on earth has she chosen to do it in front of her own ten year-old son?" To me that was unforgivably selfish. Surely she must have known that it would set up a trauma for him. This was a person who'd said she wanted to help people with childhood trauma, to steer them through their mental blocks so that they could move on with their lives. Now here she was, assigning those very blocks to Scooter.

The next moment, I began to get really worried about her because this was a sign of a human in complete desperation. I knew that whatever had driven her to this act was something she would never tell me about and if I even dared to think about going around there to check that she was all right, I would be given a very blunt message: *all my woes are your fault.* I knew she was still blaming me for letting her down: I would almost certainly get it in the neck and make things worse.

On top of this, in between his sobs, Scooter was begging me not to tell her that he'd sneaked out of the house or that he'd told me anything.

My hands were really tied. I wanted to wade in and do something, but there was no one to turn to. If I'd gone and spoken to any kind of authority figure, a doctor or even anyone else outside our small unit, Social Services would have been called and the kids might have been put into care. That would have ruined things for Scooter; as I've said, he guarded his mum like a little lion and loved her so unconditionally that if he'd been taken away from her, it would have made things a thousand times worse.

After I'd calmed Scooter down, he recovered his composure enough to run home. I assured him that I was right there and needed to be kept informed of everything, even if it meant his having to phone me in the middle of the night. We both decided not to tell Rosie as neither of us were sure how she would react.

When he got back home, he secretly phoned to give me an update and was whispering as quietly as he could into the phone, telling me that his mum was still barricaded in her bedroom and refusing to come out. Suddenly, I heard her voice in the background.

"Who are you speaking to? If that's Paul, put the phone down now!"

Scooter apologised and hung up and I didn't hear from him until early the following day. I had a night with no news whatsoever and couldn't get to sleep for worrying about what on earth was happening over in that house.

The following day, he came around and updated me. HM had come out of her room and had had some toast. She seemed a lot better, but was still very down. In himself, he seemed calmer and was trying to get back to normal.

The next time I saw HM, she was impassive and giving nothing away. She had no idea at all that I knew exactly what was going on behind my back.

After this incident, it became almost impossible to get Scooter to settle at school and he would be home within hours with an asthma attack. At the time, HM had a landlord who she claimed was violent. In reality, he wasn't a violent man at all. He was just angry and came across quite aggressively. His manner was at times exceptionally blunt and HM felt he was disrespectful to her. Her explanation for Scooter's constant absence from school was always that he was scared that he would get home in the afternoon to find that this man had come around and buried a knife in her back. Of course this would never wash with me now. I knew full well that the reason Scooter was scared of taking his eyes off his mother for any longer than half an hour at a time was because he was terrified that he would turn around and find that she'd used a knife in violence against herself.

One day my phone rang at work. It was Scooter. In a strangled voice he shouted out that HM had suddenly gone berserk, started screaming and had run out of the house and left him on his own. To make matters worse, he slammed the phone down without another word.

Scooter didn't like being on his own and was all the more terrified for honestly believing that she might never return, especially if she was suicidal. I was so worried, I decided to act.

There was no sign of my manager who was in an extremely long meeting that day. Everyone on my team had heard me answer the phone and had noted my panicky voice as I'd try to prize more information about the situation from Scooter before being cut off. So when I suddenly grabbed my coat and told them I had to go and rescue Scooter, they were extremely understanding and promised to cover for me. I knew that my manager was not the kind to be angry with me, but I'd been missing so much work because of the hell we'd all been going through, I just didn't want to blot my copybook any more.

I ran like the clappers through the centre of town and crossed the bridge over Reading's ring road, the IDR, panting and wheezing like an old bellows. I ran all the way up the road and threw myself through the gate of HM's house. I banged on the door and shouted for Scooter through the letterbox.

The door was ripped open. Pasty-faced and sneering with all the hatred and blame she could muster, HM stood there in front of me. She'd deigned to return. Beside her, Scooter stood looking impassive and trying not to show any emotion in case HM rounded on him. She spat her next words at me with total disdain:

"Yes? What do you *want?*"

I stood there confused for a moment, wondering what to say. She glared at me and waited superciliously for my reply.

"Sorry, I thought Scooter was in trouble. He phoned me to say he couldn't find you."

She stood there staring at me for what seemed like an age. She was clearly building up for some kind of acidic utterance and when it came, it was a repeat of something she'd just said, but with a new emphasis:

"What do you *want* from me, Paul?"

I think I must have been standing there with my mouth open. I don't remember saying anything. There was nothing I wanted from her and she knew that. It was her who'd plugged into me, not the other way around. She was fully aware who the vampire was. It just served her to make out that I was the leach and not her.

"Well, I'm back now," she snapped suddenly, "so you can *go.*"

She slammed the door in my face.

Chapter Thirteen

It was incredibly tense for several weeks. I tried to do as much as I could to make HM's life go smoothly, but nothing I did was ever enough. Everything I attempted went wrong and I would just end up making things worse.

The children came around most evenings and we'd watch TV and try to relax. HM needed time on her own and I was worried about both of them. At least having them there near me, I could keep an eye on them. Despite everything, we were all looking forward to Christmas as there were two films we really wanted to see. One was the very first *Harry Potter* film, *The Philosopher's Stone* and the other was *The Lord of the Rings, The Fellowship of the Ring*.

Both the children adored *Harry Potter* and HM read the books to them whenever she could. Neither of them had heard of *Tolkien* but I'd given them a rundown of the *Lord of the Rings* story and Scooter, who always made a big effort to enjoy everything I enjoyed, was now looking forward to it himself.

But then, I started to get really uncomfortable. HM was trying to scare me. One day I went around to spend some time with the children and she told me there was something in my attic, something incredibly evil. In those days, I wasn't nearly as sensitive to such things as I am now and really struggled to believe her. This entity, she claimed, was something like the tree of trapped and damned souls that haunts the abandoned art deco asylum in the film *Haunted House*. HM knew that this film freaked me out and I'd had trouble getting to sleep after watching it late one night.

Looking back, I think her intention was to try and get me to move on, to hand in my notice, to quit the flat and find somewhere else to live. I was surprised as hitherto, she'd always tried to keep me so close. I was also a little bit suspicious, but perhaps not suspicious enough.

As Christmas approached she began to change direction slightly. One day, she suggested that I leave the country and go back to teaching in Greece. I sort of shrugged the suggestion off as

I had no intention of doing such a thing. That part of my life was well and truly over. On another occasion, she suggested I go and find a new job and a new home in the West Country or move to the Hampshire town where my parents lived so that I could get as far away from the awfulness of Reading as I could. This didn't make sense either: I didn't have a problem with Reading.

It was a strange situation. HM had spent some years, I felt, subtly drawing me closer and now, quite out of the blue, I was being let go. It just didn't add up. Around this time, I was working on her biography and she was all for the idea that this book would change the world. Now her interest in it just sort of waned into nothingness, despite the hours I'd spent scanning in a manuscript from her first biography and the painstaking lengths I'd already gone to to update the story and get more information from her about her past.

One morning she rang me at 7.30 before I was due to set off for the office. She asked me to stop work on the book completely and to hand over all the computer files with the manuscript. A few days after that, she asked me to put everything that related to the rest of the work I was doing for her onto a floppy disk and to leave it around her house. She told me she felt she'd better keep control of it all in case I tried to jump ship again or "anything happened to me". This was also followed by a request for me to show her how her website worked, how to edit the files and how to upload them.

I was getting less and less work to do by the hour.

Two weeks before Christmas, HM started to be quite conciliatory towards me and even polite. It was also a very weird feeling as I'd had such a rough few months with her. I should have been suspicious but was still so incredibly disorientated by the constant mood swings that I just stopped thinking about whether or not I was in the doghouse and got on with everything, oblivious.

That week, I took both children to see the *Harry Potter* film. I got tickets for the advanced showing and the cinema was absolutely packed with kids. It felt good to be around some kind of normality for a change.

Personally I loved the film and when it ended, was positively gushing about it, thinking that I could share my enthusiasm about it with two kids who liked *Harry Potter*. But both of them were quite constructively critical, saying that too much had been left out and you didn't get to see enough of Norbert the Norwegian Ridgeback dragon who Rosie thought was excellent in the book. Scooter had wanted more blood and guts in the film and was disappointed that no one had been brutally murdered. He was only being light-hearted, but it was typical of his angle on things!

The following week, on the Saturday, I took the kids to see *The Fellowship of the Ring*. Before we set off, HM gave me a set of specific instructions. After the film, I was to allow Rosie to go to a certain shop in town to buy a set of Christmas tree lights but I myself was told to take Scooter home, immediately, without hanging around. It was almost as if HM knew in advance that something was going to go awry.

We all enjoyed the film and when we came out, Scooter and I were discussing it with great enthusiasm as we descended the cinema steps and walked out into the riverside area of Reading's Oracle shopping centre. Rosie piped up that it was time to get going and Scooter looked suddenly all serious:

"I have to go with her," he insisted.

I tried to object and told him that we'd had strict orders to go home, but he insisted that that order had been countermanded and that I was to look after Rosie to make sure she got the right lights. I had no recollection whatsoever of such a change to our plan, but Scooter was insistent. At the time, he was still desperately trying to keep control of the environment around him by "channelling" the extremely spiritually evolved entity: it was the only way he could possibly keep his mother's issues at bay.

The problem was, I was losing track of who to listen to and whose orders to follow. Was it this high being that was supposed to be helping us all who I had to obey, or was it HM herself? Because Scooter's use of the "high being" was keeping his mother's excesses in check by dishing out orders to her, I had no choice but to pretend I believed that the channelling was actually genuine. This pretence also stopped HM from going wild against me and making our lives even more complicated; if I'd stood up against her and told her I thought the being was a sham, she'd have accused me of treachery against both her *and* Scooter.

Without using my own intuition and ignoring the nagging feeling in the pit of my stomach, I chose to let Scooter and his "entity" have their way and we all headed off to the Christmas shop. By doing this, I thought I'd later be able to excuse our lateness to HM by claiming that we had orders from "upstairs", as she called them, to change the plan.

Of course, by the time I finally got both children back home, I must have been at least an hour late. As soon as we appeared at the front door it was snatched open. A demonic presence was standing in front of me in the form of HM, her face twisted with fury.

You can imagine what happened next. She screamed at the top of her voice that I'd disobeyed her, that she'd been absolutely climbing the walls in terror, worried that something had happened to the children. To make matters worse, she'd been within minutes of calling the Police. Unfortunately, Scooter didn't step forward to tell her that my orders had changed. He stood there dumbstruck as I proceeded to try and stick up for myself, getting more frustrated by the second. She just refused to listen to me and talked over every single sentence I uttered, completely unwilling to accept any explanation, however plausible. I lost my temper and raised my voice. The louder I spoke, the more incensed she became.

Realising that I was on a hiding to nothing, I stormed off just in time to hear her slam her front door so hard the windows shook. I was spitting fire.

Returning to my flat, I made a drink to calm myself down knowing that I was well and truly done for. She was still in such a precarious state, there was no telling what she might do next.

About half an hour later, I heard the sound of running feet. It was one of the children. There was a knock on the door and then the sound of running feet again. I rushed to the front door and pulled it open to find a package on my doorstep with a note from HM. I knew what this meant and steeled myself accordingly.

The letter said it was all over. HM confirmed she was about to get the break that she'd been waiting for at long last, that the work she had to do was so important there was no way that she could have poor quality, disobedient disciples around her, especially ones that were rude and nasty and showed no respect, love or compassion.

As you can imagine, I was horrified. I wasn't angry, just plain scared out of my wits. I'd really blown it this time. To my mind, and you can shout at the top of your voice that I was naïve and immature for believing this, my spiritual path was dead in the water. I was banished from sight of this woman's god and the weight of my Universal debts was such that I knew my afterlife state would be a hell realm for me, pure and simple.

I had a panic attack and went into a state of mild shock for about half an hour. Heaven only knows how I pulled myself out of it there on my own with no one to talk me through my feelings. And you know, even in those days, I could tell when I was being accompanied by guides and people in spirit. They were always around me at the time. In fact, ordinarily, they were literally packing in, watching my every move. But that evening, I realised something: they'd gone completely. It was the strangest and most unsettling feeling. I'd been totally abandoned. It was many years before I realised exactly why that was. All you need to know for the moment is that, at the time, I honestly believed it was because I'd completely and utterly smashed it all up.

Once I'd somehow recovered my composure, I decided to write HM a letter in reply to her banishment note. The package that came with the note contained a present from Scooter. It was two frosted glass tealight holders that he'd painted himself and which I'd actually promised to buy from him initially so that he could have a bit of pocket money. I felt sad that I would never be able to thank him so I thought the best I could do was acknowledge them and try to get HM to change her mind at the same time.

In my letter I apologised profusely for my behaviour and tried to see if I could mollify her. It had worked in the past and I'd managed to swing things back in my favour, even though she'd made me pay in emotional grief for my mistakes each and every time.

With a heavy heart, I walked around to hers and posted the letter in her letterbox. I returned to my place and within minutes, there was the sound of a child running in the alley, a letter being shoved hastily into my own letterbox and then the sound of the same feet fleeing back down the alley. I went to pick this letter up and found my own letter, still in its envelope - unopened - with a small paragraph written hastily in HM's hand on the rear:

I have not read this. Nor do I intend to read any more of your letters. Please do not contact me again.

The die was cast.

The sheer nastiness of this rebuttal made me angry. I strode over to her picture on the wall, one of her looking radiant in a purple sari, took it down and hurled it onto the armchair face down. As I did so, I shouted out at the top of my voice:

"Well, you can GET F***ED!"

The next thing I did was ring my parents and tell them I wasn't coming to theirs for Christmas. I told my dad what HM had done and he was sympathetic, but also infuriated and deeply frustrated. My mum sounded almost close to tears and begged and pleaded with me to come home. In the end, I just didn't have the heart to refuse, so I agreed to come.

As it turned out, I was glad I did. They tried not to be critical of me, but that was extremely hard for my dad as he just didn't know how to handle this whole weird and unwelcome situation. He gave me a lecture in the car and asked me if I'd been drawn to HM because there was some kind of demon that I was trying to exorcise from my schooldays that was still throwing me off course in life. I ducked and dived and hid as much information as possible. My schooldays are another story altogether...

It's always very calm at my parents' place and that peace and tranquillity was just what I needed. I returned to Reading a couple of days later and basically, just got on with life again. However, the composure that I'd achieved away from the mess of my everyday life sort of melted once I found myself finally in the isolation of my flat. It was also exceptionally cold over the weekend and I remember sitting in between an oil-filled radiator that I'd plugged in and a gas central heating radiator on the other side of me whilst wearing a hat and coat, two pairs of socks and a scarf. I sat through a Victorian drama on the BBC about some mad martinet who ran an almost inhumanly strict children's home and got even more depressed; my legs were pulled up to my chin, I was miserable and downright confused. I had no one to talk to either and was completely alone for about three days. On top of that, my fridge was bare and I just didn't have the inclination to go down to the Co-op and get some food. I preferred to sit there and starve.

After the festive period, I went off to work. In some senses it was a relief to get back to the office – not something I would ordinarily say in those dreary days following Christmas. I enjoyed spending time with my colleagues again. They were all as mad as hatters and I liked the environment.

A week passed and I actually began to feel better about myself. The future still seemed somewhat bleak, but I could see a light at the end of the tunnel – something I'd never expected. I began to realise that I didn't miss the Holy Mother.

All the same, I *was* missing the children. I was constantly wondering how they were getting on and if Scooter was angry with me.

I think there was a gap of about two weeks when everything was silent. Then, one evening, there was a knock on my door. It was Scooter.

For the life of me I can't remember why he'd had to come over, but I let him in and we chatted. I could tell from his manner that he was uneasy and realised that he'd come over because he was desperate to see me, but at the same time worried that I would be so furious about the way his mum had disposed of me that he would hear something like: *get out of my flat and never darken my door again...*

I could never treat Scooter like that. Or any kid for that matter.

That evening, Scooter had obviously been sent around so that HM could gauge my mood towards her. In point of fact, I was sick and tired of her, but I didn't show it. By now, the first stirrings of a desire to move away from Reading were already taking shape, but I said nothing about that to Scooter. Instead, what happened was he went home to his mum and told her I was fine and not angry. This paved the way...*sigh*...for me to be brought slowly back into the fold.

I can hear you shouting now: *For God's sake! Does this guy never learn?*

First of all I received an email from HM. It said, and I quote, "my circumstances still haven't changed..."

That's when I realised something. She believed, *honestly* believed, that by ditching me, suddenly her life would be on the up. Without my damaging presence, all the things she thought she was owed by the Universe would come rushing in: a house, money, a life, spiritual trainees of a high calibre.

When this didn't happen, she must have thought, *oh quick, get the idiot back in. He's more use to me around than in exile. I can set him to work again. He can do my shopping…free money!*

By my birthday in the first week of February 2002, after everything that had happened, there I was again. It was all back to square one.

Some years later, I realised what the whole autumn/Christmas debacle of 2001 had been about. I remembered a conversation I'd had with HM in October when she told me about a dark entity that she wanted to contact. Let's just say, for those who don't "do" the spiritual thing, that if you can understand why so many people from all walks of life go running off to satanist cults and find that they can successfully get what they want from life by using the shadow side, you'll also understand where we're moving with this. Even the most cynical and non-spiritual of my friends have heard about these satanist groups and the work they do. So I don't think I'm being too presumptuous when I say that I'm going to put a new angle on this situation now which you may well be able to relate to.

Basically, HM made a pact with a shadow entity. She needed money to do her work for her god. As this god wasn't going to cough up the goods, she decided it was time to screw it out of some "demon" or other.

Before we go on, let me just say, that she has *never* confirmed this with me or ever broached the subject since. It's just my hunch. But believe me, so much evidence points to it. Around that time, she'd been talking almost daily about a satanist group that had its HQ just around the corner. Her almost constant complaint was that this group had found out where she lived and were "on to her". I'm convinced they were "on to her" because what had actually happened was that she'd contacted them herself. When HM had given Kat and me the talk about Light and Dark a couple of years earlier, it could well have been a warning that she was prepared to use dark arts to achieve her aims of promoting her brand of divinity on a global scale. Somehow, she'd been hoping that the two of us would wholeheartedly go along with it. The problem was neither of us did. I was too naïve and Kat was just plain not interested.

So HM, in her desperation for cash, decided to reinterpret Universal Law. To her, the dark side could be used and her god would forgive her for that because any proceeds would go to "Him" in the shape of a large house for HM and an almighty global HM-style Ministry to promote "Him".

She seemed to have completely missed the point that the true nature of the Creator is one that isn't geared towards the shadow side. The truth is, although the shadow side is, in part, an expression of the nature of the Creator, *that* is only true for the lower physical dimensions, not the higher ones. The purpose is one and one alone: the darkness in this dimension of base consciousness is nothing more than a tool to teach people the nature of unconditional love. We have brought it into being ourselves through our own trauma patterns. It was never EVER, designed and brought about as a way to make money for a noble purpose.

Looking back, I now realise what had caused HM's autumn of discontent. She'd pressed ahead with her idea of "contacting her shadow being" and in doing so, had opened a Pandora's Box of horrors that had thrown her into despair. She became paranoid and jumped a foot in the air with the slightest fright. Her eyes were constantly red, her face etched with a permanent frown. Her depression was for the fact that she now couldn't escape the debts she owed and was being hounded day and night, both on a non-physical level by things that, lets say, *go bump in the night*, as well as actual individuals from the satanic group. There was every likelihood that all the money she thought she'd get from such a venture never turned up because when the group found out that she was calling herself "holy", this would have alerted them to the fact that she wasn't entirely on their side. In effect, all she got out of her dealings with the group was no cash and a sack load of grief.

Here's a little story that illustrates what happens if you start to 'dabble'. A few years ago, someone I read about in a magazine said that as a younger woman, she had an 'unwitting' brush with satanism. She'd decided she needed quite a lot of money and fast. It just so happened that around the time, she bought a copy of a New Age magazine which is generally bought by people who are skirting the edges of the spiritual side of life. There are articles for those just contemplating the possibility of reincarnation, the use of meditation, astrology and other New Age modalities. In the back of the magazine is a classified section and one of the ads was for a kit that you could buy cheaply that would allow you to perform a simple and safe ceremony designed to 'attract' money to you. She sent off for the kit and when it arrived was slightly shocked to find it meant writing her wishes on a piece of parchment, burning the parchment and reciting an incantation to some entity with a bizarre-sounding medieval-Latin name that she'd never heard of. She was suspicious because it all sounded like the sort of thing you hear about when people perform dark rites. However, the way that the kit was packaged made it all sound like a bit of fun with a very positive outcome: lots of cash!

And cash is exactly what she got after performing this ceremony. She always felt she'd carried it out a little half-heartedly and with a certain amount of scepticism, but it worked with great efficacy. The money came, and pretty much the amount she'd been hoping for. First of all, she got home from work one day to find she'd been burgled. The insurance company paid up fairly promptly. Then her mother died suddenly and left her some money in her will. Not much, but enough to bump up the coffers even further towards the amount she'd been hoping for. By the end of that year, she realised that the ceremony had in fact worked. Not in the way she'd wanted, that's for sure. Death and personal loss had brought her the reward she was seeking.

Soon her life took a turn for the worse. She was suffering from panic attacks and had the terrible feeling she was being followed. She'd wake up in the night screaming and became fearful and depressed. All her friends abandoned her as they couldn't work her out any more and found her difficult to be with. Her boyfriend had an affair and moved out. In short, her whole life went to blazes. It was only when she started going to a local spiritualist church that things began to improve. There she met a medium who told her there was something 'with' her and put her in touch with someone who, remotely, would be able to remove this entity.

After that, she was left in peace and her life improved. But it was a harsh lesson to learn.

You may well see a pattern emerging here.

As I've pointed out, the shadow side must never, ever be 'used'. One of things that you learn as you explore the great and fascinating tree of life is that the whole point of incarnating in a density of more extreme duality where the Light and the Shadows teach each other is to bring about situations where an individual soul is forced to learn and evolve. The game is rigged with traps. The shadow side of the game is cunning: offer people carrots on sticks to lure them into working against all that's good. Offer them wealth and fame, play on their desire nature, APPEAR to give them what they want and then BANG, serve them up an almighty lesson in suffering and grinding hardship. "Quid pro quo" as the famous psychopath Hannibal Lector would say.

As we've seen before, the darker side of the duality game is played to provide catalyst for souls on this great stage of ours and serves first and foremost as a platform of learning. Desire creates suffering. Stop desiring and your suffering eases.

I think it's also essential to note, and I'll go into more detail about this later, that "Darkness" doesn't actually exist per se. As we live in a holographic Universe and are creating our world as we go along, refining it to suit our learning needs, we've therefore brought demons and agents of the shadows into being ourselves through the collective unconscious. Such is our trauma in this world, severed from the rest of the loving Universe by holographic prison bars in a computer simulation that looks and feels totally real, we've allowed the monsters and chimeras of our dreams to take shape and be every bit as solid as we think we are. When I say that the human being is an immensely creative soul, I mean that we're just as likely, in this base consciousness dimension of ours, to create something "ungodly" as we are to dream up something incredibly divine. In fact, we're so keen to work through our lessons in base consciousness that we've allowed the dimension to work in such a way that it's sometimes easier to create horrors within the matrix than it is to create something divinely inspired. This will certainly change as we move out of this density. However, all you need to know for the moment is that because of this facility we have to summon up horror, this world that HM had created for herself was one that she'd pretty much thrown together in the blink of an eye by being utterly selfish.

For HM, these demonic entities were an intrinsic part of her world. She may have had an intellectual understanding of the notion of them springing from the collective as part of a platform of learning. There's every possibility she did understand the notion that they don't exist in their own right as we individualised sparks of the divine do; after all, I did hear her telling Scooter that the imps and monsters that both of them could see were only thought forms. But there's no doubt in my mind that her view of the dark side was certainly extremely dynamic. In her world, whether she cared to admit it or not, use of such energies was a sure-fire way of bringing in money. If her god wasn't going to arrange for her to win the lottery, then for good or ill, her god of the underworld would do it for her. With everything going down the pan in the autumn of 2001, the lure of dark promises was just too beguiling to resist.

First of all she set about getting rid of me. As she'd always claimed I stole her energy and dragged her down for being riddled with karma, I'm sure she would have felt no shame in using me as part of some deal: saving her own ministry in return for the soul of a sinner. She honestly believed she was a Lightworker, that she had actually earned the right to play those around her like pawns. Because she believed she was so desperate to serve the Light, she felt it was also her right to play at "God", to use the considerable power and advantage that she believed were hers to push forward with her work.

What she couldn't take into account was the fact that she'd never reached the level she thought she had. So to start hammering out deals with demonic entities when you're *not* in a place of wisdom is absolutely playing with fire. It's extremely dangerous and of course, it was never destined to work. A truly wise and spiritually evolved person would never go down such a road, anyway. Only a completely desperate, deeply misguided and flawed individual could contemplate such a course of action.

To this day, I've never been given any details, but I believe the sacking I received was a multi-faceted decision. First of all, she wanted rid of me because of my inefficiency and general lack of obedience. I hold my hands in the air and admit it: I was useless;

128

hardworking maybe, but ultimately a waste of space. Secondly, I didn't have a clue about anything. HM had to get rid of me because if I found out exactly what she'd been up to with the dark side, I'd have made the split from her myself in horror and then gone around telling everyone of her dark dealings. She knew full well I was the type of character who could well turn out to be her nemesis. When she'd warned me of her intentions to make contact with the underworld character, it was to test my reaction. If I didn't react in the way she hoped, it was OUT! And that was what happened. As I'd effectively brushed over the whole announcement and failed to give her my blessing, she felt that my lack of support was tantamount to betrayal. In reality my inner reaction to the announcement was just one of confusion: *Oh god...what now, Holy Mother...?* Of course I wasn't going to support such a hair-brained, reckless scheme.

The third facet of the decision is one that I believe to have some significance: I was too spiritual. HM knew that I'd committed myself to working for the Light and that hammering out deals with demons was simply not the way things worked in my world. I believe I unwittingly dragged round with me the positive vibration of the sincere searcher wherever I went in those days. I hope I still do. When spiritually enquiring people are working hard at their paths, a lot of darkness just dissipates around them. Their vibration is one that's natural, organic and full of hope and positive creativity. HM must have hated to admit it to herself, even though I was a bumbling fool, that was the category that I belonged to. In many respects it was good news for her because it meant that she could benefit from my puppydog, tail-wagging, tongue-lolling, panting eagerness. But the vibe from the Light that could have been billowing around me even when I was at my lowest ebb, was totally anathema to her when it came to hammering out her demonic contract. She knew it would simply cancel out all her efforts. So there really was no choice for her: say good bye to the slave and free cash machine that I'd become and clear the path for the entry of her cloven-hoofed friends.

My exit from her sphere of influence was therefore entirely engineered. Forget the fact that she'd reneged on her promise to be my Universal Mother, my special teacher and guru, my ultimate way-shower. This wasn't about me at all. As "God's" chosen one, only she mattered; everyone else could be disposed of like trash. The promises of enlightenment were shown to be what they'd been all along: an empty packet of lies. The pot was boiling over and the steam billowing out: get RID of him. An argument was therefore engineered with me and in a flash of light, I was out on my ear.

Lucky for HM though, she knew she could claw me back when all else failed. Scooter would see to that. It must have seemed a "win win" situation for her. Get rid of him, see if the underworld character coughs up and if not then grab him back before he takes off.

Let's be entirely honest though, it wasn't a winning situation at all. All it did was mark HM out as a total liar and a charlatan. Before long, she was back to her old ways, penniless and alone, hounded by satanists, abandoned by her god and now forever marked as a traitor.

Still wallowing in the doldrums, inevitably she would soon start looking around for someone else to accuse for her terrible situation. That person was someone who was even closer to her than me.

Chapter Fourteen

Even though I was back in the fold by February 2002, HM and I both agreed it was time for a change. She started insisting I move out of Reading and to be honest, by that time, I was up for it. I wasn't fed up with the town, just the way my life was going. In retrospect, even though she still had her beady little eyes on my few coppers, it was as if she also had to keep me at arm's length. I'm told she was still going around telling everyone that my vibration dragged her down and this was sold to all and sundry as *my* evil sullying *her* goodness. In reality, it was more the other way around: if I prevented her from getting on, it could well have been my Creator-seeking energy causing her to melt like the Wicked Witch of the West. Clearly, whatever it was that whispered in her ear was telling her to push me away so that she and '*it*' could set about their consciousness atrocities unimpeded.

One weekend, I went to see my parents in Hampshire and they agreed to store some of my furniture in their garage and put me up until I could find somewhere to live. By the end of April of that year, I'd moved into a comfortable one bed flat in a converted hospital just around the corner from my parents' house. My mum liked this set up as it meant that she and I could go for long walks at the weekend which we both really enjoyed. I carried on working for my company in Reading and, unsurprisingly, was still visiting HM and the children when I could and still doing HM's typing and website work.

She was also still harrying me. The slightest word out of place, the slightest mistake, I would be emotionally hung, drawn and quartered and the letters accusing me of bringing in negative entities that would keep her awake all night were still coming at the rate of probably one every three or four months.

However, at least I could breathe. I hadn't realised how much we both needed space from one another and how destructive our guru/student relationship really had been.

By this time, I'd written two more novels. The first one was untitled at the time and was about a person who I identified with and really liked as a character and who was based slightly on Squarehead. His name was Dave Lomax, a private school-educated lad from London trying to find the meaning of life, just like me. He had a problem finding meaningful, long lasting relationships (like me) and showed no loyalty to the women in his life (exactly like me!) Dave finds himself a male guru called Swami who was supposed to have been like HM, but in fact wasn't. That was because Swami was a deeply loving and caring person. He was a calm guru and one who didn't move those around him on a chessboard, emotionally bully them or lash out at people. Effectively what I'd done was create the perfect spiritual teacher, one that I really wanted and not a reflection of the one I'd ended up with. HM liked the book because at the end of it, Swami gets a large house and starts doing all the things that she herself so longed to do; he's surrounded by supportive "quality" students and is actually making a difference to the lives of everyone he teaches.

HM totally missed the point with this book. All she could focus on was the fact that Swami had suffered like her, but eventually came through triumphantly with an income and a large house. She just couldn't see the gulf in behaviour and attitude between this character and her. I'd been hoping that she'd look at the behaviour of Swami and modify her interaction with people accordingly, but she wasn't in the least bit inclined to take the hint. In fact, a time came a couple of years later when her life was still at a low ebb that she asked to read the book again. When she returned the manuscript to me, it was covered in her critical handwriting as she picked holes in everything. There was a note scrawled at the end which said that she no longer liked the book and that it needed a rewrite. I could feel her resentment as she gave that manuscript back to me. Her life hadn't turned out like Swami's. She was not like Swami herself and not admired in the way that Swami is admired by Dave and other characters in the book. She found offence at this I believe and took her frustrations out on me via the novel.

I reflected on some of the content and realised that there's a section at the end that would have brought a real ego blow to her.

HM had always told me that she was exactly like Jesus and could cure any disease and even repair broken limbs. I had never actually seen this happen, but decided to work such a scenario into the story to try and give a more rounded picture of what I'd been told an enlightened person like Swami could achieve. When Dave breaks his leg in spectacular fashion, Swami arrives on the scene just in time and literally repairs the broken limb in a flash of light.

Over the years, the few people I gave this book to said they enjoyed it, but completely refused to be drawn on their opinions for this scene. I'd kept the scene in, honestly thinking that one day, HM would pull a rabbit from a hat and, like some modern-day Jesus, fix a limb in front of me.

As it turned out, some time after she'd first read that book in 2000, she did try to pull that rabbit out…and it was pathetic.

One Saturday afternoon, she and Scooter were leaving my flat when Scooter fell down about five steps to the bottom of the stairs just in front of my front door. He didn't cry, but just looked somewhat wide-eyed and shocked. HM helped him up and seeing that he was holding his arm, rushed in her with her hand, rubbing her fingers vigorously up and down the skin. She asked Scooter if he was all right and he gasped that he was. Suddenly she turns around to me standing on the first step and says:

"Paul, you've just witnessed a miracle! His arm was broken and I've just fixed it!"

There was an awkward silence as I attempted to take stock of what I was being told. HM often complained that my reactions to everything were always muted and this bizarre outburst was no exception. I just stood there with a confused look in my eyes, my hands in a praying position around my lips thinking: *what the bloody hell..?*

It didn't take a brain of mensa to work out that I was being strung along in the most crass and disingenuous way. This situation was made worse because Scooter just shrugged and said nothing.

HM would have loved to see me fall at her feet in a swoon at such a "miracle". To be honest, even if this had been the real thing, I'd never have reacted like that, anyway. *Of course* this wasn't the real thing and HM knew it. Seeing how underwhelmed I was, she opened the door and walked home without her ego boost. It must have been such a blow for her some time later to reread the book and see a person that she so aspired to be, however idealised, perform an amazing miracle and be idolised for it both by the writer and the protagonist. I believe this heightened her bitterness at a time when she was at a low ebb with no one to worship her. It was imprudent in the first place for her to set the bar of expectation far too high for those in her circle. I do believe "miracles" of this kind are possible for the very, very few who manage to break out of this matrix; but HM was more tied to the post than I was, even in those days. So how she thought she could continue letting everyone see how chained up she was and *then* tell them that she was the new Jesus can only be a sign of her utter lack of emotional intelligence.

I cast a quick glance at what she'd done to my manuscript with all her angry handwriting on it and decided to jettison it. A few months later, I bought a paper shredder and chopped up her resentment into strips of paper once and for all.

The other book I wrote around this time was a novel I called *Breaking the Chains*. This was the story of three good friends who flee London after a terrorist attack. They take refuge in the country and start to create a community built on eco-values where everyone supports everyone else in an old-fashioned village-centred environment and where there's an abundance of love and compassion. They also watch helplessly as the rest of the country goes to the dogs whilst their world and their own lives improve because of the increased spiritual vibration they create in the village and surrounding community.

HM had no time for this book. After she read it, she refused to talk to me for a week and then called me around to her house to pick it up. As she handed me the manuscript, she said simply that she found it *lacked something*. She didn't say what. Apparently I was supposed to go away and find out from my guides in meditation what was wrong with it.

I was totally baffled. She had no constructive criticism to make whatsoever and wasn't of a mind to discuss the work in depth. Because I was still so indoctrinated by HM at the time, I listened to her words very carefully. And such was her control over me, once she'd declared she didn't like this book, suddenly, neither did I. I came to the conclusion that I had to be an utterly hopeless writer. I went home, shoved the manuscript into a box and forgot about it completely.

The novels aside, surprisingly, I did have one success with HM on the writing front. I started a forty-page booklet entitled *Armageddon Now!* This was a work inspired by my frustration and helplessness following the September 11th attacks. The first half of the book was designed as a caustic assault on the current political and social set up and the way in which it oppresses people and grinds them down in a continual and demoralising process of attrition. I gave examples of my own life when I'd been sent to court for a car-related misdemeanour which had nothing to do with me.[9] I exposed companies for their immorality in making staff redundant and offshoring jobs. I wrote bitterly about rip off Britain, about institutional ineptitude and the scourge of crime, poor educational standards and the poisoning of the population via unethical medical practices.

HM liked this book, because in the second part, I went on to propose solutions to society's ills. These solutions were based on her own teachings which I was still supposed to be immersed in. When I say immersed, I mean that loosely. In reality, I was already struggling with them and I realise, on reflection, that by trotting them out in my own book, knowing that people would then associate me with them, I was at last forcing myself to look at them in proper depth. The more I looked, the less I liked.

HM watched very closely as I finished the book. A time came when she was supervising it extremely meticulously, monitoring its content and even getting me to insert a lot of asterisks in nearly every paragraph that pointed to a footnote at the end of the book. This note emphasised that all the solutions put forward were ones taken from *her* teachings and that anyone who wanted to could phone her or contact her direct from her website ...blah ...blah ...blah.

By that time, this was no longer my book. I lost control of it completely and it became no more than a Paul Arrowbank-style write-up of someone else's musings. A day came when she took

---

[9] I was never apologised to or compensated considering the amount of money my poor old Dad had to throw at lawyers and solicitors for getting the case thrown out as one of mistaken identity.

the manuscript off me completely, demanded £100 from me and got the work printed and bound herself, obviously believing that I would never have got around to it, such was my lack of efficiency.

As soon as the book came back from the printers, I hated it. I picked it up, leafed through it and detested it with every bone in my body. From that day, I left it to rot and never dared push it on anyone, knowing that I didn't have the conviction to back up any of the proposals in its pages.

HM had wanted to ride the book all the way to the bank and to use it as a platform for her teachings. When this didn't happen, one day she rounded on me and asked me if I'd done anything at all to promote the book (and hence her). I was honest this time:

"No," I said, "I'm not interested in it anymore. The entire book is alien to me and if I could write it again, I would, but I'm not going to. I disagree with it wholeheartedly."

At this HM just rolled her eyes. She had nothing else to say on the subject. Meanwhile, the copies that she'd run stayed in the box to rot and are still there some ten years later.

The problem that I had with *Armageddon Now!* is this: in the second section, I suggested that as society begins to "right itself" following the earth changes associated with the years following 2012, we begin to reorganise communities to make them decentralised and self-sufficient. I suggested that everything should be arranged in such a way that different communities traded with one another and bartered for goods that were not available in one community, but which other communities had in abundance due to what was available to them from the point of view of resources. I stood by this assertion for a long time as it felt like a water-tight, heart-centred approach to a well-structured society. The problem was that HM didn't have time for technology and so my work, unwittingly, came over as too communist, almost implying that we would all be slaves to each other, working the land and pooling our resources in a kind of Maoist Dystopia. I did try to insist that there would be such things as ownership, where everyone would have their own house and belongings, but the suggestion that we should all have a car pool gave the game away. It seemed as though I was advocating sackcloth and ashes and a return to the dark ages.

Another problem was this: HM in her teachings was insisting that we do away with the capitalist system. I agreed and still agree wholeheartedly with this. However, her alternative was one that I came to struggle with terribly. She was suggesting that the entire world be overseen by a network of enlightened people, with *highly* enlightened people (like her) at the top of the tree, passing down advice to lower branches on a local level of spiritual beings like Spiritual Masters who have well-developed psychic and intuitive abilities. These Spiritual Masters would have enough intuition to be able to see an individual's level of Universal debt or karma the moment they met them; everyone would receive vouchers to use for food and clothes that were in direct relation to the amount of karma they had. So someone who'd had a series of successful lives and who'd accrued positive karma for their good deeds would end up having slightly more vouchers than someone who had lived a series of disastrous lives that had left them with a lot of Universal debt.

Intuitively, I had a big problem with this and since then, my studies on this subject have shown that now we're going through the initial stages of our evolutionary leap, a whole new and more fantastic scenario is taking shape which is vastly different to the one proposed in *Armageddon Now!*

The problem with this pyramidal structure of running society is that it belongs to an ethos of hierarchical control which is the very antithesis of the freedom and soul sovereignty that we will find in the coming new Golden Age. As we're in a base consciousness dimension now, you'll see what I mean. We have a small group of power wielders at the top of the pyramid. Beneath them are the heads of governments, directors of large multinational conglomerates such as manufacturers of weapons and pharmaceuticals. Alongside them are the leaders of world religions and media moguls. All these influential people feed orders down a chain of command that ends with a vast mass of the population, all of whom are dictated to as to what drugs to take, what to eat, who to go to war with, who to love, who to hate, which political party to vote for. There's no freedom, no information (unless you go out on a limb to look for it) and no possibility for true self-expression.

The purpose of incarnation in base consciousness density is to give the soul an almighty lesson in discernment. This density is set up with this pyramid structure as it's designed to cause individual souls to experience catalyst, in other words, to suffer at the hands of oppressors who work hard not to create unity, but to promote discord and separation. Base consciousness existence is veiled off from the rest of the Universe to give an illusion of disconnection. We're tricked into forgetting that we have amazing divine abilities that can be accessed in the here and now, and instead go around with our heads in a box, completely unaware how great we are. We're conned into thinking that any information coming in from an outside source is also unreliable. When I say "outside source" I mean any kind of advanced civilisation that doesn't originate from this planetary system. The mainstream media have promoted the concept of alien life as something either incredibly base and hideous or inconceivably blood-thirsty. It's almost as if we're being pre-programmed to react negatively.

To be fair we did set this whole dimension up so that we could be lied to. It's our duty in this density to work with discernment and find answers for ourselves without "outside help or interference". It's certainly the most testing density because to find answers, the individual soul is required also to practice spirituality in order to raise its level of consciousness to a point where it can use its intuition to find those answers. This process is made doubly difficult because of the pyramidal structure and its chain of command that promotes social unrest, war, lies, and misinformation. The populace at large is encouraged to wade knee deep into distraction via money, narcotics, trash TV, food and alcohol. People who set out on a journey of self-discovery that challenges all these distractions are marginalised and turned into social outcasts as their search goes against the grain. Usually the masses at large are programmed to aim for the jugular when mixing with such people, which is why you hear the cynical shout things like "why don't you get back down to earth, you lunatic!"

As I've said, in our status of co-creators, we've set this situation up with design. We live in a world of separation from each other, where our egos are all-important and our desire to feed them almost unquenchable. There's often no desire for cohesion or agreement, particularly on a political level. We're left alone with only our creature comforts and the more we dig ourselves in, the harder it is to work our way out. Those who do, must do so with tremendous catalyst after many lives of suffering and isolation. Souls that achieve such a feat are ready to graduate to a higher density.

And this is where this idea of a pyramidal structure for the new Golden Age falls down. I know that HM would be the first to say that a structure of her imagining is one in which evolved souls take over the reins of government and begin a political campaign of fairness based around peaceful and environmentally sound policies. However, that doesn't go far enough. That sort of outlook is base consciousness in vibration and still one in which separation is promoted, with a small group of individuals dictating policy to a large mass of souls.

At the moment, the New Consciousness "movement" is based around people who are trying to tread a spiritual path, waking up to the fact that they need to reach a higher consciousness. This they see as a kind of harmonious vibration that unites people into a spiritually conscious unit that thinks in one unified way, but is NOT an enslaved hive mind. It is of course, a peaceful consciousness, but it's also one that doesn't involve a single person standing head high over everyone else and dictating to "the masses" each and every thought that they're required to think. Instead, this great unit of consciousness obtains its mind energy from the greater Universe, from the original, constructive and creative thought of unconditional love that brings the entire Omniverse into being. Within this critical mass, are individual souls, certainly, but each individual mind is perfectly attuned to the whole and in unison with it.

Imagine a world where there's complete harmony. The ethos is one of tolerance and fraternity. Because humanity has left the base consciousness of control and hierarchy behind, there are no wars or injustices. There's no longer any such concept as the rule of Law. There are no politics. No one person can claim dominion over anyone in a world that flows within the natural and organic intent of the Universe. With humanity no longer imposing an iron will on nature, the planet has responded accordingly and all the adverse planetary conditions that plagued humanity during its dark age are a thing of the past. Beauty has returned to the landscape, flora and fauna abound in a vibration of so many colours, more than we ever thought existed. Humans live in abundance, the trees are laden with fruit, there's space, light, warmth. Rivers gush fresh water, the sky is clear and bright. We are true cosmic beings, mixing with our Universal cousins in a culture of intergalactic friendship. We come and go as we please, moving from place to place through thought.

This is a vision of a new Golden Age which is in our grasp should we choose to accept our mission to free ourselves from the sort of tyranny promoted by those who don't want us to thrive. We don't need leaders and we certainly don't need hierarchies or laws.

When I wrote *Armageddon Now!*, I had no idea of this concept. If I had, not only would I not have written the book, I certainly wouldn't have allowed HM to suggest that I call it *Armageddon Now!* That's the most negative title that we could have come up with. It suggests that we're all going to hell in a handcart and produces fear. In fact, it's fear that's prevented the entire population from moving on. For fear is an actual force and energy. Whereas Unconditional Love is constructive and creative, fear produces separation and lack of unity.

I'm sure HM never set out to promote herself by causing disharmony. However, her motives were entirely selfish. By sending out a message that there's Armageddon just around the corner and augmenting that message by implying that only she and a tiny handful of other so-called enlightened people are the ones with all the answers, all we're doing is promoting yet another religion and hence another base consciousness command structure that will never ever bring into being an ascension for humanity. The sort of social outlook that we're striving for isn't about one legend in her own bathtime wandering the earth blessing all the minions and imparting her own brand of teaching, expecting everyone to hang off her every word. It isn't about setting up societies and organisations that self-promote, that declare other such societies and organisations as utterly invalid and cause yet more rivalry and even greater perceived separation. It's amazing sometimes how zealous disciples of these gurus can be in their shameless promotion of their teachers' work. Spiritual people like me, completely hooked into the work of one self-appointed oracle of "God" have been known to come to blows in an effort to put the other side right. This is religion all over again. Those spiritual

140

teachers who are touring the world shamelessly promoting separation of this kind are moving against the planetary vibration of harmony that's coming in at this time and in doing so, are causing themselves and their followers damage. How I wish I'd realised that all those years ago.

I sometimes wonder what criteria HM had in mind for how we were eventually going to recognise all those advanced high beings who she'd pencilled in as the hierarchy of the incoming new Golden Age. If we were to choose her as an example, it's likely that such a hierarchy would be made up of even more legends in their own bathtimes: money-grabbing, lying, manipulative, scheming psychopaths with no love in their hearts. Clearly HM just wanted to replace an old set of dictators in suits with a brand new crowd dressed like suburban Jesuses screaming their heads off with righteous anger.

Chapter Fifteen

For a year or so, things just ticked over. HM was getting nowhere with her ministry and was still not of a mind to find out where the blocks really hid. In her head, it was still everyone else who was to blame. One person who took the brunt of that belief was Rosie who was now a fully fledged teenager. As with most teenagers, she wasn't motivated to discuss anything with a parent and was just distant and naturally uncooperative. I believe that HM mistook her lack of desire to show total loyalty as a betrayal of what she stood for. Rosie has never discussed this with me, but I always had a feeling that she may have felt some terrible peer pressure at school. She always wanted to stay on the right side of her mother and did in fact avoid wearing her skirt short and using makeup. This must have caused her to stick out like a sore thumb and could have been a source of grief for her from other pupils at school.

Because HM was beginning to see her as a potential traitor in her midst, Rosie was finding it difficult at home. She began to step out of her mother's world by refusing to do any tidying or washing up. When she came home, she would retire to her room and sit there surrounded by her clobber strewn all over the floor and watch teenage soaps. A plate of food would be brought up to her and she would leave the plate in her room rather than bring it down to the kitchen. At weekends, sometimes she would be sent to stay with me.

HM was beginning to make it clear that unless she cleaned up her act, she would not be welcome at home. It was the beginning of a rift between mother and daughter that it seemed couldn't be bridged. Neither side would back down. Rosie wanted a mother who'd accept her as someone who didn't want to walk the HM-style spiritual path and who would allow her to start doing the things that other girls of her age wanted to do. In her turn, HM felt that sharing a house with someone who didn't toe the line and accept her teachings was causing her to be pulled back from the work she still desperately wanted to start.

I have to admit, I struggled when Rosie came to stay at the weekends. It wasn't that I didn't want her there because I was only too happy to give her a break from her difficult routine in Reading. But I also needed a break as I was working all week and having trouble completing all the tasks I needed to catch up on over the weekend. Rosie was obviously unhappy with her life and she would be chirpy one moment and then quite sullen the next. Sometimes, when she was feeling really down she would stop talking completely and I'd respond selfishly by losing my temper with her. This made things worse between us and would cause her to dig her heels in even more.

In 2003, there was one area of my life that did appear to be shaping up very well. Every working day, to get to work in Reading, I'd have to take trains from my Hampshire home to Reading. One of these trains used to stop at a certain village in the Berkshire countryside, a short journey from Reading. Every time I went anywhere near this particular village, I would feel a sort of pull there, as if there was something about the area calling me in. Every morning as we approached the station, I got this strange sensation that this is where I would be spending a large and important part of my life and I would get excited. For most of the spring, I just couldn't shake off this feeling. There were several people who used to get on the train there who I felt I'd known before in previous lives and seeing them again felt incredible. I knew I would never be able to discuss that sensation with any of them.

One day, I was sitting chatting to a lady who lived in the village who also worked in the same office as me. She happened to mention that there were some ground floor flats for sale in the centre of the village. They'd been modernised and originally put up for sale at an exorbitant price by the builder. Consequently, they'd remained unsold for many months and virtually the whole village had gone to look around them with an eye to getting into the buy-to-let game. Nearly everyone had turned their noses up at them as word had got around that the builder was dodgy and a complete conman.

Two days later, I booked myself a viewing and made the journey from the station at the bottom of the hill to the top of the hill where the village is. The countryside in that part of Berkshire is beautiful and so very British: lots of quiet lanes, wheat fields and large oak trees. Next to the village itself are woods with beautiful tall Scotch pines. I knew, as soon as I stepped in through the door of one of the flats, despite it looking as though it had been modernised by a couple of monkeys, I was home.

A week later I made an offer on the flat that was accepted. By then, it was an affordable price and even though I had to scrape a deposit together somehow, I knew that I was doing the right thing as buying was going to be cheaper than renting.

Ten years later, I'm still in the village and still in my little flat. Of the four flats for sale, mine turned out to be the one that was marginally less dodgy than the other three and I still believe I got a bargain.

After a long period of difficulty in getting a mortgage offer sorted, I eventually moved in at the end of October 2003 and I was absolutely ecstatic. For the first time, I really knew that things were coming together for me and that I was finding my way at last. The problem was, I was still very much hooked into HM's life and I knew there would inevitably be grief and confusion ahead.

After I'd settled in, HM decided to resurrect her autobiography, the one that I'd been writing for her before she'd taken it away from me to dump her responsibility for my spiritual path in a trade off with the shadow side.

The first part of the book was an updated version of HM's original autobiography. That was a book that I always felt saddened by as it's an upsetting tale of a difficult and lonely childhood, followed by an early adult life when HM was kicked from pillar to post by incredibly trying circumstances and a succession of disastrous relationships. The book appears to end positively with HM saying that her enlightenment had brought her such joy and happiness. The problem is, really, I simply knew different. As we started on the new part of the book that begins with my arrival in her life, we took out the ending of the previous book as it patently wasn't true that her life was easier now that she'd supposedly reached enlightenment. Instead this second section was a write-up of all the difficulties we'd faced over the years, but with HM's own shadow over the entire text. Consequently, it reads like the most almighty blame game in the history of the biography with everyone who'd ever stood in HM's way, including Rosie, being exposed for their attitudes, their illnesses and their darkness. In the last few pages of the book, I was asked to write up my experiences of being taught by HM. I made it clear that she was strict with me and told the story of how I'd caused her to be attacked by the dark side for trying to escape from her two summers earlier. Everyone was shown up as incompetent and HM came across as a kind of all-powerful earth mother, incorruptible, always correct, God's own hand-picked oracle for planet earth.

For me, there were two problems with this book. Firstly, there were many facts glossed over and too many pieces of information that had been left out. I didn't know it, but one day, I'd feel the need to set the record straight, as you've seen.

The other problem I had was something extremely specific. HM had insisted that we put BA Hons next to my name. I had a major issue with this. HM insisted that it would make people take her seriously if they could see that the book had been written by someone "intellectual". To me, it was a sign of trying just too desperately hard; this *wasn't* an academic work. I knew from the time that HM had swept like Cleopatra into a school in Reading which Rosie was due to attend, that she'd always been labouring under the mistaken impression that university graduates are snobs that can't wait to advertise their achievements in a shameless show of superiority. This was that misconception coming through once again. It didn't seem possible to her that it isn't the done thing to plaster BA Hons over a biography as if to inflate the author's importance to bursting point. Most people would see it as a show of unfathomable arrogance.

I tried to tell HM this, but she just wouldn't have it. In fact, she became angry when I tried to put my foot down and accused me of trying to block her again. So I did what I always did and backed down. Once more, HM got her way and set herself up for another self-imposed block on her advancement.

I'll never forget seeing the printed copies of that book for the first time. I took one look at the front, saw my name with BA Hons plastered next to it and felt completely helpless. Worse still, when I opened the book to the first page, I realised something terrible had happened. I'd spent weeks and weeks before the manuscript had been sent for printing checking over it for the final time, painstakingly working through every single sentence checking for howlers. I'd made a special point of correcting a problem with a comma on the first page that I knew would give the reader an impression of amateurism the moment they saw it. A few days before HM sent the manuscript off for printing, I'd given her the floppy disk with this carefully edited version of the book on it.

Despite having spent years telling me how inefficient I was, the real truth was that I wasn't the only person with that problem. HM had made so many changes to the text of this book herself and had so many versions of it on floppies strewn around her house that she'd lost track of which one was the latest one. If she hadn't been so keen to edit and sanitise her life to such an extent, we'd have been able to work cleanly through one single version of the book. But it just never happened that way. As soon as I'd given her that final floppy with my edited version, she put it down somewhere and then accidentally picked up an older version of the book. She'd then proceeded to edit that inferior version herself, entirely missing the comma error on the first page. *That* was the version that went to the printer.

As soon as I opened the book the day it came out, I quickly read through the first two or three paragraphs. Lo and behold, there was the comma error sitting there like a pus-filled boil for everyone to see. I also knew whose fault it was. I kept my mouth shut and determined that I would never do anything to promote the book. Every time I looked at the cover, I wanted to throw up.

Some years later, a lady who came into our lives in a big way after I moved to the village, reported back to me that everyone who she knew who'd read this book had a similar reaction to it. It was full of negativity for being so hard-focused on HM's suffering. It shows her as one who's so deeply entrenched in sadness that it's impossible to see how she can help others to move on fully from their own problems. The whole book screams torment from the mountaintops and this makes it seem as though there's nothing inspirational about it at all. It also seems to insist that this suffering person is the only one with all the answers and thereby undermines itself terribly. It portrays HM as dogmatic, far too dictatorial, almost terrifying. It's not surprising that I never received a single positive comment about it and it was met with universal silence. For me, a shadow lay over the book. I just couldn't bring myself to talk about it, promote it or even admit to myself that I'd had a part in writing it.

Chapter Sixteen

In the early spring of 2004, I suggested to HM that we do some Mind Body Spirit fairs. I told her that Scooter and I would do them together and that there was no reason for her to come as all the negativity that she said abounded at such events would harm her. HM thought it was a good idea and then phoned me one evening to say that if I did manage to organise something, she would have to come along herself as, with the best will in the world, I didn't always represent her correctly as there was a depth to her work and to her nature that apparently I'd simply "missed". At this point, I began to get worried as I didn't want her to come at all. Everything she touched turned into an almighty drama and there were always ructions, accusations and tears before bedtime. Naturally, I was concerned that her inability to get along with people at large would be the greatest stumbling block.

HM herself ended up booking a stall at a fair in Swindon for early March that year. I was pressed into driving and she, Scooter and I would be present for both days of the fair. I was ordered not to tell Rosie as apparently, her "negativity" would cause the whole event to go wrong if she knew where we were going. Poor Rosie would be totally left to her own devices and unsure where her mother was. I had a feeling that there was probably a part of her that would be pleased at least to have some time to herself for once.

I wasn't happy about the driving. I hadn't driven regularly for ten years since I'd done "wine by the case" deliveries around London. I knew that my awareness skills behind the wheel had declined and the co-ordination that you tend to take for granted in changing gear and negotiating other cars was at an all time low. Inevitably, when we set off, I'd made my first driving error within minutes: I misjudged a car's speed as it approached a mini roundabout and pulled out to turn right without giving way. Naturally I was punished by this driver with the angriest of outbursts and no small amount of hooter work. I apologised to

HM and gazed at her in the rear view mirror to monitor her reaction. The sight that met my eyes was of a face that was filled with fury and malice. For some time, she maintained a vicious vigil of silence in the back seat and the negativity that she claimed innocent Rosie was constantly offloading onto her was now being created by HM herself and dished out to me generously in giant size portions.

When we got to Swindon, I was staggered at how difficult it was to find my way around and by the sheer volume of traffic. At one point, I took a wrong turn and from her seat in the back, HM railed at me with her inimitable brand of fury.

As it turned out, the MBS fair was probably the most under-attended event I'd ever been to. There was a tiny trickle of people coming through and for most of the day, we sat there whilst HM rolled her eyes and became more and more impatient and ratty.

On the second day of the fair, something happened that was to change my feelings about my life with HM once and for all. It was probably the most defining moment of my time as her student and I was given a sign at last. On this particular day, we had yet another slow morning. But at some point in the afternoon, a middle-aged lady came up to the stall. She told all three of us that she felt drawn to our corner of the room by an incredibly strong energy. She turned to HM and explained to her that she always felt there was something "with" her that had been shadowing her for years. She'd tried everything, but no one had ever been able to help her shift this entity.

If you haven't come across this phenomenon before, let me explain. Some souls that pass on, don't always wish to do so. They're not attracted by the Light and don't necessarily desire to move onto the realms of the afterlife at the moment of their passing. Consequently, these souls stay bound to this earth plane and shadow people, stealing their energy and living through them. Quite often, if they were souls that were attracted by the lure of alcohol, drugs or sex, they shadow those who indulge (or rather overindulge) in such pastimes and their presence can make those who are addicted even worse as they're subtly manipulated by the entity to find the next fix.

Some souls carry on inhabiting the earth plane after passing as they may have died suddenly by being murdered or because

149

they've been in an accident. These souls can be restless and can haunt the area where they died, desperately trying to alert the living and draw attention to their plight. It then takes the work of a sensitive or a medium to move them on to the Light and on occasion, if they sense there's someone in the vicinity who they believe can lead them to an answer and move them on, they'll shadow that person until such time as an opportunity arrives for them to be helped.

I believe this latter scenario was the case with this middle-aged lady who came to visit our stall on that day. The entity that was shadowing her was quite angry and although I've no doubt that this lady was not a drug addict or anyone with a life that would attract the attentions of a negative entity, I do believe that the entity that was with her was not very pleasant and waiting for a chance to move on, perhaps even to find another living person to shadow.

HM took charge. She sat this lady down and asked me and Scooter to stand in front of the stall so no one would be able to witness what was about to happen. She started work healing this lady behind a screen that had been erected for us and within moments, I slightly turned around to see this lady's face contort. Suddenly, she let out a horrific guttural stream of obscenities that sounded just like the demon in *The Exorcist*. I'd never seen this happen before and was shocked to see a proper bona fide exorcism happening right next to me. It probably only lasted for a few seconds, but when HM had finished, this lady was absolutely enraptured. She burst into tears of utter relief and you could really tell that the most almighty cloud had been lifted from her whole life.

For some minutes, HM allowed her to sit there and cry into a tissue. Once she'd recovered her composure, she paid up and left, full of gratitude and moving away on a cushion of air. I was extremely impressed with HM at that point and wanted to ask her everything I could about how she'd achieved such a feat. All she could do was shut me up and tell me that she was now totally exhausted and almost unable to go on with the rest of the fair. I shrugged off her reaction and ignored it when she said she wished the lady hadn't come by as the healing had polished her off.

A few minutes later, the middle-aged lady reappeared. She'd recovered her composure brilliantly and marched up to me. I couldn't believe it when she told me that she could see my aura and said it was a beautiful blue colour. She then proceeded to thank *me* for helping her. At the corner of my eye, I could see HM frowning deeply. Immediately, I shook this sudden rush of attention from the lady off by saying that I believed the energy she was feeling was coming from Scooter. She seemed thrown for a moment and turned to Scooter to take a look at him. She confirmed that he was a very advanced soul and that he had a nice energy.

Luckily, she didn't push the point. Instead, she said goodbye to me and gave me a message, saying that she knew how she felt and that there was an energy coming from me that had impressed her.

After leaving and thanking us all again profusely, HM thanked me in turn for suggesting that the vibration was coming from Scooter. She congratulated herself for teaching me in such a way that I was prepared to be humble about the thanks that this lady had given me.

But she'd been riled. As I sat there, I noticed she was not in the least bit happy. At some point, I decided to say something that was on my mind and told her that although it was a shame that the event had been poorly attended, I would have to try harder to find another way to promote her. Suddenly, she rounded on me:

"Get out of my sight! Go and sit in the car. I'm sick and tired of your negativity! All you've done today and this whole weekend is sit there and mope and think negative thoughts. Go on! Get out of this room!"

The lady with the stall next to us sat rooted to the spot to hear HM spit such an order at me. I went puce and stood up. I didn't look back at HM as I stormed off. If I hadn't been negative before, I was then. I was furious and inwardly railed at HM with every bone in my body.

I did as I was told and went off to fume in the car. It was a freezing cold day and I lost the feeling in my feet. But as I sat there on my own, I knew that something had changed. I wasn't thinking of the kind words of the middle-aged lady. It was more that, despite being dressed down in public by HM, I realised now I was over her. I no longer wanted her to be my teacher, cared about

151

promoting her or her teachings or would even bother if I never saw her again. The bond between us was broken. Deep down, I knew that she would never be able to hold me and that if she tried to send me packing again like she had at Christmas time in 2001, I'd simply walk away. I'd get the kids a mobile phone so that they could phone me if they wanted and then be done with this Holy Mother business. I didn't intend to make the move myself. I decided that I'd carry on for the moment and then just allow things to take their natural course. I knew that it might take a year or so, but eventually I'd find a way out and then I'd just get on with my life.

At some point, Scooter came and sat in the car with me.

"Mum's right," he said. "You *are* negative today and I can feel it."

I confirmed that negative was how I felt…and fed up to the back teeth. I said I was sick and bloody tired of her and explained what I'd just been thinking, that the time had come for me to move on. He begged me to reconsider and I told him not to worry, that I'd keep in touch with him by any means possible. But Scooter wasn't a fool. He knew his mother had come to rely on me and tried to mollify the situation. We had a chat in which he diplomatically explained that there were times when he was also fed up with the situation and wanted everything to be more normal in his life. By this time, he was thirteen and was just beginning to wake up to himself as an individual. He'd started to listen to music and was watching 18-rated films on video. For a kid his age, he was also more mature and advanced than the vast number of his peers. I'd never foreseen this for Scooter. I'd always had the impression that because his mother had largely kept him away from the sorts of things that other kids were into, he'd grow up quite sensitive and set apart from the rough and tumble of modern day life. How wrong I was turning out to be.

He let the subject drop and went back in to keep HM company. Meanwhile, I was glad I'd spoken to him. It was a warning of what lay ahead and it felt good that I'd made an effort to prepare him.

When the day ended, HM was quite careful with me. I had a feeling that Scooter had probably gone back to her and warned her that I was now having a rethink about my future with her. When she came out to the car later on, she was in a gentler mood and once we'd packed up and driven home, she gritted her teeth and made an effort to thank me for my hard work and for doing a good job with the driving, despite my obvious lack of confidence.

There was then a break of about two weeks to a month when HM went quiet. She didn't contact me much and I had a feeling that something was happening. Then one day, Scooter came to the village to see me and told me that the previous weekend, he and his mum had been to Salisbury together to do their own Mind Body Spirit fair, without me. Scooter told me that HM hadn't wanted me to come as I dragged her down and ruined everything for her. He also told me that her reward for not bringing me was another disaster for her. The fair had not been well attended and the two of them hadn't earned their money back for their train fare and the cost of the stall. Once more, they'd left with orders for Scooter not to tell Rosie where they were going. Rosie was now being shut out of everything.

Over the next few weekends, she was packed off to stay with me so that HM could "have a rest". HM used to call me during the week and complain about her bitterly, claiming that Rosie's dislike of her was causing her to be attacked by the dark side. She insisted that Rosie was to blame for holding her back with her negative attitude, for bringing in nasty entities from school, for not helping around the house and for not putting anything in when she was supposedly taking so much "out".

Rosie was not happy about being farmed out to the village every weekend. She was finding me boring and we'd very quickly run out of things to talk about. She refused to tell me anything about school which prompted me to think it was full of issues for her. Instead, completely unwilling to open up to me, she clammed up entirely and would just sit there and watch TV. This was my fault entirely. Rosie didn't trust me because she reckoned I told her mother about everything she did wrong and everything she said. I would occasionally complain to HM that Rosie wouldn't help me do any washing up and HM would use that as an excuse to give her a good telling off when she got home. This made Rosie think that I wasn't on her side and I believe she began to dread the sight of me. To her, I represented a Judas who supported her mum against her and I wasn't to be trusted. I did try to tell her how I was beginning to feel about her mother, but she was beyond

153

listening so I stopped talking about it. I didn't want her to think that I was turning against the family so I tried my best not to give her too many details about by new reservations.

One day, HM suddenly announced out of the blue that she was approaching Social Services to see if they could help. I was surprised about that as HM wasn't a big fan of that establishment. She always claimed that because they weren't spiritual and intuitive, they missed things and instead applied a blanket policy to every case they looked into, demonising innocent parents who had genuine issues with their troublesome kids and not doing enough to help the kids that were really in trouble.

I'm not sure what kind of a picture HM painted of Rosie, but things changed rather quickly and I began to lose track of what was going on. One week, HM was telling me that the Social were getting involved, the next, Rosie was being taken in by a foster home for what's called 'respite care' at weekends. HM phoned me a couple of times and sent a little warning message across my bows that this situation was about to take on a new dimension. She kept saying that she felt better when Rosie wasn't there, that she had more energy and was healthier and happier. To this day, I think she was preparing me for what was ahead. Again and again, she repeated that very soon, things would start to move for her and she simply couldn't afford to have anyone around her who wasn't fully supportive of what she wanted to achieve.

Then one day, out of the blue, Rosie was gone. I can't remember if it was Scooter or HM herself who phoned me to say that she'd been taken into care. All I can recall is putting the phone down after the conversation and sitting there for ages frowning. Unable to quite believe that HM would ever be so heartless, I put it out of my mind, honestly believing that she'd be back soon: I knew Social Services were always keen to reunite children with their biological parents where possible.

Over the following weeks, it became clear that a repair to this breakdown in relations was just never going to be made. HM was resigned and her mind completely made up. There was no future for her and her daughter. In fact if anything, it was almost as if Social Services were fully in agreement that Rosie should be taken away. I found that very bizarre and just couldn't understand it. Rosie had never been in any immediate physical harm from HM.

It was a couple of years before I found out why the Social Workers had gone along with HM's request for Rosie to be taken. In an effort to make sure they knew the "seriousness" of her situation, HM had admitted in interviews with them that she didn't love Rosie.

I have to say that I don't entirely believe that. To this day, it's my honest opinion that HM, *in her own way*, did love Rosie, but was - by that time - so ensconced in her belief that Rosie was a block to her, that she used the manipulative side of her character to come out with a full-blown lie, and a whopper at that. A parent who admits to not loving her child has problems indeed. HM knew that Social Workers would react to such an awful announcement by taking immediate action and removing the unloved child from the family unit.

Simply put, HM's desire for love and global honour to be paid to her as the closest thing to "God" on earth was greater than her love for Rosie. Rosie was to be removed from the scene at whatever the cost to Rosie herself. The "holy" thing came first. Other considerations, other people's lives, their needs, their feelings, all were secondary to the ultimate mission.

The next thing that happened, I heard that Rosie had been moved from a temporary foster home to a new one in another Berkshire town. She was coming back to her mum's to get some stuff from her room (that was still the way it was when she'd left) and then she was going to live with this other family. I still thought this was just HM trying to buy herself some time like she did when she used to pack Rosie off to the village to stay with me. I waited over the next few weeks to see if she'd return, but she never did. Once she'd moved in with the family, it was over. She'd been removed from the scene and there was no going back.

One day, HM rang me and explained that she felt terrible, that she'd been a failure as a mother and felt that she'd let Rosie down. I didn't comment because I didn't want to cause any more ructions but secretly, I was horrified and disliked the crocodile tears. I'd been supporting HM pretty much unconditionally for six years and by then, was really wondering if I'd been totally irresponsible. I asked myself again and again if I'd been right to fully align myself with someone who claimed she wanted to give a Universal

Mother's love to the world, to help people with their traumas, to heal them and "bring down the Light" when here she was having her own daughter put into care.

I hadn't forgotten my decision in Swindon that day to prepare for removing myself from this woman's life. But when Rosie went, I knew that the time was approaching. I wasn't having this. All I could think of was how, if HM's bandwagon took off like she always expected it to, there'd be a lot of interest in her life and that people would maul her to the bone if she was making claims about being a Holy Mother and then not being able to look after her own daughter. I just didn't want to be caught up in the inevitable controversy that would ensue. I could hear the chattering classes having a field day. "Hypocrite!" they'd be shouting. I knew this could ruin my life and Scooter's.

Not only had Rosie lost her mother, but Scooter and I had lost Rosie. I told everyone that Rosie had gone to "stay with a friend" and things were "difficult at home". But most people I discussed this with understood what had happened on a deeper level. The reaction was fairly uniform: there was something wrong with this holy woman. What kind of person in her right mind would throw her own daughter out if there wasn't a proper reason for it? The general consensus was that HM wasn't to be trusted and even that Rosie was now lucky for having escaped.

I began to worry about how Rosie was getting on. There was absolutely no news from her for me and I wondered if she was happy. On several occasions, I tried to anticipate my arrival on the morning train to work with the time I knew she'd be taking a bus from the centre of Reading to school. I concealed myself just inside the station and would look out across the road to see if she was waiting with her friends at the bus stop. Unfortunately, I never saw her. Not even once.

Because she didn't contact me in those early days, I assumed Rosie just disliked me. I came to the conclusion that she must have partly blamed me for not helping her or supporting her. Because I'd been distant to her for too many years and had always ended up hanging out with Scooter, it must have looked like I didn't care. That wasn't true at all. It was just the way things worked out and as Scooter was always so keen to hang out with me, he ended up being the first in line for my attention. Rosie was more independent. I'd always known that from day one. Because she wasn't as quick to jump on my time and energy as Scooter, she got left behind. As the years went by, she slipped further and further out of sight.

Personally, I think she had a disastrous childhood. I really don't feel good about the fact that I wasn't there for her when she needed help. Instead, I chose to flog myself to pieces for the mother who was an adult and could have looked after herself. I wasn't to appreciate it at the time, but one day, I'd need a chance to express my frustration with myself for that situation. This book, to a certain extent, is that opportunity.

Chapter Seventeen

After Rosie had left, HM began talking about moving out of Reading. She'd often blamed her problems on the town and had come to dislike it intensely, especially the West Reading area where apparently the satanist groups were still "on to her". She decided to move to the West Country and began a search for a house in the countryside around the Glastonbury area where she believed the spiritual vibration would help her.

One day she packed me off to Glastonbury with a pile of her biographies and forced me to see if I could sell them for her in the spiritual shops in the town. My dad gave me a lift and I was overjoyed that he seemed so keen to help me. I didn't show him the book. I'm not sure what he would have made of it and I was still disgusted by the BA Hons thing.

One shop I went to seemed keen and ordered a book straight away. They liked the sound of an English guru and promised that if she was up for it, there was a room upstairs where she could give talks and even Darshan.

I didn't have much more luck that day. Most people didn't seem to like the idea of Mothers calling themselves Holy and by and large, my efforts came to nothing. When I returned from Glastonbury, I told HM about the shop that had bought the book and some time later she contacted them. I'm not sure how it rolled out for her, but seemingly she struck up some kind of arrangement with them and later that year did a Darshan in their upstairs room. Funnily enough, on all the occasions when I introduced HM to people over the years, and I include certain friends in that category as well, she would snatch them for herself immediately and start working with them without telling me. Some time later, I would find out that she'd used up their good will and there'd been terrible ructions. That's when they'd either disappear completely or contact me to tell me that almost from the moment they'd been assumed into the fold, HM had spent no small amount of time destroying their image of me with a stream of complaints and vicious observations designed to undermine me completely.

In the early summer, HM found a small house in a village close to Glastonbury. It wasn't the perfect place for her as it was exceptionally small, but she was so desperate to get away from Reading, she decided to rent it immediately.

Moving was going to be a nightmare. There was still a lot of stuff in Rosie's room, but as Rosie had left so suddenly, there'd been no time to sort through it properly, so it all got left behind for someone else to throw in the bin.

As HM didn't want to drive to the new house, the plan was that she'd put her stuff into a removal van and then take trains and buses to get to her new home. I would follow a few days later in her car with items that she didn't want to go on the van. For some reason, this included a large stuffed purple hippo with baby sick stains on it that Scooter had rescued from the charity shop that was below my old "hell flat" in West Reading.

On the day that she was due to leave, I went around to Ryan Street to help her and watched as she moved her Volvo hatchback to a new parking space so that the removal van could park. The Volvo was a car that had belonged to my brother and it was ready for the big old scrapyard in the sky. HM insisted on keeping it and I was beginning to wonder if that was such a good idea. When she switched it on that morning, there was a curious rattling from underneath and I was suspicious. I told her: "that car doesn't sound right!" Even I, with my limited knowledge of cars, could spot it. HM rounded on me:

"There's nothing wrong with this car! I've had it checked over and it's fine…what do *you* know, anyway?"

I should have been suspicious. I still believe to this day that she knew full well there was something seriously amiss with the vehicle and that she was keeping something back from me, knowing that if I smelled a rat, I'd refuse to drive it down to Somerset.

That morning, Scooter and I hung out a bit. By this time, he'd discovered British rock band *Oasis* and was beginning to act and look like a teenager. For Scooter, it was *Oasis* in the morning, for lunch, all afternoon, for dinner and all evening. He knew all the lyrics and talked about the band constantly. All the same, I enjoyed our chats that morning. We reminisced with as much emotional

159

intelligence as we could muster about the years that had gone by and had a long laugh about the young lad who lived two doors down who always used to insult me when he caught sight of me coming to visit. He had a cheeky little face that often grinned impishly as he called out:

"Helllloooo, Mr Smelly Head!"

His mum was a funny lady. One day she'd accused Scooter of firing a water pistol at her through the bathroom window whilst she was sitting on the loo. Scooter pointed out that water has never been known to travel through the air at right angles and wrote her off immediately.

Despite our genuine attempts to make light of those times that morning, Scooter was unsettled, worried that he might not see me again. He promised he'd come and visit whenever he could. I think he was trying to put on a brave face for all concerned. I said goodbye to him and HM later that morning, got into the car and drove it out to the village without mishap.

Two days later, I drove it back to the house in Ryan Street and met up with Gary. He'd been off the scene for a long time and was now no longer living in HM world. He'd got his life together quite well and was training for a new career. We chatted for a while and said goodbye, but only after he'd given me a warning about the car. He told me he didn't think it would ever get me to Somerset and that it was a complete death trap. I knew I had no choice but to ignore him.

The following day, I set off for the West Country with the intention of stopping off for the night at my parents' house. It was as I was driving along the A303 north of Winchester that something happened.

I decided to stop for petrol. HM had left the tank low so that I'd be forced to fill up on my own dime and I didn't think I'd make it to my parents' house.

To this day, I honestly believe that any non-physical beings interested in supporting me in those days were packing in around me and stepped in. My decision to stop for petrol was extremely timely. Just as I slowed down and changed into a lower gear to negotiate the slip road into the service station, I heard a funny noise. I carried on driving and gave the car a little bit of gas so that I could move into the parking spot I needed. I could hear revs, but there was no acceleration at all. Instead, the car slowed down and I guided it with what was left of its momentum into the nearest parking space I could find and came to a stop. I frowned and thought: *this doesn't look good at all*. Immediately, I put the car into reverse and tried to drive back. There were revs, but absolutely no movement from the car whatsoever.

I got out and opened the bonnet. But me looking at a car engine and expecting to understand its workings is the equivalent of asking a monkey to bake a cake. I just stood there and shook my head. Seeing me looking perplexed, a Polish chap got out of the cab of his truck and came over to help. He didn't have much English but he could tell me what was wrong immediately. The prop shaft had snapped. We both looked under the car and there it was hanging loosely on the ground.

I didn't have time to worry about the wheres and whyfores of the situation. Instead, I called the AA and got them to tow me to my parents' house. They took £120 off me and dropped the car at the foot of my parents' drive. We then had real trouble trying to get it up a slope onto the property out of the way of the neighbours' front garden. As the hatchback was undriveable, the only way we could achieve that was to tow it up using my dad's Volvo estate and then use that car to nudge it into position via the front bumper.

I phoned HM and she was remarkably unsympathetic. Not only about the fact that my journey had ended in disaster, but also that I'd had to fork out for the AA. All she could think about was that she wouldn't be getting her PC when she wanted it.

I had to abandon her Volvo at my parents' place that day. Hippolytus the vomit-spattered hippo was in the front seat riding an upright vacuum cleaner like a bucking bronco and I had to leave him where he was until we could get the problem resolved.

As I took the train home, I thought about what had happened. If that prop shaft had snapped in the middle of the motorway, I don't know what I'd have done to get to safety. The very thought of it makes me squirm with horror. I also believe to this day that HM knew that it was on the way out as well. That's why she'd snapped at me when I'd mentioned my concerns about the vehicle. I also realise something else. She was quite happy to allow me to drive a dangerous car without telling me and therefore, by

161

implication, couldn't care less if I'd been turned into roadkill in the middle of the A303. All she could think about was herself. No wonder she was so reluctant to drive that car to Somerset: *"let the idiot do it. He's not holy so he's expendable. He's got karmic debt, so if he gets killed then that's his lookout…"*

Now I've had time to reflect on the events of the few weeks before her departure from Reading, I suddenly remember something she said. She told me to make sure before I made my journey that I wrote a note and left it in my flat saying that if I died suddenly, I intended to leave all my money and possessions to her. I remember this because Scooter, who didn't know her devious plan, had piped up: "…can you leave me your flat screen TV?" He was joking, of course. But you know, I don't think she was. It was almost as if she'd planned the whole thing and knew full well that prop shaft didn't have a prayer.

So not only had she tried to sell me down the river in a pact with her dark side, the vicious hag now wanted to murder me.

Even though my dad had never met HM, he stepped in to help out. The first thing he did was to get a quote for the repair of the Volvo. It was going to cost in excess of £300 to fix and HM who'd already used all her available funds for the move didn't have the money for the repair bill. Using his own money, my dad had the car scrapped and apparently, both my parents were watching the day the tow truck came to take the car away. These days they actually pay you for scrap cars, but not then. My parents paid £100 to see the car destroyed before their very eyes. A large crane was brought down to lift the car onto the truck and as the crane grabbed hold of the car via the top of the window frames, it became clear, this was one vehicle that would be going nowhere ever again: certainly not with me and a hippo in the passenger seat trundling down to Somerset.

To his eternal credit, Gary stepped in. He'd found an old Renault 5 that was being sold by the mechanics that had serviced and repaired all HM's old jalopies. They sold him the Renault for £350 and it was agreed that I'd drive it to my parents' place, load up HM's stuff and then take it to hers. I could then take public transport home.

162

Gary had originally insisted that I go halves on the Renault, but HM wasn't having it. She didn't so much ask Gary as order him to pay the full amount for the car. So I guess it wasn't really surprising that we never saw much of Gary after that. I think he was as sick of the situation as I was. So many years of forking out more and more cash for all the latest hair-brained schemes, the latest big idea that HM wanted to undertake for the advancement of her holy thing, had finally caused him to find the energy to bail out for good.

It may have been the case that Gary knew what HM's game was even better than she did. He'd gone along with it because, as Devil's Advocate, he was into the idea of giving me (and others) a good spiritual kicking and watched with relish as someone else did it with incredible panache. Perhaps he already knew he was actually helping me by throwing as much catalyst in my direction as possible. Who knows...? Whatever the reason, it was clear he was sick and tired of the shenanigans and was jumping down from the bandwagon.

When the day came to pick up the Renault, he was there to meet me. We had an amiable chat, but I could see from his eyes that the enthusiasm for the world of HM had burned out. His old habit of royally mocking me had waned somewhat as well. He seemed quite woebegone about Rosie and I could tell he was harbouring regrets about the past.

He did have time for one last jolly, though. I struggled with René the Renault from the word go. I just couldn't get used to the biting point and the pedals were too close together. Consequently, we stalled about ten times as I drove out. I could see he was getting impatient and he started shouting at me, so I gave him a bit of fire of my own - something I don't think he'd ever seen as I was always so cowed in his presence. I shouted:

"Look here, you loon; who's skinning this cat?! I hate backseat drivers!"

Facetiously, he replied:

"I'm not in the bloody back seat, I'm in the passenger seat. Now get this bloody car on the road. Are you an idiot or what?"

Suddenly I burst out laughing. There was an actual smile on his face and I realised, after everything that had happened, the Devil's Advocate had been ribbing me all along. For once I found it genuinely amusing and seeing that I was in step with his humour he softened visibly. For the first time ever we were at peace in each other's presence. I didn't see him much more after that as he emigrated, but I always think it was a slightly strange and somewhat "trying" pleasure to have known him.

There were problems with René as soon as I drove out of the mechanics' premises. A filter was blocked causing the car to shudder and keep slowing down. (You can tell I know jack all about cars, can't you.) When I got to a junction, it would stall and I would have trouble starting it again. By the end of that first day, the issue seemed to be resolving itself so the following morning, I set off for Hampshire bright and early, all ready for my long drive. By the time I'd negotiated the slip road onto the M3 at Basingstoke, I knew there would be trouble ahead. Trip number two was also going to end in disaster.

The further away I drove from Basingstoke, the more the car shuddered and slowed down. It would then speed up and then slow down again to the point that I was becoming a danger to other motorists.

Unwillingly, I turned around and made my way back up the A33 to my place, "limping" all the way along and losing my rag. At one point, I had to slow down to give way and the car stalled. There was absolutely no starting it and I felt doomed. Luckily some very kind chaps in a white van, grinning from ear to ear, helped push the car into a country lane and I was abandoned to the wiles of uncertain fate. I had absolutely no idea where the heck I was either.

Luckily, I had a mobile on me and managed to contact the boys who'd sold us the car. They decided to come out to rescue me. Unsurprisingly, they in turn got lost and it was some hours before they found me by the side of the A33, looking hassled and fed up. They were also very angry with me as I'd left my phone on vibrate and there was so much traffic I hadn't felt it go off in my pocket. They'd been desperately trying to contact me and I'd missed their calls.

Fortunately, they were very good to me. They bypassed the filter and got the car going. I was asked to get into the passenger seat and then one of the chaps drove the car at its maximum speed down the A33 and up and down the Swallowfield bypass, its engine screaming in protest as it got the caning of its life. I wanted to put my head in my hands and cry. HM's loony tune schemes always brought about this sort of malarkey and I was sick and tired of it. I felt as though she was on another wild goose chase and wasn't supposed to have fled to the West Country or be doing any of the things she'd so selfishly planned, the top of the list being jettisoning her daughter. Each and every time she failed to go along with the flow because of her desires, it was always me and those around her who picked up the tab. I knew as we burned French auto rubber up the bypass that cloudy summer's day, now she was out of the way geographically, the time had come for me to get on with my life.

The following day, I finally made it to my parents' house in one piece. Both of them laughed at the goings on but didn't really understand the true reasons for such a string of disasters. Hippolytus and I had a fairly uneventful journey to HM's village that afternoon, apart from the fact that I made a bunch of people jump in fright at a set of traffic lights in Warminster when my clutch work in that little granny car wasn't as good as it could have been.

When I found the village, I was incredibly relieved. I located HM's house at the top of a steep hill and parked right outside, leaving the car in gear in case it rolled back. Scooter came out and we had a good old chinwag, but HM was not pleased to see me. She was ratty and rude and refused to let me into the house, probably believing that I'd ruin the nice energy of the place with my evil, evil vibe. Scooter and I sat in the garden and chatted and literally within minutes of finishing unloading the car, HM drove us all to Wells where she wanted to drop me off for the bus to Bath Spa as soon as was humanly possible. She just couldn't wait to see the back of me. In fact, the feeling was very mutual.

That night, a neighbour of HM's, furious that this little French jalopy was now parked in a place where he wanted to park his car, played a very snide little trick on HM. Under cover of darkness, he inspected the vehicle and noticed that it was one day beyond its tax expiry date. The sneaky old snooper reported this to the DVLA and HM got a fine. A few weeks later, the same gentleman, who probably had just a little bit too much time on his hands, took some emery paper and worked his way around the bodywork of the car some time at night, scratching the paintwork and making it look even more of a wreck than it already was. When HM saw what happened, she didn't turn a hair. She'd hated the car at first sight and had too many other personal emergencies on her plate at the time to worry about some sneering, backstabbing old busybody.

Even though I was now off the scene, I was still expected to give HM cash every month. In my head, I got around this little issue by telling myself it was to help Scooter. If that meant there was more food in the house (he has a gargantuan appetite) then so much the better. I already knew that Scooter was low down on the list of priorities. HM had the nice bedroom upstairs whilst Scooter had to bed down in the living room. In fact, over the next few years, as he and HM madly scoured the face of the planet with no fixed abode, he was so far down on the list of priorities he would *never* get his own room, as you will see.

Although HM had moved out of Reading to get away from Rosie, Social Services, a bunch of satanists and me, it never stopped her from tapping me up at the least opportunity. To be honest, I always knew she didn't like taking money off me and dreamed of being financially independent. But sometimes, getting a few quid kept her from going under. If it hadn't been for that, and the fact that I was still doing her leaflets and website work, she'd still have dumped me in the blink of an eye. The important thing now was that she could keep me at arm's length and still tap into what few advantages there were of having me under her thumb.

Scooter phoned me most nights and I listened to his tales of woe with a sad ear. The village he and his mum had moved to was beautiful and unspoiled, situated as it was at the foot of the Mendip hills. But Scooter was bored rigid. Some of the locals welcomed him and he played tennis at the tennis club, but by and large, he felt like a spare man at a wedding. There was even one old lady with a stick who used to wave it viciously at him when she passed him in the lane, screaming at him to get out of the way. If he went into nearby Shepton Mallet, he would invariably be abused by local yobs and was always asking me what it was about him that made him the target of ridicule. I was at a loss to explain that one as I was for a solution to his terrible loneliness; being corralled up

166

with a mother who was always angry, distressed and fed up with her life couldn't have helped one bit. He never went to school or saw anyone friendly of his age for months at a time.

Scooter had insisted to his mother before they left Reading that the move to this house was just not the best idea. But HM, despite always making the assertion that everyone around her was incompetent for never listening to their intuition, was never of a mind to use it herself when there was something she really wanted. She'd been attracted by this village because it was charming and there were nice houses. But once again, because she was so keen to move there, she failed to find out from the Universe if she was doing the right thing. Because it was all "want, want, want, me, me, me," she missed all the messages that came winging their way to her, ignoring them all in favour of her own desires. Because she wasn't "listening" and had roundly ignored Scooter who's very intuitive, it all came to a grinding halt. By Christmas that year, 2004, she was given notice to quit and was back to square one.

There then followed a frantic period of house hunting. Her efforts to conquer Glastonbury had also come to nought and she'd inevitably smashed up all relations with the people at the shop where she'd given a darshan. With no one to support her, she was high and dry all over again. Eventually, with help from the 'deus ex machina' that her god had appointed to clear up the garbage she made of her life, a little cottage in another Somerset town was found.

Once more, it was not the place to be. Scooter was done out of a bedroom yet again and ended up having to bunk down in a narrow closet by the front door. At least this time he had some privacy, but he was more like *Harry Potter* at the Dursley's than a normal kid of his age. He took to wandering the countryside on his own, going for long walks and listening to *Oasis* on his portable CD player. He knew that his life was wasting away and he was becoming sadder and lonelier than he'd ever been. At the beginning of 2005, he came to stay with me for a week and was overjoyed to see me. But he just couldn't relax. He was worried about his mother and the stress caused him to get some serious nosebleeds. I had to send him back to Somerset as he was struggling far too much. Even though he was now a teenager, Scooter was still guarding his mother carefully. He'd had an early lesson in just how vulnerable she was the day she'd tried to kill herself and he wasn't going to allow such a thing to happen again. Even in the Somerset days, there were times when she'd become so depressed that she'd shut herself in her bedroom for days at a time. All Scooter could do was try and get on with his life and wade through it in the best way possible. Even though he was clearly being neglected, he didn't want to take his eyes off his mother for any longer than necessary as, despite all the hassles and disasters, she was the only person in the world he had, apart from me. As she was constantly telling him how unreliable I was, her observations of me (however inaccurate) actually registered with Scooter and he believed her. If the worst had come to the worst for him, I would certainly have taken him in, but he didn't believe that. All he ever had coming from his mother was a stream of criticism about me and of course, over time, the less he saw of me, the more his image of me became skewed.

Around this time, HM decided she wanted to learn French. I think secretly she was planning on escaping the UK, believing that her lack of fortune was down to an evil and godless British way of life. She found herself a very good teacher who had some excellent ideas for helping people remember vocabulary. The problem was, she always assumed she was not good at languages and almost immediately blocked herself. She started off great guns but then got it into her head, because she wasn't able to speak fluently after a few weeks or at least have a meaningful conversation, that she was hopeless. She asked me to help her and I spent some nights on the phone to her, talking her through the stuff she'd learnt and trying to encourage her. I also tried to tell her that if she wanted to speed up as she was insisting, that she'd have to do some graft and sit down and learn vocabulary. This wasn't what she wanted to hear. I then got an inkling into what was wrong with her attitude. Because she was frustrated with her inability to get French under her belt in a short space of time, faster than even most linguists would have learned a language, she began to get very disillusioned. Because I'd suggested to her that she needed to put her back into it, she rounded on me and accused me of putting her off. She even accused me of looking down on her for being better at languages than her. Suddenly, I became her scapegoat again and was accused of being the sole person responsible for stopping her from

168

mastering not only a language, but everything. She shouted and screamed and fired terrible accusations at me. She even brought up her classic: that because I'd treated her so badly in past lives, she hadn't wanted to bear children in *this* life and that was why she was struggling with motherhood and had had to say goodbye to her own daughter.

I was staggered by the sheer nastiness of this. She couldn't help pouring acid on everything, accusing the whole world of being the bane of her life but still holding out her hand for the take. I really began to wonder how someone who was so utterly defeatist could have made it to this "enlightenment" she made such claims to. A spiritually evolved person is grounded and has overcome their negative personality traits. This woman was still struggling with the basics; her inability to listen to her intuition, her foul temper, her accusations, her refusal to cope with life in general, her lack of basic social skills and a mothering instinct, all pointed in another direction entirely. How she ever deluded herself into thinking she'd made it to what she termed God-realisation and enlightenment was totally beyond me. At the time, I was beginning to believe that although she'd never set out to lie about the experiences and visions that had brought her to that level, she may still have tricked herself into thinking they were genuine. In fact, I came to wonder if something else entirely was whispering into her eager ears, something mischievous and deceitful that sold its twisted version of reality to her, knowing that she was so desperate, she would immediately take its words as gospel. Later, I'll show you how that really is possible...

Chapter Eighteen

One day in the autumn of 2004, HM rang me and asked me a strange question. She said:

"How do you pronounce the word R-o-n-j-a in German?" I told her that the j comes out like an English "Y": Ronya. She didn't want anything else and rang off.

A few days later, she started talking about someone called Anna, a German lady who had a spiritual teacher called Ronja. This German lady had contacted HM and wanted to know more about how she worked and how she helped people as she herself and Ronja were in deep trouble. Not only was this lady ill on a physical level but there was also spiritual distress. HM didn't give me too much information so I just got on with my life and didn't really think anything of it. Over the years, so many people had come and gone that I was losing count of them all and I knew that there was always a pattern with the new arrivals. As I've said, they'd come onto the scene, show great enthusiasm and then suddenly disappear. News would then come to my ears that they'd fallen out with HM or simply just stopped contacting her. One such person I remember was a really friendly young chap who was about to emigrate to Australia. He actually went as far as to ask HM for spiritual training as a disciple. Almost the very moment he'd made this request, she'd started to treat him in the same way she treated me and he hated it. It wasn't that he couldn't take the pressure. It was more that he found it incredibly negative and I remember him ringing me up and saying:

"She was bloody rude and nasty to me! I was horrified, Paul. I've never been exposed to such nastiness and negativity in all my life. She seemed to be in a really bad mood. That isn't the sort of behaviour I was expecting from someone of her level. I don't like it at all..."

This chap then wrote HM a letter to explain that if *that* was how she was as a person, he must formally withdraw his request for spiritual training. HM was furious. In front of me, she took his letter and burned it over the gas cooker, throwing the burning pages disgustedly into the kitchen sink and turning on the tap to douse the flames.

Because of incidents like that, I paid no attention at all to any new spiritual trainees as I knew they'd all be gone in the blink of an eye.

However, as the winter became spring in 2005, the name Anna cropped up more and more often. I began to realise, there was someone "important" on the scene and this person really sounded genuine and enthusiastic.

One day, Anna phoned me. HM had wanted her to contact me so that we could work together towards translating the pages on her website into German. She may also have had a deeper purpose in getting us together, hoping that two heads would be better than one in trying to lure more people in.

I was impressed with Anna. She had a very genuine-sounding voice and she seemed full of enthusiasm for life. She also seemed to be getting on well with HM and although she'd already been over to the UK at the end of 2004 to see HM, she was actually thinking of coming over again. I thought: *you're very enthusiastic and brave! Are you sure about that?*

Anna explained that she was happy to have been freed from her old spiritual teacher who was in a real psychic mess. She was also thrilled to have found such a seemingly caring and loving person in HM, one who was helping her with her many spiritual questions and supporting her to grow on her own path.

I tried to warn her about what lay ahead, telling her that so many people had come and gone over the years because they couldn't take the pressure. I softened my warning by saying: "it does sound like you'll be different though..."

And for a long, long time, Anna *was* different. She made that trip to the UK to see HM and the two of them still seemed to get on very well. Anna had already taken training from this Ronja lady and I understood from a distance that the situation around Ronja had been very difficult for Anna. In fact, it came to light that Anna had approached HM initially because she'd been living with Ronja for three and a half months and the latter was in a deep physical and spiritual crisis. They had been to many different healers, doctors and so-called other Divine Mothers. Most of them turned out to be bogus. Only one of them had warned Anna of the manipulation that Ronja was using. Anna says:

"At the time, I was still unable to see "reality" (meaning how people manifest themselves on the earth plane) and only saw the soul of a person. In fact, it was the only thing I *could* see. This prevented me from seeing and understanding what was really going on and how I was lured into false teachings."

As with me, initially, she was also unable to see falsity in HM. At first, she was just happy to have help with her difficult situation, to get to grips with the real reasons why she felt the need to give up her life to help another. She says she could never have imagined at the time how someone who calls herself "holy" would misuse the "word of God". She could understand such a thing occurring within the Church, but not in a spiritual teacher who claims to "bring down the Light". Consequently, she allowed HM to worm her way in.

As HM was always on the lookout for new disciples, she was only too keen to get Anna away from Ronja as soon as possible. During our phone conversation, Anna had explained what the difficulties were with Ronja and I recognised all of the symptoms. Ronja and HM seemed so very similar. I didn't say anything to Anna. In many ways, I wish I had, but I believed that Anna really wanted to be with HM and I didn't think it was my place to tell her to run away as fast as she could.

One day, HM rang me and told me she was fed up of evil England and was moving to Germany where the people were more spiritually elevated. My first and immediate (inward) reaction was: WRONG! Another hopelessly misguided decision!

She insisted that her god was telling her to go to Germany where there were "disciples waiting" and where people would definitely accept her like they accepted Mother Meera whose disciples had bought her a castle. I lied and told HM I thought it was a great idea. In fact, *she* thought I was going to beg her on my knees to stay in England. But I couldn't be bothered. The only sad thought in my head was "poor, poor Scooter."

This decision to move to Germany also coincided with the arrival of a letter from the letting agent for HM's property in Somerset. She was being given notice to quit, yet again.

Some years after these events, I discovered that after Anna had been over to the UK a couple of times, she was already beginning to change her mind about HM, or at least, the first few doubts were creeping in. When HM decided to go to Germany, I believe the decision was HM's and *not* Anna's.

All the same, Anna was happy to introduce HM to Germany and to some of her spiritual friends and was hoping that she'd be up and running in just a few weeks, having found a house and established a life for herself. Anna would then be able to put some distance between the two of them as she was extremely keen to try and walk the spiritual path on her own.

HM asked Anna to come over to the UK to help pack her stuff; without further ado she upped and left, dragging Scooter with her for his latest adventure. Bizarrely, she pointedly failed to tell Rosie that she'd left the country. I was also ordered not to tell her that her mother had gone. By this time, the two of them had lost contact completely and Rosie, who had a nice life with her new foster parents, was clearly trying to move on and start enjoying herself. It was still cruel of HM to leave without telling her.

Before her departure, I was summoned to Somerset so that I could take delivery of the little blue car. I didn't really want it as René and I had not been the best of mates and I was wondering if HM was about to hand over a death trap for me again in the hope that I would come to grief on some motorway somewhere.

Before I left for her place, she asked me to get her two pairs of jeans from a local department store for Scooter. The day before I set off, I rushed into the store and grabbed two pairs from the pile that said 32" waist, 32" leg, paid for them and fled. It never occurred to me that the store would have piled the wrong size jeans in the 32" section. So I hadn't checked they were the correct ones. As if to emphasise the fact that I'd been the most useless and incompetent disciple ever, my parting shot at HM before she was supposed to be disappearing from my life for good was to make one of my usual dog's dinners for her.

My journey to Somerset on that day was uneventful, even though I was horrendously late. HM met me at the bus stop and was polite to me but distant. Scooter was really looking forward to seeing me, but I was unintentionally rude to him and he looked

173

like he'd been slapped in the face. I think it was because being with HM again was stressful for me. All the more so when she realised that I'd bought him the wrong jeans. She gave me a withering look when she found out and I just wanted to flee.

I said goodbye to Scooter and HM walked me to the car. My visit was no more than half an hour, maximum. HM couldn't wait to see the back of me again. Poor old Scooter, he looked so lonely and dejected, but it had all gone too far. There was nothing I could do to pull him out of his mire of difficulty. As HM handed me the car keys to the Renault, I came right out with it:

"You're not supposed to be going to Germany," I said. "This is wrong."

She gave me a look of absolute fury and tears sprang to my eyes. Later on, I understood from Scooter that she interpreted that as my trying to beg her not to go because I didn't want anyone else to have her; I wanted her all to myself.

In reality, the tears were for Scooter because I was worried sick about him. I also hated the fact she was leaving without telling Rosie.

As I kangaroo hopped out of the car park (I still couldn't get the hang of that clutch) I was already missing Scooter terribly. As for HM, my heart was singing for joy, not sadness. I was free from her!

Or at least, that's what I thought at the time…

Chapter Nineteen

HM and Scooter went to live in Cologne. The plan was that they were going to stay with Anna in her flat initially and use it as a base whilst they looked for their own place.

After a ten-hour journey from the West Country to Cologne, they arrived at Anna's place and HM immediately started to cause a scene, claiming that the energy was appalling. She insisted that Anna sit down and meditate to find the source of the negativity. Apparently, there were many earth-bound souls collected together in the apartment who had anticipated HM's arrival and were waiting to be released. There were also dark energies present that were determined to cause trouble as they didn't want HM to be there.

Right from the word go, Scooter began phoning me from Anna's flat. Unfortunately, he was doing that behind Anna's back and naturally, she was footing the bill. I didn't know it at the time, but he was also giving Anna an extremely negative picture of me and simultaneously painting the most hideous picture of Anna to me such that I immediately became suspicious of her. To this day, I've never been able to get to the bottom of why that was; looking back, it may have been his mother's influence already seeping into his behaviour patterns.

Funnily enough, he was also being duplicitous with his mother: criticising her to me endlessly, accusing her of neglecting him and pouring acid over her spiritual plans and aspirations. At the same time, he was also beginning to join her in her condemnation of me, giving Anna the impression that I was a moron of the highest order.

The fact is it was true that Scooter was being neglected. Whilst other kids of his age were going to parties and mixing normally with one another, Scooter was being dragged around the world aimlessly and his life seemed to be going in no direction at all. As he sat on his own in Anna's flat, he had nothing to do but watch TV and mess around on the internet. Inevitably, the devil would make work for idle hands. My own opinion was that he became disillusioned with the fact that he saw Anna as taking away all his mother's attention. Up to that time, he'd pretty much had her all to himself. I think he may have harboured a burgeoning resentment towards Anna because of this and began to see her as a figure of fun to be mocked and poorly treated. This also manifested itself in certain tricks that he played on her, like spreading peanut butter under the cushions of her sofa, winding her up by peeping through the keyhole when she was in the bathroom and going out of his way to shock her by leaving trails on her PC that showed someone had been looking at porn sites – and hardcore ones at that. Scooter has always had an affinity with computers. I certainly never taught him to do that! Even today, I've still no idea where he learned how to use the internet so "imaginatively" at such a young age.

Meanwhile, his mother and Anna would be in another room, no doubt discussing the next stage in her life which included where she was going to live and how she would achieve her desire to rule the world. HM was constantly asking for Anna to meditate and find out what she was supposed to be doing and where she had to be. I always found this trait strange in someone who claimed to have a direct link with "God". She never seemed to get any information for herself. If someone did go away and find out through meditation what she was "supposed" to be doing, if she liked the idea, she'd jump on it wholeheartedly. On the other hand, if the solution offered was one that she didn't like, it would be roundly ignored.

I know for a fact that very early on, Anna was finding looking after the two of them extremely difficult. If HM had come and stayed with me, I'm sure I'd have ended up throwing a frying pan at her, not to mention what she'd have liked to throw at me. There was many a time when Anna had to grit her teeth in sheer frustration as she endured HM's moods, her depression and her rages. Because he was sometimes "his mother's son", I've no doubt that Scooter had moods too and the atmosphere between all three of them must have been incredibly tense. It also seemed to take ages for them to find a flat for HM. Anna wasn't working and was spending all her time looking after the two of them, putting up with Scooter's teenage destruction of her china and her sofa, dipping into her savings and never having a day off. HM seemed to be permanently on some spiritual wild goose chase or on the hunt for dark forces. Apparently in those days she saw nothing else but that. Anna later claimed it was the most draining experience she'd ever had. With every week that passed, she was driven even further into doubt and was already wondering where the beauty of HM's "divinity" lay in all the negativity.

As for me, life wasn't that much different. I was now in possession of René the Renault and he and I had learned to tolerate each other on the long journey from Somerset back home. In fact, I was already becoming quite attached to that little blue car. It was the beginning of a very favourable period for both of us. In the two years or so that I used the car, it didn't break down once and I very rarely had to spend any money on it at all, unlike HM who had constant trouble. I think I just had a more positive outlook…but I'll leave that for you to decide.

Even with HM and Scooter out of the country, I was still being roped into helping out with the website. I spent hours and hours redesigning it and tidying it up, and once, even had to take an entire day off work to finish it before some incredibly important deadline, the details of which I was not a party to in case I subliminally ruined whatever the plan was with my nasty evil little vibe.

Sarcasm apart, I have to say, that *particular* day was one that I'll never forget. It was one of those days when your whole life changes because you just so happen to be at exactly the right place at just the right time.

Someone phoned to speak to me. This was a person who was trying to get in contact with HM. I'm sure if I hadn't been at home, he may well have tried to contact HM directly and I would never have had the chance to speak to him.

The person who phoned was Percy. As soon as I picked up the phone to Percy, there was something about his voice that inexplicably appealed to me. It appeared to be so full of life and enthusiasm and there seemed to be such wisdom in his tones that I related to him immediately.

Percy seemed quite keen to contact HM. He'd already heard about her and claimed at the time that she had the key to helping him with his spiritual path. I can't really remember what we spoke about, but I gave him HM's contact details and let things take their course. To be honest, I already knew that Percy would be removed from my life by HM immediately, especially if he turned out to be talented with his spiritual abilities. Of course, it was a superb measure of Percy's usefulness the fact that once he'd contacted HM, she never, ever mentioned him to me. I knew that he was around in her life (at a distance), but he was always kept *well* away from me. I just shrugged it off as HM being HM, as usual, playing her games with people and using them for her own ends. There was nothing I could do, so I didn't worry about it.

I think it's fair to say that there seemed to be something very different about Percy. He was just too good to be true, too smooth-talking and accepting. If I'd been using my intuition, I'd have been fully aware that a woman going around giving herself titles and airs and graces was leaving herself wide open to serious damage from so many sides. It was inevitable that one day something slimy would burrow its way into her life (and mine) with a very sordid agenda designed to take her down. For the time being, that creature was very much in disguise and playing a carefully orchestrated waiting game.

I didn't forget Percy and he certainly didn't forget me. A couple of years later, when I was at my lowest ebb and really desperately needed help, Percy reappeared in my life to have some fun.

A short while after HM moved to Germany, she, Anna and Scooter went to visit Cologne Cathedral. I'm not sure of the exact details of what happened that day, but as far as I know, HM realised that there were many trapped souls there. She'd also seen an underground current from all four directions flowing under the cathedral feeding it with darkness. HM's plan was to put a permanent beacon on top of this current in order for Light to flow out of it.

During medieval times, the cathedral had been used for human sacrifice by people who believed that they could resolve issues in their lives by sacrificing humans and spilling their blood on consecrated ground. Those souls that had died violently through sacrifice were still earthbound and still inhabiting the crypts and depths of this extremely old building.

HM decided that the souls needed to be moved on, so she contacted Percy who's extremely practiced in this side of spirituality. Although Percy was in the UK, the three of them set to work. Percy opened up a gateway and with him in London and HM and Anna in Anna's flat in Cologne, they encouraged the souls to cross over to the Light. HM used her physical body to guide them through.

When they'd finished, HM became extremely ill, clutching her chest and saying she thought she was going to have a heart attack. Anna was worried and tried to place her hand over HM's heart to give her healing which she'd done successfully in the past and it had worked well. Anna herself is an advanced healer and has great spiritual ability. But almost immediately, HM brushed her aside and shouted: "Get away from me! You're *evil*. You were there, incarnated on the earth plane when the sacrifices occurred and you had a part in the deaths of all those people and the terrible things that went on!"

Anna was horrified; she says:

'I'd always had a basic underlying feeling of guilt and this was immediately triggered. I'd convinced myself that God didn't love me and this sudden rejection seemed to prove me right. At that very moment in time, all I wanted to do was die. Even more so when HM claimed that I'd also harmed both Scooter and her and that I was full of karma for my atrocities. I panicked and was so confused that I grabbed my jacket, ran out of my apartment and into the nearby woods. I then sat on a tree, weeping and full of uncertainty. All this was too much for me. The constant demands, the negativity; I just wanted it to end. Deep in my heart I felt there was something deeply flawed about these claims, that somehow, HM had got the story entirely wrong. It was some hours before I dared to return, but when I did, I was feeling depressed and trapped. Things were already beginning to become difficult between me and HM, but this situation was the beginning of a period of great doubt in my mind about her motives.'

After deeply questioning everything she'd been told, Anna still didn't feel that she'd been "evil" at the time of these atrocities. In fact, what had happened was that she was a totally innocent person (a nun, in fact) who'd discovered what was going on. One night, she'd followed a group of these satanists to see where they met and to find out more about their activities. In doing so, she witnessed their atrocities first hand and as she watched, she felt paralysed and unable to intervene, such was her fear of what would happen to her. It was this scene of Anna watching the sacrifices that had led HM to believe that she was involved in them.

Anna was now suspicious in the same way I had been when HM channelled my guide. Although there was no doubt in Anna's mind about how genuine HM's abilities were, she felt she was being used and that somehow, the truth was being twisted in order for her to be put in her place and kept firmly in line.

Relations were somewhat more strained between Anna and HM following this incident. The situation was made worse because Scooter was still going through a rude, rebellious stage causing Anna to become even more mistrustful of him. She found that Scooter was not in the least inclined towards the spiritual life. In an attempt to help, Anna spent hours listening and talking to him, trying to understand him. She took him to art classes, taught him to ice skate and took him swimming. She even taught him how to ski in an indoor "ski resort" in the hope of making his life a little lighter. But Anna was to mention some time later that Scooter came to regret opening up to her and sharing his innermost thoughts about the sadness of his life; she believes he became worried that she would report the things he told her to his mother and this was why he mocked and poorly treated her, to keep her in line. Anna was upset by this and even more seeds of disillusion began to creep into her feelings for him.

It took a long time (six whole months) for HM to find a flat that she liked. The longer she delayed, the more frustrated Anna became. She wanted her life back and was straining under the constant demands being made of her time and financial resources.

I didn't hear much from HM in those days. Scooter would phone me on occasion, but I had a feeling that he'd been ordered not to tell me anything about life out in Germany in case, for some reason, I sent across a negative vibe that caused the block to worsen.

I know that HM was giving Darshan at the time, but very few people were turning up. One day, there was a massive spiritual convention held in Bonn. Anna rented a shop for HM where they put a sign up offering free spiritual healing. They also spent all day handing out leaflets in the hope of attracting people in. As it turned out, only about thirty people entered the shop, which, considering there were potentially thousands of people around who might be interested in what was going on, should have been a sign to HM that all was not well with what she was offering.

On another occasion, HM gave Darshan at the "Lebensmesse" in Hamburg, a fair that's annually attended by more than five thousand people. Once more, Anna and HM prepared posters and leaflets, but only twenty people turned up, ten of whom were Anna's own friends.

As the fair was in Hamburg, a hotel room had been booked. But when she arrived, HM turned her nose up at it and wanted to leave. Anna was forced to call one of her friends for help and in the end, that friend organised for them to stay on the floor of a spiritual healing centre, with Scooter and Anna in one room and HM in another, as she refused to spend the night in the same room as the two of them. Halfway through the night, HM came rushing in and shouted that she couldn't stay another minute. Even though it was 2a.m., she insisted that Anna ring her friend and ask her to put them up for the night.

Luckily, this friend and her husband came to the rescue and took them all in. The following day, HM - true to type - started on the friend, trying to "hook" her in and recruit her. The friend, who was open to all sorts of different spiritual paths, listened to what HM had to say and also attended the Darshan. But later on, HM began asking for favours and pushed the boat out too far. Realising that this friend was not just going to acquiesce to her whims and requests, HM turned away from her immediately, forgetting about her kindness and claiming she was on the dark side.

People who came to Darshans during HM's period in Germany were amazed at how much energy emanated from her during the service, but afterwards, they found that she undermined all the good she achieved by giving out a strong vibration of terrible sadness and suffering. It was hard for people to reconcile such a woeful figure with someone who could bring through such extraordinary energy during the Darshan itself. When I heard this, I began to understand my own situation on a deeper level. I was still wondering why I'd stayed with HM for so long. On the one hand, I was drawn to her by this Universal energy. On the other hand, I was also repelled by her aura of misery and suffering and it was this that had made me want to run away so many times.

One day, during one of my chats with Scooter, he told me that HM was fed up with Germany and planning on moving to Austria. HM, Rosie and Scooter had been out to Austria a couple of years earlier to stay with a young lady who'd been suffering. I believe that HM had been hoping that she could jam a foot in the door of that country, however, her experiences with the lady concerned had been extremely negative. There'd been some fearsome arguments and the lady had run away from HM and left her to organise herself and get herself back to England. I didn't even need to be told what had happened between the two of them: it was all such familiar territory.

So HM, having been in her new apartment in Cologne for just six months, moved back in with Anna for three weeks and once again, the apartment, was full of HM's things. As soon as they could HM and Anna packed everything up and put it all in storage as Anna was due to fly to India for three weeks. Upon her return, her plan was to move to Munich, something she'd always had in mind.

In May 2006, she drove HM and Scooter to Vienna. By then, she was happy to let them go, but at the same time was astonished that HM didn't have a plan at all. All she'd say was "God wants me to go to Austria. There'll be disciples there."

Once again, HM's god has about to play some nasty tricks her.

The next part in the tale gets very complicated to relate as it's the usual case of decisions, reversals of decisions, lack of planning, spontaneous bizarre ideas and general mayhem. When they arrived, HM and Scooter stayed in a hotel for the night whilst Anna stayed with her Viennese family. As soon as she could, HM moved in with a lady who she thought would help her: Anna told me she had lured this lady into her life by telling her that she'd been someone important in a past life but was now suffering from traumas and needed help. It soon became clear however, that this was yet another mistake: apparently the lady walked around her house naked, something that would have inspired utter horror in a conservative "holy" lady.

During this period, Scooter was farmed out to another family near Vienna. For a while he seemed to be happy there and reported positive things back about the family to me and Anna. When he claimed that the son bullied him, I didn't pay too much attention as I knew that Scooter was always able to handle himself. But when he reported this to HM, she angrily insisted that Anna drive all the way to Vienna to collect him.

They then spent two days in another hotel, running around with no plans, chasing places to stay and trying to get information from the spirit world. A young mother with a small apartment in Graz turned up, but she didn't want HM there. In exasperation and knowing that time was running out for Anna, HM finally asked to be dropped off at the train station saying that she'd find something *somewhere* herself. Anna was then allowed to drive home.

Anna felt guilty and honestly believed she couldn't just leave her there with nothing. On the other hand, she was under pressure with only three days left to pack up her apartment; she'd cancelled the lease and was about to depart for India.

At the last minute, they received a phone call: the lady in Graz agreed that HM could come down and stay in a hotel and they would try to sort things out together. HM had hooked her in by telling her that she was a very old and special soul who needed spiritual training. As HM was short on money, Anna drove her there and then took Scooter to another contact in Linz.

In the end, Anna felt she had no choice but to let HM and Scooter continue on their own and sort themselves out. Believing that she'd done her best for both of them, she drove home. By this time, she was utterly drained and felt miserable and dejected. It was like being with Ronja again. No free will, suffering on all sides, manipulation, control and no flow to life; nothing but blockages. She felt that the Universe had always provided for her and couldn't understand at all why it wouldn't provide for HM.

From a distance, I could tell that the self-destructive edge of HM's life was still causing things to go wrong, that Scooter was being neglected again and that HM was still so utterly obsessed with herself as this messianic character that she wasn't paying attention to the all-important details. She was dragging herself down and pulling Scooter and Anna with her.

As it turned out, the lady from Graz helped find HM an apartment in Vienna, but almost immediately (as with *everything* else) she complained like hell.

When Anna returned from India she moved into a one room apartment in Munich which one of the disciples of the Indian Holy Mother Amma had rented to her. At this point, she didn't have a job, but was confident she'd find something quickly. Her experiences in India had brought about profound inner changes. She was determined to get on with her life and now hoped that with Scooter and HM living in Vienna, she could start to live again, to get a job and improve her damaged financial situation.

Inevitably, HM achieved absolutely nothing in Vienna. Any money she'd made during her time in Cologne was just whittled away on rent and food.

Two months later, Anna received a phone call from her saying: "God has told me to come to Munich. You've got so many problems that need to be sorted out and I can help you."

Anna was furious within her heart, as she told me some time later:

'Because of all the experiences I'd had with my former spiritual teacher and now with HM, I was learning to trust my intuition and my heart: if I felt anger in my heart something was really wrong and I knew that I should trust that feeling.'

She saw this tactic for what it was: HM was *still* using her. Unable to fend for herself and Scooter in Austria, she wanted Anna to shoulder her responsibilities yet again and was trying to trick her way back in. Unfortunately, Anna was just not strong enough yet to say 'no'.

The next thing I heard, Anna had managed to find HM a place to stay in the one-bedroom apartment belonging to a friend of hers who was a disciple of Amma's. This set up was only a stop gap until such time as HM and Scooter could find a place of their own in Munich. Scooter was parked with another person Anna knew who was also a disciple of Amma's, and Anna herself shared another apartment with yet another disciple.

In some respects, HM was in a goldfish bowl at this point as the people around her had genuine experience with gurus and spiritually renowned people. One person in particular who'd spent time attending Darshans with these enlightened people reported that HM certainly had healing ability, but he was appalled by HM herself.

One lady who came for healing was quite well off and owned several houses which she rented out. HM informed Anna that this lady could "lessen her karma" if she allowed her and Scooter to live in one of the houses. Anna didn't mention the "karma" angle to the lady (whose name was Susanne), but instead simply asked her if she would let HM and Scooter stay in a house as a favour. As it turned out, Susanne did have a house she wanted to sell at the time and it was vacant. Graciously, Susanne agreed that HM and Scooter could stay there on a temporary basis until more permanent accommodation could be found. However, she made it clear from the outset that the house was still for sale.

With what few belongings they had, HM and Scooter moved into this house. Immediately, Scooter took exception to the bedroom as it smelled mouldy and did what he often did, make do: he bunked down in the cellar full of spiders.

Once things had settled down, I began to hear from him again as there was a phone in the house. He told me that Anna had now found a place to live (a three bedroom apartment in the Munich area) and that he'd gone around to help her move in and do some painting. To this day, I'm not sure exactly what happened, but Anna never let Scooter (or HM) near her apartment again.

For the next six months, Scooter entertained himself, mostly going on his own to a gym and working out. It was there that he was taken in by some well-meaning sportsmen and women who'd seen him working out on his own. Over the next few months, he was introduced to a lot of people and taught kickboxing and other martial arts. When I heard from him during that period, he was often full of stories about all the things he'd been up to and for once seemed to be enjoying life. His experiences were also forcing him to grow up. Although on the face of it, the precariousness of his nomadic life was not what he needed for his education and his formation as a young adult, he was also learning to fend for himself and to mix well with his peers and people older than himself. For so long, he'd been leading an unhealthily sheltered existence. At last, life was opening up for him and he could live a little.

There were times when I knew that he was getting a little cocky, though. One day, he boarded the Munich subway system and failed to stamp his ticket. That very day, the ticket inspectors happened to come around and he says they jumped on him and arrested him. Seemingly, he tried to resist arrest and was dragged down to the Police Station and put in a cell.

Anna insists that this never actually happens in Germany; that in fact, if you're caught without a ticket, you're politely asked to pay a fine of forty euros. As none of us were there that day, I guess what really happened will never be known, but I've every reason to believe that Scooter must have really riled those Policemen and used some muscle to get himself out of a tight spot. They probably had no choice but to arrest him!

Later that day they set him free and allowed him to go home. When HM heard what had happened, she tried to defend him, but only in the most naïve fashion. She wrote an outraged letter to Angela Merkel, the German Chancellor, suggesting that Scooter had been mistreated. This action prompted no response whatsoever.

I believe this incident was the beginning of the end for HM in Germany. Somehow, it seemed to herald a new and difficult period in her time there which was to conclude in the early spring of 2006, in a series of incidents that I saw as the disastrous culmination of a decade of her life entirely wasted in an effort to start the promotional machine for her "divinity". Because she'd failed, after so many warnings, to stop that bandwagon in time, when it began to roll out of control, it did so with terrible consequences.

Anna by this time had withdrawn from HM as much as possible. In fact, the end for her came during a Darshan (actually a service HM called Bhava) which was held in the little house that belonged to Susanne. Anna came with two of her girl-friends. Apparently, the energy was extremely high, and when Anna moved forward to receive her blessing she clearly heard a voice say within her, "it's over; this is the last time - you have to move on." Anna says:

'I was strangely sad and I shed a little tear, but at the same time, I knew it was the truth.'

As always, ten minutes after finishing the service, HM was complaining again and in front of all those present.

Anna's friends looked at each other and later at home said: "we don't understand….she didn't act holy at all. Actually she was rather primitive."

They decided not to see her again.

The first time I began to get a feeling that all was not well was in the autumn of 2006. HM rang me to say that Anna had started spreading slanderous and untrue rumours about her to everyone who would listen and that she'd effectively turned against her and "joined the dark side". In reality, the only thing Anna had done by that time was write an email to HM telling her that she needed more time for herself, that she had a sixty-hour a week job that she needed to make her priority and also that after her trip to India, there were some things she needed to "feel inside". She promised to contact HM after two weeks.

Despite the fact that the future was definitely not certain, HM was still determined to stay in Germany. I couldn't see the sense in that. She had no money coming in, had long since given up even thinking about learning German and worse still was completely friendless. She wasn't even getting on with any of her neighbours, which, to be honest, was quite a normal situation for HM.

The rift with Anna also coincided with Susanne asking her to leave the house as she was now close to selling it. Rather than heed the messages that were coming to her left, right and centre, HM dug her heels in and stayed right where she was. She declared to me over and over again that she was not budging from the house and that she'd been told by "God" to tell Susanne that she was to continue to stay rent-free. She even wrote a letter to Susanne telling her about her karma. Susanne had a few quite serious health problems at the time and HM said that she would be helped with these if she played her part in the bargain and let her stay.

The problem was, by this time, Anna had truly had enough. The constant demands on her time and resources were still pulling her down terribly and she was suffering. To use her own words:

'I was suffering more for knowing that a so-called spiritual teacher misused the word of God. After having asked for a break for two weeks, I found an answer inside myself for why I gravitated towards so-called gurus. When I told HM what this answer was, all I got was: "See! This is what I mean – you've got too many problems and so much karma. You never have the right attitude when you're with a guru."'

Anna had had enough of being manipulated and controlled. She asked HM for a meeting, hoping to talk to her face to face. She wasn't afraid anymore and could see things with much more clarity. HM reacted by sending her an email that said: "God isn't allowing me to talk to you."

Anna thought: *ok then. I won't talk to you.*

One day, she asked a taxi driver to deliver carefully to HM a load of things that belonged to her which were still being stored at her apartment. Whilst packing she prayed for HM and filled the boxes with positive energy. Naturally, when HM received them, she said they were filled with darkness.

Anna's crisis in confidence about HM and the nature of her work had led her to make an extremely difficult decision: she wanted to be free of HM for good and make a permanent break. She still couldn't understand how someone who could emanate such energy during a Darshan could themselves be so woebegone and create such a heap of problems for herself and those around her. All the same, she looks back on those years with positivity, believing that she learned from her valuable experiences just how life was *not* supposed to be for her. Even though she was fully aware that she'd been conned and lied to, she found her whole HM experience was crucial for her evolution as a spiritual soul. When I asked her how she felt some time later, she was very honest and open with me:

'The stories are surely not different to yours. The basic vibration is always the same: manipulation, control, holding people back from their spiritual growth, occupying people so much with "herself" that their lives are no longer their own. If I said to her: "I have the feeling that this isn't my life anymore" the answer would be: "Anna, this is where you're supposed to be, this is your life and this is what you wanted."

188

'On some days, I had the guts to tell her various things that were on my mind. One day she asked me why she always had problems. My answer was: 'there is a very, very dark cloud above your head and it's filled with your own thoughts. Your life is a self-fulfilling prophecy of self-indulged darkness.''

HM's reaction was to brush this warning aside...

On another occasion, Anna went away and thought about what it was that had caused her to choose another guru who exploited her:

'You might think: why on earth would a grown-up person escape from one trap only to fall straight into another?

To answer that we have to understand not only someone's longing to walk the spiritual path but also the personal history of that individual that causes them to be attracted to a spiritual teacher or guru. This works vice versa with the guru. A teacher like HM has to attract people who have good hearts but who have a basic feeling of guilt, lack of self-confidence and self-esteem in order for their scam to work. If the soul wants to learn something on its path back to God that requires a teacher, it will choose that path. Depending on what needs to be learnt, the teacher is chosen. In my case, from a soul perspective, I wanted to see and feel once more what control is, how manipulation works and to find out what a high level of suffering is really like. Having been exposed to that, I could finally say: "this isn't the truth. This isn't what it's supposed to be like. There must be another way."

'This is how the soul evolves – by experience. It will then be able to distinguish which path is which.

'But I only came to understand that some years later. By experiencing and seeing so much negativity and thinking about, working against and talking of suffering, you create a totally dark life that attracts an endless amount of suffering. In my nature there is pure hope and joy and for me to see (and encounter first hand) all this self-indulged torment was a deeply awakening experience.'

Two days after Anna had sent the taxi driver over with the boxes, HM wrote an email to her which contained the same blast of fury that she'd vented on me some years earlier when I'd tried to leave myself. These letters are so full of malicious negative energy that they knock you sideways. If you aren't spiritual and are

189

trying to understand the depths of emotion that they cause you, I think the only way I can describe it is this: it's like receiving a late night visit from the Police to inform you that one of your relatives has died. Having gained your confidence, HM would find your weakest point and turn it against you, knowing exactly where you're the most vulnerable.

You might think that's overreacting, but I can tell you, as someone who was serious about his path and in his search for the source of all life, if you've come into this sphere of strong energy that HM creates, when it turns against you with spite and vitriol, it can be utterly overpowering.

Anna was taken aback by this letter which left her physical system in shock, so much so that a friend had to step in and help her with some healing. She knew full well it was an attempt to scare her into "coming back." This tactic had worked with me, and HM was trying it again now with all the strength she could muster. However, Anna's mind was made up. There was no going back. All her friends called her to tell her that her decision was right, that they'd seen the truth some time before: it had become obvious that a split would occur once HM had moved to Munich.

The vitriolic email was soon followed by a letter from HM which was calmer in tone and accompanied by a special remedy for her to help her deal with all her problems. The letter also made the claim that Anna's "soul was very sick".

Anna was not taken in, knowing that the soul itself is pure and cannot be sick; immediately, she took the letter and the remedy and placed them in the bin outside her house, "where" she says, "things like that belong."

As Anna's friends were also sure something was "not right" with HM (and in truth had always suspected as much from their very first meeting with her) they in turn decided not to contact her again. HM mistakenly took this to mean that Anna was turning everyone against her and I remember her phoning me and complaining bitterly about Anna, accusing her of having jumped ship and joined the dark side.

One day, HM asked me (in desperation it seemed) to write a "round Robin" email and send it using my name to a lot of people who she knew in Germany to try and get their support and their money. I must have sent about twenty or thirty emails out. Each and every one of these was roundly ignored. The word was spreading.

By this time, the only source of news I had about how things were in Germany, was from HM herself. Because of this, all stories had her stamp over them and were therefore either incomplete, embellished with fiction or actual bare-faced lies. Despite her best efforts, she simply couldn't prevent the truth from seeping out and I began to realise that I'd been right: the whole exercise had been an unmitigated disaster. I didn't understand what Anna was doing and was incredibly upset and angry with her for not helping HM, believing that she'd brought HM out to Germany just for herself. I now realise how wrong that assumption had been. HM had insisted on going out to Germany and Anna had no say in the matter. The choice of moving to Cologne hadn't been Anna's either. She tells me she can't stand the city. She'd only moved there because HM had given such a rosy picture of all that they would achieve together.

Anna had been completely unable to stop the train from rolling and I understand that fully. For years I'd been in the same position: without wishing to sound overly prosaic at this point, if you're a person with a genuine caring heart, it's a lot harder than it seems to stand up to HM and stop her and her great tidal wave of energy from moving into your life and sweeping everything, including your free will, away.

By Christmas 2006, HM was still living in Susanne's house rent-free and refusing to move out. She told me at the time that she was still "in training" for her level of enlightenment and that this was all part of a test. In those days, there were two novels on her PC that she'd written which were unfinished. I remember her telling me that things would start to improve for her when the novels were complete. Her god had told her so...

The books had a spiritual theme and encapsulated all her "guru first, everyone else scum" teachings. With both of them, she'd started writing with great gusto and all guns blazing, but as with all her undertakings, she had a low boredom threshold and got fed up and impatient very easily. After a while, she'd ruin things for herself by producing a last minute rushed job and then going back over her work, picking at it and adding things in as an afterthought. The problem was the outcome often produced disjointed results. This was certainly the case with the novels. The ideas were sound and there were some "sort of interesting" moments in the books, but they'd been undermined by the fact that halfway through, she'd obviously seen a word count and was suddenly striving far too hard to reach a target of 100,000 words. As soon as that happens, the "panic" shows in your writing and the last few thousand words become laboured and an unpleasant toil to read. In the case of one of the books, it ended abruptly. She'd clearly become frustrated with it, cobbled together a surprise ending which made no sense at all and then ground the work to an uneasy halt. The result was that all the headway she'd made at the start was cancelled out and the reader was left feeling frustrated and cheated out of an exciting ending. This was definitely not the work of a person who was "divinely" inspired.

To me, it was a parable for my entire experience with HM. Over the years, I came to understand that as a young person with a great deal of spiritual ability, she'd run away with herself in her enthusiasm to get on, finish the work and then get famous and start making some money. The problem with this tactic is, if you haven't dotted the i's and crossed the t's, you get a botched job. When you're trying to evolve, to do that is to open yourself up to major problems. It's the equivalent of trying to drive a lorry before learning to drive a car. With HM, that lorry was about to run hopelessly out of control.

Chapter Twenty

In February 2007, HM phoned me to ask if she could send Scooter back to England to stay with me. Immediately, I said "no". This wasn't because I didn't want to see him. It was more that I felt she needed him with her. From a distance, I could tell that she was hurtling headlong towards a brick wall and that the end of the ride for her would be traumatic. At least Scooter had a bit of German under his belt and could support her with the help of the many friends he was now making.

I also didn't want Scooter to come over because I knew that it would be a chance for her to push her way back into my life. Over the course of her time in Germany, she'd gradually pulled back from having anything at all to do with me. After all the hours and hours I'd spent setting up websites for her, she'd taken responsibility for them away from me as soon as she could and handed them over to someone who she felt she could easily manipulate and knew more about HTML than me.

HM was desperate to get me out of her life completely. Initially, when things were going well for her in Germany, she made that clear by refusing to speak to me and by criticising me literally to *anyone* who would listen, saying that I was the source of all her woes over the years. She told people that I was something akin to an evil dark master who'd set himself up to thwart all her plans, sabotage her websites and haunt her with dark visitations[10]. She also made it known that she wished she hadn't taken me on for training and that I'd been more trouble than I was worth. To be fair, she did stop taking money off me during that period which certainly showed me that she was prepared to stand by her assertions that I needed to be removed from the scene.

---

[10] I have a copy of an email that she sent someone around this time that confirms this. I sometimes read it just to remind me of her duplicity. Also, for some years I kept a message on my answerphone which had her screaming psychotically at me for about two minutes for some paltry reason. When I was up for a good laugh, I'd play it and sit there chuckling to myself...

But once Anna and her friends had disappeared from her life, despite the fact that I was probably the most dangerous, evil man ever to walk the earth, it was amazing how quickly I was brought back in once more, or "recycled" as I put it. The next thing, I was being asked for money again and now to look after Scooter for what looked like an indefinite amount of time. *She* said a few weeks. When I asked Scooter about it, he said more like six months. I knew one of them was lying and I knew which one it was. Inwardly I went ballistic. She'd said so many nasty untrue things about me and now here I was, being accepted back into the fold as a last resort: good old Paul, the idiot who can be relied upon to produce the goods, but only when all else fails.

In the end I relented purely because I could see trouble ahead and wanted to make sure Scooter was safe. So in the last week of February, Scooter, now aged fifteen, was packed off on a plane back to his town of birth to live with me.

I met him after work on Reading station and he looked terrible. He'd had flu and I could tell he was undernourished, overtired and stressed out. HM had called him fat and as a consequence, he'd apparently stopped eating. I remember him looking critically at my face. I was really suffering from hyperthyroidism at this time. I looked white as a sheet and my eyes were swollen and red. He told me I looked really old and I was horrified and saddened. As we boarded the train to the village, I steeled myself for several weeks of hell. But I talked myself through it by saying that I still really cared for Scooter and only wanted the very best for him. I couldn't see him coping on his own, he was still so young. If she couldn't look after him in her madness, then I would, whatever the consequences.

The previous summer, Scooter had come to visit me from Germany. We'd had an excellent week and I'd introduced him to all my friends. The problem was, I'd forgotten how duplicitous he can be - a trick he learned from his mother in all her years of playing people off against each other on her shoddy chessboard. During his visit, I'd taken him to a friend's 25th birthday bash and as we turned up there, he promised me he wasn't going to drink any alcohol. Over the course of the evening, all of my friends began to relax with him and finding him an affable and loveable chap started to goad him into having a drink of beer or cider. I told them it would be fine, but in moderation. The problem was that Scooter had been kept under the thumb for so many years and was not going to let me interfere with what he wanted to achieve. With the encouragement of my friends egging him on without my knowledge, he proceeded to get blind drunk and then stab me in the back, saying that I didn't understand that he'd grown up. He accused me of oppressing him and not appreciating the fact that he was now old enough to do what he wanted. This was blatantly not the truth. If anything, it was the opposite: I should have been stricter with him and put my foot down over the years. This would have shown him that I really did care and he's since admitted to me that that's exactly what he wanted all along. But not that night!

At about midnight, he got fed up and somehow managed to put on a sober voice to con me into giving him the key to my flat so he could go to bed. I gave him the key and as he made his way home, I was given a right royal rollicking by my friends who said that I didn't understand him and that I should just "let him grow up and stop interfering with the age old process of allowing a young man to find his feet." I bit my tongue as not one of them had a single idea of what we'd been through and what was still raging in our lives at the time.

At some point, as I was being talked to out in the garden by my well-meaning mates, my phone rang. It was Scooter to say that he'd thrown up in my sitting room.

Slowly and dejectedly, I made my way home about half an hour later. On walking into the room, the sight that met my eyes was nothing short of horrific. It was almost as if he'd stood in the middle of the room and spun around like a centrifuge, spraying vomit over everything. What's more, he'd collapsed onto his bed which was a makeshift pile of blankets on a rug in the middle of the floor and had been rolling around in his own sick.

I put the light on and just grabbed some antiseptic wipes. With a smile and a nervous laugh, I set about cleaning the place up. I made sure he had a bath and put all his soiled bed clothes into the washing machine.

The following day, he apologised to me profusely and was mortally embarrassed. We both decided to laugh it off and in many respects, I was glad that his first brush with the demon drink had been under the surveillance of my friends who all really like

Scooter. If it had happened whilst living with his mum, it's likely she'd have thrown him out. She never understood teenagers and wasn't of a mind to understand them either. The problem with Scooter was the way he'd been brought up left him with no yardstick to use to measure his own behaviour. As his mother's emphasis had always been firmly on herself at the expense of those close to her, Scooter and Rosie had no one to go to who had any idea of how really to commune with their peers and those more senior in years. I couldn't perform that role as I was always the idiot. Both kids had been brought up to see me being trashed by their mother and put down in public for years and years. Of course they weren't going to listen to me. Scooter seemed to love me, but didn't take anything I had to say seriously. When he came to stay at the end of February 2007, even though I still loved him to bits, I knew I was in for a hard time.

The problems started almost immediately. Over the next few days, the telephone was ringing every night. Scooter would answer it and it would be HM. He would then retire to another room and speak in confidence to her. I was not supposed to know what was happening. I assumed that this was because HM didn't want me to find out just how much things were going wrong for her in case it turned me off her. As if I wasn't already!

Apparently Susanne had been turning up and asking for her house back. In reality, what had happened was she'd gone there – maybe twice at the most – and tried to tell HM that she had a buyer for the house.

HM claimed that on some days, Susanne would turn up unannounced and if she didn't get an answer to the doorbell, would tour the house and look through the windows. Meanwhile, HM would find somewhere to hide and wait until she was long gone before coming out. She would then go back to writing her books as if nothing was wrong, thinking that once she'd finished both novels that everything would come rushing in for her: money, quality disciple stock and plenty of work. This was when she haphazardly bonded botched endings onto both of them and triumphantly pressed the Save button, honestly believing they were works that rivalled JK Rowling; if a publisher had read them and turned them down, I've no doubt she'd have had me writing an outraged letter to ask how anyone dare turn down work that was divinely inspired. As it turned out, there was no time for such shenanigans.

As soon as Scooter arrived back in the UK, HM was insisting that he start school. I was worried about the wisdom of such a decision. He'd missed so many years of education it was hard to see how he would cope with the coursework. In order to appease HM, to get him into our local school, I contacted West Berkshire Council by letter and told them I was looking after a teenager who wasn't my own son. I actually went so far as to fib to them that Scooter was a nephew. They were not having it. Immediately, they alerted Social Services and a Social Worker was sent around within days to investigate Scooter's circumstances. I didn't have a problem with this as I was only too keen to make sure that everyone knew that as far as I was concerned, nothing untoward was going on. However, HM was upset and immediately put up her guard, claiming that she would give them hell if they took Scooter into care.

When the Social Worker arrived, he was on my side immediately. I realised that they knew all about HM and certainly had a file on her as long as your arm from all the dealings she'd had with them in the days when she'd had Rosie taken away. Inevitably there would have been note taken of the fact that she was calling herself by an odd name, that she had very pronounced religious-type views, that she was also argumentative and controlling and possibly even a psychopath. During the period when Rosie had been taken into care, HM had gone head to head with the whole lot of them, implying that she disapproved of their organisation and their methods.

During the interview I had with the Social Worker, he asked me some extremely searching questions about just what HM was doing and why it was that she found herself unable to look after her own son. Of course, HM's tactic of only telling me things about her life on a need-to-know basis was backfiring on her, as now, I was forced into giving them bits and pieces of information that could have caused Scooter to be taken into care for the last few months before his 16th birthday. I had to tell them that her life was not going well in Germany, that she was about to be made homeless and had no money at all. I'm sure the Social Worker didn't like the fact that Scooter didn't have a bedroom and disapproved of the fact that he had to sleep on my floor, but he refrained from comment and instead asked me to fill in a pile of forms including ones that would mean my life would be investigated through background checks. I didn't have a problem with that as I have nothing to hide, but it felt uncomfortable. During this whole period, there wasn't a single word of encouragement from HM or even an offer of any money to look after him. I wasn't expecting any to be honest, but just an offer would have been a pleasant gesture. Instead, all HM could say was that if it was suggested that I get some benefits to help look after Scooter, it was money that belonged to HER and she should be sent it all, immediately. I purposely undermined her by confirming to Social Services that I had no intention of taking money from the State to look after Scooter. This helped my case I believe, as they would then understand that my role in the affair was altruistic and all I was doing was looking after someone I cared about.

As the days passed, the phone calls to Scooter were getting even more bizarre. HM was now claiming that she'd been contacted by a Nigerian witch doctor who wanted her to travel to Nigeria so that they could "work together". She wrote me an email that basically told me it was her intention to do just that, provided she could get the money together for a flight. I knew what this was all about. Anyone who answers an unsolicited email from someone in Nigeria and honestly expects it to be bona fide is asking for trouble. To me this was a sign that HM had now totally lost it and had gone completely gaga. She was so desperate, she was jumping on every single opportunity offered to her, even ones coming from the dodgiest of sources. Clearly, her intuition that she always claimed was so acute as an enlightened being, was either failing her dismally or being roundly ignored.

I did eventually stick my neck out over that one and told her straight: it was the wrong thing to do and would end in disaster. For once, she listened to me and quietly dropped the idea. She did ignore my other sensible suggestion, however. I told her to come back to England. She snapped back that she had no such intention: England was evil and its people nasty and immoral.

Other phone calls at the time from Germany showed that the situation was rapidly getting out of control. Whilst HM was sitting there in her squat, dressed in her coat (claiming she was freezing cold[11]) and madly tapping away at her PC trying to knock out her blockbusters, Susanne was getting extremely worried about her house. She was beginning to wonder if she would ever get it back and had started to contact people to take advice.

The situation then became even weirder. HM admitted to me that she'd been contacted by someone else: an Italian man. This was someone she said she was going to get married to; he would be meeting her at Venice railway station. All she had to do was just turn up.

No one had told me about this; seemingly it was something that she'd been planning for some time and it turned out when I pressed Scooter for information that the reason why she'd sent him back to me was that she was planning on going around the world with this Italian gentleman, that once they married, he would have a house for her to live in and be buying her some nice clothes. She would then be able to start her "work" in Italy with the support of this man and want for nothing.

I was staggered and sick to the stomach. I'd thrown my whole life at this woman and entrusted her with the most precious part of me; now here she was, a gibbering wreck, squandering the energy that so many people had thrown at her over the years, racing her vehicle over a cliff and making out as she plummeted that she still had full control of it.

As the day of this "meeting" approached, she mentioned it more and more on the phone to Scooter. She would give me little hints that it was definitely something that she fully intended to do and that I would have to look after Scooter for some months until she'd returned from her world trip and was in a position to send for him. I just turned around to Scooter and said:

"Scooter, I love you very much, but this is *wrong*. I'm not playing this game. You're going back to Germany to be with your mum."

Scooter didn't want to go and he told me so. He kept an extremely civil tongue in his head and diplomatically tried to calm me down, whilst trying not to upset his mother. I'm not sure what happened, but I believe that one day whilst I was out at work, he

---

[11] …it later turned out that she can't have been cold as her heating bills – which someone else ended up paying – were absolutely through the roof…

phoned her and told her about my reservations. The next thing I knew, the day of the amazing synchronistic encounter with a husband whom she'd never even met, just *passed*. She didn't get on a train to Italy.

Instead, she went to Munich airport and sat in the departures lounge with the intention of sending love out to everyone who went through, believing that her vibration would go with them as they travelled the world to various destinations, spreading about like lovely glittering fairy dust...

In the biography that I'd written about HM some years earlier, I started the book by telling the reader about certain amazing synchronicities that had occurred when I first started meditation in 1987/88. In February 1988, I'd gone as part of my University year abroad, to live in Rome. I was supposed to return all cultured and fluent in Italian. The problem was, I'd gone there without having sorted accommodation and finding somewhere to live was a total nightmare.

One day, in desperation, I sat down to meditate to see if I could glean any information at all about where I could go to get help. I was amazed to get an immediate and very specific answer: go to Stazione Termini on Saturday morning at 10.30...

I was quite sceptical about this but didn't put it out of my mind completely. I carried on my fruitless search for a flat for another day and then, almost as a last resort, literally forced myself to obey the order I'd received whilst quietly locked up in my hotel room the previous Thursday.

Just as I was walking along the concourse at Termini Station that morning, I bumped into four or five girls who were all from the same university as me. They'd literally just arrived and were all setting off for a local hotel to stay the night in the city centre. They were then going to start their search for flats the following Monday and I was invited to join them. I looked down at my watch just as we left the station. It was 10.30. The following week, one of the girls and I found a flat and my problem was miraculously solved.

This is a true story that shows the benefits and true power of the mind, a power that comes through in meditation when you're prepared to accept that we're all connected to the greater Universal mind, or Source Field. I was so in awe of what had happened that it was some time before I had the nerve to meditate again!

To this day, I think that this was what HM was up to. She'd taken in what I'd said in her book and believed that if it worked for a spiritual low life like me, it would work spectacularly for her, hence her totally "random" plan to meet this fictitious husband at Venice Station and later, the haphazard decision to hang around at the airport waiting for a saviour.

But all such undertakings were destined to fail. The difference between my situation and hers was clear. I was where I was supposed to be at the right time of my life, not forcing my own destiny on anyone else, just getting on with my path. HM's own concourse experience failed because she was simply, after all those years, going against the grain, refusing to listen to her intuition, not meditating properly and forcing her own plans and desires on the Universe. Not only was it failing, it was dragging everyone down. The longer she spent lying to herself and to everyone around her, the worse the situation became.

One morning, just before I was about to set off for work at 7.30, the phone rang. It was HM claiming that Anna had arrived with Susanne and the Police. She said they'd forced their way in and Anna herself, "aggressive, rude and vicious", had manhandled HM out of the house and pushed her out into the street. HM had tried to get back in to get her bag and her most needed possessions, but Anna had supposedly barred her way. The Police, she claimed, had acted like the Gestapo and wouldn't hear a word that she was saying. In sheer horror at what was happening to her, HM ran down the street screaming and frantically found a payphone so she could contact Scooter. At some point, her money ran out and Scooter just stood there in my flat, shaking his head in shock, totally at a loss.

The phone rang again; it was Anna wanting to speak to Scooter. I couldn't hear what she was saying, but I knew she was at the end of her tether and totally fed up. She told Scooter quite firmly that HM was now evicted from Susanne's house and that she would not be allowed back in. The locks were being changed. All HM's belongings would be put into store at Anna's expense, for one month and HM would have to sort herself out: either go back to

England and have the furniture sent to her or forfeit it all completely after the month was up. If no decision had been made after that time, the whole lot would go to charity. Anna then finished the call.

HM was now totally high and dry.

Over the years, I've been told that what really happened on that morning was different to the version given by HM. This is how Anna herself explained events:

'One morning, out of the blue, Susanne got a phone call from a Police Station. They said that her tenant was sitting there claiming that she, Susanne, wanted to throw her out. Susanne was so astonished, she said: "this lady isn't my tenant – she's a guest in my house."

Susanne, now really concerned, called Anna whom she'd not talked to for some weeks.

"Anna," she said, "I've just had a call from the Police. Apparently HM is there claiming to be my tenant. I'm sorry, but enough is enough. As you've introduced me to her and I don't speak English, I have to ask you to come along to clear the situation up. I'll change the lock on the front door if that's what I have to do to get my property back. I hope we'll be able to find another solution. I'll pick you up in ten minutes."

'With our stomachs tied in knots,' Anna says, 'we drove to the house. When we got there, all the curtains were drawn and there was no answer when we rang the doorbell. Susanne took her spare key out and tried to open the front door which turned out to be barred by boxes. We called out to HM to say it was us and asked her to open the door.

'At that point, we saw HM rush to the phone and heard her call the Police saying "please come quick to this address, somebody is trying to break into my house". Then she hung up, grabbed her bag and her gloves and came storming out of the door, pushing me aside, calling me "the devil and evil."

'Susanne had had enough. She quickly went round to a neighbour to get help and a witness and they both set about changing the front door lock.

'Meanwhile the phone rang and I answered it. It was Scooter claiming that I had no right to be there, that he and his mother had legal council and so on.

"Susanne has changed the lock," I said. "It's over."

'Scooter's answer was initially to say that if he'd been there, he would have changed the lock himself to prevent anyone getting in.

'I was so disgusted that I hung up the phone. It rang again. This time, Scooter tried to be more loving and begged me for compassion. I hung up, otherwise I'd have screamed.

'About ten minutes later HM came back with two Policemen. She stood at the bottom of the stairs; the Policemen were standing together in one part of the room and Susanne and I were in the corner: a perfect triangle. One of the Policemen asked what the matter was and Susanne explained as I translated for HM. When they heard that HM was a guest and not a tenant and that she'd never had to pay any rent, only phone and electric, they said:

"We're sorry madam, but this is a private matter. We have no business here, we cannot help. If you cannot show us a lease or any paper that allows you to live here, then we have no right to interfere. We may only intervene if there's a legal basis."

'Everyone was polite and calm. HM walked upstairs, took a bag with a few things and was escorted outside. But what took me aback was this: when HM faced the Police, her energy radiated love, compassion, understanding – even divinity. It was pure Light – everything I'd loved about her in the beginning and still loved about her. But as soon as she turned towards me and Susanne, this same energy changed into hate, anger, darkness and pure negativity, even though her face stayed the same.

'I was so astonished and wondered how these two things could come so close together. Later on I understood that it's a choice we make all the time, either this or that direction. I'd just never seen it so clearly before.'

HM was escorted out by the Police and the door closed on her. She ran down the street to the phone box to call the UK.

Meanwhile, back in the house, Susanne and Anna sat down and cried. Both of them were dazed and also saddened by this outcome of events. They felt guilty and wished it had all turned out differently.

When Susanne saw the state of her house she was disappointed. Astonishingly – according to Anna – she was never angry. She just didn't understand how a "divine" being could run a house down like that. In her eyes such a person should know that all things are "one"; therefore material things should be cared for as well, as in effect, they too are an expression of the Creator.

Everything was worn out and in a bad condition. Both Anna and Susanne had to work a whole day just to clean the place. The gas and electricity as well as the phone bills hadn't been paid for some time and were in arrears by over 1500 euros. Susanne was lucky that she had HM sign contracts for these services, otherwise she'd have had to pay them as well, on top of the expense of the repairs to her house.

After HM had left, their only point of contact was Scooter and they were unsure what to do with the things that had been left behind. They wanted to send everything to England, but there were no offers of help forthcoming to cover the cost. I'd have paid myself, but Scooter spoke to his mother and they both agreed that they would only need certain essential items such as the PC with the blockbusters on it and certain clothes.

In the end, Susanne took a few items of furniture to give to another tenant and gave Anna 200 euros to post the most essential items back to the UK. Anna herself went through everything and tried to remember what HM liked most. She says:

"I cried over and over again because I felt bad and didn't understand why it had all ended the way it had."

I had to go to work the morning of the eviction, so I set off at about 8:45 and arrived extremely late. When I got in, I phoned Scooter for an update and discovered that HM had just enough money to get herself into a youth hostel for the night. I asked Scooter if she was now considering coming back to the UK as this was clearly the end of the line for the Germany idea. However, even then, even when the Universe was positively screaming at HM to let go of her deluded plans for a Mother Meera-style life with a castle and adoring devotees, there was *still* no turning her around.

HM spent the night at the youth hostel. All I know is that she found it a very trying experience and didn't get much sleep. The following day, I'm not sure what she did, but she phoned Scooter in the morning to say that a man had felt sorry for her and was taking her in for one night to stay with him and his family so that she would have a bit of time to sort herself out.

It was on that day that help arrived totally out of the blue. In fact, an extraordinary scenario was shaping up. At some point in the morning, Scooter rang me at work to say that a lady (who we shall call Mrs Aleph) had phoned my number from Wales to speak to the Holy Mother. Scooter had explained to Mrs Aleph that his mother was in a bit of a scrape over in Germany, homeless and stranded. Mrs Aleph, quite a formidable woman as I was to find out later, sprang into action immediately. She told Scooter to get his mother to come back to the UK. She had a large house and plenty of room. From there, she would sort her out and help her to get somewhere to live and even offer her a chance to give some spiritual talks to people so that she would have some work coming in.

This seemed like the ideal solution. Scooter waited for his mother to call and told her excitedly that a solution had presented itself straight out of the jaws of disaster. When Scooter told me that he'd explained this to his mother, he seemed to deliver the news to me in a surprisingly deadpan way, as if all the relief that this new scenario could have brought him had somehow been sucked away. I knew who was responsible. After all that had happened, HM was clearly still clinging onto the notion that she had to stay on the continent to become some kind of international messiah and even though a fantastic solution had presented itself for her homelessness, was *still* resisting, *still* dead to the world and to the messages that were coming to her - and extremely positive ones at that. I believe Scooter may have had to apply some pressure on her to do as she was told. He was still desperately worried about her.

With all the enthusiasm of a dead fish for this wonderful and kind opportunity that was being offered to her, HM deigned to agree to come back to the UK. Mrs Aleph's husband would meet her at London's Victoria Coach Station and help her across the city. They would then take a train to Wales where she would be able to stay, not indefinitely, but certainly until she got herself sorted.

I remember saying to Scooter that he should suggest something very subtly to his mother. I told him to tell her not to treat Mrs Aleph and her family like dirt. Both Scooter and I knew that this situation was still extremely precarious and could still go wrong at any moment.

HM stayed the night with the kind gentleman who had taken her in. The following day, she set off back to the UK and left her calamitous German experience behind forever.

Chapter Twenty-One

Things went a little quiet for two days and then Scooter and I received a phone call from Wales. HM had arrived and was settling in.

There was very little news at first and for another couple of days at least, it was peaceful. Every time HM phoned Scooter, I would quickly tell him before he picked up the phone to remind his mum to try and tone down her obtuse nature whilst she was a guest in Mrs Aleph's home and to try not to abuse the opportunity she was being offered. Scooter would roll his eyes and say: "I'll try. But you know she never listens to a word I say."

The stay at Mrs Aleph's was another unmitigated disaster. HM had had no intention at all of regulating her manner to accommodate the needs and individuality of another party. Once again, it was all about her. Within days, *of course*, there were ructions.

The first I heard was that HM had phoned Scooter during the day to say that Mrs Aleph was a bitch. She'd called her a religious zealot and a fanatic and was not enjoying being talked down to by her.

Mrs Aleph was very committed to her religion and in particular the spiritual organisation she was a member of that was based in London. HM's own fanatical quasi religious views clashed immediately with Mrs Aleph's. Knowing both of them as I do, it was unlikely that a state of compromise could be reached and I had this image of them all sitting around the table in the evening having supper and growling at one other whilst trying to maintain a veneer of civility. Neither would ever back down and both were unquestionably right. One of HM's big preoccupations was that she was constantly being pulled up by her guides for not asserting herself strongly enough. She seemed to be under the impression that she could be some kind of mouse with no confidence. That was never my observation of her, to be honest. If anything, because of this celestial "expectation" on her to be more outspoken in getting her views across, she tended to stretch the bounds of social acceptability way beyond their elastic limit. When faced with someone like Mrs Aleph, who is also always correct, the most fearsome uproar can ensue.

Hats off to her, Mrs Aleph was keen to help HM, despite her dwindling opinion of her. She took her out in her car at her own expense and accompanied her while she viewed empty properties for rent in the genuine hope of seeing her and Scooter properly housed. But seemingly, HM came up with excuse after excuse as to why each and every house was no good and completely unfit for purpose. Very quickly, Mrs Aleph came to the conclusion that there was some other plan afoot, something that HM had in mind that prevented her from wanting to settle down. Mrs Aleph concluded that it was because HM wanted to stay with her and live off her like some kind of leech. She assumed that HM saw herself as "home to roost" and was simply enjoying a free ride.

I saw it differently. I felt that HM was prevaricating and procrastinating because she still wanted to go back out to the continent and settle down with some Italian who would stomp up the cash for her to do her holy thing. All she was doing was stalling for time. When she told Mrs Aleph that there was an entity under the floor of the house that was so evil it would take six months at least for her to dissipate, Mrs Aleph was extremely suspicious. Intuitively she knew that HM was fibbing and became all the keener to move her on.

Because of the stress on her family, Mrs Aleph had no choice but to start putting her foot down. The family itself was large and the children were all ages from teenagers attending university to toddlers. Mrs Aleph was also expecting a baby. As HM was sleeping in her teenage daughter's bedroom, there were problems there too. The daughter wanted her room back and all this delay was causing her to lose patience.

At some point, according to Mrs Aleph, HM's behaviour worsened. She started to sidle up to the older daughter as if trying to win her over in some kind of power play. Apparently she'd also tried the same trick on the eldest son. I'm not sure about the veracity of that however, as by the time I'd met Mrs Aleph (who insisted on recounting to me the events in minute detail) she was so utterly disgusted by HM it was hard to see if she had even the most rational view of her. After a couple of weeks of having her in her home, Mrs Aleph's dislike of HM became a kind of obsession in itself. Later on, I would see similarities in both their characters and laugh because Mrs Aleph was always spiritual enough to admit that if you have character flaws that need to be ironed out, the Universe arranges things in such a way that you often come face to face with someone else who has identical traits. Your disgust for them is a message to iron out the rough spots in your own personality. It was interesting that Mrs Aleph could see that. HM couldn't.

After a fortnight, Mrs Aleph had had enough and gave HM an ultimatum: *get out of my house!*

Admittedly, she gave her a week to sort herself out and was prepared to grit her teeth for the last few days and ignore her attitude. HM took this extremely badly and phoned Scooter who said, and I quote: "Mum, just ignore it! Do your own thing."

As usual, HM wasn't listening and heard: "Mum, just ignore her."

And that's exactly what she did. For the next week, HM refused to speak to Mrs Aleph at all and communicated through one or two of the kids. Relations broke down irretrievably.

After a few days, HM, forgetting that she was supposed to be moving on an evil entity beneath the floorboards, packed her bags and fled to a refuge for women escaping from abusive relationships. Although space was limited in this refuge, HM got a place because she made a claim that she was being emotionally abused by Mrs Aleph and all the Alephs. She didn't tell Mrs Aleph where she was going. She just upped and left. When Mrs Aleph found out that she was being accused of emotional abuse that was so bad her victim had taken herself to a refuge, she was absolutely flabbergasted. By that time, her dislike and mistrust of HM were almost unfathomable.

One day, I spoke to Mrs Aleph myself. HM had told me to send her my novel *Red*, the one that I'd just finished a few days before I met her in 1997. What had happened was HM had discovered that Mrs Aleph had contacts in the world of publishing. HM had read *Red* and although she'd always made out to my face that my novels needed *"a little something extra but, I don't know what...."* she wasn't averse to bringing them up when there was an outside chance of cash to be made. So for once, she put her neck on the line and suggested that Mrs Aleph read *Red* and see what she thought. In her phone call to me, HM told me that if Mrs Aleph had managed to place *Red* with a publisher, I could pay her back for her role in such an outcome by buying her a big house with the royalties.

Mrs Aleph and I made contact. It was decided that I meet her in London and we would talk over the possibilities. Even though I found Mrs Aleph to be extremely brusque to the point of rudeness, I agreed.

Leaving Scooter at home, I travelled up to London to meet the great Mrs Aleph in person. At first we were going to meet in Green Park. When I got there, I phoned her and she was shirty with me, telling me to wait until she'd fed her kids at her cult's HQ. So I hung around for an hour and a half in the park, twiddling my thumbs.

Eventually, she phoned and suggested we meet up in Starbucks on Oxford Street. Already fed up, I made my way there and found her downstairs, surrounded by bright and bubbly children. When she held out her hand to me in greeting, she didn't look me in the eye. There was an offhand way about her that I'm sure she never intended to come across as rudeness. But that was exactly how it registered. For a few moments, I began to worry that HM had really fled to a refuge for good reason.

Then her husband arrived. Not only did he not look at me, he could barely even bring himself to speak. When she introduced him to me all he said was: "so where's the other one then?" A reference, I should imagine, to Scooter.

Immediately, it was clear what they were after. Mrs Aleph wasn't interested in the novel. All she wanted to do was spend literally an hour and a half giving me horror stories about the woman she also referred to as HM. I wanted to talk about the book but she wasn't of a mind to discuss it for any longer than thirty seconds. I knew I was wasting my time.

I told Mrs Aleph that what she'd done for HM was an exceptionally kind gesture and apologised to her for putting herself out only to be given a right royal slap in the face. In return she was kind to me by saying that I was much nicer than she'd expected me to be given that the view she had of me from the words of HM

210

was extremely negative. I thought: *"oh great! HM never lets up, does she. She's even prepared to tell a total stranger what an idiot I am."*

It even turned out in the course of the conversation that HM had told the entire family that I was planning on stealing something from her. I immediately worked out what that was. HM still thought I would be getting benefits from the state for looking after Scooter. As she'd made it clear that all that money would have to go to her, she was *still* worried that I would put it in my bank account and she wouldn't see a penny of it. I was absolutely furious. My first thought was, *"hold on. I've been showing unconditional love for your son by harbouring him for three months at my expense. I don't have any money of my own but I'm not asking for any compensation for my efforts. And still you're going around accusing me of theft!"*

I hate to say it but surrounded as I was by crowds of people in that coffee shop, all that noise and bustle and madness, I sat there for a few seconds and made a little decision. When I got back to home, I would tell Scooter I loved him very much, but the time had come for him to go back to his mother. I just wasn't having this any more. I'd never felt so utterly betrayed in all my life.

Unfortunately, Scooter had also blotted his copybook as well. Part of our agreement was that once a week he would help me with some housework. All I expected him to do was vacuum the sitting room and hall and to clean the bathroom. I would do everything else. I also asked him if he would keep the place tidy and be prepared to wash up his dirty dishes during the day when I was at work.

When he then started telling my friends that I was a fussy old man who *forced* him to do housework they looked at him somewhat askance. This was really not what I wanted to hear. I still really cared for the chap, but I was shocked by such a display of duplicity. I thought: *"I see. Like mother, like son..."* When the time came for me to tell him to go back to his mother, I hate to admit it, I couldn't wait till he was gone.

That sounds nasty, doesn't it. Poor old Scooter. He was having a terrible time of it and had no one to turn to. All he was doing was just being a lazy, bolshy teenager and I should have understood that and been prepared to overlook it. Please believe me when I say my frustrations originated not with lovable yob Scooter, but his mother.

211

When I got home from London, I made sure Scooter was full of pizza and then told him it was time to hop it. I was nice about it and diplomatic. But I also had a plan of my own. If his mother was going to prevaricate any longer and hold out for some fantasy Italian middle-aged hunk to sweep her off her feet, then I wasn't going to wait around for it simply *not* to happen. This was about *me*. As far as I was concerned, the time had come for her to sort herself out and get real. That meant looking after her son as a proper mother is supposed to do, to provide a stable roof over his head and to give him the life he deserved. If I had to be cruel to the lovable yob to make that happen, then so be it.

Poor Scooter became extremely uncomfortable. To be fair, he wasn't wasting his time during the day. He got books on HTML and Java programming from the village library and was using my PC to teach himself. Hats off to him: when Scooter applies his mind to something, he gets results and he was learning fast. But in my mind, things had reached breaking point. It was time for him to start living a real life, to go to college and get an education. It was up to his mother to provide the basis for that, not just me. I decided to be cruel to be kind and began to close down to him emotionally in the hope he would phone HM and shout: "GET ME AWAY FROM THIS OLD GRUMP!"

And that was exactly what happened. When he left at the end of May 2007, he couldn't wait to see the back of me, bless him.

Don't worry. I hadn't ruined relations completely with him. He phoned me when he got to the refuge and we were back on track immediately. He also started showing some gratitude to me which felt good!

Now that HM had her son back with her, she finally decided the time had come to get her act together. She knew that I had Social Services on my back watching her every move and there was even talk of Scooter being taken into care. This may sound terrible, but I don't think she was prepared to countenance that, as she was hoping that with a son at home, she would get single mother benefits. Her rent would be paid and she would be able to draw income support. So having Scooter around certainly had its advantages. It also got Social Services off her back.

By way of an aside, the Social Worker who had newly been assigned to Scooter's case came round one afternoon when he was still with me to interview both me and him together. I was ready for her as, simply put, I had nothing to hide and was just doing something altruistic by looking after a homeless young person. When she asked me questions, I replied with confidence as I was sure of myself and my role in the proceedings. When she turned to Scooter, she asked him to describe himself and say what he thought were some of his strong points. I was horrified to the bone to see Scooter struggle with this. He had no answers at all. She sat there and looked at him for the best part of a minute and in that time all Scooter could do was "um and ah" and stare at the floor. If ever there was proof of the complete and total failure of Scooter's mother to help Scooter find the self-image he truly merited, it was there to see that day. Scooter was a confident chap but still found relatively little about himself that was genuinely worthy of note. His sister too, was also struggling on this front. Occasionally, she would phone me up and ask me if she was really the badly behaved and terrible kid she believed she was for having a mother who was forced to put her into care.

Given the amount of time I spent with them, I've often wondered if I'd have been able to prevent this effect in Scooter and Rosie and helped them to find a more positive self-image. Scooter says he has some good memories of me from his childhood and thinks it really doesn't matter in the grand scheme. I felt grateful about that for some time until one day he blurted out:

"Though, you could be a bit of a jerk sometimes, mate!"

Chapter Twenty-Two

Shortly after Scooter had fled from the grump, HM began to get her act together and found a house. As it turned out, it was one that she and Mrs Aleph had been to view and was in a pleasant country town.

Over the weeks, Anna had been sending across suitcases and boxes full of some of the more essential items that HM still needed from her furniture stash in Germany. None of us had any spare cash and to go over and get the rest of the items was out of the question. So Anna ended up having to do what she'd suggested from the outset: give it all to charity.

HM had lost everything. She'd moved over to Germany lock, stock and barrel and had returned in ignominy with her hands and her life empty. Anna had tried to put what she thought were essential items into the shipment but as relations between her and HM were now non-existent, she could only guess at what items were really of any value. After the last box came from Germany, it was a long, long time before I heard from Anna again. I often used to think about her and hope that she was all right. I still wasn't sure of what had happened and why she'd seemingly turned away from HM, but I knew that one day, when the time was right, I would find out the truth. HM's view of her was that she was utterly, unspeakably evil. So much so that she even accused her of taking her "Holy Mother energy" to cause the Boxing Day Tsunami.

One day, HM called me to say that she'd had a vision of Anna drowning in a whirlpool of sewage. I came to the conclusion that in fact she'd actually wished that on her. But Anna is a genuinely spiritual person and she's strong enough not to collapse in a heap from this sort of pressure. When I told her what HM had been saying, we both laughed and she simply said:

"I could feel her negative energy with me for a long time, but with the help of friends this went away. Bless them because without them, I wouldn't have made it."

The week following the summer floods of July 2007, my dad and I packed all of the boxes and suitcases into his car and took them over to the new house. I'd asked HM to make herself scarce that day, telling her I wasn't sure how well she would get on with my dad. The real reason for my making this request was in fact because I didn't want to see her. My confidence in her was now shattered and the thought of supporting her again by having to do the bowing namaste thing to her filled me with dread. I was just NOT prepared to put the stamp of approval on her atrocious behaviour by going along with the Holy Mother charade in front of my father who's a confirmed non-believer in this sort of spirituality. On certain occasions over the years, if I'd gone to my parents' house for the weekend, HM had made a point of phoning the house to speak to me. Invariably, she would get through to my dad and say – with emphasis:

"Can I speak to Paul, please. It's Hooooly Mother!'

I think a part of her believed that that would impress my dad as he's a retired army officer with a background in "rank" and all that that entails. Of course, such a shallow attempt at promoting herself was bound to fail. On one occasion, he handed the phone to me with her on the end and knowing full well who it was, said:

"It's someone calling herself *Hooooly Mother…*"

Rolling his eyes in disgust, he'd walked from the room. To a certain extent, this may also have been HM trying to mock the middle classes by putting the cat amongst the pigeons as Gary used to do. She was fully aware of how ordinary non-spiritual folk react to someone like her and she seemed to revel in the confusion that it causes.

I still feel sickened by that. Part of the purpose of me writing this book is to undo the damage that's been done by this loose cannon going around giving itself titles and airs and graces in the name of "God". For years I supported this archaic project and far from promoting modern-day spirituality and showing people what great good can be achieved from the spiritual approach, all it's done is confuse people skirting around the edges in need of a helping hand onto the first step. I can think of quite a few people who saw (through me and from a distance) what she was up to and who later turned out to be so disappointed by what they witnessed that they turned their backs on it all.

So HM made herself scarce that day. Fair's fair, when I arrived, Scooter had £100 for me from her which was money for something I'd done for her (I can't remember what) that she'd always said she'd pay back. I think that gave a slight feeling of relief to my father as he could see from the face of it that I wasn't being totally taken for a ride. In reality, I *had* been taken for a ride, but not in the way he and everyone else thought. I also avoided telling him a couple of weeks later that she'd asked for it all back again.

As the months passed, HM and Scooter settled down in their new house. Once again, there was no bedroom for Scooter. This was strange because the house had two bedrooms, but HM insisted on having the second bedroom as her workroom. Not for the first time, poor old Scooter (now over six foot in height) had to bunk down in the living room and had no space of his own. Every time HM wanted a cup of tea, she would walk through the sitting room to get to the kitchen. Scooter was to spend the next two years with no privacy at all. It didn't seem to bother him; he'd certainly had worse.

As for the work room, I heard it was never used to welcome people in. HM used it herself as a study and as far as I know, sat in there and typed out books and leaflets and all sorts of words and paragraphs for her websites, none of which were ever spiritually energised to attract anyone. She rewrote the biography that I'd spent so long on and in doing so, attempted to make the story lighter and funnier. Clearly she'd tried to take on board what Anna had told her about a cloud of negativity collecting above her head. Once again, as with the novels, she started off great guns but then soon slipped back into type, accusing everyone of being evil and betraying her. Anna was given a role as someone who resembled *Mrs Tweedy*, the evil farmer's wife in *Chicken Run* whose pie-making machine is such a source of terror to those poor chickens. Clearly, the loose cannon was still trundling out of control down the hill. Luckily, this time, most of the people who could have been run over, were just nowhere to be seen. The Germany debacle had cut everything off. As far as I could see, the Holy Mother thing was dead in the water. Only HM was keeping the dream alive, despite how jaded it looked.

Whenever I spoke to her in those days, I felt nothing from her. I supported her because I felt sorry for her and wanted to keep in touch with Scooter. A time was coming however, when such an approach would turn out to be simply hypocritical.

I was ready for a sea change, in every single respect.

Chapter Twenty-Three

The rest of 2007 just leaked away. Hats off to Scooter, with no support whatsoever from his mother, he got himself into a local college of higher education and started a course that was to help him towards his goal of gaining a qualification in a field that had become of great interest to him.

It would be best if I left Scooter's part in this story just there as he now needs his privacy and must at all costs be allowed to live his life the way he wants to, without interference. After such a disastrous childhood, it's the very least I would want for him. Suffice it to say, he is now, in every respect, a normal young person with the same outlook as many kids his age. For Scooter these days, it's all about cigarettes, drunken nights out and girls, girls, girls. He has more notches on his bedpost than many of his peers, certainly many more than me at his age!

Even though the evidence was all around showing Scooter's initiation into the real world, HM still would not let go of her plans for his divinity. He often returned home drunk as a skunk with a cigarette in his mouth having just "railed some chick" and there she would be, still desperately clinging to her plans for his ultimate canonisation as a living saint.

As autumn became winter, I did a few half-hearted jobs for HM, including setting up a website for her, but the energy had all gone for me and she knew it. She was still taking money off me, but not so much and for the first time, I began to have enough cash at the end of the month to allow me to call in a plumber if I needed one and not have to get on my knees and beg friends to help me with any DIY jobs that needed doing.

In the second week of January 2008 on a Saturday morning, I got a call from Percy. As you may remember, when Percy jumped on board the HM ship, he was immediately whisked away from me in case the two of us ever got together and posed a danger to HM. So the moment Percy announced himself that morning on the phone, it was a few seconds before I could remember who he was. When the penny dropped, I suddenly felt an inrush of relief and sheer joy to hear his voice. I had always dreaded that Percy would be one of the ones, like me, who'd been chewed up and spat out and left for dead by the side of the road. But then, another part of me had always known that there was something different about him.

We had a long chat and just picked up where we'd left off that day he'd phoned me nearly two years earlier. At the time, I was very wary of everyone and was careful what I told Percy about HM, just keeping it to the basic facts about the rest of HM's time in Germany, her experiences with Mrs Aleph and her position as it was then. In his turn, Percy said nothing and gave me no clues as to his own view of HM. Instead, he told me quite dryly that he'd left the HM scene a year or so earlier to set out on his own and explore the tree of life. I had no idea what that was at the time and didn't ask him to elaborate. As we came to the end of that conversation, we both agreed that it would be an excellent idea to keep in touch and I promised to phone him once a week on a Sunday morning so that we could touch base and compare notes.

By this time, I'd been living in the village for four years and had settled down well. It had been a bit of a rough ride at first. When I moved in, my head was in a very strange place and believe me, everyone knew it. At Christmas 2003, a few weeks after I'd moved into my flat, I started going to a local pub where I was introduced to a lot of people. This pub was a really happening place in terms of the local community. I'm not being flippant when I say that it performs an actual service; it's a focal point for so many people and there are groups of friends there who are like a family to each other. Of course, it isn't all plain sailing as, like with any local watering hole, there are characters who rub each other up the wrong way and little historical issues that range from relationship infidelities to dislike between individuals over local emergencies like shot cats, boundary disputes or just plain football rivalry. All that aside, everyone knows everyone else and their business and there's a proper community identity down there. Certainly in the days before the smoking ban and economic pressures began to hit the pub trade hard, there were times when the pub would be full to the brim on a Friday night and we would drink until late, put some music on and all sing along. Songs like *The Monkees' Daydream Believer* and *Gary Puckett and the Union Gap, Young Girl* were pub favourites and it's a great feeling sitting there on a winter's night with the fire blazing and with everyone smiling and laughing and singing along, all enmities forgotten and all the folks together. You don't get that much any more these days and I absolutely relished it after all those years of alienation and madness.

Newcomers aren't always welcomed immediately into this sort of world. I'm not saying that from a negative point of view. In any community, there's always a requirement for people to sound you out before they sense they can trust you and fully invite you in. This is a natural part of the order of things in the world of the English country village and not, as some people would have it, a kind of xenophobia or intolerance.

It was a little while before I was accepted. I made it worse for myself by not being very socially adept. I'd been out of a social scene for so long and had forgotten how to talk to people. In my world, HM did all the talking and I shut up. As most of her conversation was about her and reflected her extremely misanthropic view of the world, I'd lost all sense of proportion. I wasn't grounded either and would just stand there and talk crap whilst everyone fell about with laughter that wasn't necessarily because I was being funny.

I think people thought I was just a little odd. That didn't mean they disliked me, but it certainly took them time to learn to cope with my slightly weird ways, my intermittent vegetarianism, the way I used to howl obscenities in my sleep, my almost child-like humour and my complete and utter inability to run with the pack.

Because I had a bit of a reputation for being similar to the *Viz* character *Roger Irrelevant* (who's totally hat stand...), I began to notice one or two heads shaking. That felt strange. I thought: *oh my God, I'm an idiot.*

I had a long think about it and weighed up all my interpersonal relationships. At some point I began to wonder where this village fool had emerged from and came to the conclusion that it was because I'd stopped observing others. Not only that, I'd lost sight of what makes others tick and was out-of-step with the whole of the rest of civilisation. I'd neglected everyone for so long and felt it was time to find out what other humans felt and actually did.

220

So I mucked in with the crowd. Once people started to get used to me and realised that I was just an idiot and not dangerous, I found myself mixing with a really excellent crowd. There were so many characters around me, all of whom had something special about them that I loved: open-mindedness, acerbic humour, acid harmless criticism, generosity of spirit, boundless enthusiasm for sport, fishing, animals, ephemeral fads and late night howling karaoke sessions. I began to feel human again and realised, at long last, I was ALIVE! I think that really happened one summer when I started to see how many friends I'd made.

It wasn't all plain sailing, though. One day, a friend of mine in the village started insisting suddenly that he was going to challenge me at table football. This was someone who refused to allow you to invite him round for coffee in case you hadn't de-scaled your kettle and there were flakes of limescale in the water. Certain things had to be so precise for him; sometimes I was worried about putting a foot wrong. Despite his bizarre eccentricities, he could be excellent company.

One afternoon he rang excitedly to say he'd bought the table and wanted me to come round so he could trounce me. Nervously, I made my way round to his house and after a couple of drinks we got down to some serious competition. Unfortunately, I was just a little overzealous and bent the bar with my defenders on it. The game came to a grinding halt and my mate stood there staring wordlessly at the damage. He didn't say anything, but suddenly it was as if he'd divorced that football table! He shoved it in his garage and never looked at it again. I was so embarrassed. Luckily, I was forgiven pretty quickly as he was a good-hearted guy!

I began to realise that despite the incredible brave face that humanity puts on, we all suffer, we all make fools of ourselves. Being human was about hilarity, but also about trauma, isolation, loneliness, loss, depression, frustration and anger. I wasn't the only one who felt these things. It wasn't just me who'd been to hell and back and lived to tell the tale. I felt selfish but at the same time glad to have been shown that selfishness. I soon made up my mind that it wasn't helpful to make my life all about ME, ME, Me.[12]

A time came when I found I was part of the furniture. Admittedly, I was still known for my bizarre outbursts, eccentricities and general foolishness, but such character traits became accepted as unique to me and tolerated – even playfully mocked. It was great to feel normal at last.

It's amazing how people start to warm to you if you're prepared to make that mind flip and get onto their wavelength. Even if they never try to get onto yours, it doesn't matter. The joy you bring them will be returned to you time and time again. That's a lesson I learned for myself and not from some *Me-First, bow ye down, legend-in-their-own-dinnertime* guru or anyone going around telling me that their path and their path alone is the only one that leads to self-realisation and to higher consciousness.

---

[12] When she set out to help me edit this book, Anna had this to say about me when she read this paragraph. I think it provides a very helpful alternative angle: "Dear Paul, it would be very healthy for you to say "me, me, me," once in a while. Me, I am great; me I am joyful; me I am happy, me I am worthy. I have the feeling that you still believe that spirituality is the straight line of saying "yes" to everyone else and "no" to yourself. The path can be manyfold. For some, it's important to stand back and not do "me, me, me, I, I, I all the time – like HM; Ronja and some other Gurus. For others like you and me – who easily forget themselves completely when it comes to being there for people, to helping them, it's good and healthy to have the ME sometimes. I love myself and that is why I say NO to your behaviour, your attitudes and helping you. It depends on the path someone has chosen – spirituality can be many things. By adhering to the old belief system that spirituality is meditation, eating the right things, thinking only positive thoughts, watching only suitable films, only listening to suitable music etc. etc, spirituality becomes a dead thing. Nothing else but religious restrictions – unhealthy and breaking. Spirituality is full of life because it's alive with everything there is. With all the millions of decisions we take daily, there must be this question: "What feels right for the soul to grow?" Sometimes we do have to set boundaries certainly, otherwise people like HM can destroy you."

Chapter Twenty-Four

Just as I was beginning to feel more at home in my new surroundings, I began to feel really ill. It started in August 2005: my heart began to skip beats. It would stop for about five seconds and then kick back in with an almighty thud followed by what seemed like ten beats packed into three seconds. This weird rhythm would leave me feeling dizzy and for a few moments quite disorientated. I would recover pretty quickly and get on with my day, forgetting what had happened until the next time. At about three in the afternoon, I would get so tired I could barely stand up and then the breathlessness would start.

By the beginning of September, I could barely put one foot in front of the other and was nodding off at my desk in the afternoon. A point came where I couldn't even do any manual work without having to sit down every five minutes. One day, I passed out for a few crucial seconds at the wheel of the Renault on the way to see my parents and came to, to find myself travelling the wrong way around a roundabout just outside Newbury. Luckily there was only one car coming in my direction and I think the occupants could see that there was something wrong with me. They slowed down and stared at me aghast. I drove up the road for a few seconds and came to rest in a pub car park to get my breath back. I don't know how I made it home.

In the end I had no choice but to go and see the doctor and have a blood test. Within days I was diagnosed with hyperthyroidism and ordered to take carbimazole. I phoned HM straight away (she was still in Germany at the time) and she told me to keep well away from any poisonous conventional medicine and go and see a local naturopath to get some natural remedies.

On the face of it, this seemed like a good idea; the practitioner I went to see was brilliant. He was just a very natural physician with lots of empathy and a genuine keen interest in me and my condition. As I was paying him, he was prepared to spend a lot of time with me and his medication (which was based around bugleweed if I remember correctly) made me feel better within myself. But I was still very ill, even after three months of treatment.

To make matters worse, my manager at work was struggling to understand what was happening and was finding it hard to show sympathy. As soon as he heard I was ill, he took it badly. We'd both really been getting on well up to that point and I particularly liked the fact that he pushed me and was interested in seeing me get on and make a proper career for myself. But around that time, he'd been given a new job role that was causing him a lot of stress and extra work. He wanted me to be able to hold my own in the team and not capitulate to my own stress. But this was just not happening. To him, suddenly, it looked as though I'd turned into a hypochondriac.

The strain of this situation made me extremely emotional. One thing one notices about sufferers of this illness is that they become highly strung. I often used to start blubbing when no one else was around or fly off the handle if something wasn't going to plan. You ladies will know exactly where I'm coming from with this! I became tetchy in my working environment and made my predicament even worse by not inspiring any sympathy whatsoever in my plight because of my occasional uncontrollable outbursts. Gradually, I began to fall out with people. No one could put themselves in my place because, on the surface, I looked perfectly normal. So when I was hyper and at times banging on like an idiot, then quiet and sullen, people just assumed it was selfishness, pure and simple. That was how it was also seen by my manager who, I feel, could have done just a little research into the condition and made a slightly greater effort to find out what one of his team was going through. Even though things did get much better over time, I blotted my copybook with so many people that my career never recovered from this period and any chance I may have had of getting on seemed to have gone forever.

HM showed interest in what was happening to me by fixing one of her own remedies. This she used to do for everyone by filling a medicine bottle with mineral water. If you were there in her house, she would take the bottle into her kitchen, shut the door and do something to it in private. She would then emerge and give you the bottle, telling you to take a spoonful night and morning and to keep it in the fridge. If you weren't around, she would ask you to phone her whilst holding a small bottle of mineral water and then she'd go into meditation for a few seconds.

She did this for me many times over the years and I have to say, I can't remember a single time when it worked. She always told me that it was a homeopathic remedy that she could bring into being by simply asking "God" to turn the water into the particular remedy required. When they didn't work, she would always, without fail, tell me that it was because I was refusing to change and blocking the good effects of the medicine. More often than not, she would use the illness as an excuse to pitch in, claiming that I was the cause of all her suffering and that this was payback.

Did the remedy work for my hyperthyroid? Of course not. One load we made up over the phone (she was in Munich by that time) was supposed to mimic the effects of radioactive iodine which is used to treat the condition. Radioactive iodine is such a strong dose of treatment that it can poison the thyroid gland entirely causing the patient to become underactive for the rest of their lives. This particular natural version of it was supposedly dosed perfectly for my level of the illness and wouldn't cause the poisoning effect.

As it turned out, I didn't have a single reaction – positive or negative – to this remedy or any of the other mineral water treatments we worked on. In the end, I lost faith in them and did something I'd resisted for months: I took the carbimazole as prescribed by my GP. This actually reduced the effects of the illness within days and after a week or so, although still ill, I began to find an even keel. So much for mineral water as a "spiritual essence."[13]

I'm not saying that alternative medicines don't work. A lot of them are now prescribed by conventional doctors, but even my naturopath would admit, that if you're as ill as I was, a good option

---

[13] HM told me I was NEVER to throw these essences away by pouring them down the sink. Consequently, I had about five mineral water bottles in the fridge containing essences that I'd long since given up on that I was too terrified to touch. One day, I got fed up of them and poured every single last drop into the water reservoir of the Renault. I joked about it to Scooter who promptly told HM. Naturally, she went ballistic and didn't talk to me for a week...

is to take the conventional stuff and mix it with a bit of the alternative. This I did and found it to be top advice. The alternative I took was not, I have to say, HM's version. After so many years setting herself up as the great white hope for the chronically ill of the world, she was just playing at doctors and nurses and simply didn't have a clue about the healing arts.

When my 40th birthday arrived in February 2006, I was beginning to get fat. Quite a few people who are hyperthyroid actually lose weight because their metabolism is running so fast. That was what had happened to me initially, but with my immune system shot to bits, my metabolism all awry, my own reaction to the illness was to turn into a giant, overweight blob. I was putting on so much weight at one point that some people simply stopped recognising me. I'll never forget the reaction of one lady in my office who hadn't seen me for some months. She saw me come into the room one day and started frowning with concentration, staring at my new-found manboobs and my great wobbly beer belly. Suddenly, she goes: 'scuse me....are you Paul Arrowbank?' When I replied in the affirmative, she abruptly said out loud: 'OH....MY....GOD!'

Actually, I found that hilarious at the time; but a part of me was worried. I liked having the beefier shoulders, but every time I caught myself in a mirror or saw my reflection against a wall, I thought I'd become a darts player or a sweaty coke and fries computer geek with carpal tunnel and an 18 hour-a-day addiction to online gaming. I really didn't like the amount of bathwater I'd started to displace and the fact that I'd gone from wearing 32" waist Levi 501's in 2004 to 42" cut price supermarket sweat shop specials in 2006.

The hyperthyroid refused to clear up. By the time Scooter came to stay with me in the early spring of 2007, it was still raging away and was at least in part the reason why poor old Scooter wasn't really welcomed into my home to the extent that he'd hoped. As HM's bizarre behaviour out in Munich reached its apogee, I was going down and down with every day that passed. The endocrinologists at Reading's Royal Berks hospital started selling me the idea of having radioactive iodine treatment as they could see my health deteriorating but I held them off by telling them that my life was going through an unstable patch and that the uncertainty and stress were responsible for my lack of progress.

Looking back, I was being horrendously negative and thinking myself ill. Because of a convergence of emergencies and inconveniences that had thrown me into a place where I just didn't want to be, I was allowing my own misery to drag me down.

I had a long think about this and came to the conclusion that all I had to do was to listen to my heart. Perhaps unconsciously Squarehead's words from all those years ago were finally seeping through into my waking life. Over the next few weeks, I somehow managed to perform a bit of a mindflip by repeating a mantra inside my head designed to promote more positive thinking. It was something I'd always known how to do but had never actually used because for a long time, as much as I hate to admit it, my spiritual thing was far too logical and not nearly practical enough. I could certainly talk the talk, but walking the walk was another matter entirely. Waddle the walk maybe, but not with any great conviction or wisdom.

Gradually, after no small amount of effort, I heaved myself up off my backside and things started to shift for me. I finally did some self-analysis of the kind that HM had been trying to get me to do for years as part of her efforts to be all guru-like and in time something clicked into place. I realised properly, at long last, that all I had to do was kick the vestiges of my ill-advised allegiance with her into touch and visualise myself the way I wanted to be: healthy, happy and free from her drudgery.

That was when, out of the blue, things began to improve. First of all, HM started to arrange legal accommodation for herself and Scooter. Once Scooter had begun to sort himself out and secure a place at college, I started to feel things were settling down nicely and for the first time in years, I began to feel I could breathe again.

I recall sitting in the bath one evening and going through my problems in my head. It was funny, but I suddenly found that despite everything, there were no real issues shadowing me at all. The hyperthyroid was something that I'd simply allowed to stalk me. I was doing that by going out every weekend and having a skin-full down the pub with my friends. At three in the morning, I'd stagger home in the middle of the road with them and then spend the rest of the weekend recovering with a hangover. As I was still unconsciously kicking against the strictness of the spiritual regime of the previous few years, I joined everyone in the world of the tobacco plant and was puffing away like a bonfire whenever I had the chance.

That night in the bath, I decided that as life wasn't really that difficult after all and there were a heck of a lot of people out there a lot worse off than me, it was time to get real and treat my body as a temple.

Over the next few weeks, I stopped the smoking and cut my drinking down to almost nothing. I started taking exercise and getting out more to take fresh air in the fields and woods around my beautiful West Berkshire home. It was amazing how quickly my thyroid recovered. I could almost hear it thanking me in utter relief and came to the conclusion that I'd simply brought the illness in myself on a spiritual level in order to keep me on the straight and narrow. I'm the kind of person who likes a bit of a party and would think nothing of becoming a giant-sized elephant if it meant that I had a good time getting there. All through that period, my thyroid had been shouting at me:

"Errrr, Paul? Fatass? Get your head sorted!"

Personal triumphs aside, there was one little blip on the horizon which, looking back, was really of no consequence in the grand scheme. The problem was, at the time, it seemed like a monstrous carbuncle. That was Mrs Aleph.

Even though I was now gradually becoming more centred and in control than I could ever remember being, I still felt an inexplicable anger whenever I thought of her. I just couldn't let it go.

On August 17th of 2007, Mrs Aleph arranged a rendezvous in London so that we could talk about the novel. She'd asked me to meet her at a University Hall of Residence in Tavistock Square at a certain time in the evening and then turned up, just like the last time I'd met her, extremely late.

The meeting was a pointless rerun of the HM-bashing session of a couple of months earlier. We went to a local hotel where I bought her a drink and watched in horror as she proceeded to kick off her shoes and lay herself out on a leather sofa like the Queen of Sheba. She then set about ripping into HM again and into me, accusing me of treachery for supporting HM against her own daughter. The novel was barely mentioned despite all her promises that she could pull strings and use her contacts in the publishing world. In the back of my mind, I was now wondering if such contacts actually existed and the true reality of this situation hit home. Mrs Aleph was absolutely lapping up HM's failure. For Mrs Aleph to see that failure first hand and to be able to scream about it from the mountaintops, she was throwing extra impetus and credence at her own belief system. Having successfully blown the opposition out of the water, Mrs Aleph was now officially the one with all the answers; she talked down to me like I was a piece of dirt and I came to realise that I'd been called to London so that she could pass sentence on all of us.

After I came back from that ill-fated trip, I sent her a text message to ask her to confirm if she was still keen to pursue the search for a publisher for the novel. Of course, I never heard back from her and she hasn't contacted me since. For months afterwards, whenever I thought of her, which was invariably first thing in the morning, I'd find myself fuming at the way I felt she'd betrayed me:

I'll get you a publishing deal, Paul (simper, simper...) Ooooh, I've changed my mind. You can get lost now...

If Mrs Aleph had been more aware, she would have read the signs. Despite telling her that I was still keen on supporting Scooter and his mother, if she'd gazed in with any kind of equanimity at the situation and read the look in my eyes, she'd have seen that my liaison with HM was clearly going to fall apart at some time. Then she'd have been able to step in eventually and help out with the books using whatever contacts she may have had. But all she could think about was the damage that could be done to her reputation by all the weirdness going on around me.

I'm perfectly willing to accept that she was also just a complete and total liar and didn't have any connections in the publishing world after all. She once told me she wrote bodice rippers, but refused to tell me her pen name...

On reflection, the smell of deceit was never too far away from Mrs Aleph. Even HM, the most dextrous fibber I've ever met, called her a monumental liar. Praise indeed!

Chapter Twenty-Five

I always felt that when I reached the age of forty-two, something amazing would happen; I just didn't have a clue what and how. In terms of age, forty-two is a very important year, as are most ages that are a multiple of seven. Something began to occur for me in that year of 2008 which was to put my entire world into perspective.

Percy and I had started our weekly telephone calls a month earlier and I was beginning to find out from my own research that there's a whole Universe to be explored out there that doesn't require allegiance to any kind of abusive self-appointed spiritual oracle. During the last few months of 2007, I'd gradually begun to forgive Mrs Aleph for hanging the carrot of a publishing deal in front of my face and then withdrawing it in some kind of childish control drama. Also by February 2008, I could see enough distance between myself and HM to understand that I had more freedom than before. I was still doing the odd job for her but surprisingly, incidences of her ringing me up to trash me or to harangue me with all her self-made problems were becoming fewer and further between. With Scooter now in college and starting to get on with his life, I was ripe for my own change.

One Friday night about a week before my birthday, I went down the pub. I was standing there with a pint in my hand in the pub garden and talking to a good friend of mine. The conversation was quite animated and we were enjoying each other's company. At some point, he went indoors to get another pint and I was alone out in the garden. It was dark and miserable, but I didn't feel that cold. Instead, I leaned against the post of the smoking shelter and gazed up at the stars. It was then that something amazing started to happen. My head felt all light as if I'd just had a joint. My heart began to fill up with joy.

To be honest, I put this feeling down to the pint of beer in my hand and ignored it. By the time my mate came back with his refreshed pint, I was even more animated and we chatted and laughed as before. But for me, suddenly the conversation became so much more intense and interesting. I was looking around me at the drab-looking winter garden, the pile of cigarette butts in the ashtrays, the angular braches of the trees still bare of leaves, and it all looked amazing. I felt incredibly calm like nothing could ever hurt me again.

I said nothing to my mate and after a half an hour or so, we drifted back to our homes. I went out into my yard and looked up into space again. It was an extremely chilly cloudless night and I could see all the stars and a crystal clear moon. I felt drawn up as if something was pulling my consciousness out of my body. All my troubles seemed to be melting away and I had this incredible sense of the sheer insignificance of them. I went indoors and sat down to do some meditation. I stayed in that seat for about an hour and just bathed in the wonder of it all. For some reason, I was reminded of an advert that had often been on TV in Greece, of a man lounging happily in a child's inflatable paddling pool right at the top of a skyscraper in the middle of a bustling city. He looks serene and content with life. I laughed because that's how I felt right there and then. If a poisonous snake had slithered in and wrapped himself around me at that very time, I'd have patted him on the head and passed the time of day with him. Ordinarily I'm very wary of snakes.

The following Monday morning, I woke up to go to work and still felt amazing. The lightness and energy in my head hadn't diminished and was, even then, emanating right from the centre of my brain, seemingly expanding outwards. Work was *still* hard for me and I was *still* suffering the fallout from my former bizarre behaviour of previous months during the dark night of my soul; but I was now on a complete high. For once, all that negativity floated through me and caused no dents whatsoever in my feeling of wellbeing.

This feeling was still with me on my birthday which came and went in a bit of a haze. I didn't celebrate with a big party or drinking session with my friends. I was still pretty much on the wagon and realised that if I never had access to another alcoholic drink in the rest of my life, I wouldn't care less. This led on to another thought. When I told myself that I wasn't interested in the trappings of wealth, I now really meant it. Suddenly, all the

231

yardsticks that I'd been brought up to use to measure success in life had been thrown away. All I wanted was to feel that Universal high forever. Even if I went home that night to find all my belongings had been stolen, I would have been happy on the floor with just a blanket.

The thing is, this is a state that HM had always said she was in and yet, never, not even once, had I noticed that she would be happy and in a state of bliss with nothing but the clothes she was standing up in and just a blanket to keep her warm at night.

When I had this thought, I rang two people. The first one was HM herself. I wanted to hear what she thought had happened. What I actually got was a short silence on the end of the phone. Then she said simply:

"At last! It's taken you long enough!"

It was a strange reaction. HM always claimed there'd been massive changes in her life when she turned forty-two, so it was also odd that she couldn't see a parallel. Unlike her though, I didn't feel any different about myself: I was happy to admit I was just Joe Average and also to shout out loud that even though *something* had happened, I still had miles and miles to go before I could genuinely say I was Mr Wisdom. In fact, that's exactly how she wanted me. It would have been anathema to her to admit that someone was snapping at her heels.

That's why there was no triumph in her voice. She wasn't interested in hearing about it. She changed the subject immediately and asked me something mundane like had I managed to do the changes to her website yet. Surely as the teacher in this master/student arrangement, she should have been brimming with information about this phenomenon and what had really caused it.

As I was still in the dark about what had happened, I spoke to Percy. For someone who I thought was a good spiritual friend, his reaction to this news was remarkably muted and I just couldn't work out why. Almost grudgingly, he admitted that I was "waking up to myself".

After a few days, the euphoria subsided completely. I wasn't to know it at the time, but I'd been accorded a glimpse into what was possible for me if I could only free myself from the bonds of my own self-inflicted slavery and open up through the heart to the Universe around me. When that uplifting energy returned about a year later and stayed, I'd begun to "find myself" like never before and gained an excellent grounding in what was possible if I was ready and open for it. That return to tranquil experience, as you will see, coincided with my making a supreme conscious effort to bring about a complete break from a certain set of manacles.

Squarehead would have been proud.

You're probably wondering what the deal is with this Percy character. To be honest with you, a few weeks after we started our regular Sunday morning phone calls at the beginning of 2008, I was beginning to wonder myself. On the face of it, he seemed such a lovely, gentle and wise person, always enthusiastic to hear my voice, always absolutely brimming with energy.

But there were days when he would explain things to me and completely throw me into confusion. He started off his chats with me that January by coming in hard on the 2012 theme. If you've ever done a bit of digging on the net, you'll know that there were all sorts of traditions surrounding the date 21st December 2012 which range from a wonderful mystical and uplifting experience that would be felt by the whole of humanity (a global ascension, if you will) to the complete polar opposite: dire predictions of global catastrophe where almost the entire race was to be wiped out in a succession of climatic disasters like earthquakes, super volcanoes and giant tsunamis that would sweep away whole continents. At this point, I knew very little about this subject and was rather too keen to hear what Percy had to say. His own view on it, which appeared very set in stone, was that it was going to be utterly horrific…

For Percy, it was the sinking of all landmass around the Pacific rim, the wiping out of whole nations and more lava and human terror than you can possibly dream up in your worst ever nightmares. I was stunned. He always seemed such a loving kind of person and yet here he was almost relishing the misery and writing it all off with a perfunctory wave of his hand and the assertion that: "it's just the nature of the Universe we've created for ourselves. Death isn't the end, it's just a transition. We all have to die and we do it when the clock strikes the hour. In this case, the clock strikes the hour on 11.11am., 21/12 and then…it's all change…"

This didn't sit comfortably with me. Deep down, it felt like the mad predictions of someone who actually wanted to see death and destruction. All the same, his words were so beautifully wrapped up in spiritual terminology, it really was hard actually to see him as someone who relished pain and misery.

Like a fool, I fell for his assertion that there was nothing for Paul or Percy to worry about in 2012. We were the chosen ones – it would be all right for *us*: we would both survive in a blaze of glory to be at the vanguard of a new world movement where we'd use our spiritual wisdom to build a new society for the survivors. He didn't explain at this point exactly what he meant by "spiritual".

It was such an odd conversation; I felt depressed afterwards. Perhaps I should have used that feeling to poke myself into wakefulness. But I was still so fast asleep and utterly closed to the fact that the vultures were circling again. There seemed to be a wonderful light at the end of a tunnel and already, there I was, breaking into a run to get to it. After everything I'd learned, you'd have thought I'd have known better by that time. But my vanity was still very much in control and I'd never stopped to ask myself: *this person calls himself a Lightworker. Define "light"*...

As the weeks went by, Percy became more confident in his assertions. He gained my trust by implying that he knew what I was thinking about my life. He dipped his toe in the water and made the tiniest of seemingly inconsequential remarks about HM. For example, he asked me if I was still sure about her and if I always had a positive feeling about everything she asked me to do. I admitted that I felt most of the things she asked me to do had led both of us down a blind alley and trotted out all the reasons that HM had given me for why everything was such a mess: it was all my fault.

Very gently, Percy explained that none of her constant stream of disasters was my fault. He pointed out that she may not have thought her decisions through and that perhaps she had misheard the "voices" from "upstairs". He finally got me to admit that that may have been possible.

The further we got into this subject, the more he succeeded in allowing me to open up. In a matter of weeks from those first phone calls, the chat about HM had gone from: "has it occurred to

234

you, Paul, that HM may have misheard her information and got you working for her because she's got the wrong end of the stick" to a complete no holds barred approach: "this woman is the very embodiment of dark trickery and she's been playing you like a fiddle for years!"

So my worst fears were beginning to be realised. Here I was, listening to someone who had been given the stamp of approval from HM herself because she'd actually agreed to work with him, now telling me categorically that she was about as close as you can get to the Whore of Babylon. I couldn't ignore Percy's angle on the situation. I'd been told all this many times before, but no one had managed to break through that iron door of delusion that kept me from waking up to her. In the end, it HAD to be one of her own who achieved such a feat.

Within weeks, I stopped defending her and listened intently as Percy lectured me for literally hours on the perfidies of the Holy Mother: she had seen me coming; she'd hooked me in by undermining my confidence and claiming that only she was strong enough to take me to where I wanted to go. But all the time, she was incapable of achieving that as she had no spiritual power: all her power came from those she sucked the lifeblood out of, like a preying mantis.

Percy explained how she was a classic "darkness" vehicle thriving in this world of duality, feeding off the spiritually needy, pulling them down her path to hell and all the time covering for herself so beautifully by blaming all the negativity she attracted so abundantly into her life on them. She turned pure souls who were keen to experience the heights of spiritual achievement into quivering, gibbering wrecks and therefore blocked them utterly from spiritual advancement. This, Percy explained, was how the dark side worked and what it was set up to do: block the Light. Once it has squeezed every last ounce of hope and goodness out of you by defiling you, making you feel dirty about yourself, depressed and alone, it would then lay claim to your soul. In such a position of power, it would send you out to do its own dirty work: in my case to write and disseminate books full of nonsense where HM was shown to be a poor victim of terrible parents and abusive men who'd triumphed over adversity to become a living god, the oracle of the divine on earth.

Percy pointed out that there was no such thing. He explained that the HM bandwagon was nothing but a new religion and after 2000 years of slavery under cults that had spewed forth from the defiled teachings of Jesus, this was yet another satanic ploy to rip off humanity at a time when we were all supposed to be waking up and building a new paradigm. In no uncertain terms, I was told that I'd been shamelessly shoved out there as the "writer" with the master cowering behind me waiting for me to perform. Having tricked the whole world through the art of writing into thinking that I, Paul Arrowbank, the "great" author had found the messiah for the New Age, I was then going to be allowed to take a small amount of glory mixed in with a whole canyon-full of abuse from the media. Meanwhile the master would be hiding away behind me in her new mansion, laughing all the way to the bank and rubbing her hands in glee that her dark side had once again tricked an entire planet.

Percy never told me straight out that I needed to get away from HM. He didn't need to. He carefully left that decision to me whilst overtly sabotaging the wheels of her already extremely rickety old cart.

It was still a very confusing situation for me. Initially, Percy had rung me up back in January 2008 with the intention of getting in touch with HM again, not me. He'd explained that the reason why he'd left her sphere of influence a couple of years earlier was because he wanted to explore the "tree of Life" as he called it, alone. He needed to do that without the help of a teacher. What I needed to ask him, but never did, was this: if this woman was the closest thing to the Whore of Babylon, then why had he decided to get in touch with her again? I was still so asleep, it never occurred to me to ask that question. If I had, it would have given me a different angle on Percy.

As it turned out, when I did tell HM that I was in touch with Percy and that he wanted to speak to her, she wasn't interested. That should have rung alarm bells too. Why didn't she want to know him any more? What did she see in him that I couldn't? If it was something nasty, she certainly didn't warn me off him.

When I told Percy that HM wasn't interested in talking to him, he seemed frustrated and angry as if he'd been thwarted in some grand plan. In fact, that was when he started to pitch into her. I should have seen that as a sign too. Both of these people called themselves great spiritual beings and yet there was an unhealthy rivalry and mutual suspicion between the two of them that looked more like the sort of dangerous shenanigans you get within rival gangs in the mafia. Where was the peace and the love? Where was the true wisdom and the real teaching? I was still looking for that so earnestly and here I was, after all those years, sandwiched between two of "God's" most self-centred prophets. A time was coming when I would just get sick and tired of the whole useless shower of them; but back in 2008 that day was still just out of sight.

Chapter Twenty-Six

In the month of March 2008, about two months after my initial ecstatic state had subsided, something happened between me and HM that brought her issues into very clear focus. She'd asked me to get her a watch for her birthday. When it was her birthday, she would sometimes ring me up and ask me if I had anything in mind to buy her for a present. If I didn't, she'd ask me how much I was intending to spend, add something like £20 to that total and ask me to hand it over in cash, saying that she would either buy the present herself or just spend the cash whenever she needed it. The extra £20 she always claimed she would pay back which meant in fact that I was supposed to waive it!

On this occasion, I promised to spend £30. After the extra £20 HM tax had been added, there was just enough for me to bid on a Lacroix designer watch which she'd seen on eBay and really wanted. I'm quite good with eBay and duly won the watch from the exact listing that she'd given me. I was quite pleased with the purchase and had it sent directly to her.

The problem was she hadn't read the small print. All she'd done was look at the dial of the watch and allowed her desire nature to kick in. I'd often noticed in the past that this desire nature was at times so acute that it would override all common sense and blind her to the details. This is why she constantly set out on some latest craze or plan that never worked or came to a satisfactory conclusion. In the case of the watch, she'd been so hard-focused on the picture of it that she hadn't seen a warning within the accompanying text. The watch didn't have a strap but was of a bangle design and was one complete rigid piece. The listing also pointed out that the rest of the bangle around the dial was brown and not blue as in the picture.

Consequently when the watch arrived, I got a distressed phone call with an angry outburst: "This was NOT what I ordered!"

Once I'd calmly pointed out her mistake, she was embarrassed and said she'd keep the watch; but then a few days later, she changed her mind. I was ordered to relist it on my own eBay account and hand over the cash once I'd sold it. The whole business was time consuming and annoying. It was also exactly the sort of nonsense that would have caused me to be emotionally booted from here to kingdom come if the glove had been on the other hand and I'd made a similar mistake and caused her a similar amount of inconvenience. I'd have been accused of lack of awareness and effectively not using my intuition. Also the whole situation reeked of hypocrisy. HM was allowed to "get away with" this sort of lapse of judgement because she was a Holy Mother and could do as she liked. I, of course, as the trainee, didn't have such a luxury. This always seemed to me to be a cop out. A student will only learn from a teacher who lives by his own rules. I never expected infallibility in HM, but equally, I never expected complete lack of awareness.

To be honest, this whole incident just summed up everything I thought was wrong about the way that HM approached her life. I began to wonder what other mistakes she'd made in her training. Had she cut corners? Had she missed other messages? And important ones at that? To me it was now crystal clear that she had. She'd skated over her training in her desperation to do the Holy Mother thing.

This was brought home again a few weeks later when HM rang me at work almost howling in panic because she thought she'd accidentally ordered a whole pile of books from Amazon that she didn't want. The way it looked on the screen was apparently like she'd put a whole page worth of books into her shopping basket. Her breathless panic was a sign of a complete lack of self-control. She wasn't grounded at all. I talked her through her purchase and she calmed down only when she realised that a bill for hundreds of pounds wasn't about to be deducted from her bank account. Once again, if I'd shown the same lack of awareness, I'd have earned myself a thorough dressing down.

Just as I was about to set out on the first draft of this book, I found a letter that HM had written me on the 2nd of November 2004 when I bought the wrong items for her from Primark. You must read this. I still think it's hilarious:

Dear Paul

I did not realise that asking you to get me some slippers would reveal to me that you are not transmuting your negative traits and have been stagnating on the spiritual path to wholeness.

You have stopped self-analysis on the basis that because you can write so well on spiritual matters, you have no need to grow.

Lately I have noticed that you are becoming mentally rigid as you were in the West Reading days. You think that what you think is right and always the best way. You do not see other people's points of view or believe there is another way. So the slippers I asked for, for £1.50, became shoes for £10. The backless mules became enclosed. The centre became the side and the silky shiny satin with embroidered acorns became matt cotton polka dots.

This needs to be a big exercise for you, because if you don't change you won't be able to fulfil your destiny.

I hope you can get a refund. I'll get my own slippers in future.

Ma

For goodness sake! *Get* your own bloody slippers then. The reason why HM ended up with a load of things that didn't match her order was because I was trying to improvise. None of the things on her list were in Primark at the time and I didn't want her to go without. So I bought her other items instead to tide her over. But all she could focus on was her anger at not getting exactly what she wanted, when she wanted it. So her foot was duly stamped and I was given a trashing. This was nothing to do with my not transmuting any negative traits. I bought her a load of things in the hope that she would just stop complaining about not having any slippers. If she'd been doing what she was supposed to be doing in the first place, all her immediate needs would have been met. By having to expect everyone else to bail her out, be it with money or slippers, this was never a sign to HM that she'd gone wrong somewhere. If your needs aren't being met, then surely you should reassess and find out what's causing you to be blocked. In this case, it was her own lack of awareness and an inability to stand back and be honest about herself. As usual, it was others who had to stomp up the cash whilst she prevaricated and refused to work through her own glaring issues.

The incident with the watch prompted me to ask Percy what he thought about the situation. I honestly can't remember what he said on that particular occasion, but the result of the question brought on a topic that I would raise again and again over the coming few months in my conversations with him. It was time for me to learn the truth.

Percy had been working with HM for only a few months before he realised that her methods were not for him. This was quite a common phenomenon with HM, I noticed over the years. When someone of quality jumped on board the HM train, they would throw themselves in to working with her for a short while and then suddenly, at least from my perspective, disappear. Once the veil had duly been pierced, quality personnel slipped through HM's fingers because they very soon realised, as a Holy Mother, she was just not the full ticket.

Almost as soon as Percy had been assumed into the fold, she had him working for her. On the one level, it was full on spiritual work of the kind already discussed such as moving on disembodied souls stuck to the earth plane. On another level, there were always demands on the purse. Within days of coming onto the scene, Percy was roped into searching around to look for video games for Scooter to be sent out to Germany. There were also requests for money. Even if she knew you hadn't got much cash, HM would find some way of getting you to part with it, mostly by playing the "I'm working for God and am therefore poverty-stricken" card. I believe Percy was happy to help, but on the other hand, alarm bells were ringing.

Because she also saw virtually the entire human race as stupid, she honestly couldn't understand when people were quick to realise that her methods were suspect. So she was happy to carry on pulling these scams, knowing – not thinking – but actually knowing that no one would see her game. But Percy had been having spiritual experiences all his life. He came to her – on the face of it at least – for some serious help on the spiritual path. This was not a reason for exploitation: there was actual important spiritual work to be done by someone who said he needed to move on to the next level. To brush over that and ignore the fact

241

that he'd already arrived on the scene with plenty of abilities, by putting yourself and your own needs first as the "oracle" of God, is an insult to the seeker and a misrepresentation of how the Universe works on the Service to Others polarity.

It wasn't long before Percy was given the same line as I was. HM told him how important she was. That she'd been given the task by "God" himself to train Lightworkers for the planet. For this reason, she saw her work as sacrosanct and the needs of others were secondary: every single stop had to be pulled out by all those around her to make sure, as captain of the team, that she was looked after, housed, fed and kept in the manner to which an oracle of "God" should be accustomed.

One day during her time in Germany, HM rang Percy up and told him he had a job to do. In order for her to continue with her work, she needed money: RIGHT NOW! She asked him to use his spiritual abilities to work towards the materialisation of a large suitcase full of cash.

At this point, Percy lost interest. HM always claimed that she was not allowed to "create" for herself, that having reached such a high level of spirituality, she was egoless and no longer bound like the rest of us to the earth plane. In such an exalted position, it is, according to her, the right and the duty of the entire human race to find out what a wonderful soul they have amongst them and to react accordingly, showing gratitude to "God" by giving unconditionally to her and keeping her every single need satisfied in terms of food, clothes, housing and all the daily necessities of living.

It's possible to see how this sort of situation would work in India. That kind of spiritual culture, where people take in wandering holy men and feed them is something that has been ingrained in their culture for centuries. People who take in these holy men do it out of love and not because they've been asked to do it. However, times have changed and this is the West. We haven't come through centuries of blind service to the Church with all its collection plate demands for cash for the forgiveness of sins, its self-aggrandisement and focus on the material, to then *return* to flogging ourselves to death for a brand new set of "holy" people. When HM set out on the idea of being a guru, she didn't think this through. Those of us who have embraced the modern day Western spiritual scene (as distinct from religion) have joined up to get away from the demands for cash and all the guilt trips that are tied in with screwing the idealistic and the altruistic out of their money. I myself was brought up as a Catholic. When I lived in Rome, I was at once awe-inspired and disgusted at the wealth of the Church, particularly when vast swathes of the faithful are utterly poverty-stricken.

Put simply, HM, in her rush to reach the toppermost rung of the guru ladder, pushed aside or conveniently forgot, the Universal Law of Entitlement.

A few years ago, around the time I was being spiritually pillaged by Percy, the buzz book of the time was called *The Secret* by Rhonda Byrne. Suddenly everyone was talking about The Law of Attraction and learning that they could get what they wanted in life, the money, health, a successful job, a nice car, simply by abounding with love and gratitude. The idea is that as the Universe is a loving Universe, if you're overflowing with all that's positive about the human and showing unconditional love to all in your world, eventually, as like attracts like, the Universe would unfold for you all the happiness it wants you to have. So if it's a car you want, if it's wealth and happiness, the Universe is poised to provide. Although I loved the look and feel of the book and accompanying DVD, I couldn't help but be a little nervous. Surely this would mean having to do, dare I say it, some self-analysis. In order for people to turn into the loving and incredibly creative beings that we truly are (and I entirely agree with that assertion) the implication is that we're all going to have to make some major changes to our general behaviour.

I do think that's quite a tall order for most people, no matter how true it is. We've all come down here to be jerks at some time or another; that's part and parcel of taking an incarnation in this base consciousness world. It's hard for all of us (and I include myself in this) just suddenly to wake up one morning and go: *I'm nice now!* And then, who decides when you're on track? If you read the book and give yourself a week to turn into Mr Popular Positive, how long do you have to wait before the Universal catalogue opens? HM was convinced she was perfect and yet every week, she was filling in lottery tickets expecting that catalogue to open wide at the weekend. It never did.

I actually had to agree with Percy on this. There's another law which isn't so well known and that's the law of Universal Entitlement. This puts a completely different face on the animal. Yes, the Universe will provide, Rhonda Byrne is spot on. But only once you've cleared up the trash from the backyard of your life. In other words, despite the positive message that abounded following the publication of *The Secret*, the true message got stuck somewhere down the pipe: you'll be entitled to all the Universe can provide once you've done the homework and not just *told* yourself you're abounding in love, but actually learned to *live* it.

Sometimes, that can take years. If it's joy you want, then spread the joy, then it will be returned to you. How do you spread joy? You have to find it in yourself first. If you can't find it, where are you going to get some? If you learn to forgive your parents for example, then some of the darkness will dissipate and a good deal of joy will shine through. But that's a high old mountain to climb, especially if they've been abusive.

I believe it is truly possible to abound with joy and attract all the good things you want into your life. If you can be open-minded about your faults but also learn to forgive yourself as soon as possible, it really *is* a reasonable expectation to have. If recovery from an abusive childhood is what you're hunting for, do some research and find out what turned your parents into abusers. That's such a sure-fire way to put a different angle on the situation. As long as you give yourself time and don't rush through it to claim the cash at the end of the rainbow, it will eventually produce amazing dividends.

HM gave this sort of advice all the time, but still hadn't forgiven her mother or even spoken to her in years. With all this unresolved detritus around, she carried on regardless, setting herself up as the greatest of the great long before she'd finished filling black bin liners with personal garbage; the Law of Entitlement then simply cancelled out the Law of Attraction. There was no joy in her world. She expected it to be dished out to her in giant-sized portions and of course, as she'd set up herself up to tower over her fellow men, the Universal stock cupboard stayed firmly locked.

The irony of the Law of Attraction is that once you've worked so hard on all your negative traits and released the hidden joy from underneath, you lose interest in wealth! Suddenly, other things matter: namely those around you, your interpersonal relationships, the world at large. Maybe that was a sneaky trick of *The Secret*. What if its true motive was to lead people into a spiritual awakening? Maybe it was designed to tease them into doing some self-analysis, into releasing their negative character traits, all the time luring them on with the promise of money and wealth and more gold than you can eat. Then suddenly BANG! Everyone finds themselves in a place where, out of the blue, they shout: *I'm free! Keep your cash!*

I think I may be naïve in this assertion. I often wondered why at the beginning of the DVD for *The Secret*, it shows a group of incredibly negative black-suited insiders (the real rulers of the world) sitting menacingly in a smoky boardroom planning death and destruction to anyone who uncovered the truth. The voiceover describes this group as the ones who've existed since time immemorial and who've used the secret to become fabulously wealthy. I don't understand; they don't look very joyful and "enlightened" to me.

For her part, HM was never of a mind to explore the fact that she'd chosen a shadow path once taking her route of "positive love and Light" didn't produce the goods fast enough. Her suffering came as an inevitable consequence of the way she treated people and also because of her unconstructive thought patterns that created a living energy of negativity: she could just never see that.

When I say that HM forgot to take into account the law of entitlement, I also mean something extremely specific: she failed to find out if the style of the Eastern guru (and all the attention and razzmatazz which comes with that) was one that's not only relevant to the people she wished to teach, but also to her. She assumed that it was what her god wanted her to do and rushed ahead with her plans to bring it all into being without ever stopping to think: *is this my correct route? Am I entitled to call myself Holy? Should I expect just to be given clothes, food, money, as if it were my divine right?*

One could argue that she was certainly entitled in the same way that we're all entitled to such things. But she fell down because she made demands. Not just from people in general, but from her god.

245

And because she didn't allow people to love her, nothing came. Evolved beings are so happy, grateful and abounding in love, that others give to them freely and without condition. Nothing ever needs to be demanded by such people.

After twenty or so years of having to force the issue of her poverty onto the spiritually motivated and then seeing those very people turning away, one would have thought the penny should have dropped. After two decades of daily expectation, of constant anxious waiting and even of having to trick that money out of serious spiritual seekers and *still* ending up utterly destitute, the message should have been loud and clear: in this case, the Law of Entitlement had been roundly ignored. Some self-analysis was not done at some point on the path. For someone who was telling others constantly of her divinity and incorruptibility, the hole was gaping wide open.

But how does this happen? How does someone who is so sure in her heart that she wants the best for the whole world and for humanity come to make such a fundamental mistake?

As a young woman, HM had joined a spiritual organisation with a very good pedigree. It had taken her a long time to be accepted in as a member as this group doesn't take just anyone. These days this organisation is a mystery school that teaches healing, meditation and astrology and has a philosophy designed to help humanity radiate inner Light and to use that Light to bring comfort and healing to the world at large. HM had taken some training at the school but left when she found she'd "outgrown" the organisation and found herself to be streaking ahead of others in terms of her spirituality and her healing and general psychic abilities. She then proceeded to set herself up on her own.

When she told me this, I often wondered why. I always felt it was a mistake because there would have been guidance at the school and genuine help from fellow seekers on the path. I also felt that there had to be a tinge of frustration within HM verging on impatience that left her with the mistaken belief that other people were pulling her back and dragging her down. What I felt she should have done is stay and accept with humility the fact that her abilities were great and in advance of everyone else's. If she'd stayed, there'd have been people there who'd have taught her humility and compassion, two essential virtues for someone of a level that she began to aspire to.

In my mind, there's no doubt that as a child, HM had had a few genuine spiritual experiences, one of which, at a very young age, was a vision of a beautiful lady like the Virgin Mary who filled the whole sky. During her school days, she used to tell me, she'd had a week when she felt exalted and almost transported out of herself in joy, an experience that I've absolutely no doubt she had, having experienced it myself. These occurrences are pointers: at first they come in fits and starts and then converge towards a time when spiritual evolution starts to flower from within and stays with you.

As a young woman, it's quite likely that HM looked back on her childhood, saw what had happened and assessed her increasing healing and psychic abilities as a precursor to her own enlightenment. Because her childhood had been a difficult and lonely one with parents who were not the kindest and most loving of people, it's clear that she came to the conclusion that she'd suffered for a purpose. This purpose she would have equated with the suffering of Jesus and unknowingly, she may have started to equate *herself* with him, drawing comparisons with his life and experiences and resonating with him on a deeper level.

She may have started out with positive motives. Even though she was of Jewish origin, to resonate with Jesus would have been quite radical and probably pushed her even further forward to the extent that she might have dreamt of emulating him. For a lonely girl constantly kicked from pillar to post as she was in those early days, this would have given her much comfort from the uncertainties of dealing with one or two men who came into her life who didn't have her best interests at heart, from her poverty and her general unhappiness and disillusion.

Rather than finding her feet with the mystery school and mixing with people who'd have guided her away from thinking of herself in almost messianic terms, she began to see herself as more advanced and a cut above the rest. This may have been true to a certain extent, but at a delicate stage before a soul starts that inner flowering into enlightenment, with some people, there's a time of "wavering".

This wavering is such a subtle state that it can be missed completely. If you're not grounded and have begun to see yourself as a messiah for your abilities, then you can open yourself up to corruption. At this point, it's very easy to take a rougher path.

HM wouldn't have been aware that there was a fork in the road. It had always been her intention to serve "God" and to help heal and teach humanity. But back in those early days, unknowingly, she took the fork in the road with the sign "Service to Self" and set out on a path that would lead to horrendous spiritual blocks and ultimately to suffering and poverty.

Having put an end to all relationships and decided that she had to be on her own, she began a process that led her to isolation. She carried on working for a few years, but then stopped, preferring to devote all her time to her spiritual progress and the search for enlightenment. To leave work was a disastrous decision for a start. In her autobiography, she intimated that people didn't like her in the office because she read spiritual books and drank healthy teas. When she left, she was given a hastily arranged bunch of flowers and nowhere near the send-off she'd have liked. She implies also that most of the girls in the office had taken a disliking to her and wasted time sabotaging her work.

In many respects, you can see why she wanted to flee such a situation. However, that sort of office worker treatment doesn't just come out of nowhere. It's usually been "earned". Having spent most of my working life in an office, the ones who give themselves airs and graces or make beelines for other people's husbands or wives tend to end up being treated like that.

If your spirituality is working for you, it's more likely that people will be drawn to you rather than repelled. It isn't true that people who aren't spiritually aware will automatically take sides against you. In order to have inspired people actually to sabotage her work, she must have riled them; if she'd been doing some assiduous self-analysis to get to the bottom of her negative character traits, this is an area which was positively screaming for attention. She should have been asking herself every single day why people didn't like her and then made some adjustments to her personality that didn't compromise her integrity. You don't have to start swearing or being one of the crowd to get on with your peers. People will be drawn to you if you emanate love and compassion, even if you don't run with the crowd. It's always been clear to me that even at this early stage, HM was unable to find a satisfactory baseline with her fellow men and was reacting against their disgust with her by putting herself on an even higher pedestal.

Pulling herself out of the bustle and grind of daily life was not the best decision. It's in mixing with your fellow men and remembering how to be humble, helpful and loving towards people who don't have the same spiritual outlook as you that you learn to stay grounded and focused on the job in hand. You don't have to identify with non-spiritual people at all. All you need to do is keep humanity around you, appreciate it, care for it and rejoice in its abundance of uniqueness and sheer colourful individuality. To lock yourself away in a house and gaze out at the world walking past as you wait for that all-defining moment of "God-realisation", is to cut yourself off from the whole purpose of taking on an incarnation in the physical. As you try to raise your vibration in the silence, if you're not careful, you can start to look at those around you as beneath you and worthy of nothing but your contempt for not putting their backs into their spiritual paths as you so selflessly do. This is *lethal*. An intrinsic part of advancing spiritually is the understanding of your "being" melting seamlessly without ego into the whole. You see yourself in others (whom you start to know as "other selves") to the extent that you understand on the deepest level that we're all part of one Universal consciousness and that there's no separation. If there's a difference between you and others, it's simply one that exists in this realm where "other selves" take on different physical manifestations and soul characteristics in order to learn. But that never stops each individual from being an integral part of a consciousness unit that includes *you*. Locking oneself away in a monastery or convent, or even in HM's case, a run down terraced house in a rough area of Reading, is only increasing the sense of separation between self and other selves (ie. other people). This, per se, would have been a fundamental blockage to HM finding the enlightenment she so desperately sought.

Even though, at this point, HM would have started to walk the path of Service to Self, believing herself a cut above the rest, this doesn't mean that she'd have seen her healing and psychic abilities diminish. Anyone who came to her at this time for healing could have received a cure or an answer to a question. It's important to understand that just because the time of wavering has pushed someone in a direction away from the refined Light, it doesn't mean that they lose their abilities. If anything, those abilities then become the property of darker forces. As such, there will certainly be no dwindling in their power. In fact, the opposite is probably the case. For the shadow side is powerful in itself and those that are on that path are constantly looking to recruit. A fruitful recruiting ground is actually amongst those who are striving for enlightenment and it's at the wavering stage, if a soul isn't grounded and mixing with humanity in a healthy way, that it will strike. For years, and certainly for all the time when I was around, HM complained she was constantly being harassed and hounded by dark visitations, everything from red-eyed imps to full demonic manifestations. This was the calling card of those with whom she'd set up shop. For years, she failed to come to terms with this, covering for herself by accusing me and others like me of being the ones who brought them into her life.

HM's abilities include clairvoyance and clairaudience. It's through the clairaudience route that she would have started to hear deceptive voices. These voices would have been ones that she interpreted as good. She may have heard Jesus telling her everything was going to be fine. She may have believed she had communication from any number of saints and famous spiritual characters, all of whom would have whispered words of exhortation into her ears. What's more, they would have told her things she wanted to hear.

At some point, she would also have seen things. Once your psychic awareness starts to increase through spiritual practice, you can see things all the time, from spirits of the dead to angelic beings that can appear as points of light to your peripheral vision. For a being as advanced as HM, these would have taken the form of actual visitations. She often used to tell me about these in the early days and I need to keep the specifics of them to myself as they're still private to her.

Suffice it to say, by the time she'd shut herself off from the rest of humanity, these clairaudient and clairvoyant experiences would have been thought forms addressed to her from entities on a Service to Self polarity. For her part, HM wouldn't have appreciated that. Such was her isolation and at the same time, desperation, to reach her enlightenment and begin a kind of messianic ministry, any experience of a spiritual order would have been seized upon as the real thing and a bona fide signpost to that ultimate goal. It would never have entered HM's head to stand back and see (or hear) these interferences for what they were.

By this time, the voices would have hooked her in even further by making promises to her. They'd have told her that success would be lying at the end of the path and with success, a comfortable life with a nice, but certainly not ostentatious house, spiritual trainees to take the weight of the world from her shoulders and enough money to maintain a decent lifestyle. Such things would never have been promised to her by contact with her higher self and for a young woman who'd never had anything, the lure of this would have been incredibly difficult to resist, indeed for anyone. It's a testament to the sheer difficulty of the life path that HM chose for herself before her incarnation that she was prepared to allow these incredibly subtle promises to be thrown at her. However, over the years, she had quite a few warnings that they were not what they seemed and each and every warning was ignored.

Inevitably, a day came when HM finally sold herself to a path of Service to Self orientation. In her autobiography, she tells of an incident when she was writing out a leaflet advertising some of her treatments and the work she offered. A voice spoke to her which she always told everyone was a communication from "God" himself. It told her to put the words "Holy Mother" at the top of the leaflet.

This would not have happened. It's certainly not how the Universe works with regards souls on a path towards non-duality. The whole point of our taking on incarnations in physical realms is to provide experience and evolution for ourselves as The Creator. Therefore, an Infinite Creative Source itself wouldn't interfere in its own lessons by giving specific orders to "itselves" in such a way. These "orders" come from the ego in base consciousness, pure and simple. HM's view of the Creator by this time was one that had reverted to a kind of Biblical patriarch, a separated god that intervenes (or interferes) in the affairs of humanity, moving its favourites around a chessboard and confronting its enemies with an outrage once associated with the mountain-dwelling divinities of Classical pagans. This is a strange view to have, given that she must have known that people with a deeper spiritual understanding would be coming to her with a realisation that this level of separation belongs to abusive religions, where humans cower in fear under the might of a fearsome potentate. This is everything that a Universal Source Creator is not. If we're to advance into a new Golden Age and a higher paradigm for the entire planet, we need to get away from this view of "God" as a separately conscious being.

The voice that she heard that day as she typed out her leaflet on the old Amstrad was one that whispered to her from within the trauma matrix of the collective unconscious – the shadow side. In doing so, it guaranteed her a life of rejection, misery and separation that would bring suffering not only to her, but to scores of others who fell into her sphere of influence over the years to come. In time, she'd learn to lessen that suffering by grooming naïve characters like me, putting them out in front of her to do all the dirty work, to take the full flack and all the inevitable repercussions that abounded. She'd then be able to retreat into her divine world with whatever money came her way and come up smelling of roses whilst the rest of us tended our wounds.

As those years passed, the people who came and went all reacted to her in similar ways. When they first arrived on the scene there was fascination. People would come to a Darshan and find great energy in the room. I most certainly did. As I sat there in the silence back in the early days of 1998, I found the energy so great that it would cause my eyes to stream and my nose to run like a river. When I asked HM about this, she told me it was because I wasn't working hard enough to keep up with her great power and that my negative traits were causing me to suffer in the purity of the environment. Over the years, so many people found similar experiences. Some would find peace and calm in the silence, others would have to meditate to keep calm as the energy soared. Later, people would talk to HM and be shocked to find someone who was not at peace with herself. She would be tetchy and irritable, unsmiling, even downright rude.

If ever there was a warning to be shouted out about how the Service to Self side works, it would be in this situation. HM was certain she worked for the "Light" and it seemed, to her mind, there was no chance on earth that she could ever countenance walking the path of Service to Self. All her books talked about "God" and finding enlightenment. Behind this declaration of loyalty to the "Light", the "Dark" side worked its magic. It pulled people like me in by using HM as a conduit, by allowing subtle vibration and energy to work through her as if it was refined Light energy. As a novice, it was incredibly difficult for me to know that this great energy that she radiated was in fact one that emanated from the shadows. I had no prior experience to show me what it felt like to walk on the side of the angels. To me, a high energy was only possible for someone who walked in refined Light. I had no idea, and I'm sure others felt the same, that the shadow side is perfectly capable of impersonating the refined Light. For a complete novice, the subtlety is too great, the difference just too marginal.

Of course looking back, it *is* glaringly obvious because HM's behaviour outside the Darshan state was wild and uncontrollable and that should have been a big enough sign. But she told me (and I believed her) that it was hard for her to mix with ordinary people because her vibration was so high. *That* was why she was tetchy and irritable. She also told me (and again, I believed her) that because she was keen to get me to the highest level possible, that she had to be harsh with me. That seemed to make sense. Teachers can be hard on their students, it's an age old truth. But, if I'd had my wits about me, I'd have seen that not once, in all those years, did she ever spontaneously give me a dressing down, out of the blue, as part of a grand individually tailored lesson. Not once. All the hundreds of reprimands I received were ones dished out to me by a person who was not grounded, who was unhappy with her life, who couldn't get on with others, who was irritable and angry, who was furious for not getting what she wanted when she wanted it. This, looking back, is the sign of one who's been vampirised and even possessed. There was no serenity, no bliss. If there had been, it would have been evident in all her undertakings. An evolved being radiates unconditional love like Squarehead. That love was never present in HM as she'd allowed herself to be hijacked. The shadow side had tapped into her desire for fame and adulation as a Holy Mother, for her plans to give Darshan to thousands of people, all of whom would be throwing money into a giant collection box.

The only way HM could keep those around her in check was to play that game as it's played by those who run this world, through the base consciousness tactic of fear and control: anyone who didn't fall to their knees in reverence to her and to her god would be cast out and exiled to the outlands, damned for eternity, banished from happiness and never, ever to be saved.

I've no doubt that initially, my "friendship" with Percy helped to bring into sharp focus the gulf between a spiritual teacher working purely (albeit unwillingly) for the shadow side and one working for the greater good of the Creator. Percy seemed to know all about this and told me time and time again that a true enlightened being never demands money from those who are on a search for enlightenment. As Percy began to insert himself carefully into my life as the "new teacher" I started to wonder if he'd ever push the boat out and ask for money himself. He never did in the end, but then, his approach wasn't as crass as HM's. It was incredibly subtle, as you'll see.

Percy was also quick to point out that HM's abilities were not as she claimed. He called her a con artist and scam merchant and pointed out that you can tell a genuine enlightened person as their answers come from intuition. HM, he said, worked like Madam Mysteria in a palm reader's tent at the end of a cheap seaside pier. If you go into that tent with a shiny ring on your finger, she'll soon notice it and tell you, as if by magic, that you're recently married. As the one who's about to hand over a lot of money for a psychic reading, you're drawn in by that and think: *Wow! This lady really knows her stuff!* By extracting little titbits of information from a person desperate for pointers in life, you can build an accurate picture of their world in seconds in the style of Hercule Poirot, super sleuth. Once you become adept at such an art it comes incredibly naturally. Before you know it, you have people eating from your hand.

Percy, in his self-appointed role as the ultimate enlightened one used to come out with words of encouragement and give praise in abundance. He really knew his stuff and I believe to this day that he'd have made a fantastic teacher if he hadn't been so downright duplicitous himself. He certainly knew very well how they worked. HM, on the other hand, very rarely encouraged me with my path.

She didn't really want me to advance as that would have meant my waking up to her. This brings in another question that begs for an answer: to what extent was she aware that she was walking the Service to Self path?

I would say there were times when she was on an angry roll, when she threw plates at Rosie, times she rang me up or faced me in person screaming at the top of her voice, when she really did know. Her eyes would turn wild and she appeared to be actually enjoying surfing a wave of fury and deep-seated negativity that was impossible to distinguish from hatred. This was when she felt that dark power and rode it like the wind – with actual enjoyment. This sensation was quickly followed by her telling herself it was divine righteous anger coming through, and all from her god. I understand that there have always been truly enlightened and successful gurus who've used this righteous anger properly with full effect. But these are not people who would call Social Services and ask for one of their children to be taken away.

So she had a foot in both camps. At times she was aware, at other times, she blanked herself from it. Neither side was willing to admit that the other existed. For this reason, it was as though she was an entity on her own, showing no true fealty either to left or right, only to herself. But ultimately, that sort of angle is still a Service to Self angle. I find it hard to believe that, after all those years, she simply wasn't aware where her loyalties had ended up. Instead, she was just too stuck in her desires to care, not bothered enough to change or to contemplate this deeply. As one gets older and more entrenched in one's ways, to contemplate a life change of a kind that forces you to have to start reassessing the point of your entire existence is far too much to bear. So rather than make a change, she let it drift and told herself that because "God" was speaking to her, whether it was a demonic entity or not, she was home and dry. It's like ignoring a lump on your neck that's growing by the day. At first it doesn't hurt so it can't be anything serious like cancer. You know that you're going to have to have it checked out one day, but in the meantime, you just write it off in the same way you regard an insignificant spot, as just a slight anomaly of the skin, not worthy of contemplation. If it grows, well...you can cross that bridge when you come to it.

For me, the most telling example of the sheer gulf between HM and a proper guru came in an email that she sent Percy when he told her that he intended to leave her sphere of influence and set out to explore "the tree of life". Apparently, this is a spiritual journey that you can only take when you're ready. It requires you actually to experience what it's like to be, for example, an entity such as a crystal or a plant. Higher up, you learn to experience life as an animal and possibly even to communicate as an animal. You can only climb the tree as far as your spiritual abilities will allow you. If you want to explore higher than base consciousness and experience greater spiritual awareness, you need to have done some spiritual work and actually have earned the right…

The problem was (and this was why he had no choice but to leave HM when he did) Percy already instinctively knew that she hadn't made the grade. This was why he declared he had to go it alone. She also let herself down badly. In her email she told him:

"I would like to join you but don't know what to do or even understand what the benefits or effects are. Maybe you can teach me? …I do not want to be left behind. I can also work very fast if I understand what I am doing."

With these words, HM damned herself. For years she'd made out that she was schooled at the highest level and that she'd actually taken training supposedly from "God himself." It seemed strange that one who claimed to have been divinely taught should then be throwing herself at one of her own "students" for teaching. Also, I couldn't help but notice: she wanted to know what the "benefits and effects" were. For HM, that meant: KER-CHING! ££££…$$$$…

You don't enter into a course of serious spiritual exploration in order to reap benefits or get "effects". You do it to understand the nature of the Creator and to provide experience for the Creator. In other words, it's about soul evolution. Ultimately, you have to do it for yourself, by yourself; if your plan is to ride someone else's experience by tapping into them, how can you call yourself enlightened? This was another damaging angle to HM's dangerous game. It was never about "God" after all.

As for Percy, I still can't work out why anyone who loved the shadows thought he could explore the Tree of Life. I can only assume there must be a tree of life to explore for those on a shadow path as well which is basically something like a fake plastic tree that gives you the impression that you're really moving with your soul evolution. If anyone has an answer to that one, please feel free to contact me. For the moment, I'm just going to assume that when Percy told HM he was exploring the Tree of Life, in fact it was just him dishing up yet another giant helping of faecal matter to someone who didn't know better.

Chapter Twenty-Seven

In the autumn of 2008, I decided to take it upon myself to tell HM that I thought she'd been barking up the wrong tree. This was not Percy's idea as he was always encouraging me not to interfere *directly* in anyone's free will. However, a selfish motivation of anger was still welling within me, mixed with a feeling that someone had to say something in case another lost soul like me became drawn into her game. I decided the time had come to assert my independence. By this time, I'd pretty much stopped contacting her myself but she was still phoning me asking for updates to her websites and even for me to talk to people to promote her. Underneath the surface, there was almost an unspoken agreement between the two of us that I was close to fleeing the scene. I'd carried on doing those odd jobs because I felt sorry for her and didn't want to see her fall into complete penury again. In doing so, I knew I was still allowing myself to play a game that was doing neither me, nor her, nor anyone else any good. But once the Germany thing had died a death, I thought her life was far too precarious and I couldn't stand to see her suffer. I thought I *had* to tell her that she'd spent too many years alienating people, seeing darkness in every town and in every single person she met who didn't throw themselves in utter humility at her feet. I was tired of hearing how she was still being attacked day and night and wanted to find a way to tell her that because all her thoughts were fixated on money and so entirely devoted to emotional violence and fighting against the darkness, that she'd actually brought it into manifestation for *herself* and was now so utterly entrenched in negativity she was drowning.

One day, I wrote her a letter. In it, I compared her money situation to that of the young boy in a short story called *The Rocking Horse Winner* by DH Lawrence. The story is about a young lad who lives in a materialistic middle-class household. The boy's mother is obsessed with money and although the family lives quite well, the desire for more consumes her. She concentrates not on

258

what she has, but on what she doesn't have; consequently the constant preoccupation with *lack* of money infects the very bricks and mortar of the home and casts a shadow over the lives of everyone living within the building, none more so than for this sensitive young boy called Paul.

One day Paul receives a rocking horse as a present. Climbing onto it, he rides it faster and faster in his imagination across a far off grassy plane and slips into a kind of trance-like state. While he's in this state, a seemingly irrelevant word pops into his head. The following day, the word appears in the racing pages as the name of a racehorse. Curious to see what happens, the family place a bet at the bookies and miraculously, the horse wins.

Over time, Paul starts to exploit this lucky streak whilst riding his rocking horse and makes his mother a lot of money, all of which she spends, causing yet more need and further disappointment.

On the day of the Derby, the responsibility that Paul feels to come up with the name of the winner causes him to overexert himself and he becomes extremely ill; eventually, he succeeds in finding a name, Malabar. The horse comes in at 14 to 1, bringing in winnings of over £80,000. But during the night Paul dies as a result of his superhuman effort.

His death is clearly the result of the strain placed on him by an implacable mother motivated by greed and unquenchable desire. The tragedy also prompts his uncle to make this observation to the mother:

"My God, Hester, you're £80,000 to the good and a poor devil of a son to the bad. But, poor devil, poor devil, he's best gone out of a life where he rides his rocking horse to find a winner."

I knew as I wrote that letter to HM that I had to get off that rocking horse before it took its toll on my own health. My implacable holy mother was still expecting me to take on the role of calling in the people who would bring her the filthy lucre she desired. Even if it meant I had to sit for hours on end in front of a PC building her websites and then promoting them on the internet, desperately trying to raise their profiles and ranking as she expected me to.

When I'd finished writing the letter, I looked back over what I'd written and was stunned to find the best part of a thousand words written in my handwriting but with a strange slant to it. There wasn't a single error on the pages and no crossings out at all. Also, I couldn't remember writing most of it and came to believe that the writing may have originated from my deep unconscious, that part of you that communicates in dreams where there's always a kernel of truth in the imagery which you cannot ignore.

I rang HM and told her what had happened and she immediately went into a panic. I told her that what I was about to read out to her would cause he some pain and to brace herself. Earlier in the week, she'd rung me in tears asking me to do absolutely *anything* I could to get to the bottom of her situation and to find out once and for all what the blockage was in her life and why, after all those years, she was still at such a low ebb. To me, this was the answer and I was frustrated but not wholly surprised when she said she didn't want to hear the letter, just a summary of it given in my own words. The fact that I told her the contents had come down as a piece of automatic writing seemed to scare her.

So I told HM the story of *The Rocking Horse Winner*. I also mentioned that she needed to stop calling herself a Holy Mother, telling her that the stress of calling in all those people who were looking for a spiritual person to lean on would cause her immense damage. I told her that the razzmatazz of the guru thing was irrelevant to the Western spiritual culture where we must now learn to connect to the Source Field within ourselves through a deeper understanding of our personal experiences, through observations of our own character traits in self-analysis and quietening down the monkey chatter in our heads. I told her that she'd always been in danger of people equating her with a religious zealot in a sari with a wistful name. As I was only giving her a summary of what had come through in the letter-writing session, I could keep to myself the fact that I knew Paul in the story was in fact me. Instead, I was hoping that HM would see herself as Paul and see a warning in the story, hinting that she could kill herself with stress and flog herself to death for people who were only looking for a Holy Mother as a spiritual crutch, knowing that once those people started to pile pressure upon her, even unwittingly like me, she would start to cave in from all the darkness she saw in them. This had often happened. People like me would come to her door expecting the great white hope for the future and find an empty shell that would crumble under the slightest pressure.

HM immediately started crying and wanted to know what source this piece of writing had come from. I said I'd go away and find out but knew all I was doing was playing for time to see how the information would sink in.

I didn't hear from her for some days. When she finally phoned me, she'd done what I'd expected her to do and talked herself out of the validity of everything that I'd said, picking at every one of the points, twisting it to make it seem as though she was doing the right thing already and was still on the right track. For weeks after that she was still angrily trying to get me to find out where my automatic writing had come from. When I didn't tell her, she decided to ignore the entire incident completely.

To be honest, it upset me to hear her cry on the phone that night. But it was the combination of her misery and her consequent rejection of all help that made me decide that 2009 would be the year in which I just had to cease all communication with her.

As Scooter was still living with her at the time, there were evenings when I had no choice but to speak to her if she picked up the phone. But after a while I arranged with Scooter to phone me and I only spoke to HM when it was absolutely necessary.

Chapter Twenty-Eight

Over Easter 2009, Scooter came to visit me. By this time, he had a vast number of friends he'd made at college and was now talking and acting differently. There was a teenage swagger about his way and I felt alienated by it. I'd have been able to tolerate it however, if Scooter hadn't come over with the head on that everyone was a complete idiot and that everything was now officially about him and him alone. This was not what I'd expected from a lad who'd always been so loving and easy to get along with. He was clearly depressed and struggling with life. We talked in depth and discussed the possibility that the way he'd been brought up, in such unstable circumstances, may have had some bearing on his state of mind. Some months earlier, HM had tried to slash her wrists in front of him again and this had shaken him once more, just as deeply as it had when he'd been ten. He seemed especially to be struggling with the fact that he loved his mother very much but was having trouble reconciling this person who was a strange self-obsessed, angry and isolated woman with the person who he'd looked up to and loved as a young boy loves his mother. That unconditional love had been dissolved somehow and as far as I could make out, all he could see was someone who brought all her troubles to his door and expected him to be a post to lean on. At this time, Scooter still wanted a mother, not a needy helpless person who still made out that she was an almighty "God-realised" oracle one moment but turned out to be a collapsing house of cards the next.

I tried to support Scooter that week, but my words fell on deaf ears. He seemed to be in a very dark place and wasn't willing to find a solution outside of drowning himself in drink and casual sex. When I dropped him off at the station at the end of his stay, he reminded me that HM expected me to give him £20 so that he could buy a pair of boots. For the first time ever, I refused. Most of my motivation was selfish. I wanted to send out a strong clear message to HM that if she wasn't going to change and start a new life process that would take her to her own solutions for her insolvency, I wasn't going to step in and prop her up. But the message was also for Scooter: get off the self-obsession train. I told him I'd be there for him and I knew he was listening and believed me. That was lucky because it made things easier for him when I spent the next six weeks to two months refusing to have any communication with either of them. When the phone went, I ignored it. I felt terrible about Scooter, but not about her. At last it was my turn to throw my toys from the pram.

When I read on Scooter's Facebook page that he'd aced his exams and had got himself a place at his university of choice, I was thrilled. Communication started again and I found him still to be oversexed, drinking and smoking way too much, but more open to me. Over the summer he threw himself into all sorts of jobs and made a good amount of cash to take to university. He seemed to be enjoying life a little more and I was happy for him.

However, when I heard that HM was now demanding money from him I was incredibly upset. I told him that his money was for him to spend at university and every single penny of it would be needed; I also hinted to him that I'd had enough and when the time came for him to leave, he was to tell his mother that I no longer wanted a guru or to help with any websites or admin tasks. He's never confirmed or denied that he ever had that conversation with her, but as it's turned out, since the day he left for university, because my free secretarial services had been withdrawn, she hasn't phoned me once.

About three weeks before he left home for good, Scooter called me one night and told me that he'd been asked to give me a message. The message was this: could I find out how his mother was going to get money to pay her rent and buy food now that her single mother benefits were stopped because her son was leaving home to go to university.

I sent this message back: *I haven't got a clue…*

Chapter Twenty-Nine

Despite not having any contact with HM, I've kept in contact with Rosie in all the years she's been off the scene. The people who fostered her seemed to be wonderful folks who welcomed her into their home as one of the family. She had her own room and her own TV and PC and was allowed to go out in the evenings, to wear makeup and do all the things that a normal teenager of her age does.

Rosie has turned out to be quite independent-spirited and having got herself into college and then on to university has faced all her problems without the help of any biological parents, something that I was very lucky when I was her age to have been able to take for granted. Occasionally I got a distressed phone call from her asking me if she really was the terrible kid that she felt she must have been to have been forced to leave home. I always pointed out to her that she wasn't and reminded her that we were all in a very strange and unnatural situation and that she'd made the best of her childhood. I honestly don't remember her being a terrible kid. She was certainly wilful, but that isn't the sign of bad behaviour.

One thing that I do remember however was a nasty little incident that I got involved in when I was at the height of my blindness over her mother's "divinity". One day HM asked me to get Rosie to write a story. I was ordered to go through it with a fine toothcomb and pick out all the errors of grammar and spelling and be prepared to give Rosie a good trashing if the story was not up to scratch and throw the page into the bin. Like an idiot, I took HM by her word and thinking this was some kind of test for me, duly ripped into Rosie's efforts with gusto. I then screwed up the page and threw it into the wastepaper basket, only to see Rosie give me such a disarming and cute look of mock disgust and flee to her bedroom.

I went in to see HM who'd been listening in a neighbouring room. Her face was filled with horror:

"You totally overdid it!" she exclaimed. "I didn't mean for you to hurt her."

The following day, I tried to apologise to Rosie, but the damage was done and she pretty much blanked me for a week. Looking back however, I see this incident as something quite positive. When faced with someone being cruel to her own daughter, HM was genuinely distressed. Although I still think that HM's removal of Rosie from her life was a terrible consequence of her disastrous game, she was still trying to love Rosie. In retrospect, one thing is clear though: all efforts were buried beneath far too many selfish considerations.

Since Scooter came back from Germany, he's made several attempts to build bridges with Rosie. For a long time, Scooter blamed himself for always being the one who could do no wrong. He feels he often played up to that fact and in a world where both of them had to fight like cat and dog to gain what little parental energy was coming their way, it was always Scooter who managed to muscle himself to the front of the queue. Time and time again I've tried to talk him through this and tell him he was only doing what other kids of his age would do in such difficult circumstances, but he struggles to come to terms with it. This situation has been made worse by the fact that Rosie point blank refuses to discuss the past with either of us and would rather make small talk or sit in total silence than allow her thoughts to stray to an area of her life that still causes her a lot of pain. I've warned Scooter that it may be many years before either of them will be able to feel enough distance from the situation to be able to discuss it over a cup of coffee.

One person I did hear from again after she'd done the phone-slamming thing was Kat. One day in 2005 as I was crossing the road outside my office, I heard her shouting at me from the driver's side of a bashed up old car. I ran up and greeted her and she shoved a piece of paper in my hand with her phone number on it.

Even though we'd parted on bad terms, I was so intrigued to see how her life had gone once she'd been free of me and HM. One evening she came up to the village to see me and we had a long chat. She told me how much she'd wanted to get away from the HM days in her head and that all her years of suffering had meant finally that this was her last incarnation. I nearly choked on my pizza. I didn't say anything, but I felt so sorry for her when I heard that. It's a sign of someone who's still struggling with her spirituality. To be wishing your life away thinking that you're home and dry and can rest on your laurels is to store up issues. We have an eternity of evolution before us. If that means exploring whole new universes and brand new horizons then we simply have to move with that flow. In our perfect state, we're fully aware of this and we therefore choose lives and incarnations that we know are going to allow us to bring the maximum amount of experience to the Universe as possible. There's no sitting around in a heaven-world basking in glory and becoming complacent.

Despite our variant outlooks, Kat and I did try to get it together as friends for a short while. But then one day, she rang me up totally breathless. She'd been looking at HM's website and come across something that she honestly believed was about her. It wasn't anything bad, just a little story about someone that HM knew which was helping her to make some spiritual point or other. Kat started shouting at me, asking how I dared to be a part of this when she'd expressly asked me to delete all references to her in all of HM's books and web pages. I quickly pointed out that the story was not about her, it just contained similarities to her own life. She seemed to accept this and we left it at that until the next falling out. When that came, I was horrified by what she did.

When Scooter came to stay with me in the early spring of 2007 just after his own part in the Germany debacle, he was quite woeful about all the people who'd come and gone from his life over the years, all of whom seemed to have fled in a hurry and with no small amount of distaste for his mother and her work. Scooter said he wanted to get in touch with some of them and see how the lie of the land was for them. He wanted to know if they'd ever talk to him and be civil and not blame him personally. He also wanted to fill in the blanks of a childhood that he reckoned he was beginning to suppress in an unhealthy way as it was too upsetting to think about.

One day, he came across an old mobile phone of mine. He got it going and found Kat's number in the phonebook. Immediately he asked me if he could phone Kat just for a chat. As Kat and I hadn't spoken for ages, I was a little unsure, but not wanting to block Scooter in any way, I warned him that she may not be too nice to him, but if he really wanted to, he could give it a go. The first thing that happened was Kat's daughter answered the phone. When she heard who it was, she hung up immediately. Scooter just shrugged his shoulders and walked disgustedly from the room.

However, half an hour later, the phone rang and it was Kat. I allowed Scooter to answer it and they began to chat. I moved to another room and listened as Scooter made inroads into finding out where Kat stood. She allowed him to speak and before long, he was telling her all about his terrible life and how he just wanted to get away and do his own thing. I ran into the room where he was speaking and gesticulated wildly, waving my hands in front of his face to beg him to stop. I remembered very well how duplicitous Kat could be and this was not the way to interact with her.

In the end, he allowed Kat to fix a time for the two of them to meet up whilst I was at work. I wasn't happy for him to do that as I had a terrible feeling that getting too close to someone who was so angry with his mother would hurt him even more; however, I went along with it hoping beyond hope that Kat would now see her way clear, compassionately and with love, to help a young man begin to get his life in order.

The following day, when I was at work, Kat rang to speak to Scooter and told him that she was going to help him. But first of all, she would have to tell him who his father was. She then took it upon herself to mention someone's name in that connection and horrified Scooter to the core.

When I got home from work, he looked at me with eyes full of confusion and asked me if this piece of information was true. I was absolutely dumbstruck and furious. I'd never discussed Scooter's paternity with him as it isn't any of my business and now for Kat to wade in clearly with all guns firing, intent on causing trouble for all of us was well beyond the pale. So I rang her and asked her what she thought she was doing. I then received a pleasant little blast from the past as she began screaming at me at the top of her voice. She accused me of being cruel to Scooter by sending him back to his mother when he didn't want to go back to her; she accused HM of being an atrocious mother and an unstable psychopath. I tried to say in between the screaming that I had no choice as it was Social Services that were insistent that Scooter be reunited with his mother. She accepted this for a few seconds and then set off on another rant against me, accusing me of trying to drag her into a world that she'd hoped to leave behind. I told her it hadn't been my idea for Scooter to contact her and that I'd only allowed him to do it because I thought she'd have the heart to help him through a difficult period of his life. This was like a red rag to a bull. She started screaming again and I began to realise something. The damage to Kat was so great that she was using this situation to offload all her hatred and negativity over what had happened back in the late nineties. As I was still struggling so much myself to work through everything, I just wasn't of a mind to start dealing with someone who was, as I saw it, making everyone else's life miserable because *she* was miserable. So I cut her off in mid scream.

Scooter, who was sitting opposite, looked at me in utter shock. The first thing he said was "God, I'm so sorry, Paul..." He blamed himself for putting me through a difficult and uncomfortable situation. But I wasn't angry with him. It wasn't Scooter's fault. It was hard enough for him not to have had a dad, let alone a mother who point blank refused to discuss who that father was. I just didn't want to upset him even more by laying more guilt at his door. I found something else for us to do that evening to take our minds off what had happened and we both tried to move on.

Whenever I think of Kat these days, I remember with humour how she came on to me. I'd probably only been with HM for about five months, when one day, she came round to my flat dressed to the nines and wearing makeup. This was unusual, as normally, she wore black like a nun and fortified herself with rosary beads. Makeup was banned, not just by HM, but also in an ethos of self-denial and mortification of the emotions that she wore on her "habit dress" like a medal or armour.

I really didn't fancy Kat. This was not to say she was ugly; far from it. The problem lay with me: I couldn't get past her constant betrayals. Because she and Gary were obsessed with seeing me as having some major problems with women, she took my lack of interest to mean terror and duly appointed herself as Sexual

Healer. She often used to say her role was to heal men and to break the sexual barriers down with her special "ways".

When she sat down next to me on the floor that day, I wanted to run a mile! I moved away from her and went and sat on a chair. She didn't seem too perturbed but I knew I'd caused offence. She went home much earlier than expected that evening and I have to say, there'd been no sex: just a sack load of lectures motivated by her "slightly" skewed angle on my own mountain of issues.

You wouldn't mind only for years after that incident, she went round telling people that I wanted to have sex with her:

"I know he wants to make love to me," she told Gary. "But I really shouldn't...you know. It's not the right thing to do. I've always told Paul I'm happy being very good friends with him, but he just can't get past his lust for me..."

Talking of lust (or lack of it) HM's books advised people to scream Jesus's name, or take a cold shower to dissipate sexual urges. I've never tried this as I can't really see how gratifying such a pastime would be. Aren't such assertions a trifle naïve? What are we all to do? Turn ourselves into frigid, sexually oppressed mortifiers of flesh? Provided that no one is harmed physically and mentally and there's consent on both sides, why on earth should we go back to Victorian frigidity, the chastity belt and "close your eyes and think of the homeland..."

Here's something that will shock you. Because HM insisted that all her trainees had to be celibate, I felt I had to obey. So I left relationships behind, took her advice and meditated. It worked for me, but only because my search to understand the Creator took precedence over everything. I would never recommend it though. It's a terrible idea for most people and because we're beings that are brimming with love, passion and genuine deep feelings, it's a course of action that's against everything that we are as humans. Surely we should be promoting self-acceptance in a world where too much of this sort of religious intolerance and bigotry abound. Let's be mature about this. There are times when we need to restrain ourselves in any situation, but if self-restraint becomes unhealthy self-denial, then we're all in trouble.

After many years under her influence, I actually found it hard to go back to relationships when the time came to start living normally again. In fact, here's the shocker: I still haven't managed to. I don't blame HM for that. It's actually my own doing. Sometimes a spiritual search can take you away from real life and that isn't always the best place to be in. The simplest solution is never to lose contact with your emotions or your sexuality, to rejoice in it and make it sacred. There's nothing sacred in enforced celibacy where there's a controller standing over you telling you not to think of yourself as a loving, beautiful being.

This is one example of the bind I was in with HM's rigid teachings. If you feel ready to be celibate because you're trying to advance spiritually and if it suits what you want to achieve then that's highly laudable. But you must be ready. Although I succeeded on that front, I do sometimes think I missed out on too much experience in getting to grips with my fellow humans. Perhaps if I didn't use to swear so liberally after nodding off, I'd be with someone now..!

Chapter Thirty

In the early summer of 2009, Percy started to talk about someone who he'd met at his spiritualist church, a man called John. Percy had been recommended to John because for many years, in fact, almost from the day he was born, John had been plagued by nasty visitations and entities. He'd had a particularly rough childhood, abandoned by his parents and left to fend for himself alone in a house where every night he'd been taunted by visitations of a horrifying nature. I wish I could go into more detail about John's life, but he hasn't really given me permission to do so and a lot of his experiences are intensely personal to him.

John had come to Percy for help to try and stop these entities from tormenting him. He was desperate to move on and use his extremely well-developed psychic abilities for good. As far as I remember, he wanted to bring comfort to people by becoming a medium and helping those desperate to contact loved ones who'd passed on to the astral realms.

Percy told me that he'd finally helped John and removed the influence of a particular "demonic entity" that had been making his life hell for some time. As a result, Percy implied that John was so incredibly grateful for finding peace and tranquillity after a life full of fear and misery, that he was almost on his knees to him, thanking him for releasing him once and for all from his prison. Percy was also quick to point out that much of John's problem could be attributed to the way he lived his life: slightly on the edges of society, ducking and diving a little, taking a few legal shortcuts, possibly not being entirely wholesome in his view of the world. Percy pointed out that entities of this nature enjoy the company of those who are prepared to "economise" a little on ethics and principles. "He needs to clean up his act!" Percy claimed. "And in order to help him onto the right path, I've given him your number. We both reckon you can write a good book about his life. People will be amazed when they hear his story."

I was quite up for that actually: it sounded like John had a lot of interesting stuff to say about himself. When he phoned me a few hours later, he was also full of the idea and really wanted to start telling me his life story and opening up.

What I didn't realise was that this was a set up on Percy's part to hold John in place. He was fascinated by John, eerily so. He kept on referring to him as a Jin and explained to me that in North African cultures, this was what we know as a Genie (ie. a Genie in a bottle). Percy pointed out that John had all the energies around him to create money and that as a Jin, he attracted money into his life like a magnet. John confirmed this to me: whenever he started out on some kind of business venture, it invariably succeeded. There'd been times when he'd been quite wealthy, but because of the visitations, things had always fallen apart and he'd ended up unable to sustain the energy. He told me he'd lost many relationships and even the odd business because his life had suddenly been torn apart by the darkness that stalked him. At times, it had driven him to the brink of despair. What was creepy for me was Percy's utter obsession with John as this genie and he became quite open with his intentions:

"...see, we're gonna need as much cash as possible if we're gonna get my teaching off the ground," he said. "I need to get me and the kids out of this place and away from London. I can see myself living in a very large house. I'm going to be very successful as a famous teacher for the new era. I'll have a secretary and people to do work for me...blah...blah ...blah..."

At the time, I totally overlooked the fact that I'd heard all this nonsense before from HM. Once more, I was coming face to face with a classic Service to Self operation intent on hovering over the altruistic like flies around horse manure waiting for the drawer of that cash register to come springing open. As usual, I suspended my disapproval.

After a couple of weeks of banging on about the general excellence of John, Percy suddenly clammed up about him. I decided to ask why and, struggling to contain his fury, he announced that John had done a bunk and moved out of town. I could always tell when Percy was furious. In an effort to come across to me as this incredibly wise and caring being from the highest spiritual realms in the Universe, he would try to be placid

272

and calm, but I could tell from the vibration in his voice that he wanted to get out a knife and go on a killing spree.

"He'll be back!" he exclaimed. "He needs me. He knows he can't get away. This thing that stalks him will only go away when I'm in his life."

Like an idiot, I believed that twist on the situation and even though Percy was imperceptibly turning out to be the new HM, I still trusted his ability to help people like John. Once again, I was being utterly naïve. If John needed Percy to keep him in the Light, why had he fled?

Of course, what I didn't realise was that John had actually fled from Percy himself. The most almighty storm was whipping up around John and this time, the source of all that dark energy was right under my very nose. Percy was playing the sorcerer and calling all the elements to his command. When John fled, it was not with a flea in his ear. It was with a furious wind at his back as Percy summoned all his armies. You may think I'm being overdramatic here. But what happened over the next few months shows this to be more serious than it would seem at a mere glance.

As it turned out, John did come back. I phoned Percy one Sunday morning and he announced that John had only gone AWOL for a while to sort his head out and in doing so had run into some problems. The visitations were back and seemingly worse than ever. He'd been in a fight and had ended up in hospital. I felt really sorry for him and on the surface at least, Percy himself was showing compassion. Actually, he was wringing his twisted hands in glee. The cash cow was back in the field.

"He needs me!" repeated Percy triumphantly. "He can never really get away as he's so immoral; entities with nefarious designs will forever follow him around. Each time he does this, I'll be the one who has to sort him out. He'll always come back with his tail between his legs."

At the end of August 2009, John and I were invited over to Percy's spiritualist church and to spend an afternoon together. John and I agreed to meet up beforehand to have some lunch and then meet Percy at a coffee shop afterwards. Percy seemed remarkably uncomfortable about this arrangement and I couldn't work out why. He kept warning me to keep all conversation to basics and not to discuss anything of importance. I didn't realise it at the time, but the sorcerer was terrified that his apprentices were going to raise revolution behind his back and he was obviously riled. As it turned out, it wasn't any conversation I had with John that made me want to revolt against Percy, it was Percy himself.

When I met John at the station, I liked him immediately. He's the kind of chap who wears his heart on his sleeve and I could tell from his demeanour that he was genuinely looking for answers to his problems and trying to change his outlook on life. I could see that he was the kind who'd spent his whole life living on the edge. Percy had observed that he'd had some lives as a Viking and now I could see what he meant.

As soon as John and I started talking about Percy, I could tell that he was not as impressed by him as I was. When we'd first talked some months earlier, Percy and he had only known each other a few days and John was like me, full of joy at having met such a seemingly wise and spiritual man. But that enthusiasm was now long gone. John was suspicious of him and there was now a dark cloud appearing over John's head whenever I mentioned Percy's name. John knew that I still liked Percy and kept his suspicions about him to himself. He could see that I was still very much taken in by Percy's "thing" and clearly didn't feel it was his responsibility to wake me up. I think I'd have done the same in his position.

After lunch, John and I met up with Percy in a coffee shop. Percy and I had never actually met each other and when he first clapped eyes on me, he walked over and gave me a hug. I thought it was over-the-top myself, but I responded as positively as possible. To be honest, I'm glad he did choose to greet me in that fashion, despite the strangeness of it; it was my chance to really check out his vibration: and it was totally, completely and utterly *flat*. There really was no love there. He felt like a void. Even to look at, I just couldn't sense the divinity that he claimed for himself anywhere on him. It was like looking at a two-dimensional TV picture in monochrome. I decided to hold back my disappointment and buried my intuition as usual.

Almost as soon as we sat down in the coffee shop, John was fidgety and uncomfortable. I was accidentally rude to him because I really wanted to talk to Percy and poor old John sat there as if he wasn't wanted. Percy monopolised the conversation as always, imposing his views, emphasising and accentuating his status as he who knoweth all. At one point he brought out some rose quartz crystals for us both to keep and John looked at his as if it would turn to acid in his hand. I sat there like an over-enthusiastic puppy lapping it all up. Percy must have been laughing at me inside and loving the attentions of this zealous naïve spiritual seeker hanging off his every word. There must have been so much energy in it for him and a real coup. People like that never make any energy of their own: instead they use what we call a consumptive or vampiric modality to feed off others. He was plugging into me and I was letting him with every single last ounce of my free will.

The rest of the day passed off uneventfully. John and I accompanied Percy to his little old spiritualist church in a London backstreet and once again, I ignored my intuition. The church was cold and musty. There was no love inside it, or if there ever was, it had long since been soaked up. Percy had once claimed that he was trying to use the church as his beacon. When he told me that, he sold it to me as "a beacon of Light", but in reality, that was just code or "Percy-speak" that covered his real intentions. He was clearly working his hardest to turn it into a little beacon of darkness and complete despair in an area of London that was already in the doldrums. There was nothing aspirational about the atmosphere inside: it was dank and dead. If there were people who went there on a regular basis who did try to bring their Light with them, it must have been snuffed out in an instant and drawn like smoke up a chimney into some void.

All through the proceedings, John was incredibly uncomfortable and seemed to be under duress. As soon as the service was over, he rushed outside for a cigarette and seemed reluctant to come back in. I had a feeling that he wasn't about to tell anyone what was wrong because he saw me and Percy as mates who needed to be left alone in each other's company as we had a lot to discuss; it was only some weeks later that I realised what the truth was.

As autumn turned to winter in 2009, I carried on with my ill-starred association with Percy and continued to take in all his nonsense. He was still lecturing the living daylights out of me every Sunday morning on the phone, never allowing me to get a word in edgeways, interrupting me if I spoke for any longer than about ten seconds, cracking down hard on any sign of independent thought. By this time, I was on the internet every evening, reading up on what people were saying on the 2012 phenomenon, listening to all sorts of angles on the situation via YouTube, investigating ancient prophecies, checking out the scientific side and reading book after book on the subject. I would try to bring some of my learning into conversations with Percy but he just didn't want to know. All he wanted to talk about was darkness, manipulation, duality, the end of the world in a grand cataclysm with millions dead, war, famine, disease, poverty; in fact, anything that pertained to suffering. One of his big subjects was how he supposedly made deals with demonic entities who were standing guard as sentinels over trapped souls. To this day, I still don't understand what he means by that. Surely there's no such thing, as any soul that finds itself in a trapped afterlife state has surely, on some level, agreed to experience such a situation. The soul alone will decide what's good for it, not some meddling idiot from London. As Anna once said, why make deals with these entities anyway? What can possibly be gained from such a situation?

I think Percy thought he was some kind of spiritual anti-hero and spent all his time covering up with great bravado the fact that he was just another New Age legend in his own bloody dinner bowl...

Percy never ever phoned me, it was always me who phoned him; but on the day he did, a weekday, he pulled a really nasty one on me. I was at home one evening when he called to say that John was in trouble. John had phoned Percy in desperation and was begging him in tears for help. I don't think it would be fair to give too many details away at this point as John has not given me permission to talk in depth about this, but let's just say that he'd gone AWOL again and was cowering in his car in an extremely dark and lonely place, freezing cold and covered in a blanket. He'd phoned Percy on his mobile and was pleading with him for help. He told him he was being hounded by something incredibly demonic that was screaming at him and threatening to kill him. Percy suggested that I phone him and try to calm him down, but at the same time, goad this demonic thing into coming out and fighting:

"When you speak to John," he said, "shout at this thing, tell it to stop hiding and come out into the open. I'm not scared; tell it to come and talk to me and if it wants a fight. Well, BRING IT ON! I'm ready for it."

Honestly, he was desperately trying to cast himself in the same mould as Father Merrin from *The Exorcist:* all ready to go into battle with a contorted individual projectile-vomiting pea soup all over the place. He seemed to be absolutely lapping it up and incredibly high on some kind of tidal wave of self-importance. It must have been a real rush for the man, a little nobody from "nowheresville" playing everyone like a conductor in front of a demonic orchestra.

So I rang John. Luckily he answered the phone, but I got the shock of my life. He really was in a terrible state, weeping and pleading for help, begging me to call Percy and ask him to "get this thing off of me…*please…*"

I promised him I'd try and get him some help and we ended the conversation there and then. Within seconds I got a text from him begging me not to contact him anymore. I couldn't work out why. I only wanted to help, and in fact, by this time, I was getting really worried. I spoke to Percy again and he then advised me to call the Police.

The problem was, I only vaguely knew John's whereabouts and when I made the call, I couldn't give the lady I spoke to any details at all apart from John's mobile number. As it turned out, that was all they needed. Using whatever technology the Police use to track people's mobile signals, they hunted John down and helped him to "safety". I know this because the following day, I got a terse answerphone message from a Policeman who sounded incredibly condescending, informing me that their search had been successful.

This phone call was then followed by an extremely aggressive text from John himself, informing me that I had got him (and others) into a whole heap of trouble with the Police. They had found him and rather than getting him some help, had used the situation to bring the law down on his head. The text also asked me *"who the f*** are you and Percy working for, anyway?"*

I was staggered: I'd never intended to get anyone into trouble and had only wanted to help in the most idealistic and pragmatic way possible. I ignored the text and just kept my feelings to myself at that point, but I was hurt and felt incredibly sorry for John. I really wanted to phone him and check he was fine, but changed my mind as I just didn't want to cause any more problems with anyone.

The whole situation left me with an unpleasant taste in my mouth. Nothing was ever straightforward with these spiritual teacher people. I was really asking myself, if they were all God-realised and divinely conscious or whatever, why it was that trouble seemed to stalk them at every turn. One thing I did miss, at least for the moment, was this: when John said "please can you ask Percy to get this thing off me", did he mean, "please can Percy remove this thing that I've brought into my life", or did he *in fact* mean, "please can you ask Percy to remove this thing that he, Percy, has attached to me."

I should have had a good sit down and a ponder about that, because if I had, I'd have realised that Mr Percy Wisdom was in fact just another petty satanist playing a nasty little game, a self-styled sorcerer-thug filling his empty life with energy from sad little candle-burning late-night shenanigans in front of an altar with a dead cat.

2010 started off very quietly for me. I was not to know that it would turn out to be a momentous year for me, when finally, after all my bumbling around, I learned to walk the path on my own, using my own wit and intuition as my guide, to stop looking out for external help and for signposts. Before that happened however, I still had a rather interesting hoop or two to jump through.

During the Christmas period, Percy had sent me a delightful little Christmas card. In it, he'd wished me a Happy Christmas and a "spurtule" 2010. Next to his words, he'd drawn a somewhat childish pyramid with an all-seeing eye inside it.

Of course, I should have been suspicious. This was a guy who was claiming to be an advanced spiritual being and he couldn't even spell the word. Why was he also using that eye, the calling card of the purveyors of violent oppression and darkness within this matrix of ours?

Percy was now trying to pull out all the stops and clearly felt it was time for us to stop beating about the bush. In retrospect, I realise he must have been planning to unveil himself: the spelling error was deliberate. This man was not educated, but he wasn't a complete idiot. When he said he wished me a spurtule New Year, that's exactly what he meant: not "spiritual", but *spurtule*: his very own word for a year full of sorcery and meddling, of demonic forces and the infliction of pain and suffering. To have used the correct word would have been to wish me away from his influence.

One Sunday, Percy suggested I make my way over to his spiritualist church again as there was a very interesting medium coming who everyone called "Jeff the psychic postman". Percy described Jeff as nothing short of superb with his readings and a real natural medium.

So, at the end of February, a chilly Saturday evening, I made my way to London and met up with Percy at his nearest tube station. He didn't try to hug me this time, but his energy was as flat as ever and he made a sort of vague attempt to be enthusiastic about seeing me that didn't really work. As I followed him to some awful burger restaurant (the kind of place where everything is plastic, including the food, and the chips are encrusted with salt), for the first time, I could see a red warning light flashing in my mind's eye. I turned up in London all full of the joys of spring, but seeing Percy pulled me down. Just below the surface of my conscious mind, my suspicions were on the verge of piercing that veil of ignorance that had kept me in stasis for so long. Too much was going wrong with this venture; Percy was not doing a good job at keeping up appearances and was becoming complacent.

As we waited in line for our food Percy came out with a remarkable comment that floored me. His wife had been ill for some time and he suddenly said: *"It's ok, she'll be out of the way soon, Paul. Then we can get on with everything. We have work to do."*

As I watched him order his junk food, I wondered what he meant. I was shaken up and immediately did my usual trick of refusing to process this utterance through my intuition. Actually, I was too busy being horrified by the fact that someone who called himself "enlightened" was about to tuck into a meal that was completely devoid of nutrition. It didn't seem to bother him. Looking at him, I realised this sort of fare was staple for him. It's no wonder that with a diet like that he felt the need to plug into the energetic ones and suck them dry of their life force.

Once again, Percy monopolised the conversation and came out with some classics which were to serve me in good stead a few weeks later when the time came for me to ditch him. He called me "his resource" and openly admitted that it would be through the money that I made from writing that he would get his teaching thing up and running. He claimed that if John ever came back, he would stomp up the cash too. Strange, there was never a suggestion that he should ever come up with his *own* resources for this venture.

Over the course of the conversation, I started talking about the pyramid structure of society, with its cabal of unknown individuals who run the planet at the top, creaming off the energies and resources of those on the lower stratas and for whom there is little or no information trickling down. The ones lower down are your worker ants, if you will, the prisoners kept in a state of slavery by a matrix imposed by those at the top. I watched his eyes as I talked about this and within seconds they had glazed over and he was no longer listening. Then, out of the blue, he interrupted me and started talking about the use of the pyramid shape and structure as a Universal energy conductor. I realised in an instant that he wasn't as "in-the-know" as I thought he was. With thousands of people unplugging themselves from the matrix at this time all over the world, the man who was calling himself their future teacher couldn't even have an intelligible conversation about the simple stuff, the basics of the new Truth and Ascension movements that are superseding the New Age paradigm. Percy was totally lost, still stuck in his world of Sorcery and Enochian magic. It was also bizarre because I was convinced he was au fait with the darker interpretation of Masonry, so he should have known better.

Later on in the evening, we moved over to the spiritualist church and took our places inside. I met Jeff the psychic postman and was really impressed with him. He was an absolute natural, moving around the audience and giving people messages so deftly, they were amazed. Eventually, his attentions alighted upon Percy and he decided to give me and Percy a joint reading.

"I think you're both working together," he said. 'And it's all around this 2012 Shift of the Ages. He said he felt that we had some part to play in it, that things we were doing were in direct relation to the situation. Percy was sitting to the left of me and I could feel his self-satisfied smugness filling the room. This was *just* what he needed: a little outside influence to hook me in even further, someone with some clout to justify his claims about himself as a future guiding light.

The thing is, I was waking up now. I noticed something and I can honestly say, that for the first time since that night of fate when I made my way in puppy dog enthusiastic ignorance up to the front door of HM's house, I was about to really think for myself.

What I noticed was that Jeff was under some kind of duress. His face was turning red. When he'd been giving the readings to the other people in the congregation, he'd been standing in the same place more or less. Now, he was pacing up and down, not looking in our direction, blinking, almost fighting for breath.

What he said next shocked me.

"Which one of you put out a message to the skies recently asking for help from ETs?"

Percy almost shouted: "it was me! That's me. That's exactly what I've been doing!"

I wheeled around and faced him. I could feel a frown wanting to form itself across my face, but I stopped it for the sake of the psychic postman.

Percy had in fact claimed he'd been talking with aliens. Two weeks earlier, he'd alleged that he'd been contacted by a group calling themselves the "Zanussians" whom he assured me wanted to work with him. I asked him what sort of form this work would take and all he would say was: "I don't know at this point…"

Believe it or not the following week, I said to him, "so, have you been working with the Zanussians yet?"

There was silence.

"The who?"

I said: "you know, that alien group you said you were going to be working with…"

There was another short hesitation and then he blurted out: "Oh…oh…errrr…yeah…yeah… Um…well, we haven't started work yet."

281

If Percy was in contact with an alien group called the Zanussians, then I'm a monkey's uncle. I think, really, all that happened was he probably made himself a cup of tea one day, sat down to drink it, started thinking about what he was going to "lecture" me on the following Sunday and came up with a little ruse. *Let's make up some aliens and impress Paul with my abilities and the fact that everyone out there wants to talk to ME!*

At this point his beady little eyes would have fallen upon the washing machine. *Ah, the appliance of science! How very space age! Let's call them Zanussians from the planet Zanussi. He's bound to believe me!*

In point of fact, it was me who'd made that call to outer space. I'd been out in my garden one night watching the stars. All I said was: "this is a call to friends out there who are on the path of Service to Others....I'm ready and waiting for when the time is right."

I then went indoors and got on with my evening.

So Jeff said to Percy: "then, *you're* the one who offered yourself up for dialogue 'when the time was right?'".

My heart started to beat really wildly. Those were my exact words. I'd been heard!

To my left I could hear Percy lying through his teeth: "Yes, that was me, I'm the one who talks to the aliens..."

That was such a defining moment: it happened in an instant, I woke up to the world I'd created for myself. This man next to me who'd sold himself and his "thing" to me so artfully for two whole years – in a moment of utter vanity – had let his veil drop and I could see him for what he was: a complete and total liar.

As if to emphasise this intuitive break of mine, Jeff was clearly looking at me and actually became quite insistent. He said:

"...I think it's *you* they're telling me about, not the gentleman next to you."

Suddenly, I could feel Percy's eyes drilling into me and I really sensed his anger. He always hated any energy being directed away from him. This was his humiliation.

Jeff went on to say that I would have to go west somewhere, to Dorset or Wiltshire. I would know exactly where to be when the time was right. The words he actually used were, "when the alignment was correct."

"Make sure you take a notebook or a tape recorder when you go," he said, "and you'll learn so much from them. I wish you all the luck in the world. Keep your senses open and you'll know exactly what to do. You will go, won't you?"

I replied very emphatically in the affirmative and he moved with a knowing smile on to the next person. Meanwhile, I could feel Percy's frustration like a fire at my side.

At the end of the service, Jeff went into the quiet room behind the stage and the officiator who'd been sitting behind him on the stage as he gave his readings came down and approached me with a piece of paper in her hand.

"I've got something for you," she said, smiling. She showed me the piece of paper. "I felt compelled to draw this when Jeff was speaking to you."

On the paper was a neat little amateur drawing of a short humanoid character in quite smart dress with an unmistakeable "alien" face and wise eyes. He had very pronounced otherworldly features. Around him, she'd written some measurements to show his height. On the back of the page was the little character's name: Atz. The picture itself was remarkable, not necessarily life-like as such, just full of details that you would have to be quite imaginative to put together in a simple hastily created drawing.

You're probably thinking at this point that my description of the drawing is rather sketchy in itself. There's a reason for this. I never actually got to hold that piece of paper: Percy took it. Not only that, but he stood there staring at it, holding it in such a way that I could barely see it. In fact, he was almost determined that I shouldn't see it and even though I was craning my neck to get a good look, not once did he make an effort to turn it around for me to see. When he realised that my interest in it was too probing, he suddenly folded it over and shoved it into his shirt pocket. I looked at him in horror; the page had been for me, not him.

"It'll keep it," he said, turning away. "I'll send you a photocopy of it."

The conversation was clearly over and the nice lady who'd gone to all that trouble to draw the picture for me looked resigned as if she'd been overruled by someone with much more power and influence than her. Not once did she try and remonstrate with Percy.

At this moment, Jeff appeared from the rear room with his coat on. He came down and out of the blue, addressed me again:

"Remember, Dorset or Wiltshire! Don't forget now. You must go."

"I will," I insisted. "I live in that direction anyway, so there's no excuse!"

"Good!" he said jovially as he rushed out of the church.

Percy stood there like a zombie. On a previous occasion, Jeff had given him a lift home and Percy had been under the impression that Jeff was his great buddy who had special messages and energy for him alone. Percy also seemed to think it was a complete given that Jeff would offer him a lift home that night as well, but the latter never even offered. He just walked out and barely gave Percy a second glance.

This little action was so defining for me. I would reflect on it a few weeks later when the time came for me to kick Percy's influence into touch and hold it in mind as a sign from Jeff that I really should be working alone and not to give any more credence or even importance to this person standing next to me.

I wonder if Jeff really realises what a wonderful job he did that night. When Percy left me some time later outside the tube station, even after *everything* that happened, he was still insisting it was all about him. He was not to know that he would never see me again.

When I got home that evening, I reflected on the events of the day. I suddenly found myself in a position I'd been in before: someone I'd fallen in with, in a desperate attempt to get the answers to all my questions, was now revealing himself as a traitor. I was awakening to the reality of Percy's game just as I'd woken to HM's. If anything, Percy's excellent efforts to drag me into wakefulness over HM had been *too* effective. He'd spent hours and hours reminding me of HM's crass attempts at control and cover-up, but when it was time to step up his own game in this regard, he'd been left with absolutely no tricks left up his sleeve. He may have realised that the game was nearly up: for the last two or three Sunday mornings of our contact at the beginning of 2010, he'd been pulling out every single stop he could find.

The day after my trip to London, I called him out of sheer curiosity and he started on me with some quite poor attempts at deception. First of all, he dropped two bombshells. The first was to tell me that one of his medium friends had warned him that I was about to throw in the towel and move on from his influence.

"I don't think it's going to happen, is it Paul," he insisted. "I mean, we both have the right to move away for a short time, as long as we both get it together again after a while. Anyway, I picked something up about you in meditation the other day, but don't worry...your secret is safe with me."

This was his second bombshell revelation: the trusty old "I know something about you and I could destroy you if I wanted" ruse. To be really honest, I couldn't think what he was referring to; I've always led a fairly uneventful life; there's nothing in it that I would consider having to hide, put it that way. In the back of my mind, I had a feeling I knew this was a control tactic and glossed over it with a heavy heart, thinking, for the first time, that this individual was really exposing himself as nothing short of desperate.

At the end of our conversation that morning, I asked Percy if he still had the page with the drawing of Atz. He said he did and made a rather weak promise to send it to me.

"When you go for this rendezvous," he said, "you're going to have to take me there with you. You won't be able to do this on your own."

I told him I was in agreement with that and left it there. In reality, I was already making plans for myself. Not one of them included some idiot sorcerer from Old Smokey. I decided to give him a couple more attempts to acquit himself with a little more contact over the next couple of Sundays and to probe him a little, if only to watch him fall into a particular trap that I was about to set him.

Unsurprisingly, no copy of the picture of Atz appeared in the post over the next week. When I phoned him the following Sunday, once more he glossed over the topic and just reminded me that he would have to come with me to my meeting with the ET's. I was beginning to get angry now. Over and over again, he was talking about duality, the darkness, working with the darkness, insisting that even after the great shift of 2012, anyone who thinks that there will no longer be duality on this planet is deluded as there's darkness all the way up to the top of Universe. He insisted

285

again and again that you could reach the highest levels of enlightenment and wisdom in the Universe on the shadow path as well as on the path of Light.

I started to insist that that wasn't the case and in fact, I still make that assertion. I told him that the natural organic flow of the Universe is towards what we in this density would think of as "the positive". It's true that Percy-style darkness is a part of the expression of the Creator, but *only* as a concept in the lower vibratory dimensions of the Universe as a way of providing lessons and a vital source of spiritual evolvement for souls on the path back to reintegration with their divine starting point. We have all created these levels of "Darkness" ourselves in order to yearn for the natural "refined" Light of the Universe; this yearning is our spiritual schooling. Once it has been felt by the individual soul, that soul will have such a pull towards this refined Light that it will evolve at an ever faster rate and its triumphant return to integration with Divine Source would leave such an imprint on the Universe that it will cause the entirety of creation to evolve exponentially. Most importantly though, once these shadow realms of the lower densities have been traversed and the soul has begun its climb out of the mire, what's the point of staying in that "dark" paradigm?

I told Percy that my understanding of it was that those who struggled to reach a point of soul-balance and Unity Consciousness would become stuck in one of the higher densities and not be able to evolve any further until they'd done some assiduous soul work to find that balance. I mentioned that I'd heard souls in this state can become wanderers who *repeat* experience in the lower vibratory realms in order to reach equilibrium.

Percy wouldn't accept this and began to get incredibly hot under the collar. He started blaming me for reading too much and even accused Anna of trying to fill my head with airy-fairy New Age peace and love nonsense that was far removed from the gritty nature of "God" which he saw as a being that could be both loving and infinitely creative, but at the same time, destructive and vengeful. He insisted that every soul had a choice which polarity to choose and could then maintain that polarity, even if it was profoundly negative, right up to the final stage of evolution and

286

beyond. He told me that this is how the cabals that rule the world behind the scenes excuse their dark mind-control tactics. They believe they're enlightened on the dark side. They also believe that if ordinary mortals are so bloody stupid that they can't be bothered to do some research into how the Universe works then they actually deserve to be enslaved by those who know better.

That's why they're insane. Anyone who lives by this assertion must have been co-opted by some dark agenda themselves. I could now see that Percy had not only fallen for this deception, but was actually loving it. He even emphasised this fact by telling me that he was fed up of New Consciousness do-gooders with their assertion that the "darkness" only existed in the dense lower dimensions and refined as you rise up the vibrations. He even spent an hour or two trying to get me to go undercover and root Anna out, to expose her as a do-gooder guru in the HM style who wanted to fight against the dark and move people ever further from the reality of a Universe that he saw as structured with *extreme* duality from top to bottom. His intention, he said, was to destroy her, to take her down, just as he had taken down HM by seizing her disciple from her and cutting off her source of energy and cash. I joyfully compromised Percy's integrity by reporting this to Anna who laughed her socks off!

When the last week of my dealings with this man came, he made me realise fairly quickly in the conversation that if I stayed any longer within his sphere of influence, there would be trouble.

"I had a visitation," he claimed. "The Big Man himself came to visit me."

"The who?" I said shaking my head in disgust, unseen in the privacy of my sitting room.

"Old Nick!" he replied. "His satanic majesty... He looked so fine to behold in all his beautiful regalia. I was awestruck!"

"Oh...really!" I said, with all the enthusiasm of a dead fish.

"He says I'm about to get myself into hot water with him. Extremely hot water. I have to complete my mission or else it'll be curtains for me."

I couldn't be bothered to get him to elaborate. I knew what he was driving at. He was basically trying to get through to me that I had to jump on board his duality bus as soon as possible, or else, as he implied, he would be in trouble with "the big man".

I just yawned and rolled my eyes. All I could think of was how jaded he sounded. A sick, sad, washed up middle-aged man, lurching towards premature old-age and self-imposed misery and illness, sucking the life-blood out of his poor wife and leaving her for dead.

I let him talk and counted his mistakes and lies. He tried telling me that his Universal role was as guardian of the Universal stargates which are portals to carry beings from dimension to dimension. I just thought *"...really, this bloke is an idiot if he expects me to believe that. If he believes it himself, then he's even more deluded than I thought."*

I then set my trap for him and asked if he called himself a Lightworker. By that I meant: "are you working for the Universe in service to others?"

His reply was very succinct: "Yes, I am a Lightworker, but as you know, I also work with the darkness."

The D-word again. There was just no getting away from where Percy's priorities lay. I'd have to be deluded myself not to see it.

When someone with dark intent calls themselves a Lightworker, in fact they aren't lying. That might sound like a contradiction in terms, but it's a fact. There's a subtlety at this level of the game that those who've been doing the spiritual path for a few years eventually come to understand. As everything in the Universe is Light, we can say that there's no darkness as such, just *reduced* Light, a shadow, if you will. The realms of "reduced" Light are the ones that our religions refer to as hell. So Percy isn't lying when he tells you he's a Lightworker; he's just twisting the common understanding of the term.

One Sunday some months earlier before I woke to Percy, he told me this story in an effort to impress me. Apparently, the previous week, he'd made it to what he called Christ or Krishna Consciousness. This is a state of enlightenment which I'm still trying to find a decent definition for: you hear as many opinions on it as people claiming to have reached it. I'll leave you to do your own research on that if you feel so inclined. Suffice it to say for now, Percy tried to define it from *his* point of view, i.e. that of a person standing on much higher ground than me. He said that the moment it happened, he felt something like a lotus flower open up within him and realised that this consciousness had lain inside him all along; he'd only had to realise that and stop looking for it to come to him as if from some outside source.

That's actually quite a wise thing to say because it's accepted by those who are doing the spiritual path (as opposed to the religious path) that your divine self is within you already and just needs to be tapped into. Searching for it outside of you by throwing yourself in front of an idol or an image is looking in the wrong direction. Percy then went on to say that this entire Universe is one that's based on "Christ Consciousness".

I pressed him to give me some more information on what it actually felt like to be "Christ/Krishna Conscious" but none was forthcoming. He just didn't seem able to drill down into the subject with any conviction and kept repeating, "it was within me all along and I allowed it to open up like a lotus flower."

The problem with this is that it's an explanation that's given in many spiritual books on enlightenment. It's fine to read about it, but when you're speaking to someone who claims to have achieved this, I don't think it's too much to ask for some more detailed first hand information, some kind of deeper wisdom. But there was not a single sniff of this from Percy; in reality of course, he wouldn't have known Christ Consciousness if it had burst in and given him a haircut. His explanation was like his vibration: flat and monochrome.

The week after the "I'm Christ Conscious enlightened now" speech, he suddenly did a complete volte-face and changed his tone completely.

"I got it wrong last week," he admitted. "This isn't a Universe based on a Christ or Krishna Light at all. In fact, it's a satanic universe. The whole Universe is light, but it's a satanic light."

He then went on to explain something that had happened that week which was the next stage on from his so-called Christ Consciousness inner unfolding.

"I descended into the deepest darkest pit," he said. "I travelled right the way down through all the levels of the Universe and witnessed everything that goes on at every level. I can confirm that even at the bottom there is Light, albeit an extremely dim Light. As I travelled, I met one character in particular. Do you remember

Sunblest bread? Well, there was a serial killer down there wearing his Sunblest uniform. He had worked for the company as a delivery driver but he's dead now. He held no remorse whatsoever for his crimes and was still revelling in them, dreaming of going back out on the rampage again. His thoughts were completely twisted inwards: all he could think of was pain and death. He loves the fact that he was never caught. It gives him such dark satisfaction."

Percy often gave me little glimpses of his true nature with the intention of leading me down, but not overtly. These little seeds were scattered quite carefully around in the hope that they would sprout and produce small stems and outgrowths that would grip my limbs and pull me down when I was least aware. What he said next was a classic one of those:

"I used to work for Sunblest, you know."

This little piece of information unsettled me. I just couldn't work out what he was trying to convey. I can only leave this little story for you to ponder in your own time.[14]

To Percy, all this hell realm thing was about being a Lightworker. Along with claiming to be able to go anywhere within the shadowy realms of the inner astral, he also claimed to have his own army of monks that helped him battle against demonic entities that crossed his path. This was the sort of thing that he wanted me to get into as well. He loved the fact that I seemed to be so willing to go down with him. He didn't care that he knew he was taking me away from my own true nature which is to want to soar up and away from the shadow realms. In his own mind, he would excuse his actions by saying to himself: *this Paul wants to be a Lightworker; well, this is Light Work. He signed up with me for this!*

He also loved to hook me in by claiming that I was going to be a great writer and tapped into this desire side of my nature by implying that he could help me as a teacher. This is how these Service to Self souls excuse their pied piper actions. They tap into your desire nature and your vanity; they promise you the world, great power and money, fame and adoration. They call you

---

[14] Although if you're in the Police Force investigating serial killers, I still have Percy's real name and address, if you're interested..!

awesome and tell you about your glorious future. They also inflate their own importance to breaking point. Percy pulled a great scam:

"I don't really like to talk about it openly as I don't want anyone to fall to their knees before me, but I am the reincarnation of Egyptian sun-god, Horus. You are one of my sons, Hapi…"

By way of an aside, the Sunday morning when he told me that, something happened that made my blood run cold. During his speech about being this great ancient god, I noticed a black figure about seven feet tall walk straight out of a wall in my hallway and disappear through the opposite wall. The very presence of this thing almost stopped my heart and it was some moments before I could regain my composure.

I should have realised it at the time, but all the signs were there: I was now being subjected to the same gamut of phenomena as HM had been for years. Hers were all self-created and would have disappeared overnight if she'd given up her deluded ambition to be the ultimate holy person. Mine would have been self-created as well. They were the progeny of my own ignorance for allowing myself to be led down a shadow path yet again.

Percy would have loved nothing more than to be part of a great book-writing project where his army of monks and bread van murderers were all promoted by me as just a great and wonderful reality of living in his satanic world. He would have relished dropping these sorts of irrelevancies into the mass consciousness through a willing (albeit ignorant) accomplice and confuse even more generations of people unable to escape from the matrix that's kept us all enslaved for thousands of years. What a coup for a little nowhere man, sitting in his nowhere land. He would have excused his actions by claiming I'd allowed myself to be led down willingly, with my own vanity as my nose ring.

That last Sunday chat with Percy at the end of March 2010 also marked the end of my association with anyone peddling twisted "spurtule" teachings. I rang Anna the following day which I had off from work and we both laughed about how I'd been forced to wake up in such a curious way.

"You'll start to feel better from the hyperthyroid now," she said, "and your intuition will be sharper than before. I think you'll find happiness at last. Enjoy it. You've earned it!"

291

After our chat, I went for an hour's walk and contemplated what to do next. For the first five minutes of the walk, I actually considered ringing Percy to say goodbye to him. However, by the end of the walk, once I'd had time to mull over what he'd tried to do, I changed my mind. I didn't think I owed him anything, least of all a farewell. He'd tried to take me down a road I'd never wanted to walk and although I had to admit that in fact he'd provided me with excellent grist for my spiritual path by giving me a nasty little temptation to resist, that didn't mean I needed to thank the guy. It was a test I'd set myself and not one that he'd set for me out of love and a desire for me to advance. Advancement was never on his agenda. The opposite was the case; he'd have loved nothing more than to know at his moment of death that he'd provided service for himself and his dark master in all his regalia by sending me on a wild goose chase for millennia and possibly even cause me to regress right back on my evolutionary path. Percy walked with a stick due to some medical issues which were a long way from being resolved. In 2008 when I had a similar ailment, he'd advised me to get a stick myself. The thought of it thrilled him. If he was going to get all grizzled, bent and twisted because of his actions, wouldn't it be great to have a twin brother in bile to drag to hell as well.

As I walked along the lanes that spring morning, I remembered that I had Percy to thank for waking me up to HM. But the problem was he was also saying that I earned myself a sack-load of karma for supporting her and that the only way I could alleviate that burden was to follow him. With that thought going around in my head, I also recalled that he himself had supported HM at one time and as I was beginning to find out, had even supported her in her vicious outbursts against me, adding fuel to them, loving the division and the fallout. That was exactly why he'd inserted himself into our lives in the first place: to create mayhem and misery and to destroy not just her, but me as well. What's more, he did it with a smile on his face, telling us both that he loved us.

Percy had gradually constructed a vast edifice of deceit that had me beautifully imprisoned for quite a long time. But he just couldn't hold me. For even though he was a master builder, his edifice just wasn't weather-proofed properly. He was in such a rush and assumed too much. He saw me as easy prey, as gullible and too bound up in my own vanity to see into his game. But the problem was, in order to drag me down to his hell, he had to play out the role of the perfect spiritual teacher. In fact, he played that role so well in some respects, he woke me up as he dragged me down.

I came to the conclusion that I had to forgive Percy and HM and move on from them both. No vengeance was allowed, no bitterness. I don't know even to this day who was the bigger fool, her for being on the shadow side in her heart but being a saint in her head, or him for being dark in his heart and knowingly, consciously dark in his head with complete malice aforethought. The former was sad and the latter just plain dangerous.

Believe it or not, I congratulated myself for having brought such great teachers into existence for my path. I knew that I would have to focus on that thought for some months to come as I could see ahead of me a lot of anger for having allowed myself to be duped; I knew that I would kick myself from here to kingdom come and probably inwardly rail at both of them for hours at a time.

As it turned out it wasn't as bad as that, but there were times, perhaps for five minutes a day, when I would forget myself and find my head in a world where I was phoning them both up and giving them a piece of my mind. Actually, on some occasions it was stronger than that. Those were the days when I wanted to take a shotgun to their heads.

The following Sunday, Percy's phone didn't ring at our usual time of 9a.m. He waited about fifteen minutes for me to call him and then got fed up and rang me himself. I was at home, sitting in my armchair with my feet up. I let the phone ring off and continued sitting there. The phone rang again five minutes later and I ignored it. About an hour later, he tried again and then gave up for that particular day.

He tried again the following evening, and then the evening after that; in fact he tried every single evening for a week, even sometimes during the day when I was at work. Once the week had gone, the penny dropped and I reckon he gave up in frustration.

It wasn't all plain sailing, I have to admit. A week before my departure from his sphere of influence, Percy had given me a little demonstration of how he could worm his way into my psyche.

I woke up one night after a terrifying dream. I'd dreamt I'd been squashed into a tiny capsule and set free into outer space, unable to move, screaming my head off into a vacuum, knowing that for some reason no one would ever rescue me.

I don't often have nightmares; in fact, this was one of the few I could ever remember having outside of my childhood and the occasional bout of flu. I put the experience aside and just got on with my life, trying not to reflect on it.

The next time I'd spoken to Percy after the nightmare, he'd started off his conversation with an announcement:

"During the week," he said, "you had a vision of being locked inside a coffin, didn't you..."

On the other end of the phone I went absolutely puce. He'd already told me that he'd had an inkling I was about to cut ties with him and in an instant I knew he was trying to scare me. I had a fleeting glimpse of him in my mind's eye, late at night, sitting in front of his altar, tapping into the ether and working his craft. He'd often told me he did this, describing the flickering of late night candles and dancing shadows with dark relish. I must admit, I ignored him as I still saw him as the person I'd so desperately wanted him to be. But this time, there was no turning my back on what he was trying to say. The message was loud and clear: *You're mine and you can never escape my influence. I can get right into your head...*

I admit that despite being as upbeat as possible in the week following my flight from Percy, there were moments when I found myself looking over my shoulder. I began receiving "number barred" phone calls in the evenings when the caller would slam the phone down. Someone kept calling my mobile and when I checked the 'calls received folder', their number ended in 666.

It wasn't just that. I felt as though I was being watched, especially at night. There was definitely a curious vibration around which even today, despite being mocked by a lady in my metaphysics group about it, I cannot deny was there.

In the end, I dealt with it by doing nothing. Too many New Agers think they have to go around protecting themselves with all sorts of mantras and visualisations of protective energy fields when this sort of thing happens. But I came to the conclusion that was a pointless thing to do. All that happens when you're convinced you have to protect yourself from "evil" is that you bring it into your life anyway by being so obsessed with it. As far as I was concerned, that was HM's area, not mine.

I decided to ignore it all and just got on with my life. By thinking of other things and not dwelling on Percy or his late night shenanigans, I shut him down completely and he couldn't get near me.

In the end, I know...he just gave up.

He must have realised after a while he was on a complete hiding to nothing anyway. For ages he'd been getting shirty with me saying things like:

"Paul, I'm trying to tell you what you should be doing, but I can't tell you overtly as you have to work it out for yourself. You're too slow on the uptake, mate. Think about what I've been telling you about the work I do, the entities I deal with. You must use your intuition and start getting into this work yourself. You're slipping behind, Paul. I need you to shunt yourself up to the next level now as we can't move forward until you're fully in step with me. Wake up to all this. We haven't got time for you to drag your heels. We have work to do."

Of course I was slow on the uptake; that was his tough luck for trying to hook me into his world in the first place, especially when he knew full well it wasn't my area of interest.

I sometimes wonder if he disliked me or looked down at me for not jumping aboard. To be honest, I couldn't care less what he thinks anymore.

A lot of people will ask how I managed to be so drawn in. They'll want to know why I didn't wake up sooner when it was so glaringly obvious from day one that I was on a complete hiding to nothing. To be duped once is bad enough, twice is just downright careless!

Let me just take you back a few years to the 9th of September 1975. That was the day I started, aged nine, at a little private boarding school in the Somerset countryside. My parents sent me and my brother there because they'd heard it was a good school with high academic standards. From that point of view, they were

295

quite right. I'm really grateful for the education I had; it was second to none and most of the teachers at this school were nothing short of superb.

The problem was, during the Seventies, it was run by an unstable headmaster. This was a man in his fifties; somewhat plump, balding, he was always conservatively dressed and on the surface, controlled and dignified. He could be unerringly polite and charming – if not somewhat offhand – to parents, but once they'd all left at the beginning of term and wended their way home leaving their offspring in his charge, he turned into a psychopath. Please don't misunderstand me, I'm not talking about a man who carried out acts of physical cruelty in any way, shape or form. Beating was not allowed at this school. Instead, he was an emotional bully. His bullying was carefully controlled and so precise that you had to be quite discerning to see what was happening. In those days, it was not the done thing to turn up at your child's school and complain if the teachers were picking on your offspring, so this man had carte blanche to carry out his emotional atrocities unimpeded.

His tactics were simple: public humiliation, mass punishment, divide and rule. We were encouraged to turn on each other like the children who accuse their parents of thought crime in George Orwell's *1984*. If a child put a foot wrong, the entire school would be punished and either sent to bed early or forced onto a mass work squad where everyone would have to clean classrooms, pick weeds from between the cracks in the courtyard, climb into the nearby stream up to our eyes in mud and clear debris from the water, in fact anything where there was some kind of mass control involved. And that was just the best bit…

He would scream at individuals at the top of his voice in front of the whole school. A classic was when two kids ran away one Saturday afternoon. Panicking, he called the Police who sent out a search party across three counties. Eventually the boys concerned returned with their tails between their legs after a couple of hours hiding in a hedge just up the road. Both of them were brought in front of the whole school with the following announcement:

"These are the two FOOLS who are responsible for the entire school being sent to bed early for the next week. I trust you will make your displeasure known to them."

As it turned out, very few of the kids had anything to say to them. We knew the score and saw the little tactic for what it was.

The part that was difficult for me was the fact that to help this man run the school with an iron fist, he used a coterie of emotional tyrants, sports teacher bullies – his own little gang of three – to psychologically rough up and humiliate the kids like squaddies. So eight year-old children were told they were pathetic sissies, pansies, toerags, cry-babies and wimps. The tougher kids were encouraged to turn on the softer ones and bully them if they appeared to let the side down in sports.

The gang of three would sit on the floor in the changing rooms and watch as the boys took showers and dressed after the afternoon rugby games which always left me feeling dirty and humiliated. Their conversation was laddish and their quips and observations perfectly timed to belittle.

There was no one to turn to if you felt upset or needed a shoulder to cry on. Outward shows of emotion were immediately suppressed. Concerns over looming exams, difficulties with other children, bullying (physical and emotional) were all purposely overlooked and never addressed.

Although the school was in a large and beautiful country house, the rooms were bleak and bare: stark floorboards and lino, high ceilings with too much careless paint slapped over them, dull religious prints on the walls and cold, cold, cold.

I tried to approach my parents with the warning that I just couldn't cope. I was such a sensitive boy and the ethos of this school was entirely against my principles and character. I could see myself becoming a bully at times and felt it strange that no one cared enough to turn around to me and point out the error of my ways. More often than not, I was actually the victim and was particularly detested by one of the gang of three who did something to me once (not physical, I have to say) that terrified me to the very bone and left me distraught and insecure every single moment of the waking day. I began to get psychological hang-ups and panic attacks and would skip games and run and hide. When I was found, I was humiliated in front of the whole school under the divide and rule tactic.

My parents were unable to intervene. They tried, but the headmaster punished me even harder so I gave up complaining. I believe it was this that caused my block. I developed emotional paralysis and unconsciously came to the conclusion that the only way to survive in the world was to put up and shut up. I learned to ignore outrageous and abusive governance amongst those in authority and even to accept it as normal: the more I was expected to look up to an authority figure, the more I learned to overlook their extremes of behaviour.

I'm not trying to drum up sympathy for myself by harping on about my schooldays. I know a lot of people of older generations who suffered miserably at the hands of those old school types: your screaming dictators in tweed jackets, your ice-cold emotionless hags in twin sets. They've all gone now, we can breathe.

I just cannot get away from the fact that my prep school experience toughened me up too much emotionally. I never stopped for one minute to check if Rosie was suffering or if Scooter needed a hug. He always told me I wasn't very tactile with him and I regret that.

The worst thing was that I never properly questioned the HM regime when I should have.

Looking around me, I can see to a certain extent that this phenomenon isn't uncommon. On the one hand, these days, we're all very quick to complain if we get poor service in shops. In fact, if anything, we've learned to overdo it and are downright abusive, treating staff and their managers like serfs. But we're still far too accepting of wrongful behaviour within certain areas. How quick we are to ignore bullying in the workplace if standing up against an office tyrant means putting our own jobs at risk. We may be the kind to start screaming and shouting at a bus driver, but are we also the kind to turn a blind eye when we find that the company we work for is exploiting the third world, producing a product that can be harmful to the public, wasting tax payers' money, causing damage to the environment. How quick we *all* are to put up and shut up!

We can take this a step further: what if we're working for an organisation that's producing depleted uranium to be sprayed over the skies above cities in "enemy territory"? What if the organisation we work for is actively suppressing technology that could help humanity at large, such as free energy devices or medical breakthroughs that could save the lives of people suffering. Are there some amongst us, if an employer gave them a gun and ordered them to shoot a rival, a whistleblower or an inventor of a device that could make the internal combustion engine obsolete overnight, who would not think twice about snuffing a life out?

I personally have had to come to a terrible conclusion: and that is that I never stood up for myself. This is why I'm blowing the whistle now and on myself as much as anyone else.

If I could shout out a warning at this time of great global change it would be this: are you engaged in any kind of practice where you're actively or passively playing a part in the oppression of another party? If so, now's the time to come clean with yourself. At this time in our planetary evolution, we're being called to take a stand and there's a choice. The choice is between Service to Self or Soul Balance, between slavery and freedom. As I've explained in this very book, whether you choose to continue to polarise Service to Self or to reach that ultimate goal of equilibrium (or Unity Consciousness) your choice is valid in terms of our collective aim of providing evolution for the Universe. Service to Self calls for the Universe to balance itself out: a negative action will cause the perpetrator to have the same or similar negative action perpetrated against him. This in itself is also valid experience for the Universe but it can and should be avoided if you really want to end your suffering and move up to a higher plane of greater harmony. The ones who need to realise this the most are the groups who revel in the mistaken belief that they are enlightened ones because they run the planet as a prison camp and have millennia of experience in the art of control over the masses through wars and institutional abuse in every area of our lives. They believe they're doing "God's will" by bringing catalyst to the planet on the Service to Self path and are preparing themselves for global oppression by moving towards a world government that will operate like a dictatorship. They've also taken it upon themselves to roll out a programme to reduce the world population to a more controllable and manageable level as, at the moment, they fear the masses. Those caught up in this web of indoctrination, whether it's the "chosen few" themselves or those who bend over backwards for them, need to realise that on the one hand, they are indeed

299

serving the Creator as they claim, however, on the other side, they'll all be called to account for their actions; they're naïve if they believe they can hide from that fact.

If you go to projectcamelot.org on the net, you'll find what we call a whistleblower site. This organisation is run by two very aware people: a feisty, spiritual American lady called Kerry and a deeply caring English gent called Bill. On the site, they have interviews with people who've worked in dark areas of the global matrix we call our current consensus reality. The interviews are with people who've worked for the suppression of technology that would obviate the need to burn fossil fuels, with people who've worked in the world of military and armaments, pharmaceuticals, reverse-engineered technology, space programmes and areas where political schemes are being rolled out in preparation for a global dictatorship.

A lot of people who've become whistleblowers are waking up to the fact that they've been supporting a regime that's dark and they no longer want anything to do with it. Some have come out on a limb and revealed plans and secrets that those above them would kill to keep under wraps. A lot of the whistleblowers are brave people whose lives are in danger for speaking out. They're acting as they do because they're becoming more and more awake as the years go by. Awake to the fact that the time has come for us all to think of ourselves and our planet as one consciousness that has become splintered, disunited and dysfunctional. As we move towards a more heart-centred approach beyond the year 2012, now is the time to reassess and look carefully at the regimes and people we support. Our choice is simple: either we come clean and walk on the side of the heroes, or we take the hard path and move on down into an oppressive world that is entirely cut off from our dream of freedom and joyous self-expression. Whichever path we choose, it's valid. But one brings joy and the other abject misery.

Chapter Thirty-One

A year or so before jumping off the Percy bandwagon, I'd already begun to feel as though my life was on the up. I know that seems strange as I was still being put under so much pressure from the Service to Self brigade. I guess it's like that: the greater your trials, the grander your triumphs.

I was meditating one evening when, in the silence, that intense feeling of tranquillity began to seep into me again. It was the same sensation of lightness of being right in the middle of my head that I'd had when I was out with my mate at the pub. It stayed with me all evening and was still there the following morning when I went into the bathroom to shave and brush my teeth.

Weeks later, I was still feeling amazing. Sometimes the sensation was so strong it made me feel dizzy. However, this wasn't an unpleasant kind of disorientation; it was more like floating and not once did it ever prevent me from driving or getting about, going to work, going shopping or doing even the most mundane of tasks.

I began to notice I could intensify the feeling at will by keeping my thoughts constructive and saying positive affirmations in my head to slow internal monkey chatter. If I went out for a walk in the countryside (which I started doing every evening, eventually losing 145lbs) I would almost be lifted out of myself with the exhilaration of being in a fresh and free environment. But even in the noisy town centre or in a room full of people, I still felt incredibly centred. The only time the sensation subsided was when my thoughts strayed towards the negative. But as soon as I tipped the balance back towards the positive, I would start to feel good again.

I decided to do some investigation into this phenomenon and realised that there was a lot HM hadn't told me. I was staggered that someone who claimed she was trying to help others with their spiritual advancement would not give them any prior warning of how the ride felt. For years she'd told me that she herself would feel "not with it", "non compos mentis" light-headed and not grounded. But what I was feeling was not like that at all. If anything, I'd never felt more in control. With HM, the light-headedness was always a precursor to her saying that she couldn't cope because her vibration was sky-rocketing and that was when I was always asked to get all her shopping and run around for her as she was "in training."

Knowing that it was pointless to approach someone like her to discuss what I was feeling, I looked on the internet and found something amazing. Other people were feeling this too. I discovered it's what happens when your pineal gland starts to activate.

The pineal gland is a pea-sized pine cone-shaped gland right in the centre of your brain. It secretes melatonin, a hormone that communicates information about environmental light to various parts of the body and thereby aids the body in knowing when to sleep. In advanced ancient spiritual cultures, the pineal gland was known as a psychic centre. When this gland is activated, it's supposed to carry in Light from the Universe allowing it to flow down through your DNA and activate you psychically and spiritually, letting you perceive a higher reality and find out who you are and where you come from in a spiritual sense. People who have activated their pineal gland fully can see and communicate with those in spirit as well as astral travel, in other words leave their body and return at will.

I realised that what I was undergoing was the outer edge of this phenomenon. I came to understand that my pineal gland was not yet activated fully, but I could feel it opening up, even though I was, as yet, unable to actually "see" anything most of the time.

For someone who's always had an extremely logic-based, scientific approach to life, this was quite a shock. I know a lot of spiritual people who were born with abilities, but in my case, it's been one of starting from scratch and awakening my own energy centres through work and spiritual practice. I knew as I made this discovery that I still had some way to go, but as time passed over the course of the summer, I did begin to see things: shapes moving through walls, orbs and bright white or blue lights floating around me that became visible to my peripheral vision and which disappeared if I turned to look at them directly.

Although it was never completely water-tight, I did often find that I was beginning to sense people's inner intention and discovered to my amazement for example, that people who I thought didn't like me, actually did, but couldn't work me out and so acted offhand with me. I could tell when people were suffering and what they were worried about. This allowed me to regulate my interaction with them and get them to open up. Unfortunately, it also made me want to run a mile from some people as I could see that they had underhand intentions and were suffering because they didn't realise that their plans for those around them were not always with those people's best interests at heart. One friend, I discovered, was using several women for casual sex and keeping them all keen by telling each of them that they were the special one. Each one of these women was waiting for him to commit to them and he knew that he had no intention of being honourable to any of them. When this became clear to me, it was all I could do to stop myself from running a mile from him as I was so saddened for all the girls involved. He then complained to me bitterly that I was ignoring him and asked me what the hell was wrong. I could barely look him in the eye. I knew I had to try and be as forgiving as possible and continue to be the best friend I could to him, but I couldn't stand to see the pain he was causing and how he just didn't care about it. All he could focus on was himself and his own immediate desires as he was so deeply enmeshed in the matrix. I struggled with this for months and realised that my path would get rockier if I didn't stop sizing people up and writing them off when I sensed there was something underhand about their motives.

Conversely, I also discovered that people I'd often written off as badly behaved, rude or excessively moody, turned out to have really pure hearts. The moodiness was just frustration because things were not always going according to plan for them, but deep down their negativity wasn't aimed at anyone in particular; it was just an inability to know what to do in certain circumstances. One good mate of mine who'd always been a bit of a bad boy when he was younger, had such a pure heart I discovered, it would upset me when anyone close to him in the world was cruel to him. To mix with him in a social context you'd think he was just a football-mad booze hound with a foul mouth and a rude offhand manner. I suddenly felt such an urge to support him and encourage him, a feeling that I'd never really had for him before.

Of course, this awakening was the final straw for my view of HM. As I've said, it was all I could do to stop myself from ringing her up and shouting at her. But messages were coming through to me thick and fast: do *not* be cruel to her; forgive her and let her go. That was when I discovered that I actually had something to be deeply thankful for in her regard: I now knew what spiritual advancement was not.

I looked back over the years and realised that I'd signed up with her to find a glimpse of the light at the end of the tunnel and to begin to understand the nature of the Creator. That was when I realised the greatest and most wonderful irony of this whole business. After all the trashings, the lies, the money screwed from me, the backstabbing, the manipulation, the abuse, the neglect, the things that I'd witnessed, she'd actually given me *exactly* what I'd signed up for. Admittedly, she'd taken the suffering path for herself, but in the long run, her actions and decisions had ended up only affecting her. For me, they'd brought the desired result: I *had* advanced after all: in spite of her and because of her.

A strong willpower that had seen me stick with her during some troubled times originated in an intense desire to find the Creator and no matter that I'd taken an unintended zig-zag path to find it, that desire had produced results. A gritty intention to see it through to the end had borne fruit. The occasions when I'd tried to serve her as unwaveringly as possible, however misguidedly, could now be seen as an intention to evolve the Universe, in spite of the fact that I'd ended up serving someone else's ego. That ego had been nothing but the Source Field Creator in disguise, testing me to the limit and having a bloody good laugh.

I could almost jump with joy at the sheer bizarre ingenuity of it all. I honour you, Holy Mother!

Please don't misunderstand me. I'm not saying that I've reached anywhere near the level of "unfoldment" of those great heroes of the past, or even that exalted level that HM told me she'd reached – assuming such a thing exists. My experience is a lot more commonplace than that and not a reason for me to shout about myself from the mountaintops. At the moment, all around the world, there are people waking up as well, people who are finding that the new planetary vibration that has so long been heralded as part and parcel of the Great Paradigm Shift is bringing about a leap in consciousness. These are ordinary folks who work in offices and shops, students, housewives, people from wealthy or poor backgrounds, anyone who's open to interacting with the world through the heart. These people's stories are all over the internet if you care to look and they're talking about the same things – breaking away from the matrix that's binding them to old thought patterns, the fear of being without money, of not fitting in, of getting ill, old and dying. The last thing the ones who are waking up want to do is give themselves airs and graces and claim that they should be cherished and lauded to the skies like gods themselves. That sort of mentality is utterly alien to them. Instead, they remain calm and let everyone be. Rather than crassly push themselves forward, they stand aside and let others move on in the line, whispering quiet words of encouragement or simply just saying nothing and allowing their feelings and calm vibration to affect those around them subtly.

As soon as you become too wrapped up in the notion that you're some great and unique being that sees and knows all and thereby expects blind loyalty as if it were some kind of divine birthright, you scare away those around you who may not have the same level of spirituality that you've aspired to. Therefore you defeat the entire point of this spiritual process, which is for all of us to give each other a bump up to the next level. It's all about symbiosis and synergy: working and living together in co-operation and mutual respect, showing each other the path. This is the very crux of why we're here in this extremely difficult veiled density, the most stringent of all the densities and the one in which errors of judgement can cause us to have to repeat, again and again, the same tired, miserable old lessons from life to life until the penny finally drops. Therefore, to take on the mantle of someone else's path by *insisting* that you're their guru and that your word is the ultimate wisdom, is totally inadvisable unless you're as pure and perfect as you can be. Otherwise, all you're doing is playing. To toy with someone else's free-will, to use their honest search for your own ends, is a serious offence that will call for you to be held fully and catastrophically accountable. I don't mean that lightly. No matter if there's a positive outcome for your victim as there was for me, this road is one you should only take if you're absolutely sure you can handle the consequences.

The subtlety of my situation may be missed by quite a few people and I accept that. People have been brought up to believe that there's a very distinct separation between Light and Dark and that if you're the one, then you can't be the other. In truth, both are intertwined so very carefully it's hard to see which twine is which. They aren't always colour coded.

You have to use your intuition. I'd urge people to look at my situation and apply it to their own world. Ask yourselves some deep searching questions: have you allied yourself with a person, a company, a political faction that isn't serving your deep inner need for freedom and joy? If repression and misery is your bag, then that's your business. But if, like me, you've set out to do right by your conscience, then you need to be as self-critical and authentic as you possibly can. The shadow side is incredibly clever. Look what happens at the end of the film *The Exorcist*. Knowing that it must leave the physical body of the little girl, the demon produces one last pathetic attempt to shake off the efforts of Father Damian Karras to send it packing. It brings through his recently dead mother, projecting her weak and pleading voice at him in an attempt to shake him off with guilt. The shadow side can duck, dive and weave and be prepared to take any form it likes in order to hook you in. It's your responsibility to see through the game and to be one step ahead. Don't declare war against it and use violence. Instead, distance yourself from your situation and take stock. Ask yourself, *am I being deluded?* Think about this: if you allowed yourself to be taken in and were tricked into carrying out certain actions by someone with a dark agenda, if you were caught and there was some kind of court case or tribunal, would the excuse *"but I didn't know what I was doing"* actually wash as a valid pretext? Once you've even the slightest suspicion that you're playing a part in a dark agenda, to ignore your intuition and carry on with your role in that agenda will cause you eventually to have to stand in the dock along with your dark controller. This was certainly the case with me. I was in a very precarious position with the "Holy" Mother because she had me so hooked in that I was actually identifying with her darkness. I honestly thought that she was justified in feeding off people like the spider *Shelob* in the *Lord of the Rings* as that was her right as a divine being dishing out harsh lessons to humanity. However, another part of me that had a conscience was screaming back: *but it's cruel!* The spiritually evolved are never cruel. Those who are dishing out cruelty in the name of a god don't really wish to see humanity evolve. The fact that I managed to take some steps forward whilst exposed to such a vibration is, I would say, something unusual. I definitely wouldn't recommend it to others unless they're so utterly driven to understand the nature of the Creator that all other considerations are entirely eclipsed.

When Percy came in and used his wiles to remove me from HM, he was doing what he was Universally contracted to do[15]. Before this incarnation, I had arranged for this situation to come into my life. In order to gain a higher diploma in my spiritual education, I'd obviously decided to explore the darkest recesses of the rabbit warren, but then also to explore the Light and rejoice all the more in that Light for having melded with the Dark. Percy's role – initially – was to reach in and drag me out. If I'd ignored the warning at that point and chose to dig deeper into the warren, I'd have been lost and a lot of people around me would have continued to suffer. The reverberation of my actions would have damaged other individuals – possibly hundreds over the years – and then it would take me centuries to extricate myself. Instead, what's happened is I've spent some time immersed in the shadows and learned from it. But once that lesson is complete, it's time for the bell to ring and then to move to another class. Not to turn up for that next class is to fail the whole academic year.

It's hard to understand, but I had to see that lesson through to a satisfactory conclusion. I believe that catalyst of the kind I was subjected to should never be shrunk from, if possible. You do have the choice to flee, certainly, but you also have another choice: stand firm and immerse yourself in the catalyst whilst NOT identifying with the dark force that's working so hard on you. In doing that, you're providing the greatest experience for the Creator

---

[15] I have to admit, other people had tried to prevent my brain-washing over the years, but all of them had failed as they just couldn't come up with any watertight spiritual reasons to explain HM's behaviour. Of course I ignored them all!

and fully living the meaning of life. The most difficult part of the lesson is attempting to prevent yourself from falling so far into the darkness that you refuse to tear yourself away when the lesson has ended. This is where so many of us fall down.

Some souls spend aeons in a state of paralysis, unable to make that leap out of the abyss. The only thing I can say is that once things start to get a bit jaded, it's a message to move on. If you ignore that warning and stay, when things start to get extremely uncomfortable, if you haven't jumped, you need to be pushed. If you refuse to allow yourself to be pushed, then stay and burn. It's up to you.

This scenario is as valid for me as it is for anyone stuck with a demonic guru, embroiled in a religion that deep down they know is causing death and misery, for anyone caught up in a dogma that's self-serving, a political agenda that's destructive, a partnership that's damaging or even a habit that's detrimental to your happiness and health. Look around you by using your intuition, by checking out your dreams, by meditating and delving into your consciousness for the nearest source of help and then go with the flow. There's always help out there. You just have to be open to it and not allow yourself to be put off if the solution is weird or doesn't fit with the accepted norms of society. Be authentic and true to yourself. If it feels right to your heart conscience, then follow that road to a solution. Don't be scared of ridicule for taking a path that isn't accepted by our narrow-minded consensus reality.

Look out for the peddlers of enlightenment whilst you're on this path. There's gold in them there hills, but also a ton of lead as well. Anyone who says they can bring you to enlightenment is lying. Only you can do it. They will purposely sell you a false view of the concept to have you chasing them with your wallet open all the way to the bank.

HM herself was never of a mind to mine for the true meaning of the word 'enlightened'. She talked of her own "enlightenment" as if she'd reached the top of the mountain and passed the finishing point in a race. Home and dry, this meant that she could now sit back and rest on her laurels whilst contradicting herself in the most disingenuous way. She would think nothing of telling people that she could bring them to enlightenment like her but

308

then start off one of her spiritual books by saying: in the beginning was the word. I could tell you what that means but I won't because I'm an Avatar and well, sorry, but *you* are not.

So the message was totally cross-threaded. She told everyone she could take them but then reminded them that they would never get there, as enlightenment was her territory, her throne, off-limits to everyone bar her.

Whether she cared to admit it or not, her motives were the same as Percy's: to keep those who fell into her lair in base consciousness. Her method was to smash their self-confidence to smithereens, to lead them away from the spiritual work that would bring them to reconnecting with their higher selves and hence finding freedom and soul sovereignty.

I've come to understand that there's no such thing as an enlightened person: only an evolving or even highly evolved one. We never stop learning and those lessons will go on long after we've shuffled off this mortal coil. Anyone who's going around claiming they're enlightened has stopped evolving. In this case, it was almost as if HM had parked her car in a lay-by and was standing at the side of the road desperately flagging everyone down, howling at them: *I'm the only one with all the answers! You need me! You'll die without me!*

Meanwhile, those evolving souls speeding past in their own cars, negotiating all those unexpected twists and turns on the road of life with ease and dexterity are looking out from their windows aghast, rolling their eyes and shaking their heads with reproach:

"What the hell does *she* want?"

Percy, who was fully cognisant of the nature of his shadow side and revelled in it, used the same methods as those on the dark side of Masonry. He was wringing his hands in glee the day he sent me a prayer to say out loud whenever I "needed help". This prayer called on all sorts of Enochian angelic beings and ended with a mention of something called an inverted pentagram. I remember double checking this with him, saying that I thought that was to do with dark magic.

"It's to do with the earth," he said. "You are a being of the earth, Paul. Never forget that!"

Of course, Percy was right in one sense. I am a being of the earth, as are we all. We've come to the earth in this dimension of base consciousness to learn our lessons in a harsh reality. But when a dark magician says "you are a being of the earth" to someone who he knows is searching for a higher reality, then there's a trap within his words. By pointing your attention in the direction of downward pointing pentagrams, he's actually attempting to hold you in base consciousness. The inverted pentagram is stuck into the earth, exactly where he wants you to be. This is his modus operandi; to trick those whose souls wish to rise up into falling back down. Percy often mentioned that when he eventually got his big house and all the money that was due to him, he would have an entire room with a floor tiled in a chequered-style like a chessboard. This is another red-herring. The black and white tiled room is a symbol of the chessboard for those who've cast themselves in the roles of the master game players, the manipulators moving the ignorant around like pawns, sacrificing them, using them to destroy others. This is classic imagery from the dark interpretation of Freemasonry.

Chapter Thirty-Two

One person I'm close to who I would call quite religious has often come out with the following exclamation of horror:

"Why, oh why, does God allow such cruelty in the world? Why doesn't he just step in and put a stop to it when people are nasty to each other? I sometimes wonder if he's cruel himself..."

I've tried so many times to tell this person that WE are God. But I might just as well be whistling into a howling gale with such an affirmation for this particular soul. The answer is incredibly subtle and I do think it's time we all tackled it.

As I've said, life in this Universe is taking place in a number of dimensions or densities. I have absolutely no idea how many there are and anyone who does claim they know is probably talking from ego.

If each one of us is refined Light shining into this physical Universe from Source, we splay out beautifully like a rainbow as we shine into each density. If you look at a rainbow, it's amazing how the colours gently blend into one another, but each colour eventually becomes clear and unique in its own right as part of the whole. We could say that the bluer colours are the higher vibrations where existence is less dense, where consciousness is subtle and refined. The redder colours are the densities of grosser physical matter where existence is heavier and coarser.

Our souls are existing in each one of these densities simultaneously. Although the part of you reading this book is in a physical realm of base consciousness (or 3D), other manifestations or colours of your soul are also manifesting in the other dimensions. So you're experiencing life as a rock or a crystal in first density, know the feeling of being forged in fire, cooling, staying rigid for aeons. You're also experiencing life as an animal or a plant in second density: a cat on a window sill, a squirrel foraging, a tree by the side of a polluted road. In such a state, you aren't as keenly aware of yourself as you would be if you were human.

You're living a kind of innocence: all you're aware of is your need for sustenance and survival.

At the same time, there's you in third, reading this book with a cup of tea, shaking your head in horror. I'm telling you, and it might help you to understand, that you're also in densities higher this one, becoming lighter and finer as you move up and back towards a complete integration with Source.

Outside of this physical world of ours which runs according to Linear Time, there is no Time. You could say that everything is happening at once, as I've said. So if the Universe is a computer programme and all life and existence can be accessed in My Documents, all you would need to do to experience what you need to experience would be to open the folder to Planet Earth, choose the sub folder "Planet Earth 3D" and then choose whatever sub folders you need to open to get to the here and now. All of these folders exist on the computer at the same time. They don't follow each other like the events of a film. If it were possible for one folder on the hard drive to access and update other folders automatically with experiences that are occurring elsewhere on the drive, then that would also approximate what we're doing in the grander scheme. For experience and lessons are being fed up the tube to Source. You in 3D are passing your evolution on to higher versions of yourself and are providing evolution to the Source Field as well. "God" is therefore evolving, though as there's no Time, "God" is also fully evolved.

Too many people in the New Age and even the New Consciousness (from which this book emerges) talk about the density system as if it was a stripy pair of pyjamas: where one colour finishes, another immediately begins. There seems to be an overabundance of commentators saying that once you've finished your lessons in one density, you jump straight into the next as if by some miracle of immediate ascension. The thing is, densities aren't individualised stripes. They blend into one another like the colours in the rainbow. At the moment, this planet is playing host as far as we're concerned to a majority of 3D humans, all the animals and plants of 2D and the elements and minerals of 1D. But is that really all? Let's investigate this in more detail.

First, let's look at the nature of 3D. As well as "Base Consciousness" I also call this dimension the density of "Perceived

Slavery and Separation" as the nature of it is that we believe we're in prison. It's a prison that we're creating for ourselves as we've set things up in such a way that we purposely forget how powerful we are. The 3D human, believing himself to be alone and isolated, reliant on only his ego for survival, finds himself living in a world where his wellbeing is a result of the decisions made by a hierarchy. He has no choice but to sink or swim in a realm run by others. He is told how to think. His world is painted for him by other artists and ones that don't want him to see what lies behind the canvas. The rest of the Universe is veiled off from his sight. His spiritual evolution will be measured by how successfully he can pierce the veil and return himself to unity with his higher self and to soul sovereignty. This will have to happen in an extremely hostile environment which isn't conducive to spiritual truths and wisdom. Despite this, there are times when certain people do pierce the veil in this physical realm and communicate with higher sources whilst still enmeshed in their Slave Separation 3rd density experience. Such people have simply *remembered* that they are divinely connected to Source and set about reactivating communication with the Source Field. Humans who history has recorded as having amazing soul abilities of the kind ascribed to Buddha, for example, have pierced the veil, but such people have been the exception rather than the rule.

Thinking he's been cut off from help, the 3D entity ends up living in a control system where the ones with knowledge of how that system works, and who manipulate it for their own ends, exist at the top of a pyramid and pass on their manipulative orders to those lower in rank. As the fog is perceived to be so thick, those in the lower ranks don't believe they have access to any outer or inner wisdom and hence there seems to be little or no catalyst to wake them from their self-imposed slumber.

So the pyramid system works perfectly. Each level controls the one below. All information is strictly censored. The masses learn what the controllers want them to learn and that information is always, without fail, corrupted in such a way that it prevents an individual from waking up and piercing his head through the veil to see the grander scheme.

Look around you. The television and media in general are no more than a sludge pump for mass-produced, dumbed down garbage designed to stop you from thinking too hard. This is your classic Slave Separation density set up.

We're all bonded into this control system, this matrix. It's kept in place with a monetary system that's designed to favour mainly those who rise to the top, not always with hard slog, but with uncompromising, psychopathic natures. This order of bully keeps others in check: such people are the directors of large multinational corporations, those high up in the mass media, religions, the music industry, politics, the educational system, food and pharmaceutical companies. They're picked out for an ability to conform and mould their operations to suit the control grid. So the mass media and education are designed to dumb us down; religion and politics to scare us to death and make us feel helpless and the pharmaceutical and food organisations to poison and kill us.

It sounds horrific, doesn't it. How in hell do we survive?

Would it help if I told you that many of us are now moving between densities? I don't think this movement is going to be in one massive leap from one stripe of the pyjamas to the next. It feels like more of a rainbow-type blend. Writing as I am post 21st December 2012, it's clear that "ascension" as they call it isn't going to happen in a sudden leap as many predicted. It may take a few years, but some of us are definitely on the cusp of another density entirely.

I think if planet Earth could talk, she would say that she's offered her services in this paradigm for long enough now. It's a tough call for a planet in 3D. Earth has been subjected to some horrific experiences over the last few millennia as she allowed us to work though a 3D evolution. Wars and ecological abuse which are part of our self-imposed isolation in ego have brought about disasters on a massive scale. It must feel to her like the ravages of disease.

I also have the feeling that there have been people alive on this planet in isolated pockets who have been manifesting at a higher vibration and are already in a higher density. As they're in a loftier vibration we cannot see them even though they can see us. This is why it's a fallacy to claim that this entire planet is about to move wholesale into a 4D, or higher, paradigm. In reality, it depends what each individual soul here wants to experience, so most of us

314

will certainly move into 4D, whilst others will move onto even higher states of vibration or stay in the one they're in. I believe that the writer JRR Tolkien understood this split nature of vibration. His Middle Earth was inhabited by beings straddling different dimensions that he allowed to be able to see each other for the sake of his story. You have the forest of Fangorn, dark and heavy, Moria abounding in beings of an extremely low spiritual energy. At the same time, Lothlorien and Rivendell are home to the Elves, full of light and magic. It's interesting that the war to defeat Sauron was one that also marks the end of one density experience and the beginning of a new one. The shift is spread out over the course of many years, but when the ring is finally destroyed, a new world comes into manifestation properly: the Age of Men. The Elves move on and sail off into the West, leaving Middle Earth to the stewardship of another race.

We may be on the verge of a mass split of humanity. There are those (possibly the vast majority) who would prefer to hold on tightly to the matrix and stay within its boundaries, terrified of what lies outside. That's understandable. Some people know on a soul level that they aren't ready to wake up and that decision must be respected. Those that are awakening may live alongside those who are fast asleep for some years. Just as Tolkien's Elves share their world with bipeds of lesser ability, the awakened will probably sow the seeds of their new world whilst their 3D brothers and sisters stay immersed in the 3D game. 4D will exist alongside 3D for as long as it takes. Eventually, it will be 3D that takes the ship westwards as souls that intend to learn their lessons in a higher vibration start to incarnate here and those that still feel the need for Slavery and Separation move on to some other theatre of operations.

So what then is the nature of 4th Density? I think a lot of what I'm about to say can still only be seen as conjecture, but I'll talk about it anyway so that we can at least have a debate on the subject. To a 4D being, Time isn't fixed and linear: it's more fluid in this realm, you can move backwards and forwards at will. Matter is more malleable; souls in this realm are not fixed into one particular manifestation. Here in 3D we're identified by one physical body that we keep with us for our "four score years and ten". In 4D, we're still in a physical realm, but that realm can be more easily reshaped. Because there's a greater level of control over physical matter in this density, by its very nature, it's more harmonious. In fact, it has to be harmonious as a large group of souls existing in a state of 3D warrior ignorance operating in a realm where matter and Time can be manipulated would mean the end of everything here! Just imagine a 3D dictator like Hitler, with an ability to manipulate matter, at war with other matter manipulators...

We don't have to die in the accepted 3D sense. In the higher realms of 4D it would be possible either to move to another bodily vehicle or move on from the physical world entirely, not in one jarring moment of spiritual separation from the physical, but gently and in dignity.

Let's use the world (believe it or not) of Harry Potter to explore 4D in more detail and to try to outline what will lie ahead for us in terms of the Soul Technologies that we will eventually master.

I'm going to stick my neck out here and say that Harry Potter's magical world (although fictional) could be representative of a very early rung of the "ladder" of 4D. I think on a soul level lots of kids realise this which is why the books have been so phenomenally popular amongst the younger generation who are the ones who'll bring in the new paradigm. I think the concept of a magical world living alongside a world of 3D muggles is one that has incredibly potency and may become more and more relevant as we work our way through the shift. Please note, we mustn't fall into the trap of referring to those who still want to play the game in 3D with a derogatory word like "muggles". This isn't an "us and them" split: it's simply a major shift of perspective between one set of humans and another.

Let's forget about the broomsticks, wands and the pig Latin incantations for a moment. Put all that aside and think about Harry's magical world without the 3D witchcraft angle. 4D *is* a world of what we in 3D would call magic. Souls can appear as someone or something else. Objects can be moved or made to appear and disappear with the power of the mind. People can bi-locate or relocate from one place to another without recourse to a vehicle using an outdated technology such as the internal combustion engine. How about travel along ley lines as opposed to floo powder? What about the manifestation of a personal object

316

through the power of thought and not with the use of a wand? If you can get this, you're moving with me.

I've pointed to the fact that there's a game of extreme duality being played here in 3D. This game does take place in 4D and continues into 5D and to a certain extent into 6D; the point is that it becomes more subtle as density becomes lighter. Those polarising as Service to Self in these densities can still interfere in the free will of those wishing to rise: an excellent portrayal of that phenomenon can be seen in the character of Darth Vader in the *Star Wars* series. But when a soul takes on the role of the controller in these higher densities it's forced to confront a spiritual entropy that can only be halted by a flip of polarity followed by a search for balance. This entropy seems to take the form of a kind of disintegration. The characters of Voldemort and Darth Vader show this disintegration, but only one of them succeeds in finding a resolution.

4D Service to Self oriented beings appear to inhabit a space of their own. They seem to hive off from the rest of 4D and go about their business simply interfering and enjoying an energetic feeding frenzy in worlds of people like us who aren't able to defend ourselves. They're compromised if they continue to do this because they can't stay in 4D for eternity, revelling in their magical power and cheating death with technology. If this kind of being doesn't wish to find balance as they rise through the densities, their path to evolution may also cause them to have to repeat experience in base consciousness; they could therefore find themselves as soul wanderers in 3D doing the tough stuff like us heroes and forgetting their soul history. The loss of power and thought of imprisonment (even if it *is* for their own good) can keep them from wanting to take that leap, so they continue to drift and violate other people's space with their selfish agendas.

Perhaps those on a 3D path at this time who want to explore a higher realm on this planet are on the verge of some kind of defeat that will propel them into their new world. It could be that we have our own Voldemort, a psychopath with nothing but malice in his heart and a desire to purify the world of all those who don't match his twisted spiritual template. What if this wasn't an actual person, but the *pathology* of a Voldemort, a certain vibration of the soul that is holding us back from finding freedom and sovereignty.

317

In order to mine this theme yet further, I do believe that we should investigate the psychopath.

Firstly, I'm of the opinion that the human 3D experience has been intensified by Cataclysm Trauma. Many traditions, especially Biblical, point to a time in human history when there were areas of this planet that could have been manifesting at a 5D vibration or perhaps higher. These traditions point to a Golden Age (a Garden of Eden if you like) when the elevated human was not living in bondage, but existed in a world where there were no hierarchies. It was a world where there was no such concept as toil; everything that people needed could have simply been provided by Nature herself. I doubt this paradigm would have been uniform across the whole planet. As with Tolkien's middle Earth, 5D could have been operating for beings in one part of the world whilst in others, a pre-human of lower vibration could have lived, a Neanderthal or Cro-Magnon man. We talk about pre-history in terms of that kind of being, a native to planet Earth that evolved just as Darwin claimed, from a primate. But what if there were other things going on such as genetic seedings from outside sources, genetic splicing of these native species with genes from worlds more advanced? All of this could have been happening at once on a planet that was serving as an almighty fertile glasshouse for DNA from right across the Universe. What if all these seeds were planted here on purpose for a monumental reason: an experiment to see how everything would react to certain stimuli?

So if this Earth were a hot house where good races have seeded their DNA as part of a grand experiment, it's likely that the quarantine has largely (though not entirely) kept 4D Service to Self beings with agendas out. We may start to see more of them as we move into 4D and as the quarantine is lifted. That's not a warning. They can't really affect us. We're more spiritually advanced than them anyway, despite how it looks when they flash their tech. If a race did come to Earth at this time, telling us that they've come to clean up after us and wipe our backsides because we're too weak to do it for ourselves, my advice would be to tell them to ship on out of here: this is our world and we have the ability to look after it ourselves.

Some commentators say that if the experiment is deemed successful, the 3D Earth model could well be rolled out as the norm for spiritual advancement in other "times and spaces" in the Universe and as a way to speed up evolution. I'm not sure about that, but if it's true, it would mean that each and every one of us who's dared to come down here really is a hero!

How did we end up in 3D in the first place? Our Biblical sources tell us that an allegorical Garden of Eden for the human came to an end. It could have been that the higher form of human "fell" in vibration over a long period of time, that the subtle game once played by an Earth 5D being became fraught with difficulty as that being desired to explore the sensory world. Interfering influences (most likely 4D Service to Self) from outside our own realm came to roll out their own agendas and mine our fabulous wealth of material for some kind of selfish gain.

A new kind of human began to manifest itself. With the Golden Age no more than a memory, with those beings that we called Neanderthal or Cro-Magnon no longer able to survive in a world that belonged to them, a new way of living would have been brought into manifestation: from some source unknown to us, the new human was taught farming and animal husbandry. The foraging hunter gatherer died out and the higher 5D human now regressed and become a slave.

We know that a cataclysm took place. There are traditions not just in the Bible but in other cultures as well that talk of global destruction from water. Once the waters had subsided, all that was left was a traumatised human, scrabbling for survival in what was left of his world. I believe this was a pivotal time in human history. Cataclysm Trauma unleashed a new and unseen terror on humanity which has its effects on us even today.

The 3D experience for the vast majority of humans would have intensified after the flood. Terrified by their experiences, survivors would have had no choice but to resort entirely to their egos to survive. New societies would have begun to manifest which were run by those who knew that the traumatised human's connection to his Higher Self in the Source Field was drastically severed. These "rulers" were the first monarchs, the first emperors and oligarchs. Hidden within the fabric of these newly-forming societies were mystery schools that kept secret the wisdom of old, the true history of the planet, the knowledge of meta- and quantum physics that showed how the Universe really functioned.

Using this jealously guarded knowledge, the new ruling elites held sway over the populace and did so by mining the mysteries for methods of mind-control. The human psyche was mapped by such people long before the modern age. They introduced the 3D concept of Linear Time and set in motion the creaking wheels of the slave machine, one to which humanity is still lashed today.

I believe something else happened. Humanity began to sow the seeds of its own darkness. Forgetting that we're creator gods, we overlooked the fact that we could create the very circumstances that would set us free from bondage and instead, brought into being the bars of our cage. Our traumatised psyche manifested the monsters of our nightmares. Some called them demons, others Archons. These are energies of a vampiric and parasitic modality that attach themselves to those who leave themselves wide open to attack. If you're living in a world of ego and are too afraid to search for the spiritual truths that will set you free from the matrix, your fear can lower your defences. In this state, you forget the powerful creator god human that you really are and manifest the psychic slave masters that you believe you deserve in your guilt. When this phenomenon first began to take root all those millennia ago, the first mind-control religions came into being, ones that grabbed the human by the hair and yanked his head backwards before forcing it forwards into the dust, nose first. Traumatised humans began to bow down to false gods. Religions conjured up the images of devils and demons and hard-wired them into our collective unconscious. We began to feed these demonic thought-forms with our fears. The more we fed them, the stronger they became. The demiurge of the Bible, the vindictive, furious, warlike "God" that the religious still grovel to today came into being from misplaced worship as we begged it for forgiveness and answers to our problems. It moved out of the realms of concept and began to exist as an actual energy in its own right, an energy that's incredibly conscious thanks to our fear, trauma and guilt.

What we tend to forget is that the human is dual in nature. His body is of the earth: his DNA is part Darwinian ape, part inter-galactic. But his soul is from all dimensions. Never forget that as you walk the path. Our souls haven't just crawled out of the primordial soup. We're not just evolving spiritually from the

320

bottom trying to reach the top. We *are* at the top. In fact, we're evolving in all dimensions in all directions at once.

Watch out over the next few years as we move even further out of this 3D paradigm. Some humans will really start to show their mettle and demonstrate that we aren't spiritual low-life after all. There will be some people who will start to resonate with 5D energies and they will begin to live lives of pure joy and freedom, of boundless creativity, with abilities that we never thought possible. According to legend, we will know these people as the Warriors of the Rainbow and they will be humans from this very planet.

There is a very strong tradition that talks of how those interfering "outside forces" that genetically manipulated the human being into existence, who spliced their own DNA with ours, were allowed to do so provided they inserted within the programme our saving grace: an option, if we chose to accept the mission, for our DNA to evolve. It's this evolution, one that's pre-programmed into our genes, that's about to aid us in our search for freedom from bondage. It's *now* that we must learn to liberate ourselves from the energetic parasites, those demons and pesky Archons of our nightmares by simply bursting the bubble of religious and social mind-control. All we need to do is find the will to dissipate those energies.

This understanding of the evolutionary nature of the human genome is knowledge that has been hidden within the mystery schools for millennia. These schools tapped into the traumatised collective unconscious that has always brought into being the demiurge and the demon and developed a set of demonic rites which have evolved into Satanism. This form of demon worship is used by those working within the control grid to grind humanity down and to control it on an energetic level. Sorcery and black magic are used to transmit a vibration of fear. Now that we know that, we know who our very own Voldemort is. It's an actual force that doesn't want the human to advance or his junk DNA to come alive. "Defeat" of this vibration is at the very heart of this Great Shift of the Ages.

Once I'd fled from Percy, I wondered if he himself had ever been initiated into a satanic group. He seemed to have a good deal

321

of occult knowledge, all based around this kind of reality. He positively revelled in it. His attack on poor John, cowering inside his car, was an excellent example of how this satanic energy can be used to terrify and control. Percy always reminded me that John had quite a few lower chakra habits in terms of his slightly unethical outlook; there's every reason to believe that Percy, knowing that this Universe is a computer programme that can be infected with a virus, could have colluded with these vampiric energies to control John from a distance, to terrify him with a horrific manifested demonic entity designed to stand on his car in that isolated spot, repeatedly banging on the roof and screaming obscenities into his consciousness. That night, Percy had used me with my own energy to increase this terror on John which is why John was convinced I was working with Percy against him. All the time, Percy kept saying, "I'm the Sorcerer, he's my apprentice. He needs me, Paul. This thing won't go away without me!"

In her first autobiography, HM mentions something that I now realise is highly significant. It's a small story that just seems to have been thrown into the text on a whim and it's gone in almost a second. She mentions that she'd joined some kind of spiritual group. She doesn't specify who the group is or where they're based. The only piece of information that you can glean is that a trusted friend of hers contacted her one evening to warn her never to go near the group again. He claimed they are "on the dark side" and have existed ever since the flood.

When I re-read that section some weeks ago, my heart nearly stopped. This group is actually quite definable. You don't need to know their name or where they exist. They fit incredibly neatly under the very categories that I have just been at pains to describe. What HM may have been trying to get across in her book was that she'd been knowingly or otherwise, "assumed" into one of the organisations descended from those original mystery schools and which have their over-arching manifestation as satanism.

It could be that she had no idea. Perhaps she was utterly naïve as I was the day I first knocked on her door. I can see exactly what would motivate her. If it's true that she was like me, desperate to find the meaning of life and someone to help her, it does indeed follow that she would ally herself with some such group. She was always looking for dynamic ways to increase the speed of her path.

Perhaps this group hooked her in. Perhaps she was invited to ceremonies or rites that she thought were highly spiritual but which masked other motives. She might even have switched off her intuition on purpose and turned a blind eye to anything suspicious that was going on because a top member of the group had tricked or drugged her, telling her how advanced she was, what a wonderful high being she was and how great she would become. The group may even have seen this in her and did what they're so perfectly programmed to do: *shut her down.*

This implies that HM could well have been a highly spiritual, very powerful teacher, after all. Although I'm not sure of this, it would explain her behaviour. What she may have had when I met her were the vestiges of her original spiritual healing abilities now utterly compromised by energies that had been attached to her by whatever rites she'd been exposed to.

In the years that I knew her, she often used to tell me that she was having to remove this sort of "plug in" on many an occasion. But her way of dealing with it was pathetic. She'd go upstairs to her bedroom, there would be silence and then she'd come down five minutes later and say: *it's gone now. The Almighty has sorted it.* After another five minutes, she'd be all confused and return to her neurotic ways.

Perhaps there's another explanation entirely which I'm blinding myself to. I'm wondering if she *did* know she was being drawn into satanism. Fully aware and compliant, she allowed it to happen because her thought process was the same one that led her towards another dark group in 2001: the notion that the darkness is as much an essence of "God" as the Light. So rather than integrating the two and finding balance by NOT interfering in anyone's free-will, she assumed she could see-saw from one to the other according to what she wanted to achieve. She may have assumed honestly that that was what "God" does: showing love and mercy one moment and bringing about death and destruction the next. It may not have occurred to her that the enlightened person is actually in balance, has integrated all experience and has a non-intervention policy, only acting when it's deemed an injustice is being committed. Although she may have understood the nature of the Creator as a passive, non-judgemental consciousness, she must have ignored that concept when it came to getting what *she* wanted.

She may therefore have been motivated by the thought that after indulging in shadow practices, she could eventually move easily out of the Dark and into the Light with a box full of cash and then spend the next few decades trying to distance herself from her former choices by sanctifying herself. At this point, she may also have decided it served her agenda to make out that everyone else was filthy and immoral which is why her books damn the whole world for being sexually wanton. She put herself in place as a saviour so that she could cast herself as a Jesus and be worshipped for her spiritual prowess. With every compliment she took, she put distance between herself as the ruined, rejected character that the satanism had created; in doing so, she elevated herself in her own head to an almost god-like status. She then set about gas-lighting people like me, implanting in our heads the notion that *we* were the revolting scum, that *we* were the sullied and filthy, the incompetent, the ignorant and lacking in wisdom, the evil and riddled with karma. This was the overriding energy of all her books: one in which she's this great being as white as snow, reaching down to earth to spread fairydust over this stinking putrid mess we've made of our world. When people first met HM, like all those with psychopathy in their personality, she gave the impression that she was charming and fully in control, the most emotionally intelligent person ever to walk the earth. How quick she was to let that façade drop when she had you where she wanted. By the time she'd reduced you to a gibbering wreck and was pumping the lifeblood out of you, for five lonely minutes, she felt holy and divine, insulated from that nagging thought in her head: *I'm the dirty one...*

Percy said that this was in fact the true scenario. It was almost as if he had some kind of proof himself. But then, you've seen what kind of character Percy was.

When you start looking into the alternative media and the New Consciousness in general, you discover a wealth of information about the nature of the psychopath. Personally I always used to think it was a term to describe someone who's utterly depraved and has lost all sense of morality. I used to think psychopaths were murderers and serial killers. Seemingly this word is now used to describe one who is indeed disconnected from any kind of moral or ethical outlook, but such people don't always kill. The killer psychopath is simply one that lies at the most extreme end of the spectrum. The term has now become a reference for those who are utterly devoid of emotion for others. They'll cry for themselves and bemoan their lot, but they'll never cry for the fate of another being or animal. I've come to believe that this is the category in which I'll have to place HM and Percy.

Before I go on, it's essential that I make a difference between someone who's simply traumatised and has shut down their emotional centre for fear of being hurt again, and a genuine spiritually and emotionally devoid human with no ethical outlook. They may seem the same animal but there is a difference. A traumatised individual may act like a psychopath: they may become utterly self-obsessed and unable to relate to others, lacking in love and care for fellow humans and animals. But given the right circumstances, such people can be helped back into a state of love and humanity. I've seen several YouTube videos recently which have plastered the label "psychopath" a little too liberally over people who are simply traumatised or who've been brought up in a loveless environment. Very often your controller is not psychopathic, just a very scared human being who's suffered loss at some time in the past, loss of a parent, loss of dignity and personal contentment. They've simply developed a controlling personality to keep everyone where they can see them so they don't run out on them. This character type is terrified of finding themselves in a situation where their dignity is going to be stripped from them again, so they rigidly maintain their grip on situations and other people. They may be a controlling spouse or child because they fear loss of love from those close to them, so they over-compensate by tightening their hold on the environment around them. How do you know these people are not psychopaths? They may well have no other agendas other than to keep you close. They will still have a moral and ethical outlook and most important of all, they can be reached with time and great effort. For me, this character type will *not* reject a child of their own who doesn't conform to their agenda.

We must also be careful not to reject the ones whose behaviour is psychopathic, but who've been taught controlling antics by atrocious parenting, by mixing with the wrong crowd, by trying to keep their heads above water in a cut-throat environment. It's all too easy in the corporate world for example, to be dragged kicking and screaming into the nightmare of a fellow colleague who's simply desperate to "get on". In order to get where they need to be, they ape the actions of the psychopathic controller type and use that undignified modality to scramble over the heads and limbs of any who get in their way to the top. If you're going to diagnose such a person as a psychopath, it's best to check out their motives. They may simply be trying to live up to some horrific expectations placed on them by a family who want them to be successful in a career. They may also be covering a terrible loneliness. I've seen that happen so often. Such people have simply put their humanity on hold. If the psychopathic vibration of the corporate and political world was neutralised by humanity learning to move back into harmony with the Universe and Nature, such people would re-adjust to normality fairly quickly.

In order to mine this even further, let's use the Harry Potter books again as they're so full of wonderful allegory. Harry's school enemy, Draco Malfoy, is a perfect example of a kind of nominal psychopath. This comes across beautifully in *The Half-Blood Prince*. Knowing that he's been chosen to kill Dumbledore, we see Draco suffer true torment. It takes all of his resources of bravery and adrenaline to summon up the nerve to carry this act out and of course, as we discover, he simply cannot do it. Draco isn't really a psychopath. He simply comes from a snobbish old magical family who've only kept their position in society by going through the motions. They pay loud lip service to the darkness throughout the story, but by the end, have relieved themselves of the burden of a role that never suited them. They abandon the dark side and we're led to believe that Draco ends up as a friend to Harry, not a sworn enemy.

The Malfoys are victims of the horrendous expectation placed on them by a society that's run by the psychopath. I think their plight is also the plight of so very many of us. We have bills to pay, young kids to feed: we have to act out the mime or we sink.

I believe the time has come for us all to forgive ourselves and move on. To do that, we must root out the modality of the psychopath within society by exposing it so it cannot continue to harm us in our voyage towards 4D and higher.

Who *are* the psychopaths then?

They're the ones who can charm the birds from the trees, have the unwary eating out of their hands and then, once they have what they want, up and leave with no conscience and without the slightest tinge of regret. Psychopaths are parasites that attach themselves to anyone who has something they need, be it money, energy, resources, anything that can be prized and stolen. They target those with giving and trusting natures and bleed such people dry before speeding off into the sunset with not the slightest remorse or shame. You'll also find the psychopath in the corporate world, someone who can happily go to sleep at night having brought a company to its knees and sacked an entire workforce. The psychopath can also be the wife-beater, the drugs-dealer gangster – a person that the psychopathic control matrix has bizarrely taught us to respect through the music business.

There are one or two researchers who even claim that the psychopath isn't human. This might be a wild statement to make, but it's perfectly definable. In his true essence, the "human" is the divine, spiritually astounding being that existed long ago on this planetary system, before he began his descent into the "denser" realms. He still exists here in all of us, but as I've said, has simply been dumbed down and forced to forget his remarkable soul lineage. Luckily, he still manages to rear his head from time to time and appears in astounding works of creativity and acts of incredible love and kindness. You would never see such behaviour in your psychopath.

The psychopath appears to have lost his divine connection by comparison to your average empathic human. Your genuine psychopath won't respond to any treatment and will be as doggedly self-obsessed as ever. They will even mock those who try to help them as they never feel the need or compulsion to change. Changing means searching inside for an emotional centre. If that centre doesn't exist, why change?

The psychopath is in a bit of a bind when it comes to acceptance. My own observations have shown me that they're almost desperate to be honoured for who they are, warts and all, even for their emotional violence and self-serving agenda. They

327

find it bizarre that you should want to escape from them for these weaknesses and don't make the connection that they have to change and become loving in order to find the acceptance they crave. They react to your disgust, knowing that they've lost you, by becoming even more vicious and self-serving and increasing their own isolation exponentially. This is how the dictator is born.

The psychopath doesn't have a clear pathway to any kind of higher spiritual intention or creativity. They may pretend to, like Percy, but it's simply there to mask an agenda. This character type is emotionally dead to all externals that are not of immediate use to him. Expecting him to cry over the fate of starving children in third world countries would be naïve in the extreme.

Currently, there's research showing that the psychopath has the part of his brain that processes emotions completely shut down. My feeling is that thoughts and emotions that are associated with the brain, don't come from the brain at all. The brain itself is merely an antenna that's picking up signals from the Ether. For the human non-psychopath, those signals, faint as they will be for all of us in this veiled density, will come from the higher version of each of us. So amazing inventions, incredible works of art and music, are all emerging from the greater Source Field, from the incredibly creative, unconditionally loving energy that brings the Universe into being and which we are all part of. This is why we refer to the highly creative as divinely inspired. Thoughts of a lower vibration have their origins within the matrix and are being pumped into our reality by 3D influences that wish to create confusion and disharmony.

Art and inventions have not *just* been created in that blob of fat. By the will and intention of the artist, the brain has created neural pathways and evolved itself to pick up and process creative information from the Field. It's then given the body the electrical signals it needs to work the hands and fingers so that the creation can be given physical manifestation. The artist must be working with intent and that intent comes from having strong heart-centred emotions and reactions.

I've often wondered, on a grander Universal level, why individual souls would choose to have a life as a psychopath, why they come into this world having already made a choice that they're going to play the game to extremes.

328

Perhaps they're devolving souls on the way down from higher realms who have found terrible power on the path of service to self and have come here to understand love: their pathology is the imprint of that former power they haven't yet relinquished. In coming here they eventually relearn to connect with other selves but also sign a Universal contract with the rest of us to teach us grace by ruining our lives.

Perhaps some are not "souls" like the rest of us. Hard as it is to believe, their consciousness could be no more than the creation of some bothersome agent that wants to create havoc and ultimately to control. That consciousness is then allowed to inhabit the physical form of a human from birth. Growing up, such a person would notice that everyone else around them was busy hugging one another and rejoicing in displays of deep and wondrous warmth and solidarity. They'd find themselves confused by caring, meaningful gestures and unable to find within the trigger that should cause them to act naturally in loving relationships. For a long time, they feel confused and wonder why; then one day, they simply stop asking and become a predator, truly believing that there's no point in trying to find emotions that don't exist. From this moment on, they get what they want not by giving and taking reciprocally, but just by taking.

Or perhaps...these are souls who have chosen to be psychopaths because they want to provide catalyst for others (and hence the Creator) by playing the game to the highest level. So they come down here for a limited period to cause havoc. They then return and keep returning as normal humans to bring back balance to the Universe, going the opposite direction spiritually, becoming the most amazing loving and caring humans that ever lived. I can see exactly how that would happen.

I firmly believe that all these scenarios are possible and in HM's and Percy's cases, whatever the underlying cause, there's no denying psychopathy within their disposition. You could see it in an email HM sent Percy whilst they were working together:

"I am sure there's going to be a massive earthquake where millions will die, possibly California (the San Andreas fault line?) and the people will go completely nuts. They will be besieging people like us and we cannot take advantage of the fact that they have money, or as some will, try to bribe us to jump the queue because we will be booked out. This of course, we cannot take advantage of – 100% integrity at all times is the key.[16]"

This sort of word stew is typical of your psychopath. 100% integrity is certainly the key to hiding your true motives: cashing in on the misery of ordinary people by setting yourself up as the great white hope for the terrified.

You could also see HM's psychopathy in the way she sanctified one of her children and demonised the other in an atrocious power game. Percy also did this. His eldest son could do no wrong; meanwhile his daughter was described as the scum of the earth and unlike Rosie, actually acted that role out.

I feel I have to bring some balance to HM's case by pointing out that there was definitely a nascent creativity in her watercolour paintings; there always did seem to be the stirring of some kind of deeper aesthetic appreciation happening. But you could still see the psychopath in a lack of creative ability that caused her never to come up with answers to her problems and her consequent expectation for others to perform that role for her. You can also include her way of crying for herself and no one else, her lack of compassion, her need to control through fear and threat, her hubris and megalomania, her tendency to see others as a resource and not as individuals with needs: the list is endless.

---

[16] This is an excerpt from one of several emails that Percy sent me behind HM's back which he'd kept from his HM days. I believe his ultimate game was for me to wake up to her duplicitous nature by showing me what she used to say behind my back. Some of the emails are shocking and fill me with horror every time I read them because they show that she was telling everyone I was out to destroy her. I don't reckon she truly believed I could possibly do that; it just suited her to let everyone know how much of a victim she was. One interesting thing about these emails is that Percy has not included his replies to her in the package. In other words, he simply didn't want me to see that he was agreeing with her observations about me and may even have been egging her on by telling her that I was evil incarnate! I still have copies of these emails if anyone is in ANY doubt about the deceitful game these two characters were playing.

As someone who's been exposed to two psychopaths so closely, I can say that their vibration seeps into your own consciousness. A fully functioning psychopath can create proto-psychopaths in those around them and so vampirise their minds that they start to emulate the behaviour patterns of their "masters". This is why you must always flee from people like HM and Percy before you become too dyed in the wool. Certain people who knew me during my HM days were staggered at my occasionally "disassociated" behaviour. When I woke up, I was horrified at it myself. I feel there's every chance that HM's megalomania was created by this osmotic effect in satanism and it simply became too late for her to be pulled back.

Having been completely rewired by her own satanic cult experience, would HM have become your classic brainwashing abusive cult leader? I believe she would, however, not quite as overtly as some of the child-abusing, energy-grabbing tricksters you hear about who inspire their followers to commit suicide. HM was obsessed with how she was perceived and terrified of bad press. So any extremes of behaviour would have to be stifled. Had her "ministry" become successful, she was the kind of manipulator who would keep her nose clean whilst knowingly allowing "disciples" to abuse and mentally torture others in her sphere. She was an expert at divide and conquer, at promoting the cult of the personality, of using that cult to promote fear in those she wanted to control. There are those amongst us, and I include myself in that, who are desperate for answers, to find out who they are and where they stand in the grand scheme. Such people will stop at nothing to find the nature of the Creator and even to bask in any love that appears to be coming in from that Source via a conduit like HM. Hard as it is to believe, this character type will take the abuse and play the game. They will even be prepared to become an abuser themselves if that means the leader smiles at them for just a few measly seconds. This is the guru that HM could have become: a superficial saint presiding over a church of spiritual terror and emotional abuse. I can see her watching from the window of her mansion as a group of her close ones mete out humiliation to underlings. Standing there in the shadows, she would excuse their abusive behaviour as necessary in the war to "help" these people pay off karmic debts. Meanwhile, with her back conveniently turned on any outrages, the drawer of her cash till would be continually springing open in great guffaws of triumph.

While she was in Germany, I sent HM the famous book by Dave Pelzer: *A Child Called It*. This tells the harrowing story of a young boy who was physically and emotionally abused by a mentally ill, alcoholic mother. Beaten and starved in an emotional terror regime that lasted for years, Dave finally escaped and was taken in by San Francisco Social Services. They called his story one of the most serious cases of child abuse ever recorded in the state of California. After I sent her this book, I didn't hear from HM for two weeks and realised that I was in the doghouse. One day Scooter called me and I found out why. She'd read the book and rather than feeling horror at the circumstances of this poor lad's childhood, she'd reacted by losing her temper with me for inflicting the story on her. I knew immediately: she hated being reminded that she'd emotionally rejected her own child. Rather than reflecting on the gravity of what she'd done, she preferred to whip the messenger. *A Child Called It* is the story of the crimes of your classic psychopath. She would almost certainly have been riled by such a portrayal of her own nature, even if her mistakes were nowhere near as serious. The message of the book never sank in either. If anything, she became even more doggedly unreachable. You can tell a psychopath about his pathology until you're blue in the face and their reaction will be to shrug it off and sneer. Psychopaths don't get help as they simply don't believe their actions are wrong. If she ever reads this book, HM's reaction to it will not be: *I must address the issues raised* but *how dare that man ruin my reputation...*

I'm of the opinion that because satanism can give rise to psychopathy in people, it's historically been used to create monsters with agendas that serve the ultimate 3D Slave Separation vibration of fear, control and addiction. They make the perfect dictators. Willing or unwilling participants are simply locked into the trauma matrix. It's almost impossible to piece their shattered minds back together.

If it's true that HM was compromised (knowingly or unknowingly) by some satanic group, there's every chance that her lower chakras had been plugged into. As I say, this is quite common. This plugging in could also have happened if she'd been forced to take drugs and then been emotionally rewired by her experiences with the group. The rewiring method is extremely common in satanism and in the way these dark forces work. They will literally smash your mind to smithereens, destroy your emotional circuitry and fracture any vestige of self-belief you have left. When you're no more than a mind-controlled wreck, they will hook you into the "Archontic" machine. It could be argued that the group HM joined already knew that she would start to see herself in a messianic light. They may have watched from a distance as she sanctified herself with the word holy in a desperate effort on her part to cleanse and purify herself after experiences that must have left her feeling defiled and degraded. They simply let her get on with it, wound up the mechanism with their secret little key, switched the motor on and placed her in amongst the lambs to ravage the flock in the dead of night.

At this point, all the voices she claimed to hear of ascended masters and great Avatars of the past would have started. To her, they were real and a sign of her divinity. In reality, they were no more than the voices of your typical demonic vampire energy tricksters. These thought forms would have whispered their twisted orders into her ears and conned her into carrying out spiritual atrocities not only against others in her sphere, but against herself. Eventually, one of them would deceive her into believing it was the voice of "God" which is why she always told people with such a straight face that she could hear "His" voice. The voice would have contained just a hint of aggression in amongst its declarations of love for her. Even today, she still talks of her god as one whose name dare not be mentioned like the classic Biblical demiurge and Archontic scam artist known as Jehovah or Yahweh. Indeed, these false gods are the very ones she mentions in her books on practical spirituality, a fact that gives the game away completely, whether she chooses to admit it or not. For most of *this* book, I've wrapped the word "God" in inverted commas for a reason. There's an almighty difference between an Infinite Creator which is a non-judgemental consciousness that IS all things, and "God" which is no more than HM's very own demonic telesales commission-only con merchant who rings you up in the evening when you're trying to relax, chomping at the bit to sell you a product you don't need which is a pile of old plastic crap.

To anyone who would tell me to my face that it's impossible for anyone to be so completely drawn in by all this spiritual trickery because it sounds like a poor episode of Star Trek, then I would say this: we live in a Universe that's a hologram or a computer simulation. It's so brilliantly devised that it seems utterly real to us. But there are people out there who have knowledge of how this simulation can be manipulated in the same way that you can introduce a virus or a trojan onto a hard drive. Once that little sucker is on there, you can remotely interfere with the computer. Just because this knowledge isn't widely known amongst people in mainstream consensus reality, doesn't mean these things don't exist.

While we're on the subject of simulations, if you now think that death is a way to escape the 3D matrix, for the moment at least, I'm afraid you may have to think again. One of the last things Percy did for me was to send me a book from the library in his Spiritualist Church. The book (long out of print) had been written by a Church of England Vicar's wife in the 1930's and described her visions as a medium of what the Spiritualists call the "Summerlands". This is basically the afterlife as we call it: heaven or "Paradise".

The descriptions were beautifully drawn. People finally freed from the illnesses of old age, children prematurely dead from accidents or childhood diseases are described living a life of freedom from the physical in a world that is full of bliss. The lady author explains how when people die, they go to the halls of healing where their souls are gently administered to as they recover from the shocks and traumas of human life and death. Once each soul has recovered, they live in a wonderful paradise world of laughter and joy until the time comes for them to take reincarnation.

The world described is very similar to how one would imagine the 4th density of technology and magic, where thought creates, where anything can be brought into existence through intention. Whatever is created is then dematerialised once it has performed its purpose.

Percy spent a lot of time with me talking about the Summerlands and it was as I was about to release myself from his grasp that I discovered why.

This afterlife state is for your humans in Slave Separation after death. In other words, the same agent that has imposed a matrix upon this planet since the cataclysm that brought the previous paradigm to an end, has also imposed an afterlife state upon the human that keeps him away from higher experience.

This severely undermines what our religions say on this matter. "Heaven" is a construct. There are planes of existence so much higher and greater. But for as long as we are playing the game in base consciousness, even our afterlife state cannot bring us the true freedom that is our right as divine beings.

This has probably really shocked you. It basically means we've been recycling on rinse and repeat for thousands of years, never finding "God" as we thought we would.

The good news is that once our 3D experience ends with the arrival of our Aquarian Age, souls will start to regain their true Cosmic heritage and the veil will be lifted, not just for the physical state, but for the afterlife state as well. In fact, we'll reach a place where death, as we currently understand it, will be a gentler, less spiritually jarring experience as we move gracefully from the physical back into higher realms.

Percy's reasons for promoting both his hell realm and Summerlands concepts to me were clear: using the wonderful and enticing imagery from the book about the Summerlands, he was trying to focus my attention on a fake paradise with its ultimate promise of happiness. The fact that it's a false construct, however wonderful, is significant. He simply didn't want me, or anyone else for that matter, to look up any further than the ceiling promoted by the restrictions and limitations inherent within our religions.

This is pure psychopathic control. Although I respect and honour the work done in Spiritualist Churches, where people are given messages from loved ones they miss every day of their lives, I feel it can only ever be a stepping stone in understanding of the grand scheme, and not the ultimate authority.

For someone like Percy, it's a mechanism for use as a stick to prevent spiritual growth in those he's chosen as victims. For this treachery alone, I pray that our paths never cross again.

Part of our grand wake up in this Great Shift of the Ages is to understand the nature of psychopathic control. Once we learn to recognise this pathology in people around us in positions of authority or in those who aspire to run the world, we'll be able to deal with it properly. My own personal mission for myself over the last year or so has been to attempt to spot psychopathy in those who aren't in the most easily detectable places. I have to say, at the time of writing, I have a score of about zero out of ten. I give myself that score because most of the time, you're only wise after the event.

Watch out for those with almighty Messiah Complexes who, like HM, say they want to change the world. They will ignore the fact that the world cannot be woken up by any third party. A wake up will occur for each individual at a time that's suitable for their own soul path. This psychopath will rail at everyone for being ignorant, for suffering that cognitive dissonance that affects all humans when they're confronted with unwelcome information that challenges their cherished belief system. Such people should not be bullied or harassed. The messiah-type will try to wake certain selected individuals up with their own brand of reality coffee and then feed them their own twisted lies and agenda, immediately forcing them to go on the defensive and straight back to sleep. The frustrated Messiah will be restless and hyper, moving from passive to aggressive in the course of a single sentence. He will set about destroying you if you dare challenge him, but will eventually become bored and drift off if he cannot suck you in fast enough.

Watch out for the big talk and the minimum substance in such a character. Be on the look out for statements of grandiosity, for barefaced lies and social manipulation, for those tiny little seemingly innocuous comments dropped into your consciousness designed to make you feel small and to undermine your confidence in those around you. The true psychopath must keep you and everyone around him in an inferior position so that you *never* get ideas above your station that will topple him. Watch for the complete absence of loyalty, the restlessness, the lack of interest in the world at large. Be careful of such a person's need for destruction and the iron will they will use to carry out social atrocities. They will cover these tendencies with outer proclamations of love for us all and set themselves up as teachers, healers and rulers. This is their psycho cover up: if you ever come across anyone you're suspicious of in this regard, ask a few questions and check out their reactions. Ask them why they got into healing and what their motivations are. Push the boat out as far as possible by questioning every answer they give. Do this for as long as you feel is socially acceptable. The psychopath will get riled very early on in the conversation and start to lash back at you. Just walk out.

The psychopath is sickeningly glib. Be on the look out for a superficially sincere, charming and charismatic character who claims to be your saviour and the only one with all your answers. They'll go around telling everyone that they've set out to heal you. They're not interested in you: only in how casting themselves as your saviour will make them look. Get away from their vanity and self-promotion as soon as you smell the slightest hint of a rat. Once you're away, never, ever talk to them again or answer letters or emails. If you're dealing with a person whose pathological emotional emptiness doesn't respond to caring, loving stimuli, you'll never be able to cure them. Sack them or ditch them, delete them and divorce them. Don't say goodbye, don't let them "pass go" and do NOT let them collect £200. Move on as soon as you can. Remember, if the psychopath cannot get what he wants out of you, he'll simply destroy you. Why? No reason. That's just how they roll. Don't wait around for that to happen.

On several occasions after I myself had moved on from HM, I visited spiritual people for advice on how to proceed with my path. For a long time I didn't realise it was unnecessary to go that far, that really, it's ultimately your business and yours alone how you proceed. But sometimes it can be comforting visiting a spiritual lady who sets out her tarot deck in front of you and comes up with some wisdom and a sack load of encouragement. I was often in a place where this was offered to me for free, gratis and for nothing from lovely people who saw me walking along with my head bowed in sadness. All of them, to a man, had the same advice for me. Here are the words of one such concerned person:

"I see you have problems with a mother figure...she's not your real mother, is she. This...*mother* has something with her and it's not very nice. Whatever you do, get away from this *thing*. Don't let it come anywhere near you ever again, do you hear? It'll take every last ounce of energy and money you have. It wants to destroy you by getting into your head and rifling around in your peace of mind. It's a wonder it hasn't succeeded in all these years. I suspect the only reason it hasn't up to now is because you've lived a life of love and genuinely care about people…"

It's not just that. I've been pretty cautious in life. I know there are times to throw caution to the wind, but there are certain lines it's best not to cross. It's amazing how many gravitate towards the New Age who've taken drugs to help forget the trauma of lonely, disastrous childhoods. The drugs have actually made the situation a thousand times worse and have caused them to be compromised and deeply vampirised by parasitic energies. As they've only put a band aid over their pain and haven't got down to the heart of their problems, they then fail to get what they want and end up lashing out and attempting to destroy all the genuine empathic humans who are attracted to the New Age.

I also think a lot of people who are simply depressed gravitate towards New Age spirituality in order to find either a lost connection to their soul or unconsciously to hold on to other people who *are* empaths. Possibly even both. I've seen clinically depressed people with good hearts become so frustrated with the New Age for all its unfulfilled promises and its myriad of colourful but empty healing modalities that they've turned on both it and those around them in sheer frustration when they haven't found the inner peace they were so ardently searching for. One day we *will* be able to help these people, but only once New Age practitioners forget about the money and get down to what matters: healing people.

So the New Age is actually quite a dangerous game to be in. It shouldn't be, as the whole ethos is set up as loving, compassionate, non-violent and open-minded. It's amazing how many deeply unhappy individuals are roaming the green fields amongst the gently grazing animals of the New Age. In fact, as far as I can see, they're positively piling in. It's extremely hard to know who the empathic ones are in amongst the ones who either want the world out of you because they've destroyed their own, or want to destroy *you* because you're in a place that they've put out of reach and aren't yet strong enough to get to by themselves.

As for me, it's now clear that I was drawn to HM and her "cult" because I felt worthless and was trying to validate my existence on earth in the same way that she did, by unconsciously trying to give myself an almost messianic role. The selfish notion in my head was that I would gain love and favour for my actions and that I'd be admired for my wisdom and gifts. Instead, what I got was an almighty lesson. Feeling unloved as we ALL do, whether we care to admit it or not, I sought out the one person who claimed to have more love than anyone else in the whole wide world. As it turned out, she was empty of nearly all emotion except for the pity she felt for herself as the one so wronged by humanity. In me, this woman was looking for one who would love her so completely he would fall to his knees and worship her forever. She honestly believed this would fill her heart with the love she so desperately sought for herself. But her acute pathology could never have been neutralised by someone like me. No one in the whole world is strong enough.

As I've said, the only person who can produce the joy you seek and the love you're looking for, is you. Once you realise this and begin to dig into your own resources of joy and love and dish them out unconditionally yourself, that's when you start to feel love and validation being returned to you. Searching out this inner joy and finding that independence of spirit sometimes takes you on a horrific journey that will bring you such intense agony, it's hard to see how you'll ever survive. But the journey is worth taking and that's why I'll never ever regret the circumstances of my own lessons with HM and be forever thankful that our paths crossed. I know for a fact that Anna feels the same.

Anna told me once that when she first met her, HM tried to sell herself to her by claiming that she, Anna, needed her help and her Light. This strikes both Anna and me as typical of the false guru. You have to be wary of any religion or teacher that claims to be able to provide you with the Light or energies. It has to be found for yourself, by yourself and not any other party. Anyone who claims they're doing this *for* you is trying to trap you. Run a mile.

When Anna first came over to England to see HM, they met at a hotel. Anna had driven very far and was exhausted from her journey. The very least HM could have done is give Anna some time to get herself sorted.

But there she was, sitting in her long coat and leather gloves, her handbag at her side waiting in the lobby of the hotel for the next person to come along to validate her divinity and to pay her for it. Funnily enough, this is exactly my own abiding memory of HM: a lonely lady with a beautiful face turned hard by self-imposed adversity, sitting there with her bag and leather gloves and long sensible woollen coat, waiting and waiting and waiting for someone else to come and solve her riddle.

Anna was impressed that she had her own holy mother expecting her when she came over to England. It drew her deeply in at that time; she'd felt so neglected by her other teacher. Here was someone who really seemed to care, who came out to greet her and who, for a time at least, gave her some validation and the feeling of being loved and cherished. Like me, she had a profound lack of self-worth and self-esteem and thought she could get it this way. But as with all such undertakings, when you set out for someone else to provide you with that missing joy in your life, as soon as you start to dig deep and scratch their surface, if you're not careful, you find nothing inside for yourself but an empty space.

I can understand why people look at me with suspicion when they see that I'm on my own in life. But for a long time, I had to take this journey alone. If I'd had a wife or a girlfriend, I'd have lost them as they wouldn't have been able to sit there and watch HM and me suffer and would almost certainly have tried to intervene. Then there would have been no lesson for me. I had to follow my free will right to the end, with no interference.

I have one more sore to heal. Even though there'll be relatively few copies around, I still have to make amends for writing a book about HM in which there were half-truths and cover-ups.

In the book (which HM used to refer to her as her "biog"), I willingly allowed myself to set out HM's agenda, part of which was to demonise her daughter and canonise her son. To HM, Scooter was always going to be the one who succeeded her and would eventually have a messianic ministry of his own. I allowed myself to tell the story of how, before he was born, his spirit had appeared to HM one night to announce that he would be born to her. I'm really not sure of the truth of this. Scooter himself doesn't believe it and basically isn't interested. He's made his angle on that very plain and now wants to live a normal life and have a good career; so hats off to Scooter.

In the same pages, I also allowed myself to talk about the circumstances of HM's daughter's childhood in which she's portrayed as demanding and controlling, almost a nightmare child who never stopped crying and whose behaviour was classed by her mother as Attention Deficit Hyperactivity Disorder.

A couple of years after Rosie had been taken into care, HM decided she was going to set herself up as an expert on ADHD. She wrote a book about the subject which I believe suggested natural remedies for the condition and which was partly based on her own "experiences" with a hyperactive child. She then sickeningly wrote a letter to Rosie telling her that the reason why she'd been sent into care was because of her ADHD and implying that she'd been a problem child. I believe the purpose of the letter was to make sure Rosie was in NO doubt at all that she (Rosie) was solely responsible for the breakdown in relations between the two of them.

Rosie shared this letter with her foster mother who then rang me in paroxysms of rage, asking who the hell this woman was for putting such a label on Rosie. Rosie's relations with her foster parents were pretty strong and her foster mother knew her well. This was one child who would never need Ritalin.

With Rosie labelled as the outcast, all attention was then aimed at Scooter. As he was this great spiritual being in the making, HM built him up at the expense of Rosie and trumpeted around various stories about how Rosie had tried to kill him by pushing him into the road and down the stairs.

Utter garbage.

Rosie was never violent towards Scooter. If they had a fight like all brothers and sisters do and Rosie pushed him or hit him, it was *never* done with murderous intent.

Rosie was an innocent victim of someone else's dark drama. I still talk to her today. She's a sweetheart and wouldn't harm a fly. The reason why the white veil of divine perfection was drawn over Scooter and HM and not over Rosie and HM is, as we've seen, down to inveterate, unresolved trauma patterns.

In her "biog", HM inserted a section (without my knowing) which tells of Rosie's resentment towards her. It's a funny piece of writing; I laughed when I first found it buried in the pages of a book I was supposed to have written. It talks about how, as a toddler, Rosie had one day tried to escape from HM by attaching herself to some strangers in a supermarket car park. She'd tried to get into the car with them in the hope they'd take her home. HM implies that this was because Rosie had rejected her. To my mind, it's a lot simpler than that. HM had already admitted that one of the reasons why Rosie screamed the house down was because she could see all the imps and general nasties that projected themselves into her mother's world. The screaming was because baby Rosie was just plain terrified. I believe she was unhappy because, from day one, she knew on a soul level that she'd inserted herself into HM's pit of darkness, one that was nothing but a nest of vipers, with her own mother as chief reptile. Rosie didn't so much reject her mother as just want to run for her life.

During our early days together, HM occasionally let slip that she'd suffered at the hands of a brutal male or possibly even males. Even as the one whom she chose to write about her, I was never told any exact information about what had happened or who the perpetrator was and I just didn't feel it was my place to ask. I still don't. At the moment, at least until I know better, I have to assume that any abuse occurred during her period enmeshed within the satanist group. When I was asked to type up her booklet *Our Violent World*, I was given a thorough reprimand for changing some of the text and trying to "rewrite her history." As I've said, my intention was only to tidy up the grammar and syntax. All the same, when she scolded me for doing this, I came to the conclusion there was something sacrosanct about this book, as if it was performing some sort of blood-letting (very much like this text is doing for me). In the book, there were instructions about how to deal with an attack and how to cope with trauma. There were other sections that study the reasons for violent behaviour in men which were quite shocking in themselves as they show an underlying fury with men for their brutish behaviour. Although HM placed the blame squarely on lax morals in society and not on any individuals per se, I couldn't help but feel that there was anger there and a disillusion that was so deep, it left her with a

342

pathological dislike and mistrust of males. Perhaps that was one of the reasons why she needed to compensate by dressing her son up as a saint.

I'll always remember HM telling me how she wanted me to come up with a cover for *Our Violent World*. It was to be blood red, with a font on the front that would look like the writing on a tombstone. This was an attempt – I believe – to transfer her own terror onto the world at large. There was no suggestion that the negativity that was still shadowing her own life should be in any way neutralised. Consequently, her dark secret still haunts.

What worries me – selfishly – is that I had a part in the promotion of teachings that were overshadowed by unresolved trauma as well as in the damage that's been inflicted. Admittedly my part was only that of the one who sat at his computer and did the propaganda donkey work. I don't believe that I went out of my way to encourage any kind of emotional violence. However, I did allow HM's horror to permeate the psyches of many who may have picked up her books and those who may still do so. Once that vibration went out there, it was hard to put the lid on. That's the point of this book. I've always felt I had to neutralise that vibration at all costs.

You may think it's callous of me to expose a person's life in this way. But this was my life as well for over ten years and given the way she chose to interact with me during that time, I feel I have a right to tell people. I've been careful not to mention anything that's happened in her world since I fled from her and firmly believe that despite everything, she does now deserve anonymity and a chance, if she can, to heal in private. I certainly wouldn't condone any kind of investigation into her life unless she decides to take the greatest healing path of all and get together with another party to expose those who harmed her and to come to terms with what happened. In every respect, I wish that her life hadn't been so tortured; the thought that she desperately needs help has haunted me for years and I've always been in such a quandary about it. On the one hand, in this very book, I've amassed a thousand reasons why we should have no contact at all with her. On the other, I'm hounded by the notion that we should all be investigating new ways and methods to help those individuals I've exposed, like Percy, to reconnect with their souls. To do that, we need to take on the archontic creations of our nightmares and find some way to force them to vanish into our spiritual history. I know this is ultimately destined to happen as we haven't set this 3D world up to last interminably. All films and plays have a marked beginning and end.

But where do we start?

I really don't approve of the expression "the sins of the fathers are the sins of the sons" because it seems to damn whole generations before they're even born. But there's a good warning within these words. Trauma patterns seep down the years from person to person: children are still learning destructive conduct and attitudes from their parents and society at large and bequeathing them unchecked to younger generations, allowing them to fester, refusing to blow the whistle and shout out once and for all: THIS IS WRONG!

It's time for a change. Are the teacher "physicians" healing themselves? Unless they're prepared to look in the mirror and check out every single spot and wrinkle on their faces, they can't possibly succeed in advancing the cause of humanity and bringing about some manner of improvement to the human condition. Every year, we lock up monsters and perverts and expose their atrocities in the papers and on TV. We make and watch films about them, we find out what makes them tick. In particular, we know that some of the world's most twisted people were the progeny of twisted parenting. But still atrocities ranging from the cold and emotionless to the out and out barbaric are being carried out in our midst and very little is achieved.

I think this comes down to something simple and straightforward. We need to be honest and expose ourselves to ourselves. It doesn't have to be negative to do that. It's just a matter of being brutally down-to-earth about who we are as a race. Then, once we've succeeded in piercing our very own veils, it really is time for healing to start.

I don't believe this is a naïve assertion. Obviously, there'll always be those whose compulsive, repetitive behavioural patterns prevent them from stepping outside of the picture and looking back in. However, there are those amongst us who have this ability to stand back, who ARE ready for a kind of ascension of consciousness that will allow us to shake off the yoke of the old order. All it requires is a leap of faith, an ability to say that the old world with its corrupt and staid political regimes, its worn out, obsolete customs and allegiance to a god or gods that never really existed in the first place, can finally be swept away and replaced. What we'll replace the old world with is something that we'll have to tap into once enough of us have reached a consciousness that genuinely wants ascension to a higher vibration.

Don't be put off by the fact that I'm proposing solutions from spiritual wisdom when I've spent this entire book exposing a weakness within that very system that's caused immense damage. The very fact that someone from that arena is blowing the whistle on this weakness should lead you to understand that there's a vein of humanity within it. If I'm shouting at this point it's to proclaim to the world that we *can* use spirituality for healing. In fact, I would go so far as to say that it's our only avenue to evolution in this brave New Millennium of ours. I don't think it's unrealistic to understand that there IS a way to break the spell that has kept us in this state where we're all playing host to the parasite. We actually need to say to ourselves now: enough suffering, enough victimisation! As soon as we say that and mean it, then our souls will stop finding the need to incarnate as hunters and prey. There will be those who would still like to explore that path, certainly, but we must say to them: "it's time for you to move on. Planet Earth has had her time in 3D and the rest of us want to experience something higher now. There are other platforms of learning in other parts of the Universe set aside for you to play the parasite game."

So for the moment, let's not overly concern ourselves about who the predators are and who the unwitting prey might be in this testing 3D world of ours. Everyone knows deep inside who *they themselves* are. A choice is here now: you can ascend into a higher density having exposed yourself to yourself and decided to respect your heart centre. Or you can doggedly refuse to budge and keep that heart shut down. If that's you, be ready to ship out and take your archons with you. This is actually a personal choice, and each of us will be making that choice in full knowledge and understanding of where we stand. Percy, deep down, is entirely aware of his true nature. HM has probably found out by now. If they haven't jumped into the Light yet, I'd say it's because they don't want to. As for those who *are* making that quantum leap, we'll know them when we see them and *they* are the ones who aren't the psychopaths after all. They'll be the people who *can* be helped with unconditional care. The spiritual physicians who are in a position to help them will be fully aware they can do so knowing that they're not about to be given the most almighty slap in the face.

I think if they make the choice to stay as parasites, your Percys, and HMs should be honoured and wished well on their journeys. We might even meet them again at some point if they want. As for the rest of us, it's time to be great again.

Chapter Thirty-Three

In a Darshan with HM in about 2000, I had a strange experience. During the service, she looked at me and I was suddenly in another world altogether. As I looked into her eyes, I had this feeling of being weightless in space, of being able to see for billions of miles, through solar systems and entire galaxies. It felt for a millisecond like the whole of the Universe was inside me and I could sense every single part of it as if everything existed within my own consciousness. This feeling lasted for such a short amount of time and I have a poor recollection of it. Afterwards, I told HM what had happened and she was amazed.

When I look back, and even as I write this, I find it hard to give the experience any genuine weight. HM, on the other hand, often used it in her own writings on her site to give some credence to the work she did and even towards the end, as I moved away from her sphere of influence, was still asking me to recount to people what happened. The problem was, she had no one else around her to lend validity to her claims to be a Holy Mother and there were no ex- devotees or disciples who had any genuine stories of experiences or visitations who were prepared to come forward to share them. In fact, when I think about all the people who came and went over the last decade, nothing profound had ever happened to anyone.

I've had to come to the conclusion that this experience was no more than my imagination: I saw what I wanted to see, pure and simple. Perhaps I'd read about someone having such an experience and unconsciously tried to replicate it in a desperate attempt to validate HM to my own conscience. On reflection, all I did was make HM believe her own hype and ended up giving unwelcome credence to what she thought she'd become. This was an extremely dangerous game for me to have played, no matter how guileless I was at the time.

In the summer of 2009, on a warm night about an hour after I'd dropped off to sleep, I woke up in outer space. I was completely free of my physical body and floating above the earth.

This time, I knew it was the real thing because everything I could see was crystal clear to my sight. Usually I wear glasses or bumble around myopically so I'm used to my lines being quite indistinct. But as I floated around up there miles above the planet, I could see everything and from 360 degrees. What's more, the entire planet seemed to have an aura around it that appeared to trail off like a windsock. I remember just staying there where I was and watching as it rolled past me, thinking that its gravity would pull me down and that I'd find myself burning up in the atmosphere. The vastness of it overawed me and I felt incredibly humbled but at the same time exhilarated. And you know, it's odd: I also looked at the moon and it isn't a white ball of dust after all. It's full of strange almost eerie colours and it's incredibly beautiful.

I also wondered something else. We have photos of the Earth taken from space which show it as a kind of lonely ball just hanging there in the blackness. But there are all sorts of things flying around up there which you just never get to hear about. Someone is telling some whopping lies in the science community.

As I floated around, a voice in my head spoke gently, telling me not to worry about being pulled down by the effects of gravity as I wasn't experiencing this vision in the physical and therefore the laws of physics didn't apply as they would if I'd been in a material body. So I just stayed there and watched, marvelling at the sheer beauty of space and the feeling of being free.

When I returned to myself, I woke up and lay there in a wondrous daze. I finally knew that I hadn't had a genuine experience that evening in Darshan all those years ago. Instead, *this* was it; in so many respects, it was exactly what I'd been waiting for all my life. I know that I have so much left to do and that for centuries, others have already been to places that I'm only just experiencing for the first time; but it feels uplifting to be able to see a tiny bit for myself, even if it's just the outer edges of what's possible.

Shortly after this experience, a week or so later, I was in the bath one evening and dropped into a meditative state. I love the

348

sensory depravation of being in my bathroom. It has no windows and is a small warm room where I always find it's possible to drift off in the silence and solitude.

I found myself walking through a wasteland. It was dusk and the sun was setting. It felt cold and I was doing up the zip on my anorak and putting a woolly hat on my head. As I walked, I took stock of my surroundings. I was on the edge of a city. To one side of me was a large abandoned factory, half of which had been knocked down by bulldozers. You could see into what had been the shop floor, where once a vast assembly line had stood and giant machinery, grinding and churning rhythmically all day and night. In my mind's eye, I could see the ghosts of those who'd worked there in days when we'd flourished. They wore their sturdy boots and hard hats and threw themselves into their tasks with determination and professionalism as their fathers had done before them. But unemployment and economic insecurity had wiped away their livelihoods for good and no one worked. There was nothing for anyone in such a no-man's land and no one had any workable plans or ideas for how to return some dignity and pride to this blighted area. Now this vast building where generations had spent their working days had been torn apart and was nothing more than a shell, exposed to the elements and crumbling in the icy wind.

To the other side of me, the demolition work had left a large bare patch of ground where weeds poked up through flattened rubble and amongst discarded chunks of metal and trash, drink cans and supermarket bags, rotting clothes and rusty barbed wire. In the distance, I could see the twinkling lights of a vast housing estate sprawling out over a hill, its streets lined with the forbidding pale yellow of the street lamps. I could hear the barking of dogs and the howling of a car being driven aggressively, its brakes squealing as it turned corners at speed.

There was no one to be seen for miles around. All I had with me was a map and an address, but I knew I'd been sent on a fool's errand. The street I was looking for had been wiped off the map and all that was left was the main road I was walking along, a route that had once been lined with the entrances to factories and mills interspersed with rows of shops, the odd café, a newsagent. The only edifice still intact lay ahead of me: a solitary bus shelter with one stark neon bulb set into the inner edge, flickering and discoloured. Next to the bus shelter, a lone red telephone box with an old payphone inside it, surrounded by multi-coloured cards for call girls and personal services.

I approached the bus shelter and saw that it was covered in graffiti. There were take away boxes and greasy papers around the bench and I saw a pile of cigarette butts at one end. I could tell that this trash had been discarded recently and my belief that this was still a working bus stop was confirmed by the timetable that was still readable behind a sheet of scratched and defaced perspex.

I looked at the timetable and realised that I'd missed the last bus. Panicking, I looked back along the road and understood: I was stranded. If I retraced my steps, I wouldn't get back to civilisation before the sky turned pitch black and there was no way, once I'd distanced myself from the stark neon light of the bus shelter, that I'd be able to find the path beneath my feet.

I sat down on the bench to contemplate my predicament. I'd been told I had to go to a certain place at a certain time to meet...*someone*. I'd done exactly as I'd been ordered, but had found no one and nothing but an entire street wiped away by some destructive hidden hand. My mission was a failure and I knew for sure now that if I'd stayed at home and looked after myself, I'd have been safe and warm in a place where I was loved and cared for, not alone in the gloom, in the middle of nowhere, menaced by the elements and far from help.

I reached into my pockets and pulled out coins. I stood up and walked over to the phone box. Looking inside, I realised to my surprise that the phone was intact, so I pulled the door open and went inside.

With a heavy heart, already knowing what kind of reception I'd receive, I dialled a number and waited with my eyes firmly shut for the ring tone, bracing myself for the onslaught.

A woman answered. I pushed my 10p piece into the slot and announced myself. The voice on the other end was every bit as tetchy and impatient as I'd expected it to be:

"Why are you phoning me at this hour? You know you're not supposed to phone me after six in the evening. What do you *want?*"

"I've arrived, but there's nothing here. The address you gave me doesn't exist any more. Everything's been demolished."

"Well...that's not my fault, is it. I mean...you should have done some research, shouldn't you. Are you blaming me, Paul? What are you blaming me for? It's not my fault, is it."

"But you sent me here..."

"Look, it's late. I'm exhausted. I've been up all night looking after myself. I've got a headache. I can't deal with this right now. Don't you ever think about anyone but yourself? If you'd been aware you wouldn't have ended up in the middle of nowhere and bothering me with your problems. You're just going to have to deal with it and let me know when you're back. I can't be doing with this.... I've got to go to bed now. Don't disturb me again tonight."

Click...burrrrrrrr.

There was now no one left to phone; I'd alienated everybody and no one knew where I was anyway. Even if they'd known, I was so far away, no one could reach me, even if they wanted to.

At a loss and utterly unsure of my next move, I returned to wait beneath the flickering neon bulb of the bus shelter. I sat there and started thinking. Once this place might have been a beautiful meadow or a wide open field full of cows or horses. A time came when it had been paved over with concrete by men who were so keen to advance and to make something of themselves. Now it was just abandoned and despoiled, left to the elements and no use to man nor beast.

I sat there paralysed for what seemed like an age, bemoaning my lot and wishing for that wasteland to turn back into a sunny pasture. I cursed myself for allowing my free will to be ripped away from me and to have let myself be forced down a blind alley.

But then, just as I was beginning to abandon hope and allow the wiles of uncertain fate to take over, I heard a strange rhythmic rattling followed by a gentle *ting!* I looked around me and frowned.

It was some seconds before I realised that the phone was actually ringing. I couldn't tell it was a ring at first, it was such a coarse sound. This was a phone that had seen better days and the effects of age and lack of maintenance had left its bell in a poor state. But strangely, as clapper stopped tapping metal, there was a slight sense of its former state. The rhythmic rattle gave way to one solitary but pleasant little chime that seemed to me in my isolation to be a kind of cosmic calling card, that subtle sound that you can hear when you become sensitive to the vibration of the living, breathing Universe.

It was that subtle little "Tinkerbell" at the end of an unnatural clunking rattle that I responded to; I got up and went into the phone box and lifted the receiver. I was greeted by my own voice:

"Hello, Paul."

Still lying in my warm bath water, I sort of shook myself back to consciousness at this point. As I carried on lying there wallowing in the steam and soapy water, an overwhelming feeling of peace and calm came over me. I knew that I would still have to use all my own resources and ingenuity to get back home. But even if I had to kip all night on the bench until it was light enough to walk back to civilisation, or I chose to wait for the first bus, I no longer felt alienated. I still knew that I was about to make my journey on my own, but I now had a connection to myself that I'd never had before. There was a part of me having a cold harsh experience in this realm and another part of me that knew all. For the part of me in no-man's land to be able to speak to that higher part of me, was something special. It's a much needed "re-remembering" of who you are and even the tiniest nod from yourself to yourself. A greeting from the greater you to the expression of you that's been sent out into the dense wilderness is sometimes all you need and just enough to remind you: this life experience was never meant to be easy, but if you walk on the side of the angels, you'll never be abandoned.

In one amazing moment of clarity, I understood that freedom isn't folly: it's a state that we'll all revel in once we've realised that the human doesn't need to live in a world of control. Governments and all the impedimenta and machinery of domination are irrelevant to the human. Those who say it's human nature for the people to go to war, to commit atrocities against their fellow men and hence that we need to be directed and governed by those who know better, are WRONG, WRONG, WRONG. It's the ethos of this very control system that has turned the human into a beast. If men were set free and allowed to live according to their innate natural Universal sense of sovereignty, there would be no need for monarchs, patriarchs, oligarchs, archons. Peace and prosperity would abound. This is the very essence of this amazing shift that we're living through.

We've brought archontic influences directly into our world through Cataclysm Trauma, through guilt and fear-based thought processes. Archons, demons, long-legged beasties, however you wish to refer to them, such things only exist because we do. You don't have to co-operate with them like the Percys and HMs of this world. How quick it would be to remove such plug-ins and summon up a new Golden Age if only we didn't throw ourselves at such people. Be part of the great awakening then: learn what makes a controller tick and how you're being manipulated. If we hold a vision of ourselves as free, sovereign, divine, creative, full of love, wisdom and compassion, the matrix would simply disappear in an instant. This is why we're being told that we're the scum of the earth, violent and immoral feral beasts that need to be corralled up like fools. Those who run the show know that if we switched off our TV's, turned our back on our politicians and put down our consensus reality books, there would be no stick to beat us with and nothing to keep the lie real. 3D would disappear in a puff of smoke. I think many people are ready for this now and actually know it's going to happen. It's too late for those who are clinging onto the old world. They might as well give up and drift off to find some other theatre of operations.

Whether we choose to accept it or not, the Age of Aquarius is upon us. This era will be one of perfect Anarchy: not chaotic, terrifying, rudderless, violent Anarchy; just a vibration of auto-determination and autonomy where the timeless human will live outside bondage. All actions will come from a place of sublime creativity and will be in step with the organic and natural order of the Universe which is pure, non-judgemental, unconditional love.

When I want reminding of how brave the human is, I listen to Alicia Keys singing her solo tune *Empire State of Mind (part II)* – a song with an incredible rousing chorus. I love the fact that she sings about inspiration from big lights and the vibe of a big city whilst at the same time weaving in scenes of hardship and toil. Doesn't this sum up life? It can be SHIT down here.

I know that this is exactly how we've planned it, but it's beginning to get a little jaded now. Perhaps we no longer need to be gloriously alienated and lonely in this concrete jungle? We humans are so very alive, so full of creativity and self-expression. We're amazing: strong and bold and irrepressible! Our spirits can soar above the wasteland with such magnificence. We deserve better. I once heard a gentleman get up at an ET Disclosure Conference who said he'd been in contact with races who mentioned that we stink. No, we don't. *They* say we do because they're jealous that we've risen up through the crap smelling of roses whilst they're too gutless to come down here and do the tough stuff.

We don't have to live in an abusive world any longer if we don't care to. Soaring beautiful songs about our hopes and dreams are all very well, but the search for acceptance is one where we're making demands from a paradigm that was set up as a platform of learning in an ethos of separation from each other. Who really gets what they want in this world? I mean to the extent that fame and adulation bring complete and utter happiness and contentment? That sort of search is just a wild goose chase. There's no joy in finding fleeting approval from others.

It's time we rediscovered true contentment and learned to be our authentic selves again. All we have to do is imagine it using our incredible creative ability. We don't have to go to war against these archontic, hierarchical oligarchies – that's *not* us. We're a peace-loving, caring race. So put down those banners and loudhailers. Get off the streets, go home and change the man in the mirror. Stop co-operating with your jailers by holding in your own mind the image of your prison cell. I keep saying it and I say it again: this world of ours is a simulation. We can end the slavery at any time. If we choose, we can manipulate it into a paradise in a flash of light. See that mountain of garbage that's being added to every minute of every day by council dustcarts? By just the power of intention, we can turn that entire mess into a pasture, or a forest or a Garden of Eden, if that's how we envisage it. Why allow ourselves to be manipulated any longer when we can reform the entire world back to a paradise with no more than just our own innate loving intent?

Before I dumped Percy, I'd told him about my wasteland dream; unsurprisingly, he was very keen to take the role of the one speaking on the other end of that phone. It wasn't about me connecting to my higher self at all. To his mind, that other voice was the voice of him as my saviour, the only person to have all the answers; the one who'd taken over from that *other* person who had all the answers, who in fact didn't have all the answers after all.

Percy was so ardent for me to see him as the ultimate oracle that even in our last ever conversation together, sensing that he was about to lose his influence over me, he was almost shouting at me from a balcony like a dictator:

"I am the oracle! I am the lotus feet! I am the guide and mentor! I am Horus! I am the telephone!"

Oh, really? *Whatever!* I'm laughing my socks off.